ON FREUD'S JEWISH BODY

On Freud's Jewish Body

MITIGATING CIRCUMCISIONS

JAY GELLER

FORDHAM UNIVERSITY PRESS

New York 2007

Library of Congress Cataloging-in-Publication Data

Geller, Jay Howard.
On Freud's Jewish body: mitigating circumcisions / Jay Geller.—1st ed.
  p. cm.
Includes bibliographical references and index.
ISBN 978-0-8232-2781-5 (cloth : alk. paper)—
ISBN 978-0-8232-2782-2 (pbk. : alk. paper)
 1. Freud, Sigmund, 1856–1939. 2. Judaism and psychoanalysis.
3. Sex (Psychology) I. Title.
BF109.F74G45 2007
150.19'52092—dc22

                                        2007042838

Printed in the United States of America
09 08 07 5 4 3 2 1
First edition

For Mal (z"l), a mentor and a mensh

CONTENTS

ACKNOWLEDGMENTS

During the Winter of 1980/81, Duke professor James Rolleston, then-and-since my advisor in matters German and germane, hosted a small dinner party. Bouyed by my recent reading of Carlebach's "Forgotten Connection" and Eliot's *Daniel Deronda*, I began a conversation about an apparent pattern of converging associations between women and Jews over the last several centuries. Peggy Abrams, doyenne of the Language Lab, chimed in and introduced me to Otto Weininger and his virtual equation of women and Jews. Perhaps the intertwining representations I was noticing were more than the happenstance of my reading habits. I recalled what Ian Fleming's arch-villain Auric Goldfinger once happened to say:

"Once is happenstance. Twice is coincidence. Three times is enemy action." And so it began.

There are at least three other Duke faculty members, who have continued to provide the necessary mix of stimulation and skepticism that are needed for any intellectual endeavor: Kalman Bland, Liz Clark, and Charles Long. More involved with the working out of my ideas at the time were four individuals whose colloquy and good times kept me going through my graduate student career and whose friendship I treasure to this day: Jim Henderson, Tom Csordas, Eduardo Gonzalez, and Ned Lukacher.

When I finally left Durham, following my wife to Swarthmore, I encountered a new group of individuals, actually a new family with which I share to this day a whole lot more than my latest enthusiasm or *aperçu* and from whom I receive a lot more than their diverse cultural, literary, and historical knowledges: Scott Gilbert and Ann Raunio, Marion Faber and Steve Hannaford, Bob Weinberg and Laurie Bernstein, and Marge Murphy. During the nine years spent residing in Swarthmore, my path and project also crossed a number of others' within easy commuting range: Amy Newman, Howard Eilberg-Schwartz and Liliane Weisberg. Liliane, in particular, put the idea in my head that I may be engaged with the construction of Freud's discourse not just the interpretation of a couple of

ix

his texts. As I pursued this project Ed Fuller of the Swarthmore College Library and Stephen Lehmann at Penn's Van Pelt Library spiced up my times trolling in their archival haunts.

Also during that period, I spent a remarkable year at Rutgers' Center for the Critical Analysis of Contemporary Culture under the directorship of Carolyn Williams and with a troika of incredibly exciting fellows: Elin Diamond, Marcia Ian, and, especially, Diana Fuss. I also had the opportunity to design a class that allowed me to test out some of the readings that have made their way (and a few that didn't) into this volume. When teaching brought me down US 1 to Princeton, Firestone Memorial Library, and the irrepressible Mal Diamond, I began a couple more helpful conversations with Carl Schorske and Eric Santner, and more than a few with Jim Boon. During these years, in part through the generosity of an American Council of Learned Societies Senior Fellowship, I traveled to the National Library of Medicine and the Sigmund Freud Collection at the Library of Congress and made ample use of the staff's good services. More important I had the benefit of long exchanges of ideas and resources with Jack Cuddihy, Judith Friedlander, Delphine Bechtel, Michael Berenbaum, Jeremy Zwelling, Joel Pfister, Judith Van Herik, John Hoberman, Michael Berkowitz, Gerd Busse, Paul Roazen, Bill Pietz, Tomoko Masuzawa, Bob Baum, Robert Segal, Susannah Heschel, Diane Jonte-Pace, and the dynamic duo, Jonathan and Daniel Boyarin. Indeed a special thanks to Danny for having introduced me to Helen Tartar, then editing director at Stanford University Press, and now here at Fordham.

Since moving to Vanderbilt, I've had the good fortune of many fine colleagues—in matters Freudian, especially Volney Gay and Gregg Horowitz, and matters German, especially George Becker, Martina Urban, Meike Werner, and Barbara Hahn—and three fine deans: Joe Hough, Jack Forstman, and Jim Hudnut-Beumler. And as good as the library resources may be here, this work could not have been completed without Jim Toplon and the folks at ILL. I've also been able here to test many of this work's readings in classroom settings; I'm grateful to all of my students here for their patience and perspicacity, with a special thanks to Joanna Brichetto and Diane Segroves for their help in the production of this book. Outside of Vanderbilt, I have received much intellectual supplementation from Judith Frishman, Madge Dresser, Paul Mendes-Flohr, Anne Hoffman, Eliza Slavet, Robin Judd, Paul Reitter, Finbarr Curtis, William Robert, Frank Scherer, Diane O'Donoghue, Gerhard Fichtner, Ulrike Brunotte, and Sabine Mehlmann.

Since the project began I've also had the good fortune to spend two incredibly rich summers courtesy of the National Endowment for the Humanities. The first, a Freud-scholar's dream-wish fulfilled, at 20 Maresfield Gardens—the Sigmund Freud House and Museum in London—then guided by Erica Davies. Sander Gilman masterfully directed our reading of Freud. Beyond the glories of the British Library in its old digs and the Wellcome Library for the History and Understanding of Medicine, the interaction among the participants—in particular with Jutta Birmele, Valerie Greenberg, and Peter Rudnytsky—and the insight and support of the staff (that continues to this day)—especially Keith Davies and Michael Molnar—contributed immeasurably to this project. A visit that summer (the first of several) to the Zentrum für Antisemitismusforschung at the TU-Berlin brought me into contact with that marvelous mix of pre-Berliner Republik Berlin *ésprit* and historical knowledge, Rainer Erb. The brilliant Brothers Boyarin hosted my second NEH summer, this time at the Jewish Theological Seminary to explore Jewish Cultural Studies. They brought me together with some old abfab fellow travelers—Ann Pellegrini and Susan Shapiro—and new—Ranjit Chatterjee—at the intersection of Judaica and Freudiana as well as left me more than enough time to loiter at the Leo Baeck Institute, the New York Public Library, the Rare Book Room of the College of Physicians and Surgeons, Columbia University, and the shelves of innumerable bookstores.

Through the good graces of CIES, the Fulbright Scholar program, and the Sigmund Freud Gesellschaft, Lonnie Johnson and Ingrid Scholz-Strasser, I was able to fulfill another Freud-scholar's dream-wish and spent several months at Berggasse 19—the Sigmund Freud Museum in Vienna. The staff, especially Sylvia Weinzettel and Lydia Martinelli, greatly facilitated my research—as did the staffs of the Österreichische Nationalbibliothek, the Universitätsbibliothek Wien (including a number of its branches at Seminare and Institüten, such as the Institut für Geschichte der Medizin), and the archives of Vienna's Israelitische Kultusgemeinde during my various visits. Beyond the sharing of meals and mentalities with Joanna King, Sonia Horn, Abigail Gilman, Susi and Josef Shaked, Fritz Werner, Primavera Gruber, the truly rewarding experience of my stay was teaching what would become much of this book at the Institut für Judaistik to an incredibly diverse group of students; two in particular provided me with much succor, support, and suggestions: Ingrid Oppenauer (ironically a teacher at the Sigmund Freud Gymnasium) and Kurt Fischer (and no less ironically, who fled from Vienna about the same time as Dr. Freud, albeit in a far easterly direction).

Portions of several of the chapters first were given at Princeton University, Bowdoin College, William and Hobart Smith College, Oberlin College, the University of North Carolina, Vanderbilt University, Case Western Reserve, Sigmund Freud Museum—Wien, New York Public Library, Humboldt Universität, Spertus Institute, Smith College. And others appeared in *American Imago*, *International Journal of Psychoanalysis*, *Journal of the American Academy of Religion*, *Modern Judaism*, *Psychoanalysis and History*, and *Religious Studies Review*. I am grateful to those sponsors and editors who provided me with the opportunities to present some of what is about to follow.

Beyond the various folks at Fordham University Press (in addition to Helen: Nick Frankovich, Katie Sweeney, and J.M.), the no longer so anonymous readers, and the nameless others I apologize for having omitted, there are five people still to thank: my parents, Milton and Florence Geller, my daughter Sarah, my son Alexander, and my friend, companion, lover, wife Amy-Jill Levine.

Freud's Jewish Question and Mine

Freud famously described himself as "a godless Jew"—or, more properly, as "a completely godless Jew," *ein ganz gottloser Jude.* He so labeled himself in the second of two quasi-rhetorical questions to the Swiss analyst and pastor Oskar Pfister in an October 1918 letter. "Quite by the way," Freud asked, "why did none of the devout create psychoanalysis? Why did one have to wait for a completely godless Jew?"[1] Numerous analysts, scholars, theologians, and commentators have endeavored to parse the meanings of and relationships between Gdless and Jew in Freud's compact phrase and expansive life. Their efforts have led to a plethora of sequels to Freud's own self-description: modern Jew, secular Jew, psychological Jew, ambivalent Jew, self-hating Jew, renegade Jew, non-Jewish Jew.

These diverse reactions suggest an uncanny discomfort with the appellation "Gdless Jew." Aside from faint echoes of the history of Christian (and anti-Christian) demonic representations of the Jew—as the enemy or murderer of Gd—there are other sources of uneasiness with Freud's phrasing. The question "under what rubric does one situate 'Jew'?" poses an anxiety-generating dilemma. Is "Jew" a religious designation, thus presupposing belief in Gd? If so, then the notion of a Gdless Jew is either an oxymoron or else it is an indirect representation, such as Freud analyzed in the dream-work or noted in *Jokes and Their Relation to the Unconscious,*

and recalls Heine's witticism, cited by Freud in *Jokes*, "my fellow unbeliever Spinoza" (8:77).[2] Or, conversely, is the notion of "Jew" related to
the German term *Judentum* that condenses three fields often kept distinct
in English: Judaism (religion), Jewry (people), Jewishness (character and
custom)? If so, however it is qualified, the term "Jew" frustrates the modern desire for clear and distinct categories.

Exacerbating this discomfort is that Freud's designation of himself as a
"Jew" was not an isolated occurrence. Freud never had a problem with
affixing the label "Jew" to his person. In his letters, prefaces, and addresses
he repeatedly laid claim to that identification. For example, in a February
1886 letter, Freud described to his then-fiancée and later-wife Martha Bernays how, while engaged in a "political conversation" with the French
neurologist Georges Gilles de la Tourette, "I promptly explained that I
am a Jew."[3] Or consider how directly he commenced his 1925 "Autobiographical Study": "My parents were Jews, and I have remained a Jew myself" (20:7). In that same year he stated in a letter to the Jewish Press
Center in Zurich: "I have always had a strong feeling of belonging together with my people and have always nurtured it in my children as well.
We have always remained in the Jewish denomination" (19:291).

Nor was he averse to advising others to raise their children as Jews. The
music critic and member of Freud's *Mittwochsgesellschaft* (the Wednesday-
evening group that would later evolve into the Vienna Psychoanalytic Society) Max Graf reported that, upon the birth of his son Herbert (the Little
Hans of Freud's case study of the child) in 1903, Freud counseled: "'If you
do not let your son grow up as a Jew, you will deprive him of those sources
of energy which cannot be replaced by anything else. He will have to
struggle as a Jew, and you ought to develop in him all the energy he will
need for the struggle. Do not deprive him of that advantage.'"[4]

Often accompanying these avowals of Jewish belonging were corresponding disavowals of any religious dimension to that association. Thus,
in his 1926 address to the Vienna lodge of B'nai B'rith, on the occasion of
his seventieth birthday, Freud remarked on why he gravitated some thirty
years earlier to this group of Jewish men: "For I was myself a Jew, and it
has always appeared to me not only undignified, but outright foolish to
deny it." He continued:

> What bound me to *Judentum* was—I hate to admit it—not the faith, not
> even the national pride, for I was always an unbeliever [and] have been
> brought up without religion. . . . But there remained enough to make the
> attraction of *Judentum* and the Jews irresistible, many dark emotional pow-

ers[,] all the stronger the less they could be expressed in words, as well as the clear consciousness of an inner identity, the familiarity of the same psychological structure. (20:271)[5]

These remarks, including their enactment of the pairing "Gdless" and "Jew," as well as their unsettling indeterminacy about the nature of his Jewishness, were echoed a few years later in his 1930 introduction to the Hebrew translation of *Totem and Taboo*: "If the question were put to him: 'Since you have abandoned all these common characteristics of your countrymen, what is there left to you that is Jewish?' he would reply: 'A very great deal, and probably its very essence.' He could not now express that essence clearly in words; but some day, no doubt, it will become accessible to the scientific mind" (13:xv).

These denials of any taint of religious belief, practice, or prejudice coloring his identification as a Jew are mirrored in another set of foreclosures. In both his public and private writings Freud explicitly endeavors to separate psychoanalysis either from religion in general—here one thinks of *The Future of an Illusion* and the last of his introductory lectures on psychoanalysis, "The Question of a *Weltanschauung*"—or, more specifically, to separate psychoanalysis from *Judentum*, understood not only as a religion, but in virtually all other senses. Freud would only concede that the sociological situation of his being a "Jew" contributed to the formation of psychoanalysis. In his address to the B'nai B'rith he had also noted "that it was to my Jewish nature alone that I owed two characteristics that had become indispensable to me in the difficult course of my life. Because I was a Jew I found myself free from many prejudices which restricted others in the use of their intellect; as a Jew I was prepared to join the Opposition and to do without agreement with the 'compact majority'" (20:273–74). Comparable language had already been employed in his "Autobiographical Study" (20:9).[6]

Moreover, Freud was embedded in a number of Jewish social networks. He joined the Vienna B'nai B'rith Lodge less than two years after its founding in 1895 and became a frequent speaker there—until that venue was replaced by the initially all-Jewish and ever pre-eminently Jewish *Mittwochsgesellschaft*;[7] he and his family would spend vacations in the company of other bourgeois Viennese Jewish families at Bellevue, a *Sommerfrische* (summer resort) in what was then a suburb of Vienna, as well as frequent spas like Merano, where they would make the acquaintance of other Jewish families and future patients, among them Ida and Philipp Bauer and Hans Zellenka and his wife (or as they are known in the literature, Dora and her father, together with Herr and Frau K). These networks form part of Freud's everyday world—his engagement with their strivings, desires, anxieties, rivalries, frustrations, losses, forbidden relations, and unspoken secrets affected his dream-life and his theory-production, as well as provided him with opportunities for employment.

And while Freud would regularly confirm to his Jewish colleagues like Karl Abraham and Sandor Ferenczi their "racial kinship" (*Rassenverwandtschaft*) and common intellectual constitution,[8] he insisted on severing any connection between their shared Jewish character and psychoanalysis. In a June 1913 letter to Ferenczi, Freud readily admits that "there are great differences between the Jewish and the Aryan spirit. . . . Hence there would assuredly be here and there differences in outlook on art and life." Nevertheless, he continues, "But there should be no distinct Aryan or Jewish science. Their results should be identical; only their presentation may vary."[9] Freud remains to the last very much concerned that the claims of psychoanalysis for the scientificity—its universality and objectivity—not be placed in doubt.[10]

Conversely, Freud conceded in the 1925 article "Resistances to Psychoanalysis" that antisemitism generated significant resistance to psychoanalysis; because of its association with "one who never hid his *Judentum*" (19:22), psychoanalysis acquired a Jewish taint that made it unworthy of consideration by many in both the lay and scientific communities. This public admission had long been uttered in private, as in a July 1908 letter to Abraham: "Be assured, if my name were Oberhuber, my innovations would have found, despite it all, far less resistance."[11] While this recognition motivated a series of organizational moves—most notably the initial promotion of Carl Jung—to prevent the appearance of psychoanalysis as "a Jewish national affair" (*eine jüdisch nationale Angelegenheit*),[12] Freud at other times seemed, at least in private correspondence, rather proud of the resistances generated by his Jewishness. Afraid that his case study of Little Hans would create an uproar, Freud wryly comments to Abraham: "German ideals threatened again! Our Aryan comrades are really completely indispensable to us, otherwise psychoanalysis would succumb to anti-Semitism."[13]

These rather narrowly disseminated statements about Freud's Jewish identifications and the identification of psychoanalysis with *Judentum*— Freud's answers to his own Jewish Question—take a new and public turn after the Nazi seizure of power in Germany and its rippling effect throughout Central Europe. As he writes to the German Jewish communist author and recent emigrant to Palestine Arnold Zweig in 1934, "Faced with the new persecutions, one asks oneself again how the Jews have come to be who they are and why they have attracted this undying hatred."[14] Freud's attempt at an answer to these questions in his only text devoted to the study of *Judentum* and what proved to be his last completed work, *Der Mann Moses und die monotheistische Religion/Moses and Monotheism*, opens with the public acknowledgment of his own Jewish identity—"someone who is himself one of them" (23:7)—and continues with a self-described compulsive effort to articulate and provide a genetic account of the *je ne sais quoi* by which he had earlier defined his own Jewishness. In *Moses*, Freud repeatedly returns to the intellectuality and independence of mind, the highest ethical and moral standards, and the concern for social justice and tenacity in the face of persecution that mark the advance in *Geistigkeit* (intellectuality) and that he associates with *Judentum*.

Obviously the question of Freud's Jewishness goes beyond a list of his explicit self-references and of his protestations against seeking Jewish contamination of his work. Numerous scholars have attempted to situate those statements within the context of Freud's entire corpus of writings as well as of his biography and background in order to determine the character, meanings, and implications of his Jewishness. This work represents another such effort.

Identifying Judentum

In the chapters that follow I analyze the implications of Jewish identity upon Freud and his work. Freud was caught up in the double bind of modern Jewish existence before the Shoah: The European society into which he sought admission demanded complete assimilation to the dominant culture, even to the point of obliterating any traces of *Judentum*, yet often accompanying the demand was the assumption that Jews were constitutionally incapable of eliminating their difference. The Jew's impossible inclusion was complemented by the Jew's necessary difference. Even before the latter part of the nineteenth century, when the rhetoric of antisemitism adopted the biological race-discourse applied by the West to the rest, Jews were already ascribed an essential or ontological ethnic difference, even as religious difference, understood as voluntary, individual, and private, became a less significant determinant of public-sphere participation.[15] Jews, especially Ashkenazic Jews, were non-European; where a Northern provenance was privileged, the Jews were of the South; where a Western, the Jews were of the East. The geographical hierarchy was reproduced by a developmental hierarchy, such that the farther a group's origination was from the metropolitan core, the lower was both its level of development and its capacity to develop further.[16] Such differentiation helped create, maintain, and confirm European identities and hierarchies that could replace those eroded by the forces of modernization, secularization, and commodification. Central Europe witnessed social dislocations, economic destabilizations, growing bureaucratizations, the collapse of traditional narratives of value and meaning—the old coordinates of identity—and threats to the modern identity of the autonomous and autochthonous subject-citizen of homogeneous European nation-states—white, bourgeois, (nominally) Christian, (avowedly) heterosexual, and male. As Bryan Cheyette and Laura Marcus have written in the introduction to their collection *Modernity, Culture and 'the Jew'* with regard both to the history of the modern and its contemporary radical historical revisions, "The Jewish other is both at the heart of Western metropolitan culture and is also that which is excluded in order for ascendant racial and sexual identities to be formed and maintained."[17]

Joining the Jew's impossible inclusion and necessary difference was the Jew's uncanny gender. The political economy and moral culture of Freud's society was dictated by a class (or at the very least by a discourse that differentiated this class from the aristocracy and the people)[18]—the educated and propertied bourgeoisie—whose eighteenth-century articulation was already intimately connected with the representation of gender.[19] Authority lay in what may best be characterized as an exclusively masculine order, a *Männerbund*.[20] The masculinist and binary ideology pervading this society privileged gender difference as an originary opposition grounded in nature and hence as universally valid. Eventually supplementing this opposition was the similarly assumed-to-be natural attraction of this complementary pair: compulsory heterosexuality.[21] Upon this foundation, individual identities and social institutions were determined, maintained, and legitimated. The opposition between a male-coded public sphere— civil society and the state—characterized by rationality (i.e., freedom from desire), autonomy, and activity (i.e., aggression) and a female-coded private sphere—the family and religion—of emotionality, dependence, and passivity exemplified the economy of gender difference; their separation enforced it.[22] Consequently, in the last instance gender difference adjudicated the threats to the hegemony of the *Männerbund* posed by deviance or otherness: judged unmanly or effeminate, the other was relegated to the private sphere. To question gender identity—to allow the unmanned or unmanly into the public sphere—was in turn to question the legitimacy of the entire order.[23]

Overlapping this gender difference were ethno-racial differences and the closely correlated opposition of colonizer and colonized. Freud realized that he was not in control of many of the meanings of his masculine Jewish identification. For many Gentiles—and not a few assimilated Jews—"Jew" conveyed the image of the *Ostjuden*, the East European *shtetl* Jew.[24] This identification was in part sustained because a cultural division of labor between Austro-Germans and Jews remained even though the types of employment allowed Jews in bourgeois Vienna had changed.[25] Also contributing to this identification was the migration of *Ostjuden* in and through Central Europe, especially after the pogroms of the last decades of the nineteenth century and the first decades of the twentieth. For both Freud's Austro-German and Imperial German readers the space between the inhabitants of the colonizing metropole and those of the colonized periphery created, maintained, and confirmed those essential differences no less than the bifurcation of the metropole itself into the gender-coded public and private spheres.[26] And as with the threatened incursion of the unmanned or unmanly into the public sphere, when the colonized left the periphery, entered the metropole, and attempted to acculturate, the always precarious identities of the dominant population became more so.

Against these threats across the sexual and nationalist/imperial divide to the hegemony of the *Männerbund* and its subjects ever endeavoring to author and authorize themselves, not just popular rhetoric but also those allegedly objective epistemic discourses of disease, degeneration, misogyny, homophobia, racism, and antisemitism proliferated. The emergent scientific disciplines endeavored to administer the increasing overlap of the gender-differentiated bourgeois order and racially differentiated imperial order by affixing an identity to the body, especially to the bodies of those menacing others. As virtually everything solid melted into air,[27] the body remained, inscribed with the natural markers of gender and sexuality, nation and race. Identity was read off these inextricably intertwined signs as these sciences provided a grammar of truth that treated that body, and the reproductive organs especially, as the language by which "natural" difference was expressed.[28] "Between 1870 and 1920 science, with its claim to objectivity, its empirical basis, and its allegedly value-free knowing, constituted a cultural authority that politicized the discourse of nature— above all in relation to the nation as the *people's body* [*Volkskörper*]."[29] The primacy granted to the body and reproduction increasingly biologized the representation of the other.[30] Beyond anatomic classification, the ascription of disease and deviation, the body of the Jew and the other others became the site for their medical regulation and for the maintenance of gender and sexual ("The healthier the individual is, the more definitively he [or she] is male or female")[31] as well as ethnic and racial identity. The others were put in their place—the textbook and the clinic, the quarter (*Viertel*) and the colony, and, perhaps, the couch.[32]

Complementing nosological classification was the teleological theory of evolution, exemplified by Ernst Haeckel and his apothegm "ontogeny recapitulates phylogeny." The others had their chapter in the story of "the ascent of man."[33] Just as the different stages of the embryo recapitulated the evolutionary process, so races and genders represented different stages of human development.[34] That is, the biologization of the other entailed a hierarchization of the other that legitimated the domination of white, heterosexual men—as did the motor of evolutionary change. Darwinian sexual selection presupposed the natural necessity of not only gender difference but also heterosexuality.[35] His work confirmed the claims for natural hierarchical difference by the foremost German sociologist of the nineteenth century, Friedrich Wilhelm Riehl: "*In the opposition of man and woman is the dissimilarity of vocations and thereby social inequality and dependence put forward as a natural law.* . . . Sexual difference became the cornerstone of the entire system of *natural differences* between societies and therefore also of the state."[36] Not just gender polarization but its sharpening was both a presupposition and an index of civilization and cultural progress. The lack of gender differentiation was a sign of primitivity: "the lower a race's level of development, sexual differences [*sexuellen Unterschiede*], especially those designated by Darwin as secondary sexual characteristics [*Geschlechtscharaktere*], are generally more muddied [*verwischen*], the difference [*Differenz*] between man and woman is thus less pronounced than among civilized peoples."[37] The trajectories of cultural progress and gender differentiation converged on the European bourgeoisie and its gender division of labor,[38] with its manly men (that is, the most intellectually developed and active men) and proper woman—that is, neither too intellectual and active nor too feminine, for the last would mean being hypersexual and therefore more animalistic. The inappropriateness of Jews for European society was signaled by their less-than-virile men and their either intellectual or oversexed, and in both cases aggressive, women. According to the German literary historian, translator, author of a novel about Spinoza, and antisemitic polemicist Otto Hauser: "By no other people do you find so many effeminate men [*Weibmänner*] and masculine women [*Mannweiber*] as by the Jews. That's why so many Jewesses push their way into male professions, study everything possible, from law [and] medicine to theology, become social organizers. It's clear that a good two-thirds of these Jewish women bear ambiguous secondary gender traits. Clear traces of beard growth are frequent, while their breasts are underdeveloped and their hair short. These women made . . . the pageboy cut [*Bubikopf*] fashionable."[39] The antisemitic publicist Johannes Nordmann (aka H. Naudh) had already declared that the Jewish woman "is, if possible, even nastier [*widerwärtiger*] than the man, because she is even more unfeminine than she is inhumane."[40] At the other extreme are the depictions of the Jewess as sexual predator in the best-selling novels of Artur Dinter (e.g., *Die Sünde wider das Blut/The Sin against the Blood*; 1917) and Hans Zöberlein (e.g., *Befehl des Gewissens/Conscience Commands*; 1937) as well as Richard Strauss's 1907 opera *Salome*.[41]

Moreover, grounding gender difference in the complementary discourses of descent and of development revealed another facet of the masculinist ideology: the male expropriation of reproduction and its language from women and women-associated others.[42] The self-made autonomous men authored and authorized themselves in discipline- and discourse-formation. Yet their ideology of reproduction also mandated increasing the population of the dominant class; their disciplines and discourses betrayed the anxieties of bourgeois, heterosexual men about the demographic threat posed by the other to their hegemony.[43] Wherever one looked—government reports, scientific treatises, the *Boulevardzeitungen* (tabloids)—one could read how they feared their position atop the evolutionary and social hierarchies would be overrun.[44] They also feared that the low birthrate was also leading to an increase in mental illness. In responding to Freud's 11 November 1895 lecture to the Wiener medicinische Doctoren-Collegium, "Über Hysterie" (On hysteria), the neurologist Heinrich Weiss suggests that if Freud's theory about the sexual etiology of neurosis is true, then it should be most frequent in places such as France, where the "Zwei-Kinder System" is common and where couples (especially in the propertied classes)[45] limit themselves to only two children, and hence must either abstain from sex or engage in practices to prevent conception, either of which induces neurosis. And Weiss adds that it is indeed the case.[46]

Mirroring these race- and gender-determined distinctions was a sensory hierarchy. In contrast to the cognitive and hygienic superiority of vision, smell characterized the sexual, the primitive, the animal. On the one hand, the degeneration of smell was civilized man's mark of biological difference: "Among most mammals . . . smell is certainly the most highly developed of the senses. . . . In man it has become almost rudimentary giving place to the supremacy of vision."[47] On the other hand, the metaphorics of smell and its organ, the nose, became the mark of class and cultural difference.[48]

Jewish identity, in particular, was betrayed by the nose, the foot, the smell, and—because it was not only of the body, but of the reproductive system—the body technique of circumcision. On the imagined Jewish body, the genital, the primary marker of gender and sexual difference, was also, as the always already circumcised penis, the pre-eminent marker of ethnic and, eventually, racial difference. In his history of *Judentum* Otto Hauser argued that "indeed [*in der Tat*] circumcision is what most strikingly separates *Judentum* from Indo-Germans."[49] For the latter, this "barbaric mutilation of the human body" is "the most alien" [*am fremdesten*] of distinguishing marks; hence, liberating Christianity from circumcision is what allowed the religion to quickly spread among the peoples of the "pure Nordic West."[50] Drawing upon Tacitus's assertion in the *Histories* (5.5) that circumcision is the differentiating mark by which Jews are known and Plotinus's mocking query in the *Satires* (102), "Wouldn't you rather also circumcise us so that we can be taken for Jews," as well as archaeological finds, including Roman terracotta pottery bearing both hooked noses and circumcised penises, the racial anthropologist Eugen Fischer and the biblical scholar Gerhard Kittel conclude that "being circumcised and being Jewish were acknowledged as completely the same" in the Roman Empire by the third and fourth centuries c.e. at the latest.[51]

By that same mark the racially coded body no less revealed its gender and sexuality as it rendered its differences both visible and natural. As gender, sexual, and racial differences converged upon Jewish genitalia, "circumcision" produced the feminized male Jew (and perhaps even the masculinized female Jew) of questionable sexuality—as well as the opposing virile masculine norm. By such nostrums the Jew, along with those other others, was placed under construction.

And, hopefully, under control, for such fetishized representations of body parts and techniques sought apotropaically to foreclose the threat to European claims to autonomy and autochthony posed by the persistence of, among others, the Jews.[52] Yet like all fetishes the inscribed Jewish body uncannily preserved that which it would disavow: the continued existence of a people whose world- and salvation-historical time had purportedly come and gone. Further destabilizing the situation, circumcision is a postnatal corporeal inscription that shame—what distinguishes the human from the animal, the bourgeois from the rabble, the civilized from the primitive—demands be veiled. Even as differences between reform Jew and liberal Christian became unrecognizable, such that religio-ethical ideation and cultural upbringing no longer presented obstacles, baptism no longer provided an answer to the Jewish Question according to liberal commentator, industrialist, and, later, government minister Walther Rathenau. As Rathenau, who was denied a military commission because he was Jewish, wryly put it in his savage 1897 assault on the assimilation possibilities of those aesthetic and physical ruins, his less-than-virile contemporaries of Jewish descent: "Often the only thing that still recalls the faith of the fathers is a certain ironic external atavism, Abraham's malicious [bequest to his descendents, *Malice*]": that is, that marking on the skin that nevertheless remains hidden yet cannot be camouflaged by the Jewish talent for mimicry, that primitive sacrifice that, unlike the rest of *Judentum*, cannot be sacrificed to modernity, that practice that Rathenau no less ironically alludes to but does not expressly name, circumcision.[53]

In its ironic impossibility as what cannot be seen but must be shown and as what must be natural but is an effect of artifice, made all the more impossible by the tacit taboo of public discussion or depiction,[54] "circumcision" haunted the Central European cultural imagination.[55] Even in its apparent unmentionableness, the mutual implication of circumcision and *Judentum* surfaced in German speech. "In contemporary German [c. 1843] one says '*jüdschen*' or '*jüdischen*' instead of 'circumcise'; that means 'to make [one] a Jew.'"[56] Because it both pointedly encapsulated that which it would disavow—the misrecognition of constructed differences by which hegemony enacts itself—and remained inextricably attached to the (un)dead Jews,[57] "circumcision" became both an apotropaic monument and a floating signifier that functioned as a dispositive,[58] an apparatus that connected biblical citations, stories, images, phantasies, laws, kosher slaughterers (*Schochets*),[59] ethnographic studies, medical diagnoses, and ritual practices, among other deposits in that noisome landfill called Europe, in order to produce knowledge about and authorize the identity of *Judentum*—and of the uncircumcised.

On Freud's Corpus

Freudian discourse was at least as much shaped by the corporealization of identity as it helped shape this phenomenon. This work focuses upon the feminizing representations of and allusions to (male) Jewish body parts and techniques that traverse Freud's corpus as he sought to mediate the double bind of Jewish existence while navigating through the crises of gender, sexual, racial (ethnic), class, and self-identity that were entangled in the European "Jewish Problem." Like other black faces, Freud wore the white masks of Austro-German bourgeois sexual, gender, and familial identities,[60] identities that psychoanalytic discourse sustained as much as it provided the narratives and tools to subvert them. And like other postcolonial subjects, he internalized the intertwined dominant antisemitic, misogynistic, colonialist,[61] and homophobic discourses that regularly bombarded the Jews (and himself as a Jew) with the opposition between the virile masculine norm and hypervirile-cum-effeminate Jewish other, the healthy German and the mentally ill Jew.[62] Freud then reinscribed these images as well as those norms in a would-be hegemonic discourse (the science of psychoanalysis) that in part projected them upon those other Jews (not to be confused with Jewishness per se) as well as women, homosexuals, so-called primitives, the masses, and neurotics, and in part he transformed these representations into universal characteristics.[63]

This work is in line with a series of developments that have contributed to the revaluation of "Jewishness" as a constituent part of the analysis of a "Jewish" writer's corpus.[64] There are theoretical factors at work: for instance, under the headings of new historicism and cultural studies, approaches to texts have emerged that understand them and their producers as embedded in a matrix of cultural discourses. No less significant is what Barbara Kirschenblatt-Gimblett has called the particular "corporeal turn" of this attention to discourse, whereby "new ways to think about text as a social, corporeal, and material practice" are offered.[65] These new hermeneutical positions have also drawn on earlier rethinkings of the relationships between writers and their works. A certain S. Freud had taught them how one's productions often exceed one's intentions. In *Moses*, Freud provided perhaps his most graphic statement of this relationship and a most generous warrant for their readings. Speaking of the *Torah*, he wrote:

> The text, however, as we possess it today will tell us enough about its own vicissitudes. Two mutually opposed treatments have left their traces on it. On the one hand, it has been subjected to revisions which have falsified it in the sense of their secret aims, have mutilated and amplified and have even changed it into its reverse; on the other hand, a solicitous piety has presided over it and has sought to preserve everything as it was, no matter whether it was consistent or contradicted itself. Thus, almost everywhere noticeable gaps, disturbing repetitions, and obvious contradictions have

come about—indications which reveal things to us which it was not intended to communicate. In its implications the distortion of a text resembles a murder: the difficulty is not in perpetrating the deed, but in getting rid of its traces. (23:43)

And armed with these tools of textual forensics—and, I would suggest, an implicit ethical responsibility to undertake such textual reconstructions (after all, Freud is speaking about a sort of murder here)—I, like other contemporary scholarly detectives, am investigating the corpus of Freud's writings in search of an underlying body of *Judentum*. We look for clues, traces of the concerns (not always conscious or intentional) on the margins of his text; we keep our eyes open for the various *Entstellungen*—wrenching distortions of both form and content. We also attempt to discern what is avoided, omitted, de-emphasized. We ask ourselves: what doesn't seem to fit? what sticks out as strange? what seems not to jibe with what appeared earlier in the text?

The chapters that follow are symptomatic readings of the distortions and displacements, loud silences and quiet asides, effected by Freud's everyday engagement with *Judentum*, for he was immersed in a world in which recognition of his own Jewishness was unavoidable, if not necessarily consciously registered. Any morning he could wake up and find scrawled on Vienna's walls and *Werbesäule* (posts plastered with announcements): "Was die Jude glaubt ist einerlei, in der Rasse liegt die Schweinerei" (What the Jew believes doesn't matter, race is the source of his chicanery).[66] Daily he would be inundated with images and idioms, truisms and proverbs that drew upon a vast reservoir of antisemitic traditions that would deny him the authority and autonomy he would claim.[67] His scientific auditing and reading would be no less replete with the overflow from that same source. For example, when Freud was studying medicine at the University of Vienna in 1875, he could not have avoided the words of the honored professor of surgery, Theodor Billroth—as they were picked up and hurled throughout the medical school—regarding the unsuitability of Hungarian and Galician Jews for the pursuit of a medical education. He expressed his concern about the flood of ambitious immigrant Jews who lacked the talent, background, and financial resources to be good doctors. For the eminent surgeon it was more than a matter of qualifications: "It is often forgotten that the Jews are a well-defined nation and that a Jew . . . can never become a German. . . . It is certainly clear to me that, in spite of all reflection and individual sympathy, I deeply feel the cleavage between pure German and pure Jewish blood."[68] Nor could Freud avoid his particular family history, his particular network of friends and associates, his particular self-identifications, his particular identifications by others, the particular developments in culture, state, and society, and so forth.

In other words, Freud was traumatized. He was not a *victim* of trauma; rather, as Freud's own work on trauma recognized and later theorists have developed, he was the (often nonconscious) recipient of denigrating messages and signs that defied his immediate ability to propositionalize, integrate, or narrativize but that nonetheless left memory-traces.[69] Freud himself noted in *Interpretation*: "And the increasing importance of the effects of the anti-semitic movement upon our emotional life helped to fix [*zur Fixierung*] the thoughts and feelings of those early days" (4:196). Further, he was the object of the silences, projections, parapraxes (*Fehlleistungen*), expectations, and seemingly nonsensical statements generated by others no more able to incorporate the mnemic remains of certain experiences or the contradictions between personal interaction and nonconscious ideological presuppositions and attitudes. Whether Freud was inured by habit, blinded by convention, caught up in heroic narratives, diverted by attention elsewhere, reassured by inadequate hierarchical dichotomies such as science and superstition, modern and primitive, intrinsic and extrinsic, or confronted by category-shattering shame, violence, and dehumanization, these everyday occurrences—Benjamin, after his reading of Freud, called them "shock experiences" (*Schockerlebnisse*) that cannot be experienced as such, that is, cannot be adequately given meaning or integrated into ongoing self-narratives let alone theorized—had their effects.[70] As Freud noted as early as his and Breuer's programmatic "On the Psychical Mechanism," an insight that he never abandoned, psychopathology may arise when "a number of partial traumas forming a group of provoking causes have only been able to exercise a traumatic effect by summation" (2:6).[71]

Freud's "double" and occasional correspondent, to whom Freud confided "*Judentum* continues to mean much to me on an emotional level,"[72] the medically trained, Viennese author Arthur Schnitzler appended a most telling image to his 1913 autobiography, *My Youth in Vienna*.[73]

> It was not possible, especially not for a Jew in public life, to ignore the fact that he was a Jew; nobody else was doing so, not the Gentiles and even less the Jews. You had the choice of being counted as insensitive, obtrusive and fresh; or of being oversensitive, shy and suffering from feelings of persecution. And even if you managed somehow to conduct yourself so that nothing showed, it was impossible to remain completely untouched; as for

instance a person may not remain unconcerned whose skin had been anaesthetized [and] who has to watch, with his eyes open, how it is scratched by an unclean knife, even cut into until the blood flows.

The scenario that Schnitzler evokes is of the Viennese Jew seemingly inured to the slights, habitually parrying the blows, who wishes to reveal neither his recognition of nor reaction to those assaults, and yet despite himself, on occasion, bears evidence of the attacks. More significant, beneath the surface he is infected by these wounds. Bandaging the point of entry will not prevent the potential poisoning of his entire corpus. Homeopathy may remedy the situation, but can the cure be distinguished from repetition-compulsion?[74]

Freud's deferred engagement with the traces of his memories and others' postmemories proved an affect-laden, transferential relationship. That relationship could be one of acting-out, of unconsciously repeating the earlier practices and assumptions, but it could also be an ongoing working-through of that event and its remains: giving them meaning by integrating them into his interminable series of self-narratives and the ever expanding discourse of psychoanalysis. Thus, to recall again that long passage from *Moses*, the present of, on the one hand, that "pious" repetition and, on the other, that (technically speaking) "distorted" meaning-production is the text. This volume explores how a whole bill of "Jewish" particulars affected *nachträglich*, by deferred action, the production of a body of work we associate with the name Freud. In particular, it examines how, caught in the web of the dispositive circumcision, Freud fixed upon the transferential phantasy of castration[75] that would come to animate, as "living rock," his corpus and render meaningful the life-narratives of all as well as provide "the *a priori* condition governing interhuman exchange in the form of exchange of sexual objects."[76]

Like the author of "The Moses of Michelangelo," the author of the present work seeks to "divine secret and concealed things from unconsidered or unnoticed details, from the rubbish heap [*dem 'refuse'*], as it were, of our observations" (13:222). More than merely asserting that "the anxiety attendant on the fear of castration is a reinscription of Jewish anxieties that articulate with circumcision, and the significance of circumcision as a marker for the Jews,"[77] *On Freud's Jewish Body* undertakes close analyses of Freud's rhetorical moves: his brilliant use of narrative tropes, ambiguous figures, and selective citations, the presence or absence of curious footnotes, the choice of examples, and changes in emphases, as well as the "noticeable gaps, disturbing repetitions, and obvious contradictions"

(23:43), the officially dismissed anomalies and not-so-carefully camouflaged protuberances, that litter those same texts. It notes how Freud both enlists his readers as co-conspirators and takes advantage of what he describes as in

> the nature of our waking thought to establish order in material of that kind, to set up relations in it and to make it conform to our expectations of an intelligible whole. . . . In our efforts at making an intelligible pattern of the sense-impressions that are offered to us, we often fall into the strangest errors or even falsify the truth about the material before us.
>
> The evidences of this are too universally known for there to be any need to insist upon them further. In our reading we pass over misprints which destroy the sense, and have the illusion that what we are reading is correct. (5:499)

This work also recognizes that such could be said of itself—and indeed, as will be discussed in chapter 2, must be said.

Like Freud, I, too, assume the materiality of words, as he discusses in *Interpretation*: "It is true in general that words are treated in dreams as though they were things, and for that reason they are apt to be combined in just the same way as are presentations of things" (4:295–96). Freud repeatedly calls attention to how displaced verbal expressions allow the representation of the dream-thoughts: "Words, since they are the nodal points of numerous ideas, may be regarded as predestined to ambiguity; [and] dreams make unashamed use of the advantages thus offered by words for purposes of condensation and disguise" (5:340–41). For example, Freud later adds, a word can act as "a switch-point: where one of the meanings of the word is present in the dream-thoughts the other one can be introduced into the manifest dream" (5:410). A similar mechanism is at play in plays on words; the phonetic or orthographic similarities of different words are employed to institute linkages between seemingly divergent ideas or between licit and illicit thoughts (see 8:119–20). Such nodal points emerge in Freud's texts no less than in those other products of secondary revision, dreams.

Yet to speak of the chapters that follow as consisting of symptomatic readings is not the same as drawing upon particular Freudian passages as signifiers of a plaint afflicting acculturated Central European Jewish men between Emancipation and the Shoah, in general, and/or one particular acculturated Central European Jewish man, Sigmund Freud, in particular. These chapters depict a Freud immersed in webs of discourses, buffeted by often separated strands of the cultural imaginary, who, like every individual, Jew or Gentile, incarnated numerous often contradictory, usually overlapping subject (and subjected or abject) positions with divergent desires, values, and interests, each of which makes different demands. They explore how the double (triple, quadruple, et cetera) binds and traumatic encounters left remainders in Freud's textual corpus. These readings, however, take those particular scenes and then restage the dramas—the texts—in which they are embedded. This work depicts a Freud not as an ambivalent Jew (although, like the rest of us, traversed by numerous ambivalences)[78] but as an ordinary Viennese, one making extraordinary attempts to mitigate—both in the sense of "to moderate" as well as the frequent but nonetheless erroneous sense of "to militate against or counter"—the trauma of everyday antisemitism. Not just diagnostic acts of interpretation, such as those undertaken by Sander Gilman and Daniel Boyarin, or illustrations of a particular character type, such as the self-hating, ambivalent, or psychological Jew, these readings of the remnants and *revenants* analyze the possible contexts and conditions for the emergence of not just these anomalies but of the texts themselves.

A Historic Quest

The quest for an answer to Freud's Jewish Question in his writings precedes even *Moses* let alone the present work. It goes back at least to the 1920s, with Fritz Wittels's ambivalent *Sigmund Freud: The Man, His Teaching, and His School*; Charles E. Maylan's antisemitic *Freud's Tragic Complex*; and Isidore Sadger's *Sigmund Freud: Personal Recollections*. Since the appearance of Ernst Simon's 1957 compendium, "Sigmund Freud, the Jew," works examining Sigmund Freud the Jew have ranged from David Bakan's (1958) kabbalistic speculations to Dennis Klein's (1981) sociology-of-knowledge examination of Freud and the Jewish membership of the early psychoanalytic circle; from Carl Schorske's (1973) depiction of antisemitic constraints on Freud's career choices and dream thoughts to Jacques Le Rider's (1990) analysis of the crises of gender, sexual, and Jewish identities in Freud's Vienna; from John Murray Cuddihy's (1974) meditation on Freud's mediation of uncivil Jew and overcivil Gentile to Estelle Roith's (1987) stereotype of the traditional Jewish misogynist;[79] from Marthe Robert's (1974) charting of the ambivalences of Freud's Jewish family romance and Marianne Krüll's (1979) speculations about Freud and his father to Peter Gay's (1987) *"cordon sanitaire"* against any imputation of Jewish religiosity to an atheist Jew.[80]

In the last decade of the twentieth century, studies of Freud the Jew proliferated even more. On the one hand, there was the series of responsa to *der Mann Moses*—the chain of readings initiated by Yerushalmi's *Freud's Moses*, followed by Jacques Derrida's *Archive Fever* and then Richard J. Bernstein's *Freud and the Legacy of Moses*.[81] On the other hand, there was the series of reincarnations of *der Mann* Freud: Daniel Boyarin's *Unheroic Conduct* and Sander Gilman's diptych, *Freud, Race and Gender* and *The Case of Sigmund Freud*. Beyond these series Freud's last work has captured the attention of leading figures in Jewish Studies and cognate fields.[82]

This recent surge in revaluations of the import of Jewishness for understanding Freud and his work is in part a consequence of institutional factors in North America. One is the increase in *baalei tshuvah*, masters of the return, the return of many Jews to a religiosity they never possessed. Another is the privileging of the victim as the one remaining site of ethical authenticity. Still another is the rise of multiculturalisms that entail the recognition of both so-called Western civilization as a hegemonic institution and its coexistence with innumerable ignored or denigrated groups, discourses, and practices. While a Foucauldian realization of the inextricable entanglement of knowledge and power frequently led to anti-identitarian and antiessentialist stances, such as an understanding of cultures as intrinsically heterogeneous with porous boundaries undergoing persistent contact, more frequently the attention to conditions of oppression and concerns about agency led to the assumption of the representative and expressive character of marginalized cultural productions and producers. Yet another involves American university politics in which African-American, Chicano, Lesbigay, Jewish, Subaltern, and Women's Studies compete for legitimation and budgets.

Conversely, in an era when identity politics and positioning and their theoretical correlatives, the local and the corporeal, provide the parameters for much academic discourse and when hyphenated-American people of color among other postcolonial peoples, lesbigays, and women (including Jewish women) carve out the field of discursive objects, about what can straight, white Jewish men discourse? Are they doomed to be the defenders—which is to say, the offenders—of the hegemon? What is the position of white (or so identified from outside), straight (but maybe not), Jewish (of some sort) males in a field, Cultural Studies (albeit a field yet to be generally recognized), that seems to privilege the nonwhite, nonstraight, non-Jewish, nonmale? In other words, what about me and those like me? We, too, are establishing our canon, composed of those texts by individuals like Freud whose situation put in question these categories of identity and whose texts were generated by the attempt—conscious or not—to negotiate the boundaries and categories of identity. This work is, among other things, a contribution to such canon-formation.

More problematic is the far too frequent exclusion of matters Jewish from that seemingly all-inclusive rubric, the "multicultural." This takes various forms, such as the exclusion of Jewish groups from student multicultural organizations, the omission of Jewish Studies from Ethnic Studies, and *Judentum*'s elision from, or derision by, broadly speaking, multicultural analyses.[83] Corollary to these expulsions is the widespread belief that Jews—particularly Jewish men—have made it into, if not are identical with, the white power structure and that they form part of the so-called Judaeo-Christian tradition. As the neoconservatives and the neoliberals join in a choral celebration of that tradition, or the progressive intelligentsia proffers a Bronx cheer,[84] the marginality, otherness, and particularity of *Judentum* has been forgotten. Further, with the much reported demise of Christianity as the dominant ideology of our dominant academic discourses—and the more recent fear that it threatens an autocratic restoration—it is assumed that Christianity's longtime companion has either died along with it or is seeking its own hegemony, as was so often promulgated in rumors of old. *Judentum* has become, in the words of Freud, "to some extent a fossil" (23:88). Thus, Jews have been written out of critical feminist studies, which place the onus for misogyny on "traditional Jewish culture" and for patriarchy on the "Old Testament."[85] Even Sander Gilman,[86] who has perhaps more than anyone inventoried the leavings of European modernity's pandemic of antisemitic discourses, has let the indigenous misogynist discourses of Europe off the hook by "explaining" Freud's often stereotypical discourse on women as his defensive displacement of the discourses of racial antisemitism.

The consequences of the various supersessions of, or superimpositions upon, *Judentum* by the seemingly secular academy are manifold. These practices not only erase Jewish experience, but they also render the West thoroughly homogeneous. The erasure of internal difference thereby condemns the Jews resident therein as thoroughly collusive with a dominant culture for which, to the contrary, they have been an object of domination and to which they have represented a threatening and potentially destabilizing other. Daniel and Jonathan Boyarin call attention to how even the term "Jew" has been expropriated in recent, particularly French, postmodernist discourse;[87] in the works of Lyotard and Nancy among several others (even Derrida), Jewish particularity has been troped into universality (as the ethical or as the marginal, or, as Yuri Slezkine has recently added, "the mercurian")[88] and "real Jews" are in effect limited to the dead or to, at most, in Isaac Deutscher's here-appropriate phrasing, non-Jewish Jews like Freud.[89]

Still, why this return specifically to Freud when he is being excoriated in the pages of American journals of opinion, such as the *New York Review of Books*,[90] dismissed in departments of psychology and psychiatry, and considered *Trayf* (non-Kosher) by most feminists, positivists, and multiculturalists. For one, in the United States Freud was always already a locus of Jewish identification, as recent autobiographical remarks by such American scholars as Bruce Lincoln, Judith Gardiner, Nina Auerbach, and Elaine Marks testify.[91] Marks recalls, for example, that "for most members of my secular Jewish family, Freudian psychoanalysis played the role of a governing principle, frame of reference, and endless source of Jewish pride." Freud (together with or in opposition to Karl Marx) served for their generation—my generation—as perhaps the Jewish ego ideal: he was the genius Jew who transformed modern (i.e., Gentile) culture.

Today in our post–Cold War world, groups busily seek ethnic, racial, gender, and sexual "role models" in order to generate and market their identities. Freud would be so positioned to play such a role for contemporary Jews as they defiantly assert Jewishness in a culture that too often erases Jewish identity. Further, who better to serve as "a role model" than the *father* of the modern and, for that matter, the (post)modern identity, the theorist of identity formation, from whom most contemporary theories of the social construction of identity take off—even if that take-off point is the (often unacknowledged and dialectical) negation of their own notions of identity construction. If Sigmund Freud, this secular bourgeois *gentilhomme*, can now be demonstrated to be Jewish, Jews can more than *shep naches* (Yiddish, "to derive an exultant feeling of pride") or gain an extra boost toward the pursuit of acceptance by, and assimilation into, the dominant culture. If Sigmund Freud can be shown to have an identity that is not merely negative (the impossibility of not-being a Jew) and if that Jewishness is not merely factual, incidental, but is indeed productive of his discourse, then recent Jewish cultural history can offer something besides the Shoah and Israel as the conjoined answers to the question, "What is a Jew?" And if Sigmund Freud can be shown to have a disposition toward some form of Jewish religiosity—this desire is clearly evident in Yerushalmi's *Freud's Moses—oy Gottenyu*. . . .

And yet with regard to my attempt to discern the contours and contexts of Freud's Jewish Question and mine, it may well be that speculating about Freud's possible religiosity, no less than, with regard to the origin of monotheism, Freud's own speculating about Moses' possible Egyptian origin,[92] is more diverting than decisive. Much of the recent discussion of where to place the emphasis in the phrase "Gdless Jew" probably has less to do with Freud's letter to Pfister with which I began than with the implications of words Freud wrote in his *Diary* [*Chronik*] on 15 March 1938, less than three months before he would depart from Vienna for the last time. Perhaps even as Hitler was addressing a vast crowd in Vienna's Heldenplatz, Freud noted "Search in press and house"; two separate bands of S.A. thugs searched his home and the offices of the psychoanalytic press.

The Holocaust hovers over both the reception of Freud and the determination of, at least, North American Jewish identity.[93] Regarding the latter, Peter Novick among others has initiated a debate about the roles of discourse about the Holocaust in American life in a work of the same title.[94] While this introduction is not the place to debate the nature, motives, and extent of the purported instrumentalization of the Shoah, other aspects of Novick's work are. First, he argues that the Shoah, as the one common reference point of self-identified American Jews, has become the basis for their Jewish identity and indeed has become an ersatz religion in Jewish communities.[95] My own experience of teaching courses on the Shoah has revealed that the Holocaust is no less identified with Jewishness by non-Jews; Gentiles often inform me that they take my classes to learn more about their Jewish friends or, in a number of instances, to learn about Judaism.[96]

Second, in his account of Holocaust instrumentalization Novick seems to have adopted the *Gleichschaltung* (Nazideutsch for synchronization) of trauma and repression one finds in the likes of Frederick Crews and company; he places the onus of justifying the "inevitable development" of the ascension of the Holocaust to a central position in American life on the "sometimes explicitly, always implicitly Freudian" notion of Holocaust as traumatic event.[97] While adopting a very different posture toward Freud, Yerushalmi as well as many of the others reinvestigating Freud's relationship to *Judentum* are, as I intimated above, also seeking an alternative to Holocaust-determined Jewish identities.

Profiles in Interpretation

One of the great values of the new literature on the Jewish Freud is that it is filling in the silences that were his personal and cultural contexts—in particular, the variety of nineteenth-century Judaisms and the endemic

presence of anti-Jewish representations in scientific as well as popular discourses. The researches and reconstructions of a number of scholars have
also helped to remedy many of the earlier presentations of the religious
training and environment of Freud and his family.[98] Freud's knowledge
of the Bible and of Jewish practices was clearly greater than he would
acknowledge publicly. Further, his asserted ignorance of Hebrew and Yiddish now appears to be somewhat hyperbolic considering that the latter
was indeed the *Mamaloschen*, his mother's language of choice. Nor was
knowledge of Hebrew absent. Beyond the speculations over Freud's understanding his father's Hebrew dedication to him in the family Bible is a
striking exchange between Freud and the psychoanalyst Max Eitingon in
October 1913. On the first of October Eitingon extends to Freud "the old
Jewish New Year's greeting, *l'shana tovah*" (have a good year), with the
greeting itself written in Hebrew letters, and recalls that Freud had years
before ended one of the psychoanalytic association congresses with the
same phrase. In his response on the third, Freud has clearly understood
the Hebrew for he responds that he "could use such good wishes any time
of the year."[99] Further, comments, such as the oft-cited "I think it's called
Menorah" written to his wife after a 1907 visit to the Roman catacombs,[100]
seem more evident of a wittily ironic sensibility than of a shamelessly unin-
formed Jew. In addition, these researches have convincingly demonstrated
the inadequate and inaccurate historical understanding of earlier writers
who had concluded that based on these anything but simple and self-evident "facts"—Jakob Freud's ties to the *Haskalah* (Jewish Enlightenment
movement[s]), his possession of a Philippson Bible with its parallel Hebrew and German texts and appended German commentary, and his wedding to Amalia (Sigmund's mother) under the auspices of the leader of
Vienna's, in fact, rather conservative Reform congregation, Isaac Noah
Mannheimer—Jakob Freud had been subject to a lapse in traditional Jewish piety. He was, rather, more a modern orthodox than a reform Jew.

The major foci of the new (as well as much of the old) literature on the
how and the why of Freud's Jewish identity have been Freud's two key
lifelong identifications, his father Jakob and Moses, and the two primary
sites of their appearance in Freud's corpus, *Interpretation* and *Moses*. In his
first major work and culminating achievement of his self-analysis, *Interpretation*, Freud recounts a childhood conversation with his father. Jakob told
him how on one Shabbat when he was young a Christian lout accosted
him, knocking his *Streimel* (the fur hat worn by Hasidic men on Shabbat)
into the muck and telling him to get off the sidewalk. When his son asked
him what he then did, the senior Freud quietly replied that he stepped

into the street and retrieved his hat. Freud recalls that the young Sigmund became quite disturbed by his father's "unheroic conduct" and immediately contrasted it with the action of another Semite, Hamilcar Barca, who forced his son Hannibal to swear vengeance against the Romans (4:195–98). Since at least Robert and Cuddihy this scene of the unmanned traditional Jew has assumed the place of the primal scene for the unfolding of Freud's Jewish identity. This family romance—that is, this adoption phantasy in which the child, Sigmund, imagines that his ignoble father is but a substitute for the true and noble one—together with Freud's crisis of identification[101] are finally resolved in the deserts of Midian where the great man, the Egyptian Moses, is murdered in the climax of *Moses*.

It is no surprise that the father of the father of the Oedipal complex would become the object of analysis. Nor is it a surprise, given the highly charged character of Freud's recollection, that attention would be focused upon this apparently traumatic scene.[102] Some scholars have read this scene of impotence and passivity—unmanning—in the face of antisemitism as emblematic of the stereotypical gendered and sexual character of Jewish identity. Recently, some others have taken another approach. They have transvalued Jakob Freud's *Shabbos* encounter from a humiliation to a testimony to self-restraint—comparable to that embodied, according to Freud, by the *Moses* of Michelangelo. Daniel Boyarin mediates the two poles; he recognizes Freud's introjection of Austro-Victorian models of virile masculinity as well as the dominant representations of the feminized male Jew and consequent repudiation of his father's "feminine" behavior; however, Boyarin also recognizes Jakob Freud's behavior as exemplary of a traditional Jewish male identity that refuses to indulge in *Goyische naches*, the violence allegedly taken pride in by Gentile men.

In place of the humiliation of Jakob, the pivotal moment of the analyses of Yerushalmi among others is the interpretation of Jakob Freud's inscription in the family Bible that he presented to his son on his thirty-fifth birthday. These analysts conclude that Jakob Freud had composed the inscription entirely in *Melitzah*, a Hebrew literary form often employed in riddles. The text proves to be a carefully constructed mosaic of fragments and phrases from and allusions to *Torah* and *Talmud*. Line-by-line analyses of this inscription reveal that Jakob Freud, far from a lapsed Jew, was still immersed in the texts and practices of traditional Judaism. Further, rather than repeating the frequent representation of Freud's father as the embodiment of the passive Jew whose time has past, Yerushalmi et al. portray an individual who rises to make a claim upon his son, "a call for Sigmund's return and reconciliation."[103]

These readings by Yerushalmi and others, such as Rice, Gresser, and Ostow,[104] have indeed redeemed the image of Jakob Freud from his son's earlier biographers; the wimp who could no longer hold on to his religion let alone a job has become an inwardly resilient, life-enjoying practicing Jew. But such is not their only nor their primary goal. By attending to the inscription in the family Bible, these scholars would redeem a Jewish son. Freud's own claims for the objective, impersonal, scientific nature of psychoanalysis; the efforts of Ernest Jones and others to de-Judaize psychoanalysis, and Freud, in order to make both the man and the science acceptable to an Anglo-American audience; and Peter Gay's continuation of these traditions through a narrow, "rigorously secularist" definition of Freud's Jewishness and a no less rigorous skepticism of "any share that identity could have had in the making of psychoanalysis"—all these together necessitated a perhaps overcompensatory attempt by Yerushalmi et al. to reconstruct Freud's (and their own) more than psychological or sociological Jewishness.[105] Freud's Jewishness is no longer characterized by them as the mediation between an accident of birth and the necessities of antisemitic Vienna, universal science, and Oedipus; rather, Freud is now seen as continuously confronting—whether consciously or unconsciously—the particularities of Jewish religiosity.

This inscription in the middle of his life would set Freud (and these analysts) on a journey that would end with him attempting "to answer the hitherto unanswerable question of what makes [Freud] a Jew."[106] The earlier humiliation of his father is not, then, the repressed trauma compelling Freud to deny his fellow Jews their claims to divine election and the discovery of monotheism. For these scholars, Freud, in writing *Moses*, is heeding his father's call to return and reconcile, even as he is attempting to come to understand what motivates the Nazis' murderous antisemitism. Freud is not, as Robert, for example, claims in *From Oedipus*, seeking to combat his fear that in his old age he is becoming his father, a poor *schmo* sitting in a corner, ever at the mercy of antisemites. And they are looking at more than the manifest Jewish content in the work that Freud was completing as the twisted road to Auschwitz was under construction—namely, *Moses*.

Long dismissed as an expression of a writer long past his prime, *Moses* is, admittedly, a most curious work; it is composed of a mixed multitude of styles and marked by "noticeable gaps, disturbing repetitions and obvious contradictions" (23:43), such as Freud's oft-cited failure to note Karl Abraham's work on Akhenaten.[107] The work contains as well a host of questionable historical, ethnographical, and Lamarckian assumptions. It bears the characteristics of the compulsiveness that drove Freud to this project as it tormented him "like an unlaid ghost" (23:103). Indeed one cannot help but think that Freud's discussion of the dynamics of textual distortion in the *Torah* applied as much to *Moses* as it did to the *Five Books of Moses*. So what kind of Jew wrote *Moses*? The picture Yerushalmi draws, following Philip Rieff,[108] is of Freud the "Psychological Jew" who has unambivalently embraced Jewishness—intellectuality and independence of mind, the highest ethical and moral standards, concern for social justice, tenacity in the face of persecution—if not Judaism.[109] Yet Yerushalmi, too, would ground his psychological Jew in some material religious *realia* such as Jakob Freud's inscription. Yerushalmi holds out for the possibility that evidence is available to confirm some essential—or at least positive—religious content to Freud the Jew. Consequently, in a provisional postscript, he notes how the existence of items of Jewish content in Freud's possession had recently come to his attention.

> I do not know if Freud bought these ritual objects or inherited them from his parents. I do not claim for a moment that the fact that Freud owned two kiddush cups and a Menorah means that he ever used them for the purposes for which they were intended, any more than I would think he necessarily worshipped his Egyptian deities. That the Jewish objects were part of his most private ambiance seems, for the moment, sufficiently noteworthy and (such are the surprising vicissitudes in the unfolding story of Freud), may, with the discovery of further facts, even prove significant.[110]

He clearly desires to found Jewish "national character" and the character of a Jewish role model on more than a collection of attitudes or a psychological disposition. Yerushalmi, who in *Zakhor* detailed Jewish memory in liturgy and practice, seeks to restore what Freud has with his "memory-traces" substituted for: "direct communication and . . . education by example" (23:128).[111]

Oddly, Yerushalmi, like others who have sought to ground Freud's Jewishness religiously, neglects that other material site of Jewish religious identity, that other trace that Freud abundantly discusses in *Moses*. That material correlate emerges unnamed but clearly pictured in a third primary site for the analyses of Freud the Jew: the famous footnote appended to Freud's "Analysis of a Phobia in a Five-Year-Old Boy."[112] In that note Freud first propounds his theory that "the castration complex is the deepest unconscious root of antisemitism." He continues, "for even in the nursery little boys hear that a Jew has something cut off his penis—a piece of his penis, they think—and this gives them the right to despise Jews" (10:36n1). That material remainder is circumcision.

A number of analysts,[113] based on their readings of historical and Freudian discourses on circumcision, among other body parts and techniques, argue that Jewish identity, whether postmodern or premodern, is not just a matter of mediating the particular and the universal or the secular and the religious; it is also constructed out of the cultural representations and performances of body, gender, and sexuality. And the identity of Jewish males was composed of, if not puppy-dogs' tails, then circumcised penises, for no signifier of Jewish difference was more important to the determination of turn-of-the-century male Jews like Sigmund Freud than circumcision. The identification of the male Jew with his (assumed-to-be) circumcised penis functioned subjectively as well as objectively: "the internalized self-contempt that the colonized male comes to feel for his disempowered situation [was] represented in the case of Jews by the affect surrounding circumcision."[114] That affect was horror. For many of Freud's non-Jewish contemporaries, that a people would ritually practice genital mutilation was no historical accident: it suggested something perverse in their essential being. Worse, constellating about the figure of circumcision was that most threatening representation—to both Jew and European—of the feminized Jewish male,[115] or, following Daniel Boyarin, the "femminized" Jew (i.e., the performance of Jewish maleness, which is other than normative European masculinity and thus is represented within dominant discourses as effeminate).

The "Little Hans" footnote, the *locus classicus* of the feminizing threat posed by circumcision, does not just draw parallels between the origins of antisemitism and those of misogyny. Freud marks the convergence of hatred toward Jews and women with a reference to Otto Weininger and his "remarkable book" *Sex and Character*. In Weininger's much-discussed and much-reprinted tome of 1903, the figure of the feminized Jew achieves its to-that-point most elaborate formulation; he characterizes women and male Jews with virtually identical, virulently negative attributes, often analogizing the one to the other—*"The Jew, like Woman, has no personality."*[116] Gilman reads the reference as arguing that Weininger—not Freud—"is like the little (non-Jewish) boy . . . who hears about the Jews cutting off their penises, except that he, of course, knows that it is true," and therefore draws the conclusion that if they have already taken a little off the top they could take the rest. Weininger becomes fixated at this infantile stage. Hence, "Jewish neurotics like Weininger focus on the negative difference of their bodies from ones that are 'normal,' and use this difference, like their evocation of the bodies of women, to define themselves." "'Normal' Jews, like Little Hans" (see 9:135), by contrast, are "made to understand that the real difference is not between their circumcised penises and those of uncircumcised males, but between themselves and castrated females." Gilman's Freud is gazing at Weininger gazing at his own penis, and, here as elsewhere, Freud's "need to distance the challenges to the special nature of the Jew's body through his creation of a universal 'male' body transmutes categories of race into categories of gender."[117] Thus, Gilman's Freud, like any analyst, is amid the fray but not of it. (This also applies to Gilman's readings of Freud's texts; he situates them amid the mass of antisemitic effluvia but rarely provides the close readings of Freud's texts that would demonstrate compellingly that they are—*and they are*—embedded in this cultural morass.) Gilman's Freud is Moses, who would slay the overseer beating upon the Jews and emancipate himself and his people from such victimizing images; he is the doctor combating the epidemic of antisemitic discourses by rendering them harmless—to male Jews.

Daniel Boyarin more appropriately sees Freud gazing at his own penis and places him in a colonial scenario where "knowledge of [his] own circumcision must inevitably produce in the Jew a sense of inferiority vis-à-vis the Gentile, a sense of inferiority that Freud himself shared." To feel inferior is to be placed in the feminine position that Freud identifies with the homosexual. He "accepts the characterization of Jews as differently gendered, as indeed female, and tries to overcome this difference." Whereas for Gilman Freud merely displaces the anti-Jewish responses to circumcision, for Daniel Boyarin Freud is in the thrall of homophobic panic. Freud occludes the Jewish identities of Little Hans (Herbert Graf), Weininger, and, above all, himself, and in their place constructs Oedipus: "The Oedipus complex is Freud's family romance of escape from Jewish queerdom into gentile, phallic heterosexuality." By screening his circumcision, like his identification with a series of "Jewish" non-Jews, from the Semitic Hannibal to the Egyptian Moses, Freud was able "to remain Jewish in name but be entirely transformed in such a way that the Jewishness would be invisible."[118] Whereas Gilman concludes his *Case* (and thus his two-part work) with a paean to Sigmund Freud, the Jewish scientist who refused "to disavow his sense of Jewish identity,"[119] for Boyarin Freud's Jewishness is the very site of a disavowal; Freud constructed psychoanalysis, and himself, upon the refusal of a certain Jewish identity that is marked by circumcision—the *Mensh* who is gentle rather than Gentile, the "feminized" rather than the effeminate Jew. Boyarin finds the circumcised penis as the mark of both a certain always already, never-not-yet ideal Jewish identity and its repression.[120]

As can be seen in both Boyarin's and Gilman's texts, a primary, if not primal, response to the fluidity of (post)modernity is to seek some ground upon which to anchor that Jewish identity, or at least some bedrock that resists the pressures of fragmentation and dissemination and that delimits signification. Because it is inscribed on the body of every Jewish male, perhaps no signifier of Jewish difference resists those pressures more than circumcision. Yet while the act of circumcision binds the young male to the covenantal community and inscribes him into and with a tradition, it apparently does not satisfy the demands for the construction of a (post)modern religiously Jewish self. One significant factor contributing to its insufficiency is that it is only performed on males.[121] A number of other problems with ascribing a significant role to circumcision in Jewish identity formation arise from the differential aspect of circumcision—it separates and distinguishes (specifically, male Jews from others) as much as it binds and inscribes. Most often perceived by contemporary culture,[122] and thus to the acculturated Jews who have introjected this perspective, as a sign of difference, circumcision indicates a purely negative relation, understood both semiologically and ethically, rather than serves as the emblem of a desired positive identity.[123] By extension, as a mark of difference circumcision determines Jewish identity by its relations with the identities of other peoples and thus subverts any claims for an autochthonous Jewish identity. Further, emptying out even the differential character of the circumcised signifier is that the Jews are not the only, nor by any means the most populous, group to practice circumcision—whether in the United States, where the circumcision of the majority of newly born boys still takes place, or in a world with more than a half billion circumcised Muslim men.

Also further problematizing the value of circumcision's differential quality is its association with secularity and Spinoza, the "first great culture-hero of modern secular Jews" or, until Freud, "the arch-heretic of Judaism [in] modern times."[124] Freud's "fellow unbeliever" Spinoza, writing in the *Tractatus Theologico-Politicus*, the predecessor of *Moses*, credits circumcision both for separating the Jews from other peoples—thereby incurring their hatred—and for preserving them. An additional problem with circumcision is that it is material, corporeal, and practical in a culture that privileges the spiritual; although Jewish orthopraxy is now recognized, it is not the site for attempts to universalize Judaism's value. The privilege accorded the spiritual and intellectual devalues circumcision another way. Since the eight-day-old child does not authorize the procedure, circumcised Jewishness lacks the sense of autonomous choice that modernity (and Protestantism) associates with identity. Finally, there may be embarrass-

ment over discussing genitalia as well as a desire not to assign such significance to a practice and a mark with such shameful associations; then again,
it may be that circumcision creates an uncanny impression—for Freud its
evocation of castration—that makes individuals uncomfortable in speaking
about it.[125]

"Circumcision" appears more than twenty-five times in *Moses*: Freud
employs it as a "key-fossil" (*Leitfossil*; 23:39), as the evidence that allows
him to trace the Egyptian origins of monotheism and Moses. For Freud
circumcision both identifies the Jewish people and makes them a people
apart; it is the sign of neurotic compromise; and it is the symbolic substitute for castration. Yet, it fails to make Yerushalmi's index and only appears
briefly in his summary descriptions of Freud's text and of Ernest Jones's
"The Psychology of the Jewish Question."[126] Yerushalmi does implicitly
refer to circumcision by citing the letter to Arnold Zweig in which Freud
first broaches the Egyptian origin of Moses. Marthe Robert had employed
that 18 August 1933 correspondence to argue both for Freud's ambivalence about being Jewish and for *Moses* as the culmination of Freud's family romance.[127] In the letter, Freud comments on Zweig's own ambivalent
feelings toward his Jewishness: "One defends oneself in every way against
the fear of castration. Here a *piece of opposition* to one's own Jewishness may
still be hiding cunningly. Our great master Moses was, after all, a strong
anti-Semite and made no secret of it. Perhaps he was really an Egyptian."[128] Yerushalmi seeks to undercut the alleged opprobrium of Freud's
last assertion and thus Robert's claim: "If as [Freud] believed, monotheism
did not evolve gradually, then it had to come to the Israelites abruptly and
from the outside or . . . it had to be 'given' to them by a 'great stranger.'
In this . . . he is in curious accord with the Bible, only there the great
stranger is God himself."[129] In countering Robert's "psychoanalyzing"
and its threat of an ambivalence that would diminish Freud's value as a
Jewish role model, Yerushalmi does more than merely repeat the offending
passage from the letter. Rather he quotes the entire passage with its invocation of castration, yet resists commenting on that content. Whether
placing the passage against the footnote to "Analysis" or the discussion in
Moses of how circumcision, by "recalling the dreaded castration," is among
the "deeper motives [i.e., both ancient and unconscious] for hatred of the
Jews" (23:91), one clearly is not indulging in a psychoanalysis of Freud to
recognize that the "piece of opposition" is the missing foreskin.

Yerushalmi's foreclosure of circumcision from Freud's discourse of Jewish identity soon took a curious turn. Jacques Derrida, whose obsession
with circumcision was amply documented in the autobiographical "Cir-

confession,"[130] offered an encomium to Yerushalmi's *Freud's Moses* in *Mal d'archive/Archive Fever*. In classic deconstructive fashion, Derrida would read Freud's *Moses* through an earlier strong reading: in this case, *Freud's Moses*. Consonant with his interests, Derrida teased with the figure of circumcision throughout his essay; for example, in discussing the necessity of the archive to have an exterior he tossed out: "Is a circumcision, for example, an exterior mark? Is it an archive?"[131] The second citation in his exergue, which he announced will concern circumcision, was that same inscription by Jakob Freud that is the focus of Yerushalmi et al. Derrida's promised evocation of circumcision, however, had met with resistance. I imagine that Derrida would like to see *Metzitzah* (the ritual sucking of blood from the newly circumcised organ) behind the *Melitzah*—viewing the text perhaps as the *Mekhitzah* (the screen that separates men from women) or as a screen-memory. He hopes to meld the factual—that is, specific references to Sigmund Freud's circumcision—with the figural, with the matrix of associations generated by circumcision. Thus regarding the inscription Derrida writes: "and the very first sentence recalls, at least by figure, the circumcision of the father of psychoanalysis, 'in the seventh in the days of the years of your life.'"[132] But Derrida yields—at least in the manifest body of the text—after consultation with Yerushalmi and leaves the particulars to the footnotes: "I decided I should make this prudent addition ('at least by figure')[133] after a friendly talk with Yerushalmi, who several months later in New York, correctly warned me against a reading which would seem to identify here a *literal* or *direct* reference to the dated event of a circumcision."[134]

    This retreat is only temporary. In the course of his essay, that footnote moves into the body of the text, and Derrida places Yerushalmi in the position of Jakob Freud: "Like Freud's father, the scholar wants to call Sigmund Shelomoh back to the covenant by establishing, that is to say, by restoring the covenant. The scholar repeats, in a way, the gesture of the father. He recalls or he repeats the circumcision, even if the one and the other can only do it, of course, by *figure*."[135] As the "singular archive," circumcision would be substituted by Derrida for those "memory-traces" of Freud in which, following Yerushalmi, reside Jewish identity.[136] Although Derrida remarks that this "memory without memory of a mark returns everywhere" and holds "the enigma of circumcision [and] its literalness . . . to be irreducible, in particular in the rereading of Freud," he concedes that he "must put it aside here."[137]

The chapters that compose *On Freud's Jewish Body* do anything but put it aside. Yet a certain irony need be recognized with regard to the "irreducible literalness" of circumcision in this rereading of Freud. While Franz Maciejewski, in his *Psychoanalytic Archive*, has picked up on Derrida's "irreducible literalness" and concluded that "the sought-for common focus" of the Jewishness of Freud and the early psychoanalytic movement, their "shared intellectual constitution" and "consanguineous Jewish traits," as well as the primacy ascribed to castration, is to be found in "the *fact of circumcision* [*Tatsache der Beschneidung*] as the traumatic central event of Jewish socialization and ethnogenesis,"[138] in the chapters that follow I focus on the value of "circumcision" as a dispositive for the Central European imagination between Emancipation and the Shoah—whether the would-be-hidden circumcised penis or its displacement upward into visibility, the Jewish nose. The ascription of this ritual inscription more than signified Jewish difference, it established it for the non-Jew—even when the practice did not take place.[139] Consider this passage from Jacob Wasserman's autobiography *My Life as a German and a Jew*:

> Imagine a laborer who, when he asks for wages, never receives them in full although his work in no way falls below that of his fellow, and whose question as to the reason of such injustice receives this answer [*mit den Worten bescheidet*]: You cannot demand full pay, for you are pockmarked [*blatternarbig*]. He looks in the mirror and sees that his face is entirely free of pockmarks. He retorts: What do you mean? I have no pockmarks whatsoever. The others shrug their shoulders and reply: Your record declares you to be pockmarked, so you are pockmarked.[140]

Similarly, institutional assumptions about, and the assumed institutionality of, circumcision dictated the terms for the interpellation of the Jew into modern Central European society. At a crucial moment in Freud's work, circumcision proved no less a phantasy than the castration for which it symbolically substituted. While the assumed circumcision of Little Hans (Herbert Graf), the object of speculation and assumption surrounding that third scene of Jewish identification, is the "proof stone"[141] upon which rests Maciejewski's thesis that circumcision is the core trauma that Freud's theorization of the castration and Oedipal complexes screen, there is no record that Little Hans was in fact circumcised (nor for that matter were Freud's biological sons). No amount of mitigation, properly understood, ultimately mattered; circumcision was always already a mitigating, improperly understood, condition of Jewish life in Central Europe.

My Jewish Question

This project began over twenty-five years ago, like so many other academic endeavors, in the working out of a dissertation proposal, then entitled "'And He will let him have delight in [lit. *will let him scent*] the fear of the Lord' (*Isaiah* 11:3): Toward a Philosophic History of Shame." My focus had been on the relationships between normative European society and its indigenous others, especially women and Jews. Specifically I intended to trace what I perceived as the association, turned increasingly into the identification, of women and Jews—most frequently of male Jews with women—to the detriment of Jewish communities as such a connection became a primary component of anti-Jewish discourses.[142] Otto Weininger, I surmised, could not have been the first to analogize women and Jews, to question the innate virility of Jewish maledom.[143] I foresaw a trajectory that would take me from Marlowe's Jew of Malta and Shakespeare's Shylock through Lessing's Nathan—and their daughters—through the three figures who would ultimately become the focus of my dissertation: Schlegel's Lucinde, Hegel's Antigone, and Gutzkow's Wally,[144] and onward to Eliot's Daniel Deronda, Weininger, and Freud's Moses. The Shoah marked the terminus of this series and the catalyst for the underlying question, "Why the Jews?"

What was it about *Judentum* and/or its despisers that motivated such hatred and/or fear? Even if anti-Jewishness was a function of some scapegoating mechanism, why specifically the Jews? Did it lie in some (alleged) action, such as the murder of Gd? Was it some specific Jewish belief, whether in monotheism, the unrepresentable, or the ethical? Was it Jewish immodesty (*Unbescheidenheit*)[145]—the assertion of Jewish chosenness (embodied and incarnated by ritual, eating habits, endogamy) in the face of Gentile nationalism? Or was it related to the simple fact that, while there are no more ancient Romans (if we exclude that fascist interlude of the second quarter of the twentieth century), Greeks, or Babylonians, there still exist groups who call themselves Jews and identify with the community that inhabited Palestine two thousand and more years ago? That is, is Jewish persistence decisive in the persistence of anti-Jewishness?

My training in History of Religions led me to rethink these questions at a more general level: what are the effects of relations with others who are always already here, who are still here, and with whom it is necessary both to maintain (the other must remain other) and to misrecognize this ongoing relationship? In sum, what problems arise for the dominant culture—a culture with claims to autochthony and self-sufficiency—to have persistent and necessary[146] contact with other groups? To contain the threat presented by this contact the dominant group, I suggested, engages in exchange—the exchange of representations. The exchange of such gifts regulates the economy of the border encounters of different groups; however, these exchanges do not occur between ego and alter as anthropology typically define them, but rather they take place between hierarchically opposed rival subjects. Representations of those other others (such as women and Jews) are the coins of exchange in what are fundamentally (male) status contests. These agonistic encounters also maintain the border as well as author and authorize the participants. Only recognized, allegedly autonomous subjects are allowed to play.[147]

What ultimately led to this theoretical breakthrough that allowed me to mediate the general problematic about the role of representations of the other with the specific historical and literary observations of those representations—the increasing connections between women and (male) Jews—without resorting to theories, like Hans Mayer's about "outsiders," that subsume both women and Jews under some third category, or those that seek correspondence between representation practices and historical happenstance, such as the coincidences of late-eighteenth- and late-nineteenth-century emancipatory efforts and societal responses,[148] was a public lecture by George Mosse at the University of North Carolina, Chapel Hill, during the winter of 1984–85, in which he previewed his then-forthcoming book, *Nationalism and Sexuality*. I had never before or since found myself so excited by an academic talk. While his combination of anecdotal thick description and history of *mentalités* enchanted and confirmed, it did not satisfy. He had all of the dots, but a weak engine to generate the connections. *"It's all there; can't he see it?"* I screamed inside my head that night and to my trying-to-sleep wife every morning for the next week.

Dissertations being what they are—tasks to be done within a given period of time—I limited the body of the text to an examination of how and why three nineteenth-century bourgeois German men—Schlegel, Hegel, and Gutzkow—were acting like Trobriand Islanders, although exchanging images of women instead of shells. I was going to continue to work chronologically and move from its concluding focus, Gutzkow's representations of women, to how such representations led in part to his being represented as Jewish when fate intervened. During a Spring 1987 reception at Swarthmore College for external honors examiners I entered into a conversation with Princeton Professor of Religion and psychotherapist Mal Diamond about Freud's *Moses and Monotheism*. My reading and endeavoring to teach it had opened upon a mystery.[149] Simply put, "What's going on there?"

For Mal, not much, but I was fascinated by how the text enacted the textual distortions Freud ascribed to the *Tanakh*, the extensive concern followed abruptly by a virtual abandonment of his *Leitmotif*, the *Leitfossil* circumcision, the gendered aspect of Jewish identity, and his unanswered question of Jewish persistence. At the end of my rather long listing of intriguing aspects about the text, Mal asked if I would like to lecture on *Moses* to his Religion and Psychology class sometime. Well sometime came in the form of a call later that September when he repeated the offer. "Great. When?" "Next week," he replied.

In order to find some thread to weave together my diverse observations I scoured the Swarthmore College library shelves until I came across the marvelous collection from the 1980 Colloque de Montpellier *La psychanalyse est-elle une histoire juive?* and Jean-Pierre Winter's contribution "Sur 'Moïse et le Monothéisme' Psychanalyse de l'antisémitisme." What most struck me in the article though was its epigraph: a quote from the Pléiade edition of Spinoza's *Tractatus Theologico-Politicus* that began:

> As for the fact that [the Jews] have survived their dispersion and the loss of their state for so many years, there is nothing miraculous in that, since they have incurred universal hatred by cutting themselves off completely from all other peoples . . . by preserving the mark of circumcision with such devoutness. That their survival is largely due to the hatred of the Gentiles has already been shown by experience. . . . The mark of circumcision is also, I think, of great importance in this connection; so much so that in my view it alone will preserve the Jewish people for all time. [Then following another Winter-inserted ellipsis, the passage continued:] Of such a possibility we have a very famous example in the Chinese. They too have some distinctive mark on their heads which they most scrupulously observe. . . .[150]

Aha! Here was perhaps a clue to Freud's text: the problem being of course, that Winter provided the Pléiade pagination and not the Spinozan chapter. Eventually I did find the passage and filled in what proved to be a most telling elision: "indeed, did not the principles of their religion make them effeminate [*effoeminarent*] I should be quite convinced that some day when the opportunity arises . . . they will establish their state once more, and that God will choose them afresh." I seemed to have found the answer to my mystery: persistence, circumcision, and problematic gender (and even "curious omissions") all in one sentence by a possible precursor for Freud's activity in *Moses*: the great Jewish-born analyst of human passions, who drew conclusions from the historical-critical exegesis of apparent biblical contradictions that would not meet favor with his *Landsmen*, someone

who sought to distinguish between Judaism and the Jewish people, someone whose highest avowed value was the pursuit of truth, someone whom
posterity has greeted with either great acclaim or great disparagement—in
short, Spinoza.

To that point in my research and theoretical development, my focus
had been on gender and the primacy of the gender division of labor, with
its gender-coded spheres for the formation and maintenance of bourgeois
male hegemony. From this perspective, at the heart of the matter, of the
series of distortions that is the text *Moses and Monotheism*, was the traumatic knowledge that Freud sought to repress and a primary deep source
of the antisemitism that so problematized his situation as a Jew: an identification secreted behind the ever-present, never-acknowledged solution,
circumcision, to his problem of how the Jews "have been able to retain
their individuality till the present day" (23:136–37). As a consequence of
the syllogistic identification of the circumcised male Jew with woman (via
the mediations of circumcision as castration, as emasculation, as being effeminate), gender difference, so necessary to both Freud's theory and to
his society, was jeopardized. Thus, to acknowledge this cultural fact, this
historical truth that—as I phrased it then—"Jew equals woman" would
entail the repudiation of psychoanalysis. To acknowledge the solution
(that is, circumcision, which screens the repressed identification) to the
problem of Jewish persistence would be to anticipate the Final Solution.
That is, two factors—the circumcised Jew problematizing the gender division of labor that undergirt Central European society and the collapse of
traditional Jewish-Christian relations as foundational to society—threatened
to shift the relationship of the Jews to their host-culture from a neurotic
to a psychotic register. While traditional relations entailed the repression
of the Jews, a remnant was nevertheless required for Christian salvation;
that is, the two groups were doubly bound together—Jesus would only
return when the Jews converted, yet the Jews would only convert when
Jesus returned.[151] Without this countervailing neurosis, and, despite a cultural identification, incapable of fulfilling woman's biologically necessary
role in social reproduction, the threat posed by the circumcised Jew portended the psychotic reaction of foreclosure—extinction. Rather than face
the implications of circumcision upon the fates of psychoanalysis and of
the Jewish people, as Freud says with regard to the Jews and their knowledge of the Egyptian origin of circumcision, "the truth about circumcision
must also be contradicted" (23:30). That lecture to Mal's class led to a
presentation at the 1988 American Academy of Religion annual meeting,

a *Modern Judaism* article, a series of other investigations of Freud's work, and, ultimately, to the work before you.

In the interim, as elaborated above, I came to realize the more-than-epiphenomenal role of race and sexuality, as well as the greater threat presented by the ambiguity of *Judentum*'s gender, race, and sexuality than by the bald identification of Jews and women or of Jews and women who are either nonreproductive or engage in "bad" reproduction.[152] Hence, rather than begin where my own investigation began, with Freud's last completed work—or with circumcision for that matter—*On Freud's Jewish Body* begins with Freud's Vienna and the everyday psychopathological interaction of Jew and Gentile. Chapter 1 examines the parapraxes made by, to, or about the Jewish-identified individuals discussed by Freud in *Psychopathology of Everyday Life*. Each of these errors and slips is occasioned by what he terms a *"mésalliance"* between a Jew and a Gentile. Such incidents of distorted language betray unresolved ambivalences and unformulated anxieties endemic to Jewish-Gentile interaction in Freud's Vienna. Freud's focus upon the conflicts within what should be the most pleasurable and intimate relationships between Jew and Gentile, namely sexual and connubial relations, diagnosed the intrinsically problematic character of Jew–Gentile interaction in his Vienna. It is from this situation that it all begins—even psychoanalysis.

Chapter 2 explores the question of the origins of psychoanalysis and of Freud's Jewish identity in *Interpretation of Dreams*. Rather than attending to that frequently cited recollection of Freud's, the encounter between his father and the antisemitic lout, this chapter engages the most interpreted of all of Freud's dreams, the specimen dream, "The Dream of Irma's Injection," and examines the possible conditions for its emergence. In part, like many interpreters since the publication of Max Schur's groundbreaking "Some Additional 'Day Residues' of 'The Specimen Dream of Psychoanalysis,'" I focus on the triangle formed by Freud, his confidante and otolaryngologist Wilhelm Fliess, and their shared patient Emma Eckstein, as well as on that other often triangularly represented figure, the nose. Since the first presentation of this material at the 1989 American Academy of Religion annual meeting and its later development and publication, a crucial datum has come to my attention. The first versions of this chapter drew upon Schur's 1966 typescripts of what was until 1985 Freud's *unpublished* correspondence with Fliess. Part of my argument revolved around a Latin word, *Foetor*, that Schur mistranscribed as the nonsense word *Foetos* and that out of which I, lacking the little Latin that the German-trained Schur had at the very least, blithely spun into a tight network of crises surrounding Jewish and masculine identity. Imagine my relief when I realized that the parapraxis was Schur's and not mine; nonetheless, while some adjustments have had to be made to its argumentation, the analysis, I believe, still holds.

Still while neglecting to check Schur's German transcript against the later official version ultimately had no major effect on my underlying thesis, remedying that omission did point out the value of scholarly persistence. Beyond the matter of academic diligence (let alone, integrity) is the realization that one never knows what else one might stumble across. Thus, while seeking out the provenance of a note from Freud's *Nachlass* that appeared to be a precursor of the famous footnote in the Little Hans case study, I uncovered the previously unrecognized first review of Freud and Breuer's *Studies on Hysteria* in a prominent Viennese medical journal, which in turn led to the discovery that the Irma Dream may be even more thickly embedded in the social networks and other factors that conditioned Freud's Jewish identity than had been previously suspected. Consequently, the excursus into noses that protrudes from chapter 2 is paired with another on the implications of the dream-work's use of *weiss* (white) for an understanding of the sleeping Freud's Jewish context.

Chapter 3 remains with the nose as it examines Freud's return to the nose in his 1927 essay on "Fetishism." In particular, it focuses on what appeared to have been a curious oversight in the literature:[153] Freud's underinterpretation of his opening example, the fetishized "Glanz auf der Nase." My analysis, which brings Freud's essay into conjunction with his case "History of an Infantile Neurosis" through their shared patient, Sergei Pankejeff, the Wolf-Man, provides the occasion to realize that sometimes a nose is not just a nose or necessarily just any penis as it examines the relationship among fetishism, circumcision, and castration and argues how Freud as a Jew anticipates more recent discussions of the role of fetishism in racialist and postcolonial discourse.[154]

In a major theoretical reworking of his notion of anxiety the year before the "Fetishism" essay, Freud had juxtaposed the Wolf-Man with his other famous child patient, Little Hans, as, respectively, exemplary instances of the negative and positive Oedipus complexes (20:101–10). Chapter 4 addresses Little Hans's case history and, in particular, its famous footnote on circumcision and antisemitism, castration and misogyny. Unlike previous interpretations, this chapter attends to the very anomalousness of the note: not only the question of why Freud explicitly mentions "Jews" during a period (c. 1905–16) when he eschews public mention of such matters— including not only the contemporaneous study of the "Rat Man" but also the discussion of Little Hans and castration the following year in the *Leonardo* essay—but also why the footnote would re-emerge in the 1919 revision of that *Leonardo* essay. Moreover, the chapter explores how Freud makes every effort to ensure that Little Hans not be perceived as one suffering from what he would later theorize as the negative Oedipus complex. In examining this case originally, I came to realize most clearly that not only was the relationship between the representations of the Jewish body and gender identity inextricably interrelated with sexual identity, but while feminization cannot be reduced to homosexualization, Freud betrays anxiety about any substantial overlap. Further, I then recognized that by generating an implicit structural complementarity between fetishism and circumcision, Freud was also further distinguishing circumcision from homosexualization. Since the earlier version of this chapter I had the opportunity to visit the archives of the Viennese Jewish community; there I discovered that according to their records Herbert Graf (aka Little Hans) had not been circumcised—at least not ritually[155]—thereby rendering the anomalous invocation of circumcision all the more curious. That find rather than separating Jewish identity from circumcision confirms the recognition of how bound Jewish representation is to the dispositive of circumcision.

The next chapter shifts the focus from the anomalous presence of a Jewish reference to an anomalous absence in one of Freud's case studies: the Schreber case. An NEH Summer Seminar on Freud's reading under the direction of Sander Gilman at the Freud Museum in London provided me with the opportunity to peruse the books that Freud perused, to read his marginalia, including those that were in turn marginalized when Freud drew upon those readings in his own works. Chapter 5 juxtaposes Freud's "Psychoanalytic Notes" with the notes that he left in his copy of Schreber's memoir. It examines the way Freud's case study both assiduously avoids any mention of Schreber's Jewish identifications in the memoir and displaces the former judge's *Entmannung*, an unmanning that he understood as a transformation into a woman, into an emasculation that Freud read as castration. This classic case study of psychosis argues for the emergence of paranoia as an effect of repressed homosexual desire for the father while eschewing any association between this particular paranoiac, Schreber, and those who have been subjected to that symbolic substitute for castration, circumcision, namely, the Jews.

The last two chapters shift the focus from Freud's case histories to his studies of group psychology and the psychoanalysis of culture. Chapter 6 explores the possible implications on Freud's corpus of his surprising patronage and eventual repudiation of a leading theorist of homosexuality and male groups (*Männerbünde*), Hans Blüher, whose outspoken antifeminism and incipient racialism were soon outshown by his blatant and widely disseminated antisemitism, a shift widely echoed in the antisemitic, *völkisch* turn of *Männerbund* theories as well as the racialization of homosexual identities. It tracks the diminishing role of homosexuality in Freud's theorization of the brother band that overthrew the primal father from its emergence in *Totem and Taboo*, with its characteristic—at times forced—absence of Jewish reference, during the period of his correspondence with Blüher through his subsequent writings on cultural origins until its disappearance when Freud finally employs his theory in his speculations about the ancient Hebrews and the origin of *Judentum*.

That last study of Freud's is the focus of the last chapter of this book and, as noted above, the first of this project. The great question mark that remained from the original essay—was Freud indeed familiar with the passage from Spinoza with its particular conjunction of motifs that I argued underlay Freud's text?—has, if not been resolved, at least been given a greater degree of probability by my study of its reception history in "Spinoza's Election of the Jews." Still much has been written on *Moses* since I presented my observations to Mal Diamond's Psychology of Religion course—much of which I have discussed above—and the emphases of my work too have shifted as my study of Freud has morphed from the originally envisioned "The Nose Job: Freud and the Feminized Jew" (what Daniel Boyarin has hilariously referred to as "Noses and Monotheism").[156] For one, I have attempted since its initial presentation to nuance (live down?) my seemingly bald assertion that "this historical truth that Jew equals woman" beyond merely reiterating its original context as an apposition of "this cultural fact." More significant is how my research since has brought more attention to how embodied Jewish gender identity is bound up with sexuality—although, as in *Moses*, it remains rather marginal to my argument in this chapter. My explorations in the phenomena of trauma and fetishism have supplanted exchange theory as the primary interpretive keys for understanding the emergence of Freud's corpus just as trauma and fetishism began having their effects on Freud's own thinking at the time of *Moses*; the problematics of dealing with difference that underlies both fetishism and exchange remains foremost. Finally, I query whether the recent ethico-spiritual readings of *Moses* are engaged in acting out much like Freud's text itself.

In my concluding remarks, I will turn to the last section of one of the last psychoanalytic works that Freud completed and published in his lifetime, the 1937 study, "Analysis: Terminable and Interminable," and his invocation of the "bedrock" that marks the limit and the limen of psychoanalysis. Freud there comes to a final reckoning with his three primary, now deceased alter-egos, Wilhelm Fliess, Alfred Adler, and Sandor Ferenczi over what he holds to be the stumbling block of both therapeutic and character analyses: sexual difference, that in the last instance proves to be the castration complex. Freud's phrase translated in the *Standard Edition* as "bedrock," *gewachsene Fels*, literally (and figuratively) signifies growing or living rock. This image of the unplumbable point of an analysis harkens back to the Dream of Irma's Injection as well as evokes the fossil that emerges in Freud's discussions of fetishism, circumcision, and *Judentum*. Such living rock will be traced back through biblical allusions and forward to anomalies in *Moses* that betray Freud's interpellation into his modernity and our (post?)modernity.

Yet, it remains the case that while I will tie Freud's implication that castration is the bedrock of psychoanalysis to his attempts to work through his Jewish identity, such historicization neither addresses the truth value of psychoanalysis nor contradicts alternative readings such as those that would find the specter of the mother haunting Freud's texts. Besides my obvious use in my reading of Freud's corpus of particular rhetorical tropes, those unconscious processes Freud sees at play in the dream-work and in symptom formation such as displacement, condensation, and representability, or, more generally, distortion, I am a firm believer in the overdetermination of any articulation—whether by Freud or by myself. Beyond the truth or falsity, rightness or wrongness, of Freud's theories or methods, what remains the case is that since *Studies on Hysteria* whole generations of readers and nonreaders have either interpreted their worlds in Freudian terms or found it obsessively necessary to counter those interpretations.

New Genealogies

> No retrospect will take us to the true beginning; and whether our
> prologue be in heaven or on earth, it is but a fraction of that all-
> pre-supposing fact with which our story sets out.
> —George Eliot, *Daniel Deronda*

For centuries the Jews have identified themselves as the "People of the Book," desiring to overlook—especially in the wake of emancipation, the processes of acculturation and assimilation, the development of racial discourse, and, ironically, the decreased familiarity with the Book (*Tanakh* and *Talmud*)—that they were also the people of the body.[157] Caught between book and body, the contemporary crises and quests for a (post)modern Jewish identity manifested by this new literature on Freud are perhaps like those undergone by George Eliot's Daniel Deronda, the eponymous hero of one of Freud's favorite books. It takes some three-quarters of this eight-hundred-plus-page novel for Daniel to discover that he was of Jewish descent. Yet as Lennar Davis has quipped, "What this has to mean . . . is that he never looked down."[158] On one level then the novel reproduces that modern Jewish oversight of body by spirit and, as discussed above, the corollary disregard of circumcision in the quest for a Jewish identity, but there are other implications of Deronda's secreted circumcision for understanding the new Freud literature.

Eliot writes at the beginning of her novel: "Men can do nothing without the make-believe of a beginning."[159] Indeed, without the apparent ignorance of that trace of Deronda's origin there would have been no story; further, once Deronda learns of his beginnings, he spends the remainder of the novel attempting to adequate himself to this knowledge. Eliot's commentary on the nature of narrative also has insights in the psychology of contemporary individuals. Many, too, seek out origins to find their identity: it is all in their childhood or in the life of the man who led them to look there—namely, Freud. Knowledge of their singular origination tells them who they have always been. They would like to assume some form of continuity between said origin and their present, but Nietzsche has disabused us of the assumption that we can translate a notion (in itself problematic) of natural genealogical sameness between then and now into the more cultural realms of ideas and identities.

And so has Freud, as Yerushalmi has significantly and quite properly emphasized.[160] Freud's concern was more with tradition, with the problem of transmission, than with origin.[161] His problem was how to conceive a discontinuous identity or, otherwise put, a repetition or reinscription that is both the same and different. In *Moses* the Jews are not the motley crew who murdered the Egyptian Moses but the people who a thousand years later anamnestically, albeit unconsciously, reappropriated and transformed that origin. Without recognizing that origin these children of Israel reenacted it and thereby formed their identity. Freud would posit a memory-trace to mediate the discontinuity. Yerushalmi suggests Freud imagined a Lamarckian Jewishness: "the powerful feeling that, for better or worse, one cannot really cease being Jewish, and this not merely because of current anti-Semitism or discrimination, and certainly not because of the

Chain of Tradition, but because one's fate in being Jewish was determined long ago by the Fathers, and that often what one feels most deeply and obscurely is a trilling wire in the blood."[162] But in place of some hypothetical acquired memory-trace, perhaps that genital inscription and the uncanny impressions it makes provided a constant reference to an event beyond memory and one that, through deferred action, produced the Jewish people.

That ever-present inscription plays such a role in Eliot's novel. The discerning reader knows of Deronda's Jewishness from the start: whether from Eliot's opening "all-pre-supposing fact" or from Deronda's misrecognized enactment of identity when introduced. He returns Gwendolen's pawned necklace to her in a handkerchief, "a large corner of [which] seemed to have been recklessly torn off to get rid of a mark" of identity.[163] The never-said of circumcision is readily displayed and shapes the construction of the plot, whether in epigraphical reference, the missing monogram, or in Deronda's later—but prior to learning of his Jewish mother—interactions with the London Jewish community. Eliot looks down, and these children of Freud, too, are looking down and remarking upon the traces of *Judentum* in Freud's texts and contexts. They endeavor to demonstrate that Freud is always writing out of the "all-pre-supposing fact" of his multiple situations as a Jew. Consequently, where *Moses* is the site in which Freud most explicitly and most extensively addressed the nature, place, and time of the Jews, that work is more the culmination of a career than the exceptional instance of thinking in Jewish.[164]

Yerushalmi et al., in their Deronda-like quest for a positive Jewish identity, take a more biographical route and focus upon Freud's manifestly Jewish identifications with Jakob and Moses as well as upon his explicit, though rarely public, comments on Jewishness. By contrast, the chapters below, like a George Eliot, inhabit the margins and machinations of Freud's corpus and attend to the interplay of a life and its contemporary social and scientific discourses that not only represented Jews but were structured by the usually deprecatory relationship between *Judentum* and *Germanentum* or between *Judentum* and *Christentum*. Taking circumcision as my *Leitfossil* I, like a Freud, pursue the secreted mark of Jewish identity and of the trauma of being Jewish in an antisemitic environment and then map its displacements. Moreover, these studies demonstrate how Jewish identity is thoroughly interwoven with sexual, gender, corporeal, ethnic, and racial identities; they thereby help bring our understanding of Freud the Jew more in line with other contemporary understandings of identity construction, in particular theories of trauma and fetishism, and the relation of that construction to the production of texts.

CHAPTER I

The Psychopathology of Everyday Vienna: Familiarity Breeds Psychoanalysis

Nun ist die Luft von solchem Spuk so voll,
Das niemand weiss, wie er ihn meiden soll.

But now the air is so full of these ghosts
That no one knows how to escape their hosts.

—GOETHE, *Faust*, II.V.5, epigraph to Freud's
Psychopathology of Everyday Life

In 1919 Freud devoted an essay to "das Unheimliche," the uncanny, in order to explore what arouses terror, dread, horror. At the beginning of his examination Freud makes a curious move that has affected studies of the uncanny ever since. He does philology: "The German word '*unheimlich*' is obviously the opposite of '*heimlich*' [homely], '*heimisch*' [native]— the opposite of what is familiar; and we are tempted to conclude that what is 'uncanny' is frightening precisely because it is *not* known and familiar" (17:220). Freud then provides a long citation from the entry for "heimlich" in the 1860 edition of Daniel Sanders's *Wörterbuch der Deutschen Sprache*. At the end of this passage he adds: "What interests us most in this long extract is to find that among its different shades of meaning the word *heimlich* exhibits one which is identical with its opposite *unheimlich*" (17:224). To still any of his readers' doubts that may remain of this magical conversion of something into its opposite, Freud cites from the standard dictionary of the German language, Grimm's *Deutsches Wörterbuch*, s.v. "Heimlich." As one reads the excerpted entry, *heimlich* shifts from what is characteristic of a "place free from ghostly influences [*gespensterhaft*]" to that of a realm apperceived by one who "believes in ghosts" [*Gespenster*] and thus finds it to be "*heimlich* and full of terrors." Grimm's editors themselves add that "*heimlich* comes to have the meaning usually ascribed to *unheimlich*" (17:226).

From these definitions and Freud's subsequent discussion, several aspects of the uncanny bear significance for understanding the situation of Viennese Jews during Freud's professional career. First, the uncanny is terrifying; it is something ghostlike. Ghosts or specters were among the figures by which Jews were represented. Second and more significant to this analysis, sometimes what motivates the terror is the uncanny object or experience's underlying familiarity. Freud ties the second form of the uncanny to the fear of doubles. The tacit familiarity for Central Europeans of *Judentum* lay in more than its function as the necessary and proximate other or older would-be superseded sibling by which *Christentum*, a comparable condensation of the communities, beliefs, and practices of Christians, continued to define itself. With the advent of Emancipation, Jewry lost more and more of its manifest difference without losing its structural otherness necessary for first Christian, and then German, self-definition.

After exploring how these uncanny characteristics conditioned the antisemitic atmosphere of Freud's Vienna, this chapter turns to Freud's *Psychopathology of Everyday Life* in order to explore how for Freud Jewish psychopathology emerged not from any inherent disposition, as a number of his contemporaries asserted,[1] but at the interface of Jewish-Gentile relations. As noted in the Introduction, from their perspective Austrian Jewry were caught in a double bind. From the Gentile perspective, Jews in Germanophone Austria-Hungary, regularly characterized as a Gast*volk*, a guest people, or as a parasite upon the Gast*volk*, the host people,[2] came to be viewed, like nihilism for Heidegger, as an *unheimlicher* Gast, an uncanny guest/host. Consequently, as with any encounter with the uncanny, Gentile encounters with Jews were mediated by dread, anxiety, and fascination, by the projection of all that would be strange on the all-too-familiar.

A Specter Haunts Europe

In the 1880s a German-language pamphlet by the Russian Jewish physician Leon Pinsker began circulating among the Jews of Austria-Hungary. Its author had been driven to despair over the fate of the Jewish people following the violent pogroms that ripped through the Russian Pale of Settlement in 1880–81. Pinsker concluded that the Jews could not trust in Emancipation but must emancipate themselves; he disseminated his reflections and remedies in the pamphlet "Die Autoemanzipation" (Auto-Emancipation). His diagnosis of the Jewish situation in Europe would emphasize the perceived ghostlike character of *Judentum*.

Pinsker's essay offers a series of images that reflect how, by their very persistence, Jews have brought upon themselves the hatred of the rest of humanity. Israel had not died after the loss of its state, of its actual existence; rather it had continued its existence—as a spirit: "Among the living nations of the earth the Jews occupy the position of a nation long since dead."[3] Here Pinsker drew upon the Christian tradition that *Judentum* had been superseded (*aufgehoben*) as well as on eighteenth- and nineteenth-century German philosophy, in which images of *Judentum* as dead proliferated.[4] Pinsker then evokes the frightening image of "the uncanny [*unheimliche*] form of one of the dead walking among the living." This "ghostlike apparition [*geisterhafte Erscheinung*] . . . makes a strange and peculiar impression upon the imagination of the nations."[5] Pinsker lays the blame for the long-festering prejudice against the Jews, hatred of the Jews, fear of the Jews on Wundt's ethno-psychological notion of an inborn fear of ghosts (*Gespensterfurcht*); Judeophobia (*Judophobie*) is rooted in and naturalized as demonopathy.

Pinsker's work appeared thirteen years before Herzl's Zionist classic, *The Jews' State*, and greatly influenced the development of Jewish student movements in the interim. The Austro-Hungarian Jewish university student organization Kadima (Forward), for example, formed in 1882 to espouse not just Jewish pride in the face of growing antisemitism, but also Jewish nationalist sentiments in the empire. "Auto-Emancipation" helped these students articulate a response to their exclusion from various German-nationalist student reading societies and fraternities as well as provided a rejoinder to the assimilationist tendencies of family, friends, and fellow students.

Jewish nationalism crystallized the desire to pursue what was denied them in the empire. Although the bulk of social, economic, and civic restrictions as well as other special legislation regarding Jewish life had been lifted with the emancipation decrees of 1867, Jews suffered from one crucial legal disadvantage. Following Article 19 of the 1867 Imperial Constitution, the Jews, unlike other nationalities, such as the Ruthenians and the Czechs, were recognized as a people (*Volksstamm*) but not as a nation (*Nationalität*); hence they had neither language nor territory rights. Every recognized nationality had the right to teach its children in the "language customary to the land"—Croat, Czech, German, Magyar, and so forth. Austria-Hungary recognized eleven national groups and their languages, but the state did not confer such status on either the Jews or their languages, Hebrew and Yiddish. Throughout the empire the vast majority of urban Jews learned and spoke German. Pinsker's diagnosis and suggested remedy emboldened and embodied these uncanny imperial citizens.

Does Familiarity Breed Contempt?

What is so scary about the familiar—other than the prospect of boredom—has been explored, among other places, in Hoffmann's tales of doubles (*Doppelgänger*), de Maupassant's "The Horla," Otto Rank's *The Double*, the classic silent film(s) *The Student of Prague*, and, of course, Freud's essay on the "Uncanny." Freud notes Rank's conclusion regarding the "invention of doubling as a preservation against extinction" during the stage of primary narcissism. "But when this stage has been surmounted, the 'double' reverses its aspect. . . . It becomes the uncanny harbinger of death" (17:235). The defense mechanism of projection exteriorizes such threats. To Rank's pioneering work, Freud adds other sources of the double during the course of ego development, such as the lingering phantasies, whose realization "adverse external circumstances have crushed" (17:236). Freud, more significantly, suggests that the double may originate in a critical agency that emerges within and splits off from the ego—more commonly known as the conscience; in later work he would call it the "ego ideal" and the "super-ego." This agency views the ego as an object. Regardless of the material content of the double, "when all is said and done, the quality of uncanniness can only come from the fact of the 'double' being a creation dating back to a very early mental stage, long since surmounted" (17:236), hence its (un)familiarity.

Another crucial factor in the development of the threatening double was the contradiction between the ideology of the self-authorizing and -authored autonomous individual and the biological, social, and psychological necessities of an other for the emergence of that self. The dependence of the individual on its relationship to that pre-existent other undermines its claims for autonomy and transforms the original into something derivative, at best a copy. The other and its necessity must be suppressed, foreclosed, jettisoned. Further, since nothing is more familiar than the individual self and since that individual can, by definition, only be singular, then the double is out to get the self, to replace the "original."

As recent research on nationalism and ethnicity has determined, the threatening, uncanny double also has a collective component. Like the individual self, neither national nor ethnic identity is intrinsically self-determined; rather the identity of a nation or ethnic group is constructed in relation to what it is not, to what has been marginalized or excluded and designated as other.[6] Yet if the identity of the nation or group is not self-contained and cannot be articulated outside of relation, then neither can the particular difference of its others. Underlying differences are processes of identification; what necessitates the antagonistic and seemingly clear-cut differentiation of one group from another is the narcissistic threat of perceived commonalities. That is, what is exaggeratedly represented as most foreign may be what is most familiar, as Freud suggested in his discussions of the narcissism of minor differences. In *Civilization* Freud provided both a rather instrumental explanation of the phenomenon—"a convenient and relatively harmless satisfaction of the inclination to aggression, by means of which cohesion between the members of a community is made easier"—and an example. The latter he offered rather facetiously—in 1930, I suppose, one could still speak facetiously of such matters: "In this respect the Jewish people, scattered everywhere, have rendered most useful services to the civilizations of the countries that have been the hosts" (*Wirtsvölker*; 21:114; cf. 18:101 and note).[7] When Freud returns to this phenomenon as one of the causes of antisemitism eight years later in *Moses* he is no longer quite so facetious and its irrationality is more striking: "the intolerance of groups is often, *strangely enough*, exhibited more strongly against small differences than against fundamental ones" (23:91; emphasis added). Indeed, the recent literature on ethnicity and nationalism has drawn out the implications of Freud's argument: "what appear as ethnic or national 'differences' are . . . more or less elaborate and effortful attempts by groups to forget, deny, or obscure their resemblances,"[8] in particular, attributes they would censor or disclaim.

Strange Bedfellows

And this was the situation in the last third of the nineteenth century in Vienna, where there were two groups attempting to shape their own collective identities. One consisted of the German-speaking Gentiles. As part of a century-long struggle throughout the German-speaking world to discover a group identity underlying the hundreds of principalities, duchies, and would-be empires—seeking a union of *Blut und Boden* (blood and soil)—Austro-Germans sought to define themselves as Germans over and against the other nationalities of the empire. The newly emancipated Jews of Austria for their part also sought to adopt the "universal" culture of the German bourgeoisie. *Judentum*'s continuing function as exemplary other, as the always already antitype of Austrian Catholicism, however, fomented a crisis.[9]

The Jews and Germans shared a long history together—and apart—in Vienna.[10] There were permanent settlements of Jews in Vienna by at least the twelfth century as archaeologists of the square known as Judenplatz have uncovered. Their status, the restrictions on life and labor, always remained at the mercy of whoever was the current ruler—until, that is, the massacres, holocausts (in the literal sense of burning alive), and expulsions of 1421 that in part were motivated by a blood-libel accusation.

Gradually a few Jews were allowed back—so long as they paid their protection money (*Schutzgeld*) to the emperor. Eventually, in 1624, they formed a Jewish quarter—a ghetto—on the other side of the Danube. In 1670 the Jewish quarter was bought out from Emperor Leopold by the city of Vienna, which then expelled its inhabitants. The Viennese renamed the area Leopoldstadt in his honor, and built churches with the stones from the demolished synagogues. Again some Jews were soon returning, but only the wealthiest were allowed to reside as "tolerated subjects" in return for a substantial payment up-front and annual taxes. These old-new inhabitants included a group of Sephardim from Turkey as well as Ashkenazim. These *Hofjuden*, or court Jews, such as Samuel Oppenheimer, Samson Wertheimer, the Eskeles family, and the Arnsteins, functioned as chief financial agents and bankers to supply the growing imperial financial needs. By the middle of the eighteenth century and the rule of Empress Maria Theresa, the Viennese Jewish population grew to around four thousand.

Though their numbers had increased, their position in the imperial capital became more restricted under Maria Theresa. A series of *Judenordnungen* (Jewish ordinances) were enacted, among them: no direct ownership of land, no automatic rights of residence for the sons of "privileged" Jews, the requirement to remain indoors until late morning on Sundays and holidays, and the wearing of beards by married or widowed Jewish men. Her son, Joseph II, however, inaugurated a shift. He issued his *Toleranzpatent* (Patent of Toleration) in 1782. These new rules by no means instituted an era of emancipation; this was no era of civil and political rights in which virtually all restrictions on employment and residence would be lifted. Rather it was a pragmatic move to improve the backward economic situation of his empire by transforming the productivity of the Jewish population by disciplining them through state education, ceasing the use of Hebrew and Yiddish in public and for commercial purposes, requiring the adoption of German surnames, and diversifying the occupations of Jews so that they could be of most use to the empire. This Germanification met with a great deal of support from the *Maskilim*, the followers of Moses Mendelssohn and the participants in the Jewish Enlightenment (*Haskalah*), who saw this as an opportunity for greater social and cultural integration. It opened avenues for the Jewish acquisition of secular education (*Bildung*). This prime value of Gentile *Bürgertum* was readily appropriated by the Jews of Vienna.

Many of the old restrictions remained, including: the special taxes, the prohibition on marriage by any but the oldest son, and the denial of state citizenship. The operative word here is *Verbesserung* (improvement), as in the presumption that the Jews needed to be improved; of course, the optimist would say, that they felt that Jews *could* be improved—at least to a point. The purpose of many of these schemes, whether in Austria or Prussia, was to transform the Jews into good colonial workers who could help transform the backward regions of the empire into productive sites for imperial exploitation.[11] And this was especially important at this time when the Habsburg Polish holdings were growing, including the 1772 annexation of Galicia and its over 200,000 Jews.

Between 1782 and the arrival of the family Freud in 1859–60, the Jewish community of Vienna began to have an increasingly important role in the growth of industry, commerce, and finance; they also began to attend the university and enter into Viennese intellectual and journalistic life, though they still lived under a number of restrictions, not least the limitation on the number of Jews allowed to live in Vienna. A number of young Jews participated in the 1848 revolution as well as in the subsequently created parliament. With the development of this association of politically active Jews with Gentile liberals, there emerged a redefining of Jewish identity along religious as opposed to cultural, corporate, or ethnic terms. Their religion was *Judentum*, but their culture was *Deutschtum*, and their fundamental value was *Bildung*. Prior to the parliament's consideration of emancipation legislation as part of a general liberal legislative package, however, the counterrevolution foreclosed that possibility (and, ultimately, removed the parliament itself).

What really began to change the character of Jewish Vienna was the lifting of restrictions on Jewish travel, residence, and the purchase of real estate in 1859–60. Just prior to the arrival of the family Freud, there were approximately six thousand Jews in a city of about a half a million people. Waves of Jews from the impoverished provinces of Galicia as well as from

Bohemia, Moravia, and Hungary streamed into the imperial capital. Generations who had experienced ghettoization, extensive civil, economic, and vocational restrictions, and a traditional Jewish lifestyle found themselves emancipated citizens with access to secular education as well as to the liberal professions. By the time Freud completed his university studies in 1879 there were approximately 70,000 Jews in a city of 700,000; when *Interpretation* appeared in 1900 the number of Jews doubled again on account of the city's annexation of many suburbs, new waves of immigration of Polish and Russian Jews fleeing pogroms, and the migration of great numbers of Gentiles from throughout the empire seeking employment. In 1910, when Freud and the psychoanalytic movement had finally achieved international renown, Vienna was a city of over two million inhabitants, 175,000 of whom were listed as Jews.

Sigmund Freud's life mirrored this trajectory. Born in Freiberg (Pribor), Moravia, he and his family moved to Vienna when he was three. They lived in the district of Leopoldstadt, where the vast majority of Jews from the periphery of the Austro-Hungarian Empire had emigrated and where most of the lower-class Viennese Jews such as the Freuds resided; Leopoldstadt figured "the Jewish ghetto in the popular imagination."[12] Despite their tenuous financial situation, his parents ensured that young Sigmund acquired a bourgeois *Bildung* at gymnasium and university; he then pursued a bourgeois career path and, after marriage, resided in a bourgeois district.

Just as Austria-Hungary was breaking out of its feudal, corporate identity, so, too, was *Judentum*. As Viennese Jewry, at least among members of the middle and upper classes, began to delimit their *Judentum* to a private, albeit publicly registered, faith confession-cum-possession to conform with the modern Catholic and Protestant norm, ritual practices and halakhic requirements that distinguished these new citizens from their compatriots were openly questioned. When a Viennese Jewish father petitioned the civil authorities directly to register his son as Jewish without circumcision, they overruled the prior refusal by the directorate of the Viennese Jewish community. While the community's rabbis ultimately conceded the official designation, they called upon their colleagues from across Europe to decide upon the halakhic and ritual implications of this ruling. Taken up with other questions surrounding Jewish practice in modern Europe first in the Leipzig (29 June–4 July 1869) and then the Augsburg (11–17 July 1871) synods, it was resolved "that a boy born of a Jewish mother who has not been circumcised, for whatsoever reason this may have been, must be considered a Jew, and be treated as such in all ritual matters, in accordance with the existing rules regarded binding for Israelites."[13] Such exemplary rulings and adaptations led Viennese Jewish religious leaders like Adolf Jellinek, on the one hand, to speak of the universality of Jewish teaching; on the other hand, support of the liberal state (and of the monarchy) began to replace religious observance as the community's most characteristic practice—and remained in place for that generation, even as, following the *Krach* (crash) of 1873, the ensuing economic depression eventually led to the collapse of liberal governance and the rise of political antisemitism.

Attitudes toward, and the structural positioning of, *Judentum* also drew upon a long history of Christian hatred of Jews. The Jews were viewed as deicides, as cursed, as demon spawn, as betrayers, whose miserable circumstances confirmed the truth of the church. These differentiating images found support in gospel accounts that were themselves products of Christian self-definition—a differentiating of themselves from *Judentum*. Within the Austrian context, perhaps most important were the preachings of the (in)famous late-seventeenth-century Habsburger court preacher Abraham a Sancta Clara. He offered some choice words about the Jews— years after they had been expelled from Vienna. His depiction of the Jews as "the scum among all godless unbelievers" (*der Abschaum aller gottlosen und ungläubige Leute*) and his accusation that "they pray several times a day for God to exterminate the Christians by plague, hunger, and war" (*sie beten alle Tage mehrmals, Gott wolle uns Christen vertilgen durch Pest, Hunger und Krieg*) and other choice bits from his "Ho! And Fie on the World" (*Huy! und Pfuy die Welt*) sermon became staples of Viennese antisemitic discourse.[14]

From the nineteenth-century German Gentile perspective, the struggle for self-definition might be distilled as follows: the German individual desperately wants to become "himself," and the other, the Jew, is perceived as also wanting desperately to become that same German self. While the question of individual and national identity was by no means the only crisis experienced by German Gentiles during this period of general social and economic upheaval and transformation, a primary response to this question—antisemitism—also became the code that signaled the suffering of, and solution to, the myriad problems afflicting German-Austrian society; however, the recognition that antisemitism served as a shibboleth does not assume that antisemitism merely functioned indexically.[15] The German Gentile experienced a deep-felt anxiety about being controlled—and ultimately replaced—by that uncanny other. Since identity formation is about drawing lines—both between self and other and by surrounding the self with "like" selves—when identities are becoming more defuse, as they were during this period, lines, boundaries, and walls tend to be more sharply, violently drawn and fiercely defended.[16]

Against the threat presented by the (un)familiar, several strategies have been developed. One such strategy, which was employed in late Habsburg Austria, is to paint the other so that he or she would be clearly defined; such ascription passes for description. As has already been noted, there was no shortage of discourses, both popular and scientific, that endeavored to define the Jew. Another primary strategy is the avoidance of mixture, for any intermixture is understood as contamination. This defense manifested itself in a discourse of purity that feared defilement by miscegenation (the products of intermarriage and other such affairs), a subversive *Verjudung* (Jewification), and/or a flood of "immigrants." As Georg Ritter von Schönerer, a leader of Austria's political antisemitism movement put it, *"Durch Reinheit zur Einheit"*—unity through purity. Austrian Jews, awash in such representations as well as structurally excluded from, or directed to, particular social relationships and positions, found it all but impossible not to internalize such denigrating identifications. Split and split off, Jews became doubles to themselves.

Nowhere, perhaps, was the issue of boundary-transgression, especially in Jew–Gentile relationships, starker than in intermarriage; here, Jew and Gentile (whether Christian, German, or German-Christian) met at their most intimate, and here the question of coexistence would be most directly negotiated. It would prove a major crux of later racial discussion, especially with regard to the fate of future generations and the threatened poisoning of the gene pool, degeneration of the race, et cetera. Intermarriage was also the site where the question of continued existence came up: whether or not *Judentum* had a future, as the German Zionist physician Felix Theilhaber put it in 1911.[17] Although the number of conversions (whether to Catholicism, Protestantism, or *"Confessionslosigkeit"* [no religious preference]—the latter two being the "lesser evils") was greater in Vienna than in other European cities of the time, two factors need to be considered.

First, Austrian law forbade marriages between Christians and Jews unless either the non-Jewish partner converted to the Jewish confession (or registered as *"confessionslos"*) or the Jewish partner converted to some form of Christianity (or again registered as *"confessionslos"*). Second, intermarriage was relatively rare, and the number of converts—including those who converted for career advancement—relative to the size of the community was tiny. In 1910, for example, fewer than 10 percent of marriages involving Jews were with a non-Jewish partner, and only 512 (in a community of over 175,000 Jews) changed their religious registration.[18] But the numbers did accumulate over the years and an indistinct class formed who, although regarding themselves as totally assimilated, whether Christian or unregistered, would still be regarded by others as remaining "essentially" Jewish. Researchers estimate that by the time of the *Anschluss* (the 1938 annexation of Austria by Germany) approximately 50,000 Gentiles (equal to about 20 percent of the entire Jewish population) were suddenly regarded by the Nuremberg Laws as Jewish.[19] Despite empirical evidence somewhat to the contrary, Theilhaber's concern that intermarriage, understood also as a sign of self- and group-disavowal, boded ill for the Jews was shared by many.

Speaking of Whom . . .

Throughout *The Psychopathology of Everyday Life* Freud seeks to find meaning in some of the most seemingly meaningless or nonsensical of phenomena, such as parapraxes (*Fehlleistungen*) and slips of speech (*Versprechen*). His study uncovers some of the underlying or repressed motives as well as the processes by which these phenomena emerge. Several of these discursive disruptions appear to be precipitated by contact between Jew and Gentile—especially contact of the most intimate kind. Indeed, instances that entail ongoing or anticipated sexual relationships between Jew and Gentile are the only occasions when individuals explicitly identified as Jewish are subjected to Freud's clinical commentary. More than a few of the parapraxes and Freudian "slips," curious forgettings and mistakes, involve what in one instance Freud refers to as a *"mésalliance"* (6:67),[20] that is, either a mixed marriage or an affair between Jew and Gentile. In the three other instances of its appearance in *The Standard Edition* (2:303, 3:75, 10:175) Freud had employed this French term as a figure for more clinical matters; it figured the "false connection" symptomatic of neurosis between affect and ideational content.

Freud devotes his second chapter of *Psychopathology*, "The Forgetting of Foreign Words," to a thick description of one such instance. He frames the ensuing narrative in a purported contrast between one's being less likely to forget something in one's own language (*in unserer eigenen Sprache*) than words in a foreign language (*in einer fremden Sprache*). Yet in the course of this work, Freud regularly undermines this seemingly self-evident distinction (that is, the preponderance of his examples suggest that we are at least as prone to make mistakes in our own language). Throughout his study the familiar/*heimlich* and the foreign/*unheimlich* are interwoven so as to subvert, perhaps, any absolute distinctions. Although it is the foreign that is represented as the threat, the anxiety arises from the failure to maintain the difference. The following analyses demonstrate that the uncanny (*unheimliche*) Jews (re)present such a crisis of clear and distinct identities.

In Freud's extended illustration of the forgetting of foreign words, he recalls an encounter with a young man who would cite Virgil: "Last summer . . . I renewed my acquaintance with a certain young man of academic background. I soon found out that he was familiar with some of my psychological publications. We had fallen into conversation . . . about the social status of the race [*Volksstammes*] to which we both belonged" (6:8–9). Freud does not here or anywhere else in this work explicitly state which "race" among the many dwelling in the multiethnic Austro-Hungarian Empire is being referred to.[21] Consequently, Freud's elliptical phrasing does not necessarily entail a self-identification as a Jew. As the anecdote proceeds and as analysis will indicate, Freud's discussion of several details both underplays their strong Jewish associations and fails to connect those associations with his and his companion's shared ethnicity.

He continues: "And ambitious feelings prompted him to give vent to a regret that his generation [*Generation*] was doomed . . . to atrophy, and could not develop its talents or satisfy its needs" (6:9). Freud's young companion sounds one of the most potent themes of the German- and Austrian-Jewish literature of the period: the "generations" problem. The sons who were reaching their maturity in the first years of the twentieth century evince despair and disappointment over their future. More than the continuation of adolescent angst and melancholia, these men were at a loss as one-time hopes had turned into lingering delusions of Gentile acceptance and/or into denials of growing Gentile enmity among their fathers' liberal generation. The most notable literary exemplar, perhaps, is the 1908 novel *The Road into the Open* (*Der Weg ins Frei*) by the man Freud considered his *Doppelgänger*, Arthur Schnitzler.

Freud goes on:

> He ended a speech of impassioned fervour with the well-known line of Virgil's in which the unhappy Dido commits to posterity her vengeance on Aeneas: *"Exoriare. . . ."* Or rather, he wanted to end it in this way, for he could not get hold of the quotation and tried to conceal an obvious gap in what he remembered by changing the order of the words: *"Exoriar(e) ex nostris ossibus ultor."* At last he said irritably: 'Please. . . . Why not help me? There's something missing in the line; how does the whole thing really go?" (6:9)

Freud was most willing to help him with the correct quotation—
"Exoriar(e) aliquis nostris ex ossibus ultor" ("Let someone arise from my
bones as an avenger")—and to explain the hidden motivations for this
moment of forgetfulness.

This young man was familiar with Professor Freud's works and desired
to put their author to the test after Freud's having just borne witness to a
shameful forgetting of a verse that should have been so familiar to one
with a university education (*einer akademischen Bildung*). Freud's acquaintance challenges him to uncover why he (the young man) forgot the in-
definite pronoun *"aliquis"* (someone). Through a series of free associations
by the young man the conversation moves from *aliquis* to *reliquien* (relics),
Liquidation (liquifying), and *Flüssigkeit* (fluid). The young man continues:
"Simon of Trent, whose relics I saw two years ago in a church at Trent. I
am thinking of the accusation of ritual blood-sacrifice which being
brought against the Jews [*die Juden*] again just now, and of Kleinpaul's
book in which he regards all these supposed victims as incarnations, one
might say new editions, of the Savior" (6:9–10). Freud's language of ethnic
belongingness is again elliptical. He has the young man say that the accusation was raised against *"the* Jews" and not raised against "my people."
This instance of vague ethnic references obscures the fact that the speak-
ers' shared Jewishness conditions the chain of associations. Moreover,
Freud chooses not to dwell on the Jewish blood flowing from the rash
of libels that had been directed at Central and Eastern European Jewish
communities during the previous two decades—Tisza-Eslar (1882), Xan-
ten (1891), Polna (1899), and Konitz (1900).[22]

It was just such an accusation that helped justify the pogrom of 1421 in
Vienna. All the property of the Jews passed into the hands of Archduke
Albert V, and, as previously mentioned, the stones of the destroyed synagogue were used in building the university (of Vienna, from which Freud
graduated). Hundreds were murdered, and most of the survivors who had
not fled were expelled; those children who were not expelled were forcibly
baptized. A community that once numbered between 1,400 and 1,600 individuals was extinguished, and the city became notoriously known in Jewish tradition as "Ir ha-Damim" (the city of blood). These massacres,
expropriations, forced baptisms, and expulsions were collectively referred
to as the Wiener *gezerah* (the evil decree of Vienna)[23] by the surviving
Jewish population, and perhaps by Freud as well.[24]

The more recent accusations would have been relevant to the young
man's earlier *kvetch* (griping) since these events challenged claims to the
"cultural progress" of modern Europeans and the parental generation's

deluded optimism. Freud also omits mention that several of the purported victims were young Gentile women rather than young boys; such references would have infused a (normative) sexual element to the accusations. Despite the recalled visit to the reliquary and the accompanying mention of the famous classicist Rudolf Kleinpaul's 1892 volume *Human Sacrifice and Ritual Murder*,[25] Freud opts against interrupting the flow of associations and allows them to remain only just so much cultural capital (*Bildung*) that one acquires as an educated man.

The young man then moves on from Saint Simon to a list of various other saints and church fathers—Augustine, Benedict, Origen, Paul (which they hear echoed in the reference to Kleinpaul)—and then to Saint Januarius and the vial of his blood that miraculously liquifies on a certain holiday. Finally he comes to the crux of his associational chain: "Well, something *has* come to my mind . . . but it's too intimate to pass on. . . . Besides I don't see any connection, or any necessity for saying it" (6:11). This of course is the key, for when the young man mentions that he is waiting to hear news from a woman friend that may cause difficulties for both, Freud guesses that he is afraid to learn that she has missed her period. He then briefly recalls the series of associations and adds, "St. Simon was *sacrificed as a child*" (6:11). The young man later adds that not only is the woman Italian but she comes from Naples, where the statue of Saint Januarius stands.

When Freud leaves the young man and returns to the text he provides this explanation for the origin of this forgetting:

> The speaker had been deploring the fact that the present generation of his people [*seines Volkes*] was deprived of its full rights; a new generation, he prophesied like Dido, would inflict vengeance on the oppressors. He had in this way expressed his wish for descendants. At this moment a contrary thought intruded. "Have you really so keen a wish for descendants? That is not so. How embarrassed you would be if you were to get news just now that you were to expect descendants from the quarter you know of. No: no descendants—however much we need them for vengeance." (6:12)

Freud's summation generates curious echoes of an earlier scene in *Interpretation* where he also addresses the need for the filial generation to revenge the oppressors of the paternal generation. Framing Freud's recollection of his father's recounting to his "ten- or twelve-year-old" son his passive acquiescence to an assault by a Christian lout, Freud identifies himself with a different Carthaginian than Dido—namely, the young Hannibal. In this lead-in to the anecdote, which happens to be the primary locus in analyses of Freud's ambivalence toward his father and *Judentum*, is an account of how, when confronted by the "anti-Semitic feelings" of his fellow gymnasium students, the young Freud realized that he was a member of an "alien race." He saw in Hannibal and his war on Rome a model for Semitic tenacity in the face of oppression.[26]

In a fascinating article, "Freud's 'Forgetting of Foreign Words,'" Harris L. Gruman also follows the young man's Dido reference through to Freud's discussion of his identification with Hannibal in *Interpretation*. Though the ambivalence characteristic of the tension between Freud the scientist and Freud the Jew in fin-de-siècle Vienna catalyzes his discussion, Gruman focuses upon three "parodic narrative inversions" at play in Freud's example—inversions "of historical epic, the duel narrative and the joke." His analysis culminates in an understanding of Freud's encounter with the assimilation-desiring Jewish young man as a therapeutic intervention where "applied paranoia neutralizes the pathological resentment of clinical paranoia."[27] However, by also attending to the resumed discussion of Freud's Hannibal identification that follows his father's anecdote, one might question whether Freud's—and, by extension, the young man's and other contemporary Germanophone Jews'—ambivalence is so therapeutically resolved. In seeking a counter to the scene of his father narrating weakness and capitulation, the young Sigmund finds the account of Hannibal's father making his son swear vengeance against the Romans. Adding significance to both story and frame, Freud, as noted in a subsequent chapter of *Psychopathology*, makes one of his most telling slips: he mistakenly writes Hasdrubal, the name of both Hannibal's brother and of his brother-in-law and predecessor, rather than Hamilcar Barca, Hannibal's father. At the end of the encounter in *Psychopathology*, although Freud elides that they are his people, too, when he refers to the oppressors of "his people" (which is to say, the people of his companion), he is replaying his own earlier scene. Hence, neither wreaking vengeance nor cohabiting with Gentiles is any more a viable response to the oppressors than is passive acceptance. Ambivalence and not assimilation is the best one can expect from Jewish–Gentile relations, and that is the way to neurosis and stillbirths; that is, reading the young man's desire for the termination of any possible pregnancy symbolically,[28] there appears to be no future for the Jews.

Resorting to Silence

Freud also finds meaningful misstatements by or about Jews that take place in summer resorts (*Sommerfrische*). These vacation spots were major sources of status for the Jewish educated bourgeoisie (*Bildungsbürgertum*),[29] especially since so many did not allow Jews as guests. While these examples all function illustratively both with regard to the meaningfulness of these parapraxes and to Freud's methods (for example, free association), they also appear to suggest that interactions between Jew and Gentile are doomed to psychopathology.

The two particular examples that Freud cites also arise in the context of mixed marriages. One deals with an anticipated marriage that was to take place "in spite of the differences in their social position and race [*Standes- und Rassenunterschiede*]." A poor but handsome Gentile school teacher writes a letter to his brother but, instead of being sent to the brother, it arrives in the hands of his Jewish fiancée, the daughter of a wealthy villa owner from Vienna. It reads: "The girl is certainly no beauty. . . . But whether I shall be able to make up my mind to marry a Jewess I cannot yet tell you" (6:223). Needless to say, the wedding did not go on. Freud here provides a brief picture of the Viennese class structure: confirming the statistical studies that have examined the Jew/Gentile breakdown of various forms of employment normally associated with the liberal bourgeoisie—that Jews were numerically underrepresented among school teachers.[30] The scene also possibly echoes some of the stereotypes of the ugly Jewess (*hässliche Jüdin*), who together with the beautiful Jewess (*schöne Jüdin*) formed a complementary fin-de-siècle imaginary field of female Jewish types, and of the Jews attempting to buy themselves (through wedding dowry) into social acceptability.[31]

The second example is more developed; it is a story that Freud's colleague Viktor Tausk rather ironically entitled "The Faith of Our Fathers" (*Der Glaube der Väter*). The protagonist is a Jewish man who converted to Christianity to get married, since his Christian wife would not cross over to *Judentum*. Again, marriages between Jews and Christians were not per se allowed. Their two sons were baptized, but as they got older, their father informed them of their Jewish descent so that the antisemitic influences in their primary school (*Volksschule*) would not turn them against him. The recounted incident takes place at a summer resort where he and his family are staying. Unaware of their Jewish descent, the hotel hostess unleashes a series of antisemitic utterances. Here is the guest's dilemma: should or shouldn't he stand up to his hostess and demonstrate his boldness and the courage of his convictions to his children? Then he weighs the pros and cons, mainly the cons: creating a scene, turning the hostess against him and his family and, as a consequence, receiving horrible service at the resort. He feared the kind of experience Max Nordau suffered at the North Sea resort and gathering spot for the Prussian aristocracy and their entourages at Borkum. During the summer of 1893, Nordau was the leading cultural critic in Europe and his recent work, *Entartung/ Degeneration*, was an international bestseller; nevertheless, at his first dinner there,

> he found a letter at his place. Unsuspecting, he opened it. It was anonymous and requested him to leave Borkum at once. "We do not wish to see Jews here." [The n]ext day there was a second letter. He opened it in his room. From now on he found letters wherever he went, open or sealed. He pretended not to see them, but to be busy with his friends. They were now delivered to his room, more grossly vulgar, in verse or prose, from day to day, a very web of persecution. He tried to stick it out to save the feelings of his friends. But at the end of ten days he left. . . .[32]

In any case, the father in Tausk's anecdote does not want to subject his sons to the litany of antisemitic comments intoned by his hostess. So he sends them off: "Geht in den Garten *Juden*" ("Go into the garden, *Jews*"), instead of "Geht in den Garten *Jungen*" ("Go into the garden, youngsters"; 6:92–93).[33] Rather than sparing his children from the indirect and possibly direct opprobrium of the woman, he has made them—and himself—into potential targets. Even baptism and intermarriage did not provide him with a shield against antisemitism.

There is another instance of a *mésalliance*, one drawn from his psychoanalytic practice, that Freud mentions; indeed the word "*mésalliance*" is the unconscious representation that catalyzes a chain of associations, like "the genealogical tree of a family whose members have also intermarried" (3:198). It culminates in a slip of the tongue (*Versprechen*). While derivatives of the root "Jew-" (*Jud-*) do not appear in this example, an unmistakable synonym does: "non-Aryan" (*nicht-Arierin*). Freud's patient has a dream of *a child who would commit suicide by means of a snakebite*; she associates the manifest content with a lecture on first aid for snakebite that she had attended. When asked what kind of poisonous snakes were discussed, the patient responds *Klapperschlange* (rattlesnake). Freud finds that unlikely since rattlers are not native to Europe, let alone Vienna. As their exchange continues Freud makes an interesting aside that may be considered a recognition of the stereotypical ascriptions to which Jews had been subjected: "It is usual for us to lump together everything which is non-European and exotic" (6:66). Not surprising in light of Freud's elliptical references to his own Jewishness, by means of "us" Freud makes himself the subject and not the object of such practices. Eventually the chain of associations leads to reminiscences of the play *Arria und Messalina* by the Viennese playwright Adolf Wilbrandt. From this the essential content of the dream could be deduced: "Certain recent events had made her apprehensive that her only brother might make a socially unsuitable marriage, a *mésalliance* with a non-*Aryan*" (6:67).

Freud would also signal such visibility and identification of the Jew qua Jew in these interactions in another from his collection of Freudian slips; it was not manifestly addressing a sexual *mésalliance*, but who knows? An individual describing the relationship of two friends, one of whom is Jewish (*Jude*), says: "They live together like Castor and Pollak" (6:69). Obviously the individual had substituted this derogatory epithet for Poles, Polack or Pollak, for the other Gemini: Pollux. Pollak suggests that the Jew was of Eastern provenance, although he may not have been. At this time the *Ostjude*, or Eastern Jew, had come to be considered the normative or true Jew. Despite the seemingly natural affinity, even identity, of Germans and Jews, Jewish difference is always made manifest.

Although engaged in the analysis of the parapraxes of individuals, one that presumed the common psychological disposition of all, Freud's choice of examples suggests that he was also aware of a collective psychopathology betrayed by those same parapraxes. That Jewish (and Gentile) individuals would have lapsed into errant communications may well have indicated that the pursuit of intermarriage or interethnic love affairs either signaled or generated unresolved ambivalences and unformulated anxieties. Such affects would themselves be effects of the encounter between the dominant Gentiles and their uncanny doubles, the Jews, in Central Europe. There is nothing in itself "wrong in mixed marriages," as Freud told Joseph Wortis in 1935;[34] however, the conversion, whether whole- or half-hearted, necessary for intermarriage would have indicated the Jewish individual's ambivalence or self-hatred. Again, Freud, although nonobservant, never repudiated his Jewish descent; indeed, he felt that religious conversion represented a different form of conversion hysteria.[35] Yet, Freud's focus should suggest neither that such *mésalliances* were an exceptional form of Jewish-Gentile interaction nor that Jews alone were adversely affected by these everyday interactions.

Conversion Cannot the Cut Erase

Let us recall Schnitzler's most uncanny figuration of the inescapable ascription of the deprecating label "Jew" to his fellow Viennese Jews no matter how assimilated they may have been: "It was impossible to remain completely untouched; a person may not remain unconcerned whose skin had been anaesthetized but who has to watch, with his eyes open, how it is scratched by an unclean knife, even cut into until the blood flows."[36] There was no way out of the efforts to render the all-too-familiar as different. His contemporaries could not be blind to the antisemitic assaults against which they had become anaesthetized. More significant, even as they might dismiss the attacks because of the manifest absence of pain and perhaps resign themselves to living with a scar that may distort their countenance—but one that they can attempt to cover up—a more insidious injury has been inflicted. Because the knife is dirty, a poison has entered their system that unbeknownst to them might at a later date do them serious harm. To extend Schnitzler's figure a bit further: the first symptoms of such a tetanus infection would be spasms and tightness of the jaw muscles affecting speech. Consequently, it is not so much Jewishness as it is the hostile interaction between Jew and Gentile that betrays itself in conversation,[37] in language acts such as those analyzed by Freud in *Psychopathology*.

The problem may well have been less individual and more social. These uncanny *mésalliances* could have arisen out of individual psychopathology; nevertheless, they could just as well have conditioned, and been conditioned by, group psychosis. By blurring the lines of distinction—especially as the dominant group sought so hard to maintain them—the acculturating, yet persisting Jews presented a narcissistic threat to collective identity: "Jews and non-Jews became over the course of centuries so alike that the persistence of the Jews in their own group identity becomes an offense [*Ärgernis*], even a narcissistic insult [*Kränkung*] to the non-Jewish majority."[38] The bargain that the Jews had made to attain Emancipation— acceding to the demand, "Be like us"—had proved Faustian. Though it may have appeared as if an era of rationality had dawned with the advent of Emancipation, night as ever framed the day; for, as the epigraph to *Psychopathology* announced, ghosts were about and no one knew a way out. Before the violence would escape social and cultural restraints later in the century, the first distorted signs of the return of repressed and unresolved ambivalences, as well as of unformulated anxieties, slipped into the discourse of everyday Vienna. Freud's *Psychopathology of Everyday Life* let slip the distorted desires, demands, and dreads that shadowed the masks of his fellow Viennese. This analysis of Freud's discussions of explicitly Jewish-identified individuals and their strict delimitation to illustrating parapraxes associated with what should have been the most pleasurable and intimate relationships between Jew and Gentile suggests that, by focusing upon this conflicted conjunction, Freud diagnosed the intrinsically problematic character of Jew–Gentile interaction in his Vienna. The next chapter diagnoses how Freud, having internalized this problematic situation for Viennese Jews, from the start of his psychoanalytic career symptomatically externalizes and acts it out on his body and in his body of work.

CHAPTER 2

Not "Is Psychoanalysis a Jewish Science?" But "Is It *une histoire juive?*"

Artists tell us that the best way to make a caricature of the Jewish nose
is to write a figure 6 with a long tail.

—*The Jewish Encyclopedia* (1905 ed.)

Die Judennase ist die Figur sechs (= *Sex*) mit einem langen Schwanz.

—A German paraphrase of the above

This chapter draws its title from the 1980 Colloque de Montpellier that
was directed by Jean-Jacques and Adélie Rassial. The title of the conference played on the ambiguous phrase "une histoire juive." It can be translated as "a Jewish joke," "a story about Jews," and/or "a moment in Jewish
history." Psychoanalysis has had a long association with Jewish jokes.
Freud was a notorious collector and regaler of them, and they formed a
major focus of his study *Der Witz und seine Beziehung zum Unbewußten/
Jokes and Their Relationship to the Unconscious. Jokes* followed Freud's previous two meaning-recovering interventions into fields of the supposedly
meaningless: dreams and parapraxes. Consider this joke, not from *Jokes*,
but rather, with a minor change of locale, one reputedly told by Harvard's
first Jewish professor of philosophy, Harry Wolfson:

> In the middle of the nineteenth century a traveling salesman had arranged
> several appointments in a small town in Moravia—let's call it Pribor or
> Freiberg. When he arrives he discovers that his watch is broken. How is he
> going to make all of his appointments without knowing the time? So he
> sets about walking through the town looking for a watch-repair shop. Fi-
> nally he spots the sign of a clock over a little shop and sees several time-
> pieces in the window. He walks in and sees an old bearded man bent over
> a book at a table. "Excuse me," the salesman says. "My watch has stopped

and appears to be broken. Would you be able to repair it?" "I'm sorry, young man, but I cannot," the old man replies. "Is there anyone else in your shop who can repair it?" "I'm sorry, but there is no one else in my shop." "This is a watch shop, is it not?" "I'm afraid not, young man." "But why, then, is that sign over your shop and why are there timepieces in your front window?" "Well, young man, I'm a *mohel*. What would you like me to hang over my door or put in my window?"

We may laugh because this "tendentious" joke allows for the indirect expression of both a sexual (allusion to penises or parts therof) and an aggressive (evocation of castration through the allusion to its "symbolic substitute" [23:22], circumcision) content. It "make[s] possible the satisfaction of an instinct (whether lustful or hostile) in the face of an obstacle that stands in the way. [It] circumvent[s] this obstacle and in that way draw[s] pleasure from a source which the obstacle had made inaccessible" (8:101). It works so long as the listener already knows that a *mohel* is a ritual circumciser. This restriction provides an additional source of pleasure for those who know: "our laughter expresses a pleasurable sense of the superiority which we feel in relation to" (8:195) those others. In mixed company a joke such as this, which requires knowledge that a marginalized or oppressed group alone may be privy to, can provide a creative venue for that group usually denied the power that comes with knowledge. This "joke will allow us to exploit something ridiculous in our enemy which we could not, on account of obstacles in the way, bring forward openly or consciously" (8:103). Perhaps adding to the pleasure, this joke—all jokes?—like circumcision itself both displays what it cannot talk about and talks about what it cannot display. This joke also has a self-critical dimension that Freud remarks is often characteristic of Jewish jokes. It asserts that the (male) Jew cannot and should not show his Jewishness—indicated by the determinate Jewish attribute, circumcision—in public.[1]

Like dreams, which, as Freud repeatedly noted in *Interpretation*, make unashamed use of the advantages offered by verbal ambiguity for purposes of condensation and disguise, Jewish jokes often exploit plays on words (polysemy) in their depiction of the tension between how Jews perceive themselves and how they are perceived by others. One such joke that Freud tells in *Jokes* is a classic: "Two Jews met in the neighborhood of the bath-house. 'Have you taken a bath?' asked one of them. 'What?' asked the other in return, "is there one missing?'" (8:49). The joke plays on both the ambiguity of "taking a bath" and two anti-Jewish stereotypes: that Jews are dirty and that they are thieves. Freud confesses to accepting the truth of the former—at least with regard to Galician Jews (as opposed to Viennese Jews like himself);[2] although, he later transforms this self-criticism into a virtue. Jews "know their real faults as well as the connection between them and their good qualities, and the share which the subject [that is, the joke-teller] has on the person found fault with creates the subjective determinant . . . of the joke-work" (8:111–12).

There is perhaps a more significant joke that Freud repeats and that perhaps better than any illustrates the logic of the unconscious as well as the logic of antisemitic discourse and its construction of the Jew. It is a joke that appears twice in *Jokes*, but it had already made an appearance in *Interpretation*. As Freud concludes his analysis of the specimen dream (*Traummuster*) with the realization that the secret underlying this exemplary dream was his wish for self-exculpation of any responsibility for his patient Irma's condition, he writes:

> I noticed, it is true, that these explanations of Irma's pains (which agreed in exculpating me) were not entirely consistent with one another, and indeed that they were mutually exclusive. The whole plea—for the dream was nothing else—reminded one vividly of the defense put forward by the man who was charged by one of his neighbors with having given him back a borrowed kettle in a damaged condition. The defendant asserted first, that he had given it back undamaged; secondly, that the kettle had a hole in it when he borrowed it; and thirdly, that he had never borrowed a kettle from his neighbor at all. So much the better: if only a single one of these three lines of defense were to be accepted as valid, the man would have to be acquitted. (4:119–20; cf. 8:62 and esp. 205)

Perhaps it was in such a kettle that Freud cooked up psychoanalysis: for where and when can we say psychoanalysis began? Some might argue that it begins in 1896 with the first use of the term in a pair of medical journal articles: "Heredity and the Aetiology of the Neuroses" and "Further Remarks on the Neuro-Psychoses of Defense." Others would backdate the origin to the case of Anna O. (Bertha Pappenheim), who actually was not Freud's patient, but rather the patient of his senior colleague Josef Breuer in the early 1880s. Anna developed her own "talking cure"—telling stories until they awakened important, previously forgotten memories and released powerful emotions that could not be expressed.[3] Freud fully adopted this cathartic method to treat hysteria a decade later in 1892 when he helped his patient Elisabeth von R. to freely associate and reveal repressed wishes.[4]

The source, however, that is most often cited as the birthplace of psychoanalysis is Freud's analysis of his specimen dream, more commonly known as the "Dream of Irma's Injection." In a 12 June 1900 letter to his Berlin friend and confidante Wilhelm Fliess, an ear, nose, and throat specialist, Freud, after returning from the *Sommerfrische* where his family had been and were still staying—the villa known as Bellevue in the Vienna suburb of Grinzing—makes reference to dreaming that dream five years earlier and wonders,

> Do you suppose that someday one will read on a marble tablet on this house:
> Here, on July 24, 1895,
> the secret of the dream
> revealed itself to Dr. Sigm. Freud.[5]

Freud came to the realization that the purpose of the dream-work—the processes (condensation, displacement, representability, symbolism, secondary elaboration) to which the latent dream-thoughts and day residues are subjected in order to escape repression and construct the manifest dream—is the fulfillment of wishes, unconscious wishes. As he wrote at the end of his analysis of the dream in *Interpretation*: "*When the work of interpretation has been completed, we perceive that a dream is the fulfillment of a wish*" (4:121; emphasis in original).

Revealing that secret had a number of implications for the formation of psychoanalysis. Since we all dream, neurotics are not the only ones with repressed desires that have psychic effects; we all do. Further, as Freud concludes in *Interpretation* and, indeed, as he concludes *Interpretation* with—perhaps referring to the book as much as the technique—"*The [I]nterpretation of [D]reams is the royal road to a knowledge of the unconscious activities of the mind*" (5:608; emphasis in original).[6] Psychoanalysis, thus, was more than a psychotherapy; it was *the Geisteswissenschaft, the* human science and science of the human.

This chapter undertakes a series of interpretations of that specimen dream, which Freud described as the first one, upon which he systematically subjected every detail to free association and analysis. The dream arguably inaugurated Freud's self-analysis, and it certainly initiates Freud's own discussion of dream analysis in *Interpretation* with further discussions of aspects of the dream woven through the rest of the text (4:106–20, 123–24, 140, 163, 165, 173, 180n1, 271n1, 292–95, 306, 310, 314, 316–17, 322; 5:341, 513, 534, 595, 657). My analysis will examine how the interrelationship of dream-thoughts and day residues about gender identity, Jewish identity, and the body, as well as how the masculinist ideology of Freud's Vienna, the "objective" authority of knowledge, the labeling power of nosology, the expropriation of reproduction, and the telltale signs of the nose all contributed to the emergence of the manifest dream—and, perhaps, psychoanalysis.

Dream a Little Dream of Me

Sometime during the night of 23–24 July 1895, Freud dreams that he and his wife are receiving numerous guests; among them is his patient Irma. Taking her aside, he becomes alarmed by her symptoms, in particular the "extensive whitish grey [*weißgraue*] scabs upon some remarkable curly structures which were evidently modeled on the turbinal bones of the nose [*Nasenmuscheln*]" (4:107). He calls in his male colleagues. After examining her body, the doctors diagnose her infection and nonsensically predict that the toxin (*Gift*) will be (rather odorously) eliminated through the supervention of dysentery. They then identify the cause of Irma's ailment: one of Freud's consulted colleagues had used an unclean syringe to inject Irma. The dirty *Spritze* contained a preparation that reeked, according to Freud, of associations to strong-smelling substances. Among these chemical preparations was trimethylamin, whose formula he visualized in heavy type $(N[CH3]3)$ and whose role in sexual chemistry had been pointed out by "another friend" (4:116), whom Freud implies was not present at the dream scene. In addition, this "friend," obviously Wilhelm Fliess, Freud adds, "had drawn scientific attention to some very remarkable connections between the turbinal bones [*Nasenmuscheln*] and the female organs of sex" (4:117).

The origin of Irma's plaint is also the source of the dream's familiar designation: "the dream of Irma's injection." In *Interpretation* Freud would employ it as a "specimen dream" (*Traummuster*) to exemplify his method of interpretation. It is both the first thoroughly analyzed dream of Freud's groundbreaking text and the first of his own dreams that Freud subjected to a "detailed" (*eingehend*, thorough) analysis (4:106n).[7] As a consequence of its significant placement in his text and life, it is also the dream most thoroughly analyzed by Freud's later commentators.[8] Further enticing readers to continue Freud's own dream work is his confession at its conclusion: "I will not pretend that I have completely uncovered the meaning of this dream or that its interpretation is without a gap" (4:120–21). The text of his analysis confirms this incompleteness. Thus, while Freud's analysis elicits from the dream a wide array of associations, the final interpretation is restricted to the motifs of professional rivalry and guilt. He concludes that the dream represents his wish both to absolve himself of responsibility for Irma's condition and to stick the onus on his colleagues.

The dream-text and Freud's accompanying commentary have generated a number of controversies—particularly about the identity of Irma—and many other interpretations: these range from Freud's valorizing his theory of the sexual etiology of neurosis to his confronting a life-stage crisis of generativity, from his own problematic identification with a neurotic woman patient to his efforts to restore his idealized relationship with Fliess that had been jeopardized by the latter's botched operation upon Freud's own patient Emma Eckstein, from orality and the displacement of maternal loss to anality and the repression of homoerotic desire.[9]

This chapter's discussion takes as its lead the recognition by Didier Anzieu that "the Irma dream makes a kind of inventory of the body. . . . [It] spells out the identity of both the body of the dream and the dream of the body."[10] In particular, I isolate one item of that inventory, the repeatedly mentioned nasal turbinal bones, the *Nasenmuscheln*, that are covered by the "whitish grey scabs." These body parts generate associations with a number of the motifs and alluded-to individuals noted by Freud and his successors: personal responsibility and scientific authority, creativity and sexuality, Wilhelm Fliess and Emma Eckstein. The *Nasenmuscheln* also call attention to the nose. The prominent role the nose plays as an interpretive key to the dream has been pointed out by Mahony in his thorough analysis of Freud's visualization of the formula for trimethylamin:[11]

> The N, the hetero-atom that Freud reflected on orthographically, olfactorily, medically and symbolically, establishes crucial links, extending from Fliess the rhinologist and his all-embracing theories about the nose, to the nasal operation of Emma, Freud, and Fliess, to the smelly bottle of liquor. Or, said somewhat differently, the letter N, the chemical sign for nitrogen, which also orthographically represents the first consonant of the word *Nase* ("nose"), significantly enough represents a sound the linguistic decoding of which inevitably constitutes a kinesthetically nasal performance.

But the *Nasenmuscheln* do not allude to just to any nose; rather, they evoke the Jewish nose, *die Judennase*. *Muscheln*'s near homophones—*Mauscheln* and *Muskeljuden*, both turn-of-the-century figurations of (male) Jews that will be discussed below—resonate with ethno-racial as well as gender and sexual overtones. In *Interpretation*, Freud repeatedly calls attention to how displaced verbal expressions allow the representation of the dream-thoughts: "Words, since they are the nodal points of numerous ideas, may be regarded as predestined to ambiguity; [and] dreams make unashamed use of the advantages thus offered by words for purposes of condensation and disguise" (5:340). A word can act as "a switch-point: where one of the meanings of the word is present in the dream-thoughts the other one can be introduced into the manifest dream" (5:410).[12] This chapter pursues the curly trail of those whitish-grey, scab-ridden *Nasenmuscheln* from the metaphorical, scientific, and sexological determination of the (Jewish) nose and smell, through Emma Eckstein's apartment, past Jewish social and professional networks to a significant subtext of both Freud's dream and his Vienna: the construct of the feminized (male) Jew whose presence in the public sphere threatened the gender (and ethno-racial) difference sustaining the masculinist, bourgeois European order, the *Männerbund.*

The Judennase *and the* foetor Judaicus

The Jews have not always been known by their noses. According to Dennis Showalter, "the 'Jewish type' . . . only emerged during the seventeenth century. Before that the Jews were identified symbolically rather than physically: by tall hats, money bags, and similar items. The creation of physical forms of caricature began with giving all male Jews beards—a pattern reflecting accurate observation as much as antisemitism. The process of distortion began with the nose."[13] This shift from symbolic to physical identification was not the consequence of any increased Jewish presence; rather it signalled both the erosion of feudal-aristocratic society, in which identity and status were symbolically indicated, and the shift from a theological to a rational/natural ground of meaning.[14] Characteristic of this period was the widespread belief in physiognomy. This "science," advanced by Johann Caspar Lavater in 1776, discerned people's true natures by their features. For Lavater, "the moral life of man discovers itself principally in the face."[15] In the late eighteenth century, physiognomic verities became commonplace and, despite either the universalistic intent of Lavater or the radical empiricism of many of his scientific disciples, they were employed in the social stereotyping of the dominant culture's others. The Jews became categorized by their physiognomy—their noses.[16] As the leading chronicler of Jewish caricature Eduard Fuchs remarked: "It is impossible to deny that the extraordinarily big, and usually also conspicuously [*auffällig*] formed, namely hooked [*hakenmässig*], nose is characteristic of the Jews as a whole."[17]

Conversely, the *Jewish Encyclopedia* (1901–6) devoted an entry to the nose and focused not only on statistical analyses of the predominance of straight over aquiline or arched noses in all Eastern European Jewish communities but upon the caricaturist's focus on "Jewish nostrility" as what distinguishes the Jewish from the Roman or Gallic or any other ethnically coded proboscis. Citing the English anthropologist and *Encyclopedia* editor, Joseph Jacobs, that "it is not so much the shape of its profile as the accentuation and flexibility of the nostrils," the entry-author and American anthropologist Maurice Fishberg continues with Jacobs's account of "a curious experiment": "Artists tell us that the best way to make a caricature of the Jewish nose is to write a figure 6 with a long tail; now remove the turn of the twist . . . and much of the Jewishness disappears; and it vanishes entirely when we draw the continuation horizontally."[18]

That the nose should become so prominent in representations of a person or a people is no surprise. The nose, generally, is considered "the physiognomic *principium individuationis*, the symbol of the specific character of an individual, described between the lines of his countenance."[19] It is "the most conspicuous body part as well as, at the same time, the one most capable of expression" (*ausdrucksfähigste*).[20] For Lavater, the nose was "the fulcrum of the brain";[21] 120 years later, Wilhelm Fliess begins his 1897 work on the relation between the nose and the genitals by also calling attention to its central location: "In the middle of the face, between the eyes, the mouth, and the osseous formations of the fore- and midbrain, there is the nose. Connected to the rhinopharyngeal space, it communicates with the ear and the larynx."[22]

Moreover the German language is rife with idioms and proverbs as well as superstitions about the nose as a visual index—without any original Jewish context; for example, "In einer kleinen Stadt kennt einer den anderen an der Nase" ("In a small town one knows the other by his nose"); "Man kann's ihm an der Nase ansehen" ("You can read his character in his face [nose]"); "sich an der Nase fassen" ("to confess one's guilt, to reprove one's self"; lit. "to fix [it] on one's nose oneself"); "die Nase voll haben" ("to be fed up with" or "to have a nose full of").[23] Further, the traditional belief that the possessors of large noses also possess large penises was pervasive.[24] Yet, while the so-called Jewish nose is not universally characteristic of Jews—as not only the already mentioned *Jewish Encyclopedia* endeavored to demonstrate, but even the racist antisemite Houston Stewart Chamberlain concedes, "The nose alone is no reliable proof of Jewish descent"—it remains ever present in the popular imagination.[25]

In one of the most popular novels of the nineteenth century, Gustav Freytag's 1855 *Soll und Haben/Debit and Credit*, the main antagonist, the Jew Veitel Itzig, "had a curious preference for crooked (*krumme*) alleys and narrow pavements. Here and there behind the back of his travel companion he beckoned with brazen familiarity to the dolled-up young girls who stood in the doorways or to the young fellows with crooked (*krummer*) noses and round eyes who hands in their pockets loitered about the streets."[26] Freytag's description hooks Itzig into a tradition of antisemitic representations exemplified by Wilhelm Busch's notorious depiction of the Jews (in the first chapter of *Die fromme Helene/Pious Helen* [1872]): Freytag's "harmless appearing, doubtless ironically intended indication, loses its harmlessness, when one recognizes with what prejudice the adjective 'krumm' is bound: 'And the Jew with crooked (*krummer*) back, / crooked (*Krummer*) nose and crooked (*krummer*) legs / snakes his way to the stock market / profoundly corrupted and soulless.' "[27] Jacob Burckhardt, the great historian and one of Freud's favorite authors, was no less caught up in the nasal representation of the Jews. In a letter to his friend, the architect Max Aliot, he describes his visit to Frankfurt where "Kalle and Shickselchen and Papa with their famous noses, appear on the balcony between females borrowed from the Pandroseion."[28]

Jewish writers were quite aware of the identification of the Jews with their noses. Moses Hess, in his 1862 proto-Zionist tract *Rome and Jerusalem*, undercuts the belief held by many Jewish Reformers that the German perception of the Jewish religion as ritualistic and atavistic was the primary obstacle to emancipation. He writes: the German "objects less to the Jews' peculiar beliefs than to their peculiar noses. . . . Jewish noses cannot be reformed."[29] It would be another thirty-six years, 1898, before the German-Jewish surgeon Jacob Joseph would undertake the first rhinoplasty to relieve the melancholy of a young man whose Jewish nose prevented him from passing in Gentile society.[30]

Heinrich Heine also identifies the nose with the Jewish people. In his 1840 *Denkschrift/Memorial* for Ludwig Börne, Heine recalls the late author describing Jewish converts to Christianity: old daughters of Israel who wear crosses that are "even longer than their noses." Later, he recounts Börne's comment that "The renegades [*Abtrünnigen*] who deserted to the new covenant need only smell a *tsholent* to feel a certain homesickness for the synagogue."[31] In a similar vein, Heine's contemporaneous continuation of his prose fragment *The Rabbi of Bacharach* is rife with nasal imagery and beliefs. The gatekeeper to the Frankfurter ghetto is Nasenstern (Schnozzle Stern); his partner is Jäkel the fool who has a "nasally voice" (*näselnde Stimme*). Nasenstern's "incredibly long nose" (*fast unglaublich lange Nase*) facetiously substitutes for the key to the ghetto gate; the voluptuous and promiscuous Ellen Schnapper "has fallen in love with his nose" (*hat sich in seine Nase verliebt*), and, because of his (Schnozzle Stern's) imagined reproductive prodigality, in 300 years Frankfurt would be hidden beneath the numerous Nasensterns. Heine has odors just pour out of Ellen Schnapper's kitchen, which ultimately motivate the apostate courtier Don Isaak Abarbanel to declaim, "My nose is not a renegade" (*abtrünnig geworden*).[32]

These last passages from Heine shift the focus on the *Judennase* from form to function, from shape to smell, and reflect a metonymic broadening of its symbolic field.[33] For the European cultural imagination, however, the earmark of the Jews was not so much their sense of smell as it was their smell itself. The Jewish stench, the noxious *foetor Judaicus*,[34] betrayed the Jew. The noted nineteenth-century German ethnographer Richard Andree, in *On the Ethnography of the Jews*, traces the emergence of this odious ascription to the ancient Greeks and Romans, who—unlike contemporary Italians—hated garlic and garlic-eaters.[35] This custom, he suggests, may well explain the locus classicus of the *foetor Judaicus*, Marcus Aurelius's (in)famous comment on the "malodorous Jews" (*foetentium Judaeorum*) as reported by Ammianus Marcellinus.[36] In explicit contrast to such antisemitic polemicists as his contemporary Gustav Jaeger, who claimed that there were particular racial smells,[37] Andree writes that the probable origin of the fabled Jewish stench lies in the Jews' "well-known preference for leeks and the like" (*die bekannte Vorliebe nach Lauchspeisen*).[38] As evidence he cites Numbers 11:5, in which the wandering Israelites bemoan their diet of manna: "Remember how in Egypt we had . . . leeks and onions and garlic." But even such dietary explanations did not prevent antisemites in the late nineteenth century from generating a more perfidious tie of the Jewish stench to garlic. The widely disseminated "Song in Praise of Garlic" (*Ehren unn Lobleid oufn Knoblich*) mocks: "Garlic, garlic, bold herb / [you] strengthen your Jew's heart and mind / and profit him with / the genuine, kosher Jewish stench."[39]

The physiognomics of caricature were soon joined by a metaphysics of olfaction:[40]

> My instinct for cleanliness is characterized by a perfectly uncanny [*unheimliche*] sensitivity so that the proximity of—what am I saying?—the inmost parts, the "entrails" of every soul are physiologically perceived by me—smelled.
>
> This sensitivity furnishes me with psychological antennae with which I feel and get a hold of every secret: the abundant hidden dirt at the bottom of many a character—perhaps the result of bad blood, but glossed over by education—enters my consciousness almost at the first contact.

The most celebrated modern disseminator of the *foetor Judaicus* was perhaps the German philosopher Arthur Schopenhauer,[41] who talks repeatedly of being overcome (*übermannt*) by it. Even Spinoza, one of his favorite philosophers, does not escape its taint: "Here [Spinoza in part 4 of the *Ethics*] speaks even as a Jew understands it, following Gen. 1:9, such that the *foetor Judaicus* thereby overcomes [*übermannt*] the rest of us who are so accustomed to purer and worthier theories."[42] Indeed, "Spinoza . . . could not get rid of the Jews: quo semel est imbuta recens servabit odom ([A smelling bottle] long retains the smell of that which filled it)."[43] In Schopenhauer's essay sequence "On Religion," a most telling and repeated phrase appears: "A man must be bereft of all his senses, or completely chloroformed by the *foetor Judaicus*, not to see that, in all essential respects, the animal is absolutely identical with us and the difference lies merely in the accident, the intellect, and not in the substance, which is the will."[44] This last utterance suggests two interrelated implications of the association of the Jew with the nose: the animalistic (sexual) Jew and the Jewish threat to gender identity.

First, even as Schopenhauer rails against the Jews' presumption of their superiority to the animal kingdom, he reduces them to animal-like status.[45] By ascribing odorousness to the Jews, he expels them from the confines of civilized humanity.[46] This ascription simultaneously binds the Jews to the "primitive" and atavistic sense of smell in word and deed: on the linguistic level, in German (as in English) *riechen* (to smell) signifies both the emission and the perception of an odor;[47] and, from a phenomenological perspective, a smell and its perceiver become united.[48] And olfaction, like its object, is tied to animality. Whereas smell is highly developed in animals, it has become almost rudimentary in the human, a biological fact that nineteenth-century comparative brain anatomy proved—at least for the European. According to G. Eliot Smith, "sometimes, especially in some of the non-European races, the whole of the posterior rhinal fissure is retained in that typical form which we find in the anthropoid apes."[49] Smell lies in a "most ancient . . . a remote and almost disused storehouse of our minds."[50] Consequently, to attend to smells inordinately is to resort to primitive processes; it is a sign of biological degeneration.

Preoccupation with smells is a sign of cultural degeneration as well. According to Max Nordau's anatomy of fin-de-siècle culture *Entartung/Degeneration*, "Even the nose, hitherto basely ignored by the fine arts, attracts the pioneers, and is by them invited to take part in aesthetic delights."[51] Obsessions about odors gripped the French representatives of this "degenerate" epoch, such as the novelist Huysmans and the noted defender of Dreyfus, Zola.[52] Nordau also notes that the followers of a particular German variant of degenerate culture—antisemitism—have nightmares about body odor.[53] Despite infusing the self-proclaimed antitheses of Jewry with the odorous stigmata of *Entartung*, Nordau and his contemporaries implicitly render, by this connection of smell with degeneration, the Jews as fallen from the evolutionary pinnacle embodied by bourgeois European maledom.

The association of the Jews with the primitive sense of smell also entailed an association with sexuality. Since for animals smell is an essential ingredient of that most animalistic of activities, sexuality, the sexologists of the late nineteenth century added that "a certain histological conformity [exists] between the nose and the genitals, for both have erectile tissue." The "intimate association" of nose and genitals was also observed in the relationship between source and sensation.[54] Ellis cites Gustav Klein, who "argues the special function of the glands at the vulvar orifice . . . is to give out an odorous secretion to act as an attraction to the male, this relic of sexual periodicity."[55] Ellis's reference to the *odor di feminina* indicates that the primary focus of discussions of odor and sexuality was feminine odor and sexuality. Although sexologists usually conceded that "much of what has been said concerning the *parfum de la femme* applies to the sexual exhalation or scent of men,"[56] the vast preponderance of attention was directed toward women's odors. Hence to speak of a particular Jewish odor was to evoke the primitive, the sexual, the feminine.

As the sexological literature attests, the connection of scent to sexuality was subject to biological and medical investigation. Various embryological and evolutionary theories were proposed: "As early as G. Valentin's 1835 handbook of human development, the chronological parallels in the development of soft-tissue areas and cavities of the fetus had been noted."[57] Through the evolutionism propounded by scientists like Haeckel, the common and early development of nasal cavities and genitalia in the fetus were signs both of their mutual implication and of their comparative primitivism. Haeckel himself expounded upon the connection between smell and sexuality. He "theorized in his *Anthropogenie oder Entwickelungsgeschichte des Menschen* that 'erotic chemotropisms'—that is to say, chemically based sex stimulants affecting taste and smell—were phylogenetically the 'primal source' of all sexual attraction in nature."[58] Haeckel's theory of primal smells was hailed by the sexologist and author of *Odoratus Sexualis*, Iwan Bloch, in his 1902–3 *Beiträge zur Aetiologie der Psychopathia sexualis*.[59] Even the commonplace association between a large nose and a large penis got tied into smell: large noses smell more and hence are sexually more excitable.[60] The increased attention directed at matters nasal led the *Gazette hebdomodaire des sciences médicales de Bourdeaux* to conclude, if half facetiously, in its report of Dr. Oméga's letter to the editor of *Archivii italiani di laryngolia*: "a new science is in the process of being born: who knows if in the twentieth century we will not have chairs of comparative rhinography in our universities?"[61]

Out of this scientific focus on sexuality, smell, and, by implication, the nose, emerged the work of Wilhelm Fliess and that of his predecessor, the American laryngologist John Noland Mackenzie:[62]

> Mackenzie believed that all such afflictions of the nasal mucous membranes were probably "the [phylogenetic] connecting link between the sense of smell and erethism of the reproductive organs exhibited in the lower animals." It was in this implicit phylogenetic connection that Mackenzie specifically attributed perversions of smell to pathological reversions to "the purely animal type." Summing up the phenomena on nasal pathology in general, and those of the "nasal reflex neuroses" specifically, Mackenzie suggested that such disturbances are probably a direct result of the major reduction in olfactory acuity that has accompanied human evolution and the advent of civilized life.

Freud, in a letter to Fliess (11 January 1897), provides a similar summary of the connections inherent among smell, animality, perverse sexuality, and psychopathology:[63]

> Perversions regularly . . . have an animal character. They are explained . . . by the effect of erogenous sensations that later lose their force. In this connection one recalls that the principal sense in animals (for sexuality as well) is that of smell, which has been reduced in human beings. As long as smell . . . is dominant, urine, feces, and the whole surface of the body, also blood, have a sexually exciting effect. The heightened sense of smell in hysteria presumably is connected with this.

From this miasma of biological speculation about the relationship between smell and animality arose an implicit connection among Jews, their noses, and "primitive," ergo degenerative, sexuality; that is, between Jews and a sexuality that did not support, or that threatened, the male European's gender (and sexual) identity.

This conclusion suggests that, for his readers, Schopenhauer's references to the *foetor Judaicus* associate Jews not only with the animalistic but with questions of gender identity as well. The phrasing out of which the *foetor* emanates echoes this second connection. Schopenhauer employs gender-indicative language. The evocation of gender identity in being *"über-mannt"* (lit. "overmanned") by the *foetor Judaicus* is obvious. But his other preferred term, *"chloroformiert,"* and his comparison of Spinoza with a smelling bottle are no less so. Ellis notes that "during menstruation girls and young women frequently give off an odor which . . . may smell of chloroform."[64] Moreover, as the sexological literature reports, "It is known to all that during her menses woman gives off an idiosyncratic repulsive odor."[65] Thus, through the chloroform-like, repulsive *foetor Ju-daicus*, the Jew again becomes associated with women.[66] "Chloroform," moreover, provokes other questions about gender identity that were a matter of much discussion during the late 1840s when Schopenhauer was composing the essays in which *"chloroformiert"* appears.[67] At this time, chloroform became the anaesthetic of choice for women in labor.[68] Comparing Spinoza to a smelling bottle has a complementary connection with women. Whereas chloroform puts the soon-to-be mother—a dominant nineteenth-century stereotype of women—to sleep, the smelling bottle restores the fainted hysteric, another dominant stereotype, to her senses. The *foetor Judaicus* put its male victim in a female role; it put male gender identity in jeopardy. To be "overmanned" by the *foetor Judaicus* was to be unmanned. Consequently, noses—and their bearers—would become an object of nosological classification and medical administration.

In addition to iconic and olfactive indices, the *Judennase* had a more sanguine connection to sexuality, gender identity, and the biologization of the Jew: the bloody nose as male menstruation. Sander Gilman and others have chronicled the traditional Christian calumny of Jewish male menstruation that continued at least into the eighteenth century.[69] The rumor (*Gerücht*) that "around Christmas only Christian blood could help menstruating male Jews" provided one of the explanations for Jewish ritual murder.[70] Interest in the subject rekindled toward the end of the nineteenth century, especially in the work of Magnus Hirschfeld, for whom it "came to hold a very special place in the 'proofs' for the continuum between male and female sexuality."[71] The link between the medieval theory that Jews needed Christian blood to replace the blood lost in (male) menstruation and the contemporary theory of bisexuality was found in the study of nosebleeds. In his *Relations between the Nose and Female Sexual Organs* (*Die Beziehungen zwischen Nase und weiblichen Geschlechtsorganen*) Fliess argued that nosebleeds in prepubescent, postmenopausal, and pregnant women are not merely vicarious menstrual discharges; rather, they demonstrate that "the process of monthly uterine bleeding is only a link in the chain" of human periodicity.[72] He goes on to cite, as proof of his theory that men like women have menstrual periods, the case of a man who had periodic nosebleeds that his friends referred to as his "menstruation."[73] Indeed, Freud, ever ready to provide his friend Fliess with evidence for his theory of periodicity, informs him in a 20 July 1897 letter of Freud's own "menstruation with occasional bloody nasal secretion before and after."[74] Cases like this were, according to Fliess, "consistent with our bisexual constitution,"[75] to which Freud concurred: "I avail myself of the bisexuality of all human beings."[76] They were also consistent with the threat to gender identity posed by chloroform-smelling menstruation and, implicitly, by those who menstruate: "Menstrual blood, on the contrary, stands for the danger issuing from within the identity (social or sexual); it threatens the relationship between the sexes within a social aggregate and through internalization, the identity of each sex in the face of sexual difference."[77]

These permutations of the *Judennase*, the *foetor Judaicus*, and male menstruation combined to question gender (and sexual) identity in a society that at least since the 1860s had endeavored to force individuals through legal, medical, and administrative means to have an unambiguous gender (and sexual) identity.[78] For a man to be bisexual, or to have a "strong homosexual current,"[79] that is, to share qualities characteristic of the ideological construct "woman," threatened the gender difference that, together with other naturalized differences (including sexual), undergirded masculinist bourgeois European society. The bleeding Jewish nose with its suggestion of male menstruation and bisexuality stigmatized the male Jew as effeminate.[80] Yet the scientific exploration of bisexuality implicit to the representation of Jewish nasality threatened to universalize Jewish difference—and therefore undermine the order founded upon the production and maintenance of particular differences of gender, sexuality, and race.

I Was Schur about Emma's Foetos *[sic], or Tracing the Implications of a Mistranscription*

After riding some curls of nineteenth-century cultural and scientific history, we return to Freud's Vienna and to a series of events that began almost six months prior to the dream of Irma's injection: Fliess's operation on Emma Eckstein's *Nasenmuscheln* to remedy her gastric distress[81] and its aftermath. These events both anticipate many of the elements of Freud's dream and recapitulate much of the preceding discussion of noses, smells, gender (and sexual) identity,[82] and reproduction.

By the time Fliess journeyed to Vienna in late January or early February 1895 to operate on Eckstein and Freud, he and Freud had already been meeting, corresponding, and exchanging research for almost eight years. The preceding two years had marked an intensification of their relationship; both men were increasingly involved in comparing notes and noses. Leaving aside Fliess's rhinological specialization, their correspondence revealed, between their shared nose-related ailments and involvement with cocaine, a virtual obsession with the nose and nasality. Freud endeavored to incorporate Fliess's insights about the nose into his own psychological theory. He had already at the end of 1892 treated a patient suffering from olfactory hallucinations. Indeed, his discussion of the case of Lucy R. (2:106–24) is where Freud clearly describes the active process of repression for the first time.[83] From this early recognition of smell as a possible sign of repressed ideas, Freud's theory of repression acquired an increasingly olfactive air: "To put it crudely, the memory stinks just as in the present the object stinks; and in the same manner as we turn away our sense organ (the head and nose) in disgust, the preconscious and the sense of consciousness turn away from the memory. This is repression."[84] And just as smell betrayed the conflicts within Lucy R.'s situation of employment, so, too, did Fliess and Freud's professional preoccupation with noses and psychopathology betray their shared fate as Jews within the Central European medical establishment. Jews like Freud and Fliess who sought status and upward mobility by pursuing a medical career were generally confined to the lower rungs of the medical academic hierarchy. Rhinolaryngology, dermatology, syphilology, psychopathology, sexology, all of the specializations that dealt with primitive sense organs and sensations; all of the sub-disciplines that had contact with the socially unacceptable; all of the vocations that were not marked by the objective, disinterested, technical mastery that characterized surgery or neurology—these were the preserve of the Jews.[85] Yet Fliess and Freud's revaluation of the importance of nasality would restructure the strictures on Jewish medical mobility. By restoring the nose to an important role in the makeup of civilized modernity, Freud and Fliess would redeem the nosebearers as well.

Other factors than this common quest for medical respectability led to the intensification of their relationship. Fliess's charisma, his comparative professional success, and Freud's feeling of isolation and corresponding need for an audience,[86] for an "Other,"[87] led to a "transference-like relationship," in which Freud idealized his Berlin friend.[88] In their correspondence, and outside it as well,[89] Freud assumed the role of patient. Considering the predominance of female patients in Freud's practice as well as the general and gendered structure of medical relationships—masculine subject and feminine object—he thereby took on an all but "feminine" persona.[90] Freud continuously yielded to the opinions of his "Daimonie" (letter of 24 July 1895, the morning after the dream of Irma's injection).[91] He would come to describe their relationship in terms of "homosexual investment" or cathexis.[92] This relationship between two Jewish men recapitulated the shared belief in human bisexuality. But in ideologically heterosexual, gender-differentiated Vienna, any intimation of male-to-male intimacy rendered the offending parties unmanly.[93] Within the binary logic of masculinist ideology, they were feminized. Freud's male relationships—with their inherent potential for feminization—would play a large role in the dream of Irma's injection and Freud's later theories and relationships.[94]

Freud's theoretical formulations at this juncture—he was working through his theory of the sexual etiology of hysteria as well as completing his *Studies on Hysteria* with Breuer—were guided by the hegemonic ideology of reproduction.[95] Reproduction, neurosis, and its treatment were intimately connected. Freud hypothesized that the so-called actual neuroses were caused by the impairment of normal sexual activity, defined as heterosexual intercourse for the purpose of reproduction. Anxiety and neurasthenia arose not only from too much sex, exemplified by masturbation, or too little, the fate of unmarried women, but also from contraceptive sexual practices such as coitus interruptus and coitus reservatus, that is, with condoms.[96] He also knew that Breuer had ended his therapeutic relationship with Anna O., the most famous study on hysteria, when she confronted him with the claim that she was hysterically pregnant with his child.[97]

Freud's concern with reproduction extended to the metaphors employed in describing his work: for example, in his 12 June 1895 letter to Fliess, Freud states that "reporting on [the psychological construction of defense] now would be like sending a six-month fetus of a girl to a ball."[98] On a more personal level, Freud was ever concerned about the effects of pregnancy on Martha's health, on their sex life, and on his ability to support a family. Epitomizing how the ideology of reproduction impinged upon both his theoretical and his personal life is a comment in his 25 May 1895 letter to Fliess: "I felt like shouting with excitement when I got your news. If you really have solved the problem of conception, just make up your mind immediately which kind of marble is most likely to meet with your approval. For me you are a few months too late, but perhaps it can be used next year. In any event, I am burning with curiosity about it."[99] Fliess's solution to unwanted pregnancy was to induce labor by stimulating the *Nasenmuscheln*.

His answer to Emma Eckstein's gastric distress was the partial removal of those same *Nasenmuscheln*. Several weeks later (4 March 1895) Freud wrote to Fliess, "Eckstein's condition is still unsatisfactory." Freud convinces himself to call in another physician to Eckstein's apartment, who diagnoses that access to the site of the operation is impeded, thus making drainage difficult. "To judge by the smell [*Geruch*]" emanating from her,[100] Freud accepts his conclusion. According to the letter of 8 March 1895 Eckstein's condition had seriously deteriorated. Freud begins the letter by summing up his previous correspondence: "I wrote you that the swelling and the hemorrhages would not stop, and that suddenly a fetid odor [*Foetos* (*sic*)] set in, and that there was an obstacle upon irrigation (or is the latter new [to you]?). . . ."[101] The *Foetos*, this bearer of bad tidings, suddenly makes an appearance, like an actor entering on stage (Freud writes "*auftrat*"), a stage upon which Freud would soon play out the problem of gender identity.

Two days later, he adds, he had to call in Dr. Rosanes, an ear, nose, and throat specialist like Fliess. "There still was moderate bleeding from the nose and mouth; the fetid odor [*Foetos* (*sic*)] was very bad." Smell remains the key index of the severity of the situation. "Rosanes . . . suddenly pulled at something like a thread, kept on pulling. Before either of us had time to think, at least half a meter of [iodoform] gauze had been removed from the cavity. The next moment came a flood of blood [*Verblutung*]."[102] Following this nasal hemorrhaging there is no more discussion of the smell: with the removal of the gauze comes a corresponding elimination of the *Foetos* as well as the implication that an alternative scene is being enacted. That is, *Foetos* is a virtual homophone for *Foetus*, or fetus. Through this phonetic connection the *Verblutung*, by definition a scene of (nearly) bleeding to death, also suggests a scene of birthing or rather, of miscarriage, of abortion. This symbolic depiction conforms to Fliess's contention that both nosebleeds and labor were forms of "transformed menstruation"; birthing is described as a "magnified version of menstrual flow." Freud and Fliess shared the "*Schibboleth*" that allowed them to recognize these relationships among nose, sexuality, and birth.[103] Further contributing to the impression that Eckstein's nasal hemorrhaging represents a birthing is the iodoform gauze left in by Fliess, the source of the *Foetos*.[104] Iodoform is closely related chemically to that other strong-smelling substance frequently present in birthing rooms—chloroform.

Unfortunately in the staging of the previous paragraph's interpretation, one of its leading dramatis personae appeared under false pretenses. As I discovered to my great embarrassment, just hours before I was to lecture my class at the University of Vienna on this scene, the text in the German edition of the Freud-Fliess correspondence read otherwise than I had presented: in both passages instead of *Foetos*, I found *Foetor*. Had I pulled a "man in the Rorschach shirt"—Ray Bradbury's classic story of the psychoanalyst whose entire theoretical edifice was built upon the repeated mishearing of his patients' words—and substituted a (nonexistent) form of the Latin word for "fetid odor" in anticipation of the remarkable correspondence between Freud's word choice and my analysis of the episode and subsequent dream? Had I engaged in some (un)professional wish fulfillment like Freud in his interpretation of his dream?

As I reconstructed what had transpired when I was initially working on this analysis, I recalled that I had relied on Max Schur's transcription of the German original in his 1966 article,[105] because I did not have access at that time to Masson and Schröter's then-recently published German edition. While I could now acquit myself of an ethical lapse, I was still confronted by the ruins of an interpretation. Yet, while my ignorance of Latin could explain my blithely reproducing Schur's mistake, what could explain the transcription of a nonsensical Latin term—twice!—by a physician who would have had taken Latin at least six hours a week for eight years as a young gymnasium student,[106] as well as have had years of subsequent practice in the use of Latin medical jargon? Rather than dismissing Schur's mistake as a mere accident, perhaps it should be seen as a meaningful parapraxis. Since in outing the Emma Eckstein episode he was betraying what he considered as the site of the Irma Dream's conception, perhaps he was picking up on the birthing imagery that was rife in this and other of Freud's letters. Hence, by providing his mistranscribed genetic account of the specimen dream, Schur had provided me with a *Schibboleth* to cross over into this additional level of meaning at play in Freud's account.

Inversions of Gender and . . .

In an atmosphere still pervaded by the fetid emission, Freud continues by describing his encounter with another bodily discharge: "At the moment the foreign body came out and everything became clear to me—and I immediately afterward was confronted by the sight of the patient—I felt sick. After she had been packed, I fled to the next room. . . . The brave

Frau Doktor [*tapfere Doktorin*] then brought me a small glass of cognac and I became myself again. . . ."[107] In this scene Freud was less than manly or professional. The gender (and gendered role) inversion is heightened by the courageous bearing of the *tapfere Doctorin*, both woman and, probably, untrained physician's spouse.[108]

That gender roles are at stake in this aborted birth scene becomes clear when Freud, after describing Eckstein's subsequent care, returns to recount what happened after "I became myself again." Eckstein "had not lost consciousness during the massive hemorrhage; when I returned to the room somewhat shaky, she greeted me with the condescending remark, 'So this is the strong sex' [*Das ist das starke Geschlecht*]." Freud becomes very defensive in his commentary on her remark: "I do not believe it was the blood that overwhelmed [*überwältigt*] me—at that moment strong emotions were welling up in me." He endeavors to restore his professional—and masculine—status. Yet his alternative explanation, the surge of affects, undercut his defense. The source of this welled-up emotion is his relationship to Fliess, and he situates himself in a "feminine" position: irrational, dependent, passive, powerless. "That this mishap should have happened to you [Fliess]; how you will react to it when you hear about it; what others would make of it, how wrong I was to urge you to operate in a foreign city where you could not follow through on the case; how my intention to do my best for this poor girl ['my child of sorrows'] was insidiously thwarted and resulted in endangering her life—all this came over me simultaneously."[109]

Fliess, by leaving the gauze in the wound, is the father of the "*Foetor*"; Freud is the mother or midwife. Freud's "feminine" defensiveness, however, had to be itself defended against: "I only want to add that for a day I shied away from letting you know about [the scene]. . . ."[110] Yet once again he was overcome by a feeling ascribed to women, shame:[111] "then I began to feel ashamed [*mich zu schämen*], and here is the letter."[112] In the aftermath of Fliess's surgery, Emma Eckstein's hemorrhaging nose becomes the stage upon which problems of gender identity are played out.

Through the end of May Freud continues to report on Eckstein as well as endeavors to absolve Fliess of all responsibility for her condition. His letters are filled with accounts of his cocainization, case histories to validate Fliess's nasal theories, and discussion of the impending births of both Freud's last child and Fliess's first. When 24 July comes, Freud queries Fliess about the entire inventory of his concerns: "What is happening to the nose, menstruation, labor pains, neuroses, your dear wife, and the budding little one?"[113] But there is no mention of Eckstein, nor is there any mention of the dream of the preceding night—the dream of Irma's injection.

Identities and Social Networks: Weiss-*washing the Irma Dream*

The role of the *Nasenmuscheln*, the significant presence of strong odors, the medical intervention, the casting (out) of toxic substances, and the questioning of gender identity all find their parallel in the dream of Irma's injection. Was Irma Emma? In the course of his analysis Freud associates her with a number of people, including a governess; Irma's friend whom he would have preferred to treat; a patient who has the same name as his eldest daughter, Sophie; an old woman who has the same name as his middle daughter, Mathilde; as well as his wife. When he takes up the analysis of the dream again in *Interpretation* he refers to Irma as a "collective figure" (4:292) and adds a few more associations. Emma Eckstein is not mentioned in either account. Some later investigators have found a clue to Irma's identity in the word "Ananas" that appeared on the bottle of liqueur whose foul smell Freud credited with initiating the series "propyl . . . propyls . . . proprionic acid." Freud appended a note to his mention of the word: "I must add that the sound of the word 'Ananas' bears a remarkable resemblance to that of my patient Irma's family name" (4:115n1). Since none of Freud's patients is known to have a last name in any way close to this, it has been assumed that Freud was merely diverting attention from the patient whose first name would bear a "remarkable resemblance": Anna Lichtheim. She was the daughter of Freud's beloved teacher Samuel Hammerschlag, a current patient, family friend and widow like Irma, and the person for whom Freud would name his last child, the child Martha was carrying at the time of the dream.[114] When this identification is made, however, Irma's identity tends to be downplayed in the interpretation.[115] She is merely the occasion for other dream-thoughts to be represented, including "sexual megalomania," as Freud himself confesses in a 9 January 1908 letter to Karl Abraham: "the three women [who are condensed in the figure of Irma], Mathilde, Sophie and Anna, are my daughters' three godmothers, and I have them all!"[116] Another school of thought takes its cue from Schur and identifies Irma with Emma. These interpreters cite among other clues Freud's comment that "I had had Irma examined by [Fliess] to see whether her gastric pains might be of nasal origin" (4:117). For this school, the identity of Irma is the interpretive key, and the dream a way for Freud to work through the trauma Fliess's botched surgery caused to their relationship.[117]

Yet there is another possibility that moves beyond the usual suspects to other members of Freud's extended social and professional Jewish contacts. An "Irma" does appear among the *Nachlass* in the Sigmund Freud Collection at the Library of Congress in a folder of assorted notes, the first page of which bears the rubric *"Aus älteren Aufzeichnungen* von 1897 an" (From older sketches from 1897 on; first three words underscored in original). Attached to the second page is a sheet containing a note entitled *"Eine Quelle des Antisemitismus"* (a source of antisemitism; underscored in original). It reads:[118] "The fact that anti-S[emitism] is generated in the nursery [*Kinderstube*] is clear. Irma has a physical horror of any Jew. When she was a child they said (in Ofen [= Buda, Hungary]) if there was any trace of *Incontinentia alvi* [i.e., fecal incontinence] on a child's vest: the Jew has wiped [*abgewischt*] his mouth on it again." Moreover, not only does a patient called Irma appear in this note, but elsewhere among the *Nachlass* Freud records an *"Alter Tr[aum] von Irma"* (Old dr[eam] of Irma; underscored in original).[119] Is there a connection among these coincidences of names?

Both Emma Eckstein and Anna Hammerschlag-Lichtheim were, unlike the Irma of the note, Vienna natives. Who, then, is the Hungarian-born Irma who emerges out of the notes left in Freud's *Nachlass*? In the letter of 8 February 1897 Freud mentions to Fliess that he currently has a female patient (*eine Kranke*) from Budapest.[120] Unfortunately, there is no other evidence to corroborate such an identification of the note's Irma with this patient. Freud preserved the names of his patients from 1896 to 1899 in a *Kassabuch*, a record of his accounts. No Irma, however, appears in this book.[121]

It is possible that the note (*"Eine Quelle"*) about Irma's experiences in the nursery was written prior to 1897. Although the first sheet of the folder, which bears the heading "From older sketches from 1897 on," is uniform, the remaining three sheets are undated composites with other pages, such as the one carrying the note *"Eine Quelle,"* pasted or otherwise attached to them. Some notes appear to predate 1897. On a paper pasted to the fourth sheet in the folder is the note:

3 Oct. Dr. ? brings me a contribution toward the explanation of superficial anaesthesia [*Hautanaesthesie*]. A young woman's n[umbness] in both arms ceases when under hypnosis she thinks of the key that her beloved husband had pressed in her hand. It strikes me that this case is similar to that of [?]

pat[ient] with anosmia a[nd] the subjective smell of pudding [*Riechanaesthe-sie u dem subjektiven Geruch nach Mehlspeise*]. Thus [symptom and reminiscence] suspended together [*Zusammenschwebung*]. Moreover, my old theory of hyst[erical] lameness [*hyst Lähmungen*], the rejecting [of] particular associations [*Associationsbesetzung*].

The "pat[ient] with anosmia a[nd] the subjective smell of pudding" clearly refers to the woman whom Freud called Lucy R. in *Studies*. And the reference to his old theory about hysterical lameness caused by the rejection of particular associations could very well refer to his analysis of the motive for the symptoms of another patient discussed in *Studies*, Elisabeth von R. (see 2:165–67). Even by the time *Studies*, which included this theory of the etiology of hysteria, was published, Freud began to think that his theory was obsolete. The *Studies'* hypothesis was, according to Freud's 8 October 1895 letter to Fliess, manifestly superseded by a belief in the traumatic effects of a prepubescent sexual experience.[122] When Freud delivered his lecture "Über Hysterie" (On Hysteria) at the Wiener medicinische Doctoren-Collegium during the course of three meetings on 14, 21, and 26 October 1895 he went public with his new theory. Hence the note from 3 October may have been composed as early as 1895.

The absence of an extant list of patients for the first years of Freud's practice renders locating a patient by the name of Irma prior to 1896 (when Freud began his *Kassabuch*) difficult. Based on available information, however, none of Freud's early patients appears to bear this name.[123] Could the note's "Irma" be a pseudonym just like the dream's "Irma"? To take the speculation one step further: could the pseudonym of both the note and the dream be borne by the same person?

There is one early patient who, though already bearing a pseudonym other than "Irma," shares a key identificatory mark with the note's Irma. Ilona Weiss, or, as she is known in *Studies*, Elisabeth von R., was born in Budapest.[124] Moreover, "I must add that" orthographically and phonetically *Ilona* and *Irma* "bear a remarkable resemblance"; they share identical first and last letters as well as two phonetic couplets, the liquid consonants *l/r* and the nasal ones *n/m*. The connections grow stronger when one considers her case history.

Ilona Weiss became Freud's patient in the autumn of 1892 when Freud "was asked by a doctor [he] knew to examine a young lady who had been suffering for more than two years from pains in her legs and who had difficulties in walking" (2:135), like another patient Freud would later treat, Emma Eckstein.[125] Their sessions culminated in Freud's conclusion that relief of her hysterical symptoms would follow from abreacting the "repressed idea" of her morally unacceptable love for her brother-in-law. Ilona Weiss's treatment lasted until the beginning of the summer of 1893, when she and Freud parted by mutual agreement: "We both had a feeling that we had come to a finish. . . . I regarded her as cured and pointed out to her that the solution of her difficulties would proceed on its own account now that the path had been opened to it. This she did not dispute" (2:159).[126]

Some weeks after ceasing treatment, however, Ilona Weiss had a serious relapse; her mother wrote to Freud that "the treatment had been a complete failure" (2:160). Later reports indicate that soon thereafter Weiss's symptoms had again disappeared, and a colleague reported to Freud "that she is to be regarded as cured" (2:160). Freud's account concludes: "In the spring of 1894 I heard that she was going to a private ball for which I was able to get an invitation, and I did not allow the opportunity to escape me of seeing my former patient whirl past me in a lively dance" (2:160). Freud felt vindicated in both the interpretation and treatment of her illness. Gay concludes, "Freud the physician-researcher, ambivalent about his career in medicine, could take satisfaction in her restored vitality."[127]

Freud's work with Ilona Weiss was the first case in which he made free association his modus operandi. It also led him to recognize the erotic nature of pathogenic phenomena (2:146–47, 168–69), although he had not yet realized the sexual etiology of neuroses.[128] In his biography of Freud, Ernest Jones describes the case as the "first one where [Freud] dispensed with hypnotism and used the new ['concentration'] technique;[129] it was also the first one where he felt satisfied with the completeness of what he termed the 'psychical analysis.'"[130] With this case the method of systematically generating associations with each symptom of a hysterical ailment became a principal component of the analysis of neurosis, and Freud would later translate this method to the analysis of each component of a dream—including the "Dream of Irma's Injection." As Schur comments: *"What Freud may have been attempting for the first time with the Irma dream was the systematic application of free association to every single element of the manifest dream, after which he connected these associations until a meaningful trend emerged."*[131] The approach to the case of Elisabeth von R., then, parallels Freud's interpretation of the Irma dream, the "first complete analysis he made of one of his dreams."[132]

Freud's disintegrating theoretical and personal relationships with his senior colleague and collaborator Josef Breuer also play parts in both the case of Elisabeth von R. and the Irma dream. The shifts in technique as well as the attention directed to defense and sexual etiology that mark Freud's treatment of Ilona Weiss exacerbated the developing breach between him and Breuer.[133] This gulf would manifest its unbridgeable dimensions in Freud's derisive representation of M. (Breuer) in the Irma dream and its accompanying analysis (4:111–15, 119). Grubrich-Simitis speculates that although Ilona Weiss was chronologically not the last of Freud's patients discussed in *Studies*, Freud placed his case study of her last and, hence, immediately prior to Breuer's theoretical chapter in order to serve as a counter or reply.[134]

Several aspects of Freud's engagement with Ilona Weiss are also echoed in the dream itself. The dream takes place at a large reception, which mirrors the private ball at which Freud had last seen Ilona Weiss. Once Irma arrives Freud takes her to "one side, as though to answer her letter and to reproach her for not having accepted my 'solution' yet. I said to her: 'If you still get pains, it's really only your fault.' She replied: 'If you only knew what pains I've got now . . .'" (4:107).

In his case study of Elisabeth von R., Freud describes a similar confrontation with a resistant patient: "She cried aloud when I put the situation dryly before her with the words: 'So for a long time you had been in love with your brother-in-law.' She complained at this moment of the most frightful pains, and made one last desperate effort to reject the explanation: it was not true" (2:157). Indeed, Freud credits Elisabeth von R. for enlightening him about the role of resistance in analysis: "In the course of this difficult work [with Elisabeth von R.] I began to attach a deeper significance to the *resistance* offered by the patient in the reproduction [*Reproduktion*] of her memories . . ." (2:154; emphasis added).[135] Later in *Studies* Freud elaborates upon the relationship between resistance and symptom formation as well as the patient's responsibility for both:

> Thus a psychical force, aversion on the part of the ego, had originally driven the pathogenic idea out of association and was now opposing its return to memory. The hysterical patient's 'not knowing' was in fact a 'not wanting to know'—*a not wanting which might be to a greater or less extent conscious.* The task of the therapist, therefore, lies in overcoming by his psychical work this resistance to association. (2:269–70; emphasis added)

Correlations between Ilona Weiss and Freud's dream also emerge on the level of the dream-work. As already noted, in *Interpretation* Freud repeatedly calls attention to how displaced verbal expressions allow the representation of the dream-thoughts; he describes words as "nodal points" (5:340) and "switch-point[s]" (5:410). In Freud's dream the source of

Irma's pains are all coded white, that is, *weiss*: "a big white [*weißen*] patch
. . . extensive *whitish* grey [*weißgraue*; emphasis added] scabs" (4:107). Admittedly, in his analysis Freud does not associate the "white" with Irma
per se. When Freud analyzes the "white patch," he treats it as a single
element; he does not separately consider the hue from that which it colors.
Moreover, the associations Freud generates from that image are with illnesses: not Irma's, but those of her woman friend and of his daughter.[136]
This symptomatic *"weiß,"* nonetheless, identifies her true ailment ("a severe organic affection"; 4:114) and thereby, within a medical discourse
that designates (whether by synecdoche or objectification) the ill by their
illness, identifies her.[137] This diagnosis of an organic illness rather than a
hysterical reaction to Freud's treatment also signals his ultimate vindication: "The dream acquitted me of the responsibility for Irma's condition
by showing that it was due to other factors . . ." (4:118). And thus this
scene recalls that other scene—Ilona Weiss at the ball—in which Freud
could again claim vindication despite a precipitous turn for the worse after
the conclusion of treatment (2:160; 4:118–20).[138]

Bedtime Reading: The First Review of Studien über Hysterie

The signifier *"weiß"* has affinities with more than Ilona Weiss, and those
connections, more immediate to the time of dreaming and in this instance
tied to a Jewish colleague rather than a Jewish patient, may well have precipitated the appearance of these symptomatic *weiß*'s. Just before dreaming of Irma, Freud might have been confronted with the judgment of
another Weiss, Heinrich Weiss, in a review of Freud's latest work. *Studies*,
in which Elisabeth von R.'s case appears, was published in May 1895.[139]
Less than two months later the first substantive response to *Studies* appeared as a feuilleton bearing the work's title "Studien über Hysterie" and
signed W. in the Sunday 14 July 1895 number of one of the leading Viennese medical journals, *Wiener medizinische Presse*. The publication of the
review was little more than a week prior to the date Freud ascribed for his
dream. W.'s essay demonstrated a familiarity with the history of theoretical considerations of hysteria and of unconscious representations. It begins
with a discussion of the great French neurologist Jean-Martin Charcot and
the philosopher and author of *The Philosophy of the Unconscious*, Eduard von
Hartmann,[140] and then turns in the next paragraph to Moriz Benedikt's
notion of "second life."

W. continues the introduction of his review with a few remarks on everyday phenomena like memory and hypnotism to provide an ideational context for Breuer and Freud's concern with unconscious representations. Then the author states: "But under pathological conditions also lie representations outside of consciousness, representations which are capable of calling forth not merely strong corporeal phenomena but also the accompanying affect." Breuer and Freud are described as two of the most significant (*bedeutentendsten*) Viennese physicians and as masters of observation and of case presentation (*Darstellung*). Borrowing Freud's own judgment the author depicts that presentation as novelistic.[141]

Rather than addressing the specifics of the case histories, W. cites extensively from Breuer's theoretical contribution (esp. what becomes 2:245–46). In line with his prefatory remarks, he focuses upon the *Abspaltung* (splitting off or rendering unconscious) of a piece of the psychic apparatus and its influence both upon the contents of conscious representation and upon the suggestibility of the patient. Then after dealing with the mechanics, he addresses the sexual content of the repressed (*verdrängte*; i.e., rendered unconscious) representations and the symptoms that emerge as defenses against the repressed. After remarking upon the therapeutic value of catharsis, the author concludes with a virtual citation of Freud's final apothegm: "Much will be gained if we succeed in transforming your hysterical misery into common unhappiness. With a [nervous system] that has been restored to health you will be better armed against that unhappiness" (2:305).

Although the article is signed only W., internal evidence suggests that the author is Heinrich Weiss.[142] Heinrich Weiss was a Jewish neurologist who had graduated from University of Vienna Medical School (1878) several years before Freud (1881). He was the protégé of Benedikt, whose work was given prominence in the feuilleton. Weiss worked in Benedikt's neurology section at the Poliklinik. Under his tutelage Weiss presented a series of cases of aphasia and other nerve-related illnesses before such professional audiences as the Wiener medicinische Club (Medical Club of Vienna), the Wiener medicinische Doctoren-Collegium (Vienna Medical Doctors-Colloquium), and the K.k. Gesellschaft der Ärtze (Imperial and Royal Society of Physicians). These were later reported in the *Wiener medizinische Presse* as well as frequently referred to in Benedikt's contributions to the journal.

That a protégé of Moriz Benedikt responded favorably to *Studies* may have provided Freud with feelings of pride and vindication. After all Benedikt was at the time perhaps the foremost Jewish neurologist in Vi-

enna and a frequent contributor to the *Wiener medizinische Presse*. He was
a polymath; during his long career Benedikt's explorations ranged from
medical forensics (he was known as the German Lombroso) to hypnotism
to electrotherapy to hysteria. Benedikt had given the young Freud a letter
of introduction to Charcot and the Salpêtrière. As several footnotes to
Studies indicate, Benedikt also anticipated Freud and Breuer's insight into
the connection among sexuality, memory, and hysteria: "We have found
the nearest approach to what we have to say on the theoretical and therapeutic sides of the question in some remarks, published from time to time,
by Benedikt" (2:7n3; cf. 2:210n1). In one such publication, written a year
before Freud and Breuer's preliminary communication of 1893, Benedikt
summed up his theory of hysteria: "Its basis consisted of an inborn and
acquired vulnerability of the nervous system but its actual cause was either
a psychic trauma (in men or in women), or a functional disturbance of the
genital system or the sexual life, which a woman will keep secret from her
nearest relative and her family doctor."[143]

Weiss's Benedikt connection may also have weighted the association
with that other bearer of the signifer "*weiss*," Ilona Weiss, since Freud's
write-up of her case bears extensive traces of his familiarity with Benedikt's
work, especially the value of catharsis and the role of the secret. Freud
begins his account of his treatment of Ilona Weiss (2:138–39):

> When one starts upon a cathartic treatment of this kind, the first question
> one asks oneself is whether the patient herself is aware of the origin and
> the precipitating cause of her illness. . . . The interest shown in her by the
> physician, the understanding of her which he allows her to feel and the
> hopes of recovery he holds out to her—all these will decide the patient to
> yield up her secret. From the beginning it seemed to me probable that
> Fräulein Elisabeth was conscious of the basis of her illness, that what she
> had in her consciousness was only a secret and not a foreign body.

Diverse Identifications

Another aspect of the dream is tied to that loaded signifier "*weiss*": Freud's
identification with Irma (1:113).[144] In this instance the connection is
through neither his case study of Ilona Weiss nor (as far as I have been
able to reconstruct) his relationship with Heinrich Weiss. Another Weiss,
the late physician Nathan Weiss (1851–83), had great personal significance to Freud. The son of Isaac Hirsch Weiss, the Talmud scholar and
lecturer at the Vienna Bet ha-Midrash, Nathan Weiss committed suicide

at the start of what many thought would be a brilliant career in neurology. Freud attended his funeral in September 1883 and reported upon it extensively to his then-fiancée Martha Bernays. Jones reports, "It was the death of Weiss . . . that emboldened Freud to decide on a neurological career."[145] Apparently both Freud and Breuer decided that Weiss's death had created an opening in the highly race-conscious hierarchy of Viennese medicine for a Jewish physician to specialize in neurology. Freud would take Weiss's place.[146]

And Irma's. Irma clearly has a composite identity, inclusive of Emma and, I would add, Ilona, but the identification process that this dream enacts and that brings together the earlier scene of Freud's apparent unmanning with the motif of questioned gender identity is Freud's own conflicted identification with a woman. This analysis occurs during his analysis of dream-elements that deal with particular body locales. Thus, when discussing the passage in his dream-account, "a portion of the skin [*Hautpartie*] on the left shoulder was infiltrated (I noticed this, just as [my colleague] did . . .)." Freud recognizes the shoulder-infiltration as his own rheumatism and further specifies, "I noticed it in my own body" (4:113). The doctor and, by extension, his colleague detect this *Hautpartie* on Freud's body. Freud has become the patient: "he, the doctor and man, fuses with the image of the patient and woman."[147] By fusing with Irma, Freud confirms as well that he had relinquished male authority[148] by calling upon other men to examine and help his patient.[149]

Yet this identification with Irma is a conflicted one. Freud is struck by the dream-wording, which refers to the body (that is, the "left shoulder") rather than to abstract coordinates "left upper posterior." His puzzlement over the use of nontechnical language, on the one hand, acknowledges the objectification of the female patient by medical examination and its "objective" discourse. On the other hand, the omission of medical body topography indicates Freud's wish to distinguish himself from the traditional object of medicine and therefore manifests his resistance to the implications of being identified with a woman patient, namely, being subjected to "homosexual submission and humiliation before male authority."[150] The surface of Freud's body that is observed and contested over is also the skin of a Jew; and what infiltrates the *Hautpartie* is Freud's isolation within a Jewish medical preserve, like neurology. That is, the locus of medical treatment and Freud's professional concerns converge on dermatology, a field nicknamed *Judenhaut* (Jew-skin).[151]

Freud's Jewish- and gender-coded identification with Irma through the spot on her shoulder hooks into two other body sites mentioned in the analysis. In the dream-segment he writes: "She then opened her mouth properly and on the right I found a big white patch; at another place I saw extensive whitish grey scabs upon some remarkably curly structures which were evidently modeled on the turbinal bones of the nose." According to Freud, Irma's friend "would have yielded sooner" (*würde also eher nachgeben*)—a clearly feminine position—and "would then have opened her mouth properly, and have told me more than Irma." Following this scene of yielding and confessing, Freud notes that he had curtailed his analysis; he then adds, "There is at least one spot (*Stelle*) in every dream at which it is unplumbable—a navel, as it were, that is its point of contact with the unknown" (4:111n1). It is also the male fetus's point of contact with the mother: they are fused together. At this junction distinctions, gender distinctions, blur; the male is passive and dependent—"feminine." Identification with woman is something that cannot be known or let be known.[152]

Discussion of this "spot" is immediately followed by discussion of another one, the so-called genital spots (*Genitalstellen*), the turbinal bones, or *Nasenmuscheln*.[153] Here, too, Freud associates Irma's body with his own: "The scabs on the turbinal bones recalled a worry about my own state of health. I was making frequent use of cocaine at that time to reduce some troublesome nasal swellings . . ." (4:111). The implications of the *Nase* in *Nasenmuscheln* in cultural and gender terms have already been explored. But *muscheln* resonates as well with two diametrically opposite images of turn-of-the-century Jews: Theodor Herzl's *Mauscheln* and Max Nordau's *Muskeljuden*. For Herzl, "*Mauschel* [pl., *Mauscheln*] is the curse of the Jews."[154] *Mauschel* is antithetic to, if tragically confused with, his idealized image of the Jew. *Mauschel*, derived from the derogatory term for nasally Jewish-accented German and its purported content, deceptive economic dealmaking, is the cringing, mocking, arrogant, selfish, mendacious *Schnorrer* (beggar), ever on the lookout for an underhanded deal and quick profit. Nordau's *Muskeljuden* made their appearance at the Second Zionist Congress in 1898. He exhorted his audience to "pull up your socks" (lit., "make men of yourselves"; *Ermannt euch*) and create again a "Jewry of muscle" (*Muskeljudentum*).[155] Then he set about organizing Jewish *Turnvereine* (gymnastic associations) to transform the nonvirile Jews who had long left the ghetto into "deep-chested, sturdy limbed, sharp-eyed . . . muscle-Jews" (*Muskeljuden*).[156] These "muscle-Jews" seek to differentiate themselves from such feminized Jewish types as the atavistic ghetto Jew and the decadent coffeehouse Jew as well as from the unmasculine Jews pictured by Walter Rathenau in "Höre Israel": "unathletic [*unkonstruktiven*] build," "narrow shoulders," "clumsy feet," "soft [*weichliche*], roundish shape."[157] Arousing the anxieties of Herzl, Nordau, and Rathenau were the consequences, for all Jews, of the entry into the public sphere of the now-emancipated, perceived-as-feminized Jew. Freud's turbinal bones evoke his feminization, not just as a late-nineteenth-century male, but as a late-nineteenth-century Jewish male.

The reference to the *Nasenmuscheln* also evokes one other intrinsically "feminine" body process: birthing. Again, according to Fliess these "genital spots" were intimately related to the birthing process: "an important connection . . . close and reciprocal rapports."[158] The process of conception is alluded to at both the beginning and end of the dream. When the dream opens, Freud and his wife are receiving guests. The German term for "receive," *empfangen*, is rife with associations to conception; for example, the *unbefleckte Empfängnis* is the Immaculate Conception. Unfortunately in Irma's mouth, a traditional womb-vagina symbol, is "a big white patch," *"einen großen weißen Fleck."* The other allusions to birthing are no less maculate. The elimination of the "toxin" through the supervention of dysentery clearly evokes parturition.[159] Freud would later write to Fliess that birthing—or miscarrying—is dirty, diarrhetic: "everything related to birth, miscarriage, [menstrual] period goes back to the toilet via the word *Abort* [toilet] (*Abortus* [abortion])."[160] And the cause of the conception, the unclean syringe, is a dirty squirter or penis [*Spritze nicht rein*].

These images of befouled or failed birth conflict with Freud's desires to create. His works are his creations, his children with Fliess: Fliess is introduced into the chain of associations as "another friend who had for many years been familiar with all my writings during the period of their gestation [*meine keimenden Arbeiten*]" (4:116). And he wishes to re-create himself; such is the goal of his self-analysis, which may be said to have begun with this dream. Yet in this dream, when Freud assumes the woman's role, conception is no longer scientific; it becomes dirty, if not aborted. The imagery of conception both is modeled after and distinguishes itself from women's fertility.

There is a conflict in this dream between Freud's desire to be a member of the *Männerbund*, represented by the authoritative, probing male medical examiners, and his identification with woman, the neurotic, nasal, victimized—Jewish—patient. He wishes to (re)join his confrères. According to the dream such men, on the one hand, assert their socially sanctioned male aggressiveness against women and the unmanned and, on the other hand, desire to usurp from women the ability to reproduce: they desire to create themselves as independent individuals. And through his analysis of the dream he succeeds: he willingly confesses his aggression (4:120) and applauds his own new production, "the achievement of this one piece of new knowledge" (4:121). Yet Freud remains plagued by the impossibility of desire within the *Männerbund*; male intimacy is overlaid with a socially encoded feminine role—yielding, passive, desiring of men.[161] The dream reveals the fragile nature of the gender identities supporting the Vienna of the late nineteenth century. The dream's focus on Irma's/Freud's body shows how the body became the field upon which the various disciplines and institutions sought to construct gender identity necessary to sustain the *Männerbund*.[162] The *Nasenmuscheln* and related nasal imagery point out how the feminized body of the male Jew, as an individual and as a group, threatened that construct.[163]

Yet an averted threat, a repressed threat, a disavowed threat can be productive. Not only did the Dream of Irma's Injection help clear "the royal road to a knowledge of the unconscious activities of the mind" (5:608) by inscribing Freud in the *Männerbund* of expertise, but it also betrayed the process by which Freud was generating apotropaic defenses against the ongoing trauma of his own Jewishness (*Judentum*) as lived and as ascribed. Although the dispositive circumcision does not make an explicit appearance in *Interpretation* and his transferential phantasy castration only slips in to the first edition by way of a pair of famous parapraxes about a castrating Zeus (4:256; 5:619),[164] the part performed by castration in that first edition has long been acknowledged: "Publishing *The Interpretation of Dreams* is a way for Freud simultaneously to display his castration and to defend himself against it. *The Interpretation of Dreams* is an apotropaic defense that is to protect Freud against castration and death, against the detractors, against anti-Semitism."[165] The particular form it takes, as this chapter has shown, is what he will articulate as the "repudiation of femininity" (for example, 23:250, 252).[166] Circumcision noses its way in as a nose, as *Nasenmuscheln* that are to be extirpated. After all, "I should like to draw attention to the frequency with which sexual repression makes use of transpositions from a lower to an upper part of the body. . . . Comparisons between nose and penis are common" (5:387). The next chapter begins the examination of Freud's transpositions from upper to lower.

CHAPTER 3

"A glance at the nose":
Freud's Displaced Fetishes

Freud opens his 1927 study of fetishism with a discussion of "the most extraordinary [*merkwürdigsten*] case": a young man who "had exalted a certain sort of 'shine on the nose' into a fetishistic precondition." Freud continues:

> The surprising explanation of this was that the patient had been brought up in an English nursery but had later come to Germany, where he forgot his mother-tongue almost completely. The fetish, which originated from his earliest childhood, had to be understood in English, not in German. The 'shine on the nose' [*Glanz auf der Nase*] was in reality a 'glance at the nose.' The nose was thus the fetish, which, incidentally, he endowed at will with the luminous shine which was not perceptible to others. (21:152)

There are a number of most extraordinary aspects about this passage—not the least being that Freud waited some twenty-two years after writing in *Three Essays on the Theory of Sexuality* (7:153) that "no other variation of the sexual instinct that borders on the pathological can lay so much claim to our interest as" fetishism, before he specifically dedicates a study to the topic, and that study a mere six pages long. Perhaps more significant is that the story of the nose fetishist is simply not needed. Although the prominent position of, and Freud's hyperbolic claim for, the case would suggest that it would play an exemplary role in his discussion of fetishism, Freud fails to connect it with the ensuing argument; he no longer even refers to it. Moreover, its mention is as "surprising" as the source of the young man's choice of fetish. That is, the essay begins with Freud commenting: "in the last few years I have had the opportunity of studying analytically a number of men whose object-choice was dominated by a fetish." Alas, he adds: "For obvious reasons the details of these cases must be withheld from publication; I cannot, therefore, show in what way accidental circumstances have contributed to the choice of a fetish" (21:152). Rather than immediately embarking on the explanation that would soon follow—"In every instance, the meaning and the purpose of the fetish turned out, in analysis, to be the same . . . a substitute for the woman's (the mother's) penis" (21:152)—Freud provides the details of one of these cases, "the most extraordinary case." The decision to interpose the story of the nose fetishist hence seems to be marked by the same caprice that marks, in the original ethnographic reports on the African fetish,[1] as also in Alfred Binet's influential essay on sexual fetishism, "Le Fétichisme dans l'amour,"[2] the fetish. At most, this example seems to play the role of a subsidiary finding in Freud's discussion, just as the fetish does, according to Freud, in his patients' analyses ("*spielte . . . der Rolle eines Nebenbefundes*"; 21:152).

Still, although instances of nose fetishism are rare,[3] that a nose, shiny or otherwise, might be a fetishistic substitute for the penis is suggested by the sexologist Magnus Hirschfeld: "Often there is connected with the fetishistic prepossession for large noses a more or less unconscious phallic cult, or the old folk belief, which is in no way organically founded, that the size of the nose is indicative of the size of the male organ."[4] Freud, one might suppose,[5] would make such an assumption about noses. And he does in *Interpretation* (5:387): at least with regard to typical dreams, "Comparisons between nose and penis are common." Moreover, since at the end of his "Fetishism" essay Freud writes, "In conclusion, we may say that the normal prototype of fetishes is a man's penis" (21:157),[6] one might assume, then, that nose fetishes would be subsumed under this rubric of normality. But with regard to the man with a shine for shiny noses, he makes no manifest link. Indeed, it is as if Freud intentionally avoids such a connection. That is, whereas Freud has uncovered a homophonic displacement (from glance to *Glanz*) as the occasion for the particular object-choice, he omits mention of another homophone that points directly at the underlying cause that engenders all fetishism. The missing word is *glans*, the Latin term for penis.[7]

What would motivate the omission of such an obvious association? Some have argued that the absence of the word *glans* betrays a *mise-en-abîme* structure at play in Freud's text; that is, the elision reproduces the entire logic of fetishism. Thus Charles Bernheimer writes: "The text's exemplary denial of the Latin word *glans*, of the word that explicitly evokes the fantasy of the mother's penis, is the equivalent of the fetishist's denial of the difference between the sexes."[8] Other moments of the account of the young nose fetishist support the contention that it reproduces Freud's notion of the fetish. For example, Freud seems to go out of his way to call attention to the epistemic problematic of fetishism (and of the word *glans*): namely, to see what is not there. Thus, after shifting the focus of his analysis from the *Glanz* to the *Nase* (nose), he adds, seemingly gratuitously ("incidentally" [*übrigens*]),[9] that the young man had endowed the fetishized nose "at will with the luminous shine [*Glanzlicht*] which was not perceptible to others." The *Glanz*, like the maternal *glans*, is invisible.

Although such analyses of Freud's account accord this "most extraordinary case" an exemplary role, it might be stretching matters a bit to assume that Freud had such modern commentaries in mind when he included the discussion of the nose fetishist. Still, Bernheimer's depiction of the fetishistic character of Freud's account combined with the case's "overvaluation" (cf. 7:153), its contiguous relation to the main argument, and its capricious selection suggest that Freud has exalted this exemplary instance into a fetish. But what is Freud disavowing through the construction of this fetish, and why the story of a nose? The remainder of this chapter endeavors to answer these questions and thereby to understand Freud's insertion of this exemplary nose into the business at hand—indeed, to explore the implications of a theory of fetishism that is led by the nose. In the process it will uncover feminizing metonyms of the male Jewish body, by which, as we have already seen and will continue to see, the Central European social and scientific imagination constructed the Jew; it will also continue this work's examination of Freud's problematic relationship to that construct.

Sniffing Out Theories of Fetishism

Before dealing with these questions, a few more words on fetishism are needed. The fetish, according to Freud, is a sexually overvalued object that represents the absent maternal penis. It is a substitute that is constructed to resolve the castration complex (cf. 21:155). The crisis that creates the complex arises when the little boy perceives that a woman does not possess a penis—and that consequently "his own possession of a penis [is] in danger" (21:153). The boy is confronted with, in Freudian and conventional terms, sexual difference, and his narcissistic enjoyment of an undifferentiated, self-enclosed world is rudely interrupted. His reaction will lead him down one of three paths. He can become either a homosexual, or a fetishist, or a member of the "great majority [who] surmount" the castration complex (21:154).[10] With the resolution of the castration complex, that is, with the recognition of sexual difference, the boy not only assumes a gendered and sexually oriented identity, he is inserted in the social order. In his "Fetishism" essay Freud alludes to the societal implications of the (re)cognition of sexual difference; he analogizes the little boy's protestations of disbelief when confronted by the mother's missing penis to a different encounter: "In later life a grown man may perhaps experience a similar panic when the cry goes up that Throne and Altar [*Thron und Altar*] are in danger, and similar illogical consequences will ensue" (21:153).[11] And in Freud's Vienna the gravest threat to "Throne and Altar" was to question the rigid gender-coded differentiation of roles and spheres, the "sexual difference," which both marks and legitimates the bourgeois social order. Yet it seems curious that Freud would compare the infantile desire to elide sexual difference with the adult desire to preserve it; on the surface the two situations seem antithetical. In point of fact, however, the adult male abhors difference as much as the young boy. Within the masculine social order of bourgeois society men preserve the narcissistic phantasy of wholeness: this world and its discourses reflect male values and hegemony.[12] Women are objectified representations of what is not male; such representations are fetishes that substitute for the difference that would threaten male claims to identity and authority.[13] In sum, the fetish has both an individual and a societal dimension.

For the fetishist—and the bourgeois male—female difference is not, however, absolutely elided or foreclosed (*verworfen*). What allows the construction of the fetish is what Freud calls "disavowal" (*Verleugnung*). The little boy—it is always a little boy—has both retained and given up his belief in the maternal phallus according to the paradoxical logic of "I know very well, but all the same . . ."[14] "In the conflict between the weight of the unwelcome perception and the force of his counterwish, a compromise has been reached" (21:154). The fetish as a substitute for the absent penis embodies that compromise; it both denies and affirms the mother's castration (cf. 21:156). Like a scar that remains after a wound heals, the fetish both covers the injury and serves as a reminder of it. In Freud's article "Fetishism" the most extraordinary case is such a remainder.

In order to discover of what Freud's fetishistic account of the fetishized nose acts as a reminder, the presence of the nose needs to be paired with the absence of odor as either example or explanation of fetish object-choice. In contrast to nose fetishes, fetishes related to smell are rather prevalent. Thus, the sexologist Iwan Bloch wrote: "Among the bodily functions which are capable of acting as fetishes, the smell, the emanation of the body, unquestionably takes the first place."[15] Indeed, Freud's earlier analyses had also emphasized the role of odor. In a footnote added in 1910 to his *Three Essays'* discussion of fetishism,[16] he wrote:

> Psycho-analysis has cleared up one of the remaining gaps in our under-standing of fetishism. It has shown the importance, as regards the choice of a fetish, of a coprophilic pleasure in smelling which has disappeared owing to repression. Both the feet and the hair are objects with a strong smell which have been exalted into fetishes after the olfactory sensation has become unpleasurable and been abandoned. Accordingly, in the perversion that corresponds to foot-fetishism, it is only dirty and evil-smelling feet that become sexual objects. (7:155n2)

Pace his December 1909 preface to that second edition of the *Three Essays* that asserts that he "has resisted the temptation of introducing into [the new edition] the results of the researches of the last five years" (7:130), Freud appears to be drawing upon his 1909 "Notes Upon a Case of Obsessional Neurosis," his study of the Rat Man, to compose this one of the "few footnotes" supplementing the 1905 original. In the penultimate paragraph of "Notes," Freud adds "one more remark": "It turned out that our patient, besides all his other characteristics, was a *renifleur* (or osphresiologiac)" (10:247); that is, "in his childhood he had been subject to strong coprophilic propensities" (10:247n1), and smells still turn him on. As in the later note Freud then goes on to speculate about the "organic repression" of childhood osphresiolagnia and its possible phylogenetic source in "man's assumption of an erect posture."[17]

Freud does make one more comment in this 1910 supplement. "Another factor that helps towards explaining the fetishistic preference for the foot is to be found among the sexual theories of children: the foot represents a woman's penis, the absence of which is deeply felt" (7:155n2). What Freud "resisted" adding to the second edition of the *Three Essays*, but which would be mentioned—to the exclusion of all other factors[18]—in the discussion of the "fetishistic reverence" of foot and hair in the work he undertook as he completed his emendations, *Leonardo da Vinci and a Memory of His Childhood*, is mention of the castration complex (11:96).[19]

When Freud returns to the question of foot and hair fetishism in his 1927 essay, every trace of smell has been removed. Instead, he focuses on two other factors: first, he shifts sensory registers from the olfactive to the visual.[20] Second, the sole object of our "inquisitive boy's" attention is the mother's genitals: "the longed-for sight of the female member" (21:155), that is, of her (reputed) penis. What had been in 1910 "another factor" besides the repression of pleasure in smells had become by 1927 the explanation. As Freud writes, "To put it more plainly: the fetish is a substitute for the woman's (the mother's) penis that the little boy once believed in and . . . does not want to give up" (21:152–53). To put it even more plainly: Freud's text has been deodorized.

Smell also played a very significant role in a major source of Freud's own considerations of fetishism: Alfred Binet's "Le Fétichisme dans l'amour." From the start, odor permeates the latter's essay. Thus, when first discussing the associationist psychology that underlies his analysis, Binet is careful to emphasize, like Freud after him, that particular fixations and accompanying excitations are "independent of the memory of what generated" them; to make this point he cites Descartes' discussion in his *Treatise on Passions* of an aversion to the odor of roses.[21] Indeed, for Binet the fetishistic fixation on odor is paradigmatic of the potential disjunction between sexual excitation and conscious memory.[22] Smell is even more prominent in Binet's descriptive passages. He distinguishes between *grand fétichisme* and *petit fétichisme*. Exemplifying the former is a young man who had a preference for big noses with huge nostrils; typifying the latter is the marriage of an unlikely pair, whose union, Binet suggests, is the result of "an olfactive sympathy."[23] He deals rather extensively with olfactive fetishism, and he comments on the extensive rapport between the sense of smell and love cited in both biblical and ethnographic sources. Further, lovers of smell, as a general class, are his prime examples of how the fetishized object is an end in itself, of how—in contradistinction to Schopenhauer, specifically,[24] as well as to the general consensus prior to Freud—a universal form of sexuality can be determined by something other than the instinct to reproduce. Finally, the development of the sense of smell is among Binet's three general causes of fetishism.[25] The other two are heredity, which "prepares the ground necessary for the germination and growth of love sickness [but which] is incapable of giving this illness its characteristic form,"[26] and the association of ideas and sentiment engendered by social custom. Although Freud adopts and retains many of Binet's insights into fetishism, by the time of his own "Fetishism" essay the odor has dissipated.

What the absence of smell—along with the presence of the nose—points to is a miasma of tropes of Jewish difference. I have chronicled in the previous chapter how throughout the nineteenth and early twentieth centuries, the Jew was figured by the *Judennase*, the Jewish nose, and the *foetor Judaicus*, the Jewish stench. The use of these metonyms of Jewish difference (that is, noses and smells) by Freud and Binet as exemplary fetish objects suggests a connection between the Jew and the fetish, and that for which the fetish substitutes: namely, the recognition of (sexual) difference. If we return to Binet's essay, we find a number of motifs besides smell that are related to how Jews were represented in the nineteenth-century cultural imagination. For instance, Binet employs the language of (self-) betrayal (*se trahit*) and dissimulation (*se dissimule*) to describe, respectively, *grand* and *petit fétichisme*. Such language was routinely employed to describe the Jewish threat to European culture; the so-called assimilated Jew was in fact a dissimulator whose loyalty in the last instance was to his fellow Jews, and hence he was a traitor to his adopted state.[27]

Binet's continuous references to Schopenhauer also resonate with Jewish associations: as noted in the previous chapter the German philosopher notoriously invoked the *foetor Judaicus*; further, his discussion of the Jewish stench also carried suggestions of problematic gender identity and sexuality. As Binet makes clear, fetishism, like the Jew, contradicts the philosopher's metaphysics of love and his notion of the generative instinct. Further compounding the connection between the fetish and the Jew is Binet's determination of the general trajectory and ultimate consequence of fetishism: being outside of nature (*hors nature*), degeneracy, sterility, and the perversion or absence of reproduction.[28] These conditions are also associated with the Jews. Another prominent characteristic of the antisemitic inventory of Jewish traits and, for Binet, no less specific to fetishism, is "the tendency toward abstraction."[29] Finally, the most curious connection is Binet's concluding analogies between kinds of love and stages of religious development: he compares normal love, composed of a "myriad of [fetishistic] excitations,"[30] with polytheism; and he compares fetishism, at that time considered among the bottom rungs, if not *the* bottom rung of the ladder of religious development,[31] in its most pronounced, singular, and "perverted" form, with what was considered the pinnacle of religious development, monotheism.

The Enlightenment-based notion of religious fetishism also shared a number of traits with the contemporary depiction of *Judentum*, most nota-

bly untranscended materiality and meaningless ritualism. Both the fetishists and the Jews, it was understood, worship the material, and their
religions were viewed as "perversion[s] of the true principle of social
order: [self-] interest."[32] The rampant characterization of the Jewish religion as a fossil bears marks of an implicit comparison with fetish religion.
In addition, the label "fetishistic" was applied by Enlightenment thinkers,
such as Kant, to opposing religious systems, including that of the Jews.[33]
The notion of commodity fetishism also had an implicit connection with
the Jews; for Marx, fetishism characterized the ideological appearance of
those capitalistic social and economic relations that the so-called practical
religion of the Jews epitomized.[34] Consequently, from a number of different contemporary, "scientific" perspectives, the discourse on fetishism
overlapped with that on *Judentum*—including, at least structurally, from
Freud's. In *Civilization*, the "people of Israel" are placed in the same structural position as the "fetish." In a "remarkable" contrast between them
and "primitive man," the "people of Israel" like the "fetish" are ascribed
the blame for any misfortune that befalls, respectively, themselves and that
"primitive man" (21:126–27).

Being Fliessed Again

If we shift from the general notion of fetishism back to the specificity of
that exemplary nose in Freud's essay, several other Jewish subtexts open
up. One prominent subtext is Freud's earlier relationship with Wilhelm
Fliess, the Jewish rhinolaryngologist from Berlin. As discussed in the preceding chapter, Fliess sought to draw homological connections between
the nose and female genitalia as well as to extend his theories of biological
periodicity and bisexuality from menstruating women to all people, regardless of age or gender, by way of the nose. The periodic nosebleeds of
men as well as of prepubescent, pregnant, and postmenopausal women
joined menstruation as expressions of general body rhythms.[35] In his letters to Fliess, Freud wrote almost obsessively about noses: their conges-
tions, suppurations, and effluvia. He remarks on how the condition of his
nose reflects his psychic health as well as on how Fliess's surgeries upon
that same organ affect his physical health. Freud even developed an olfactive theory of repression: certain memories stink. According to Sander
Gilman, two factors in particular contributed to Freud and Fliess's mutual
overvaluation of the nose. One motive is the transvaluation of a figure of
Jewish denigration: the Jewish nose. For them the *Judennase* is neither just

an object of derision nor merely a sign of either decadent hypervirility or (since, in the logic of the time, excess maleness signified that to which its concomitant sexual excess was presumed to lead) decadent weakness and effeminacy. Rather, through their research the nose (and so, by implication, the Jewish nose) becomes a source of scientific truth and a site for easing human misery. The second factor is the revaluation of medical specialties, like rhinolaryngology and neuropathology, which, because the medical establishment considered them to be of lesser importance, had become preserves for Jewish doctors.[36]

Yet, just as, one might say, it was the nose that joined Freud and Fliess, it was also, as we have seen, a nose, Emma Eckstein's nose—and Fliess's botched operation upon it—that would instigate their eventual rupture. Freud reported to Fliess over the next four months about her very slow recovery while trying at the same time to recover Fliess's reputation. Eventually Freud managed to shift the blame onto Eckstein and in the process to claim validation for Fliess's theories. Thus, fourteen months after the operation Freud wrote to Fliess: Eckstein's "episodes of bleeding were hysterical, were occasioned by longing, and probably occurred at the sexually relevant times (the woman, out of resistance, has not yet supplied me with the dates)."[37] Nevertheless, despite Freud's psychic expenditure to preserve both his idealization of Fliess and their relationship, his efforts retained a trace of doubt about Fliess that in time led to their break. Freud's correspondence—like a scar covering Eckstein's excised nose—appears to have been the working out of a fetishistic logic: his discourse about her nose substitutes for the one "castrated"—or, at least, clipped or circumcised—by Fliess (that is, for the true account of Eckstein's nose, for woman's truth) and acts as "protection" (21:154) against the loss of his own ideal: namely, Fliess and the "truth" of his theories.

Freud's fetishized discourse, like his discourse on fetishes, betrays as well a concern about gender and sexual difference. In the preceding chapter I examined how the bloody aftermath of Eckstein's operation and Freud's reworking of the event in his dream of Irma's injection problematized Freud's own gender identity. Indeed, to shift to the fetishistic register of this chapter, Freud notes that Eckstein wielded the maternal phallus when she said to him when he returned to the near-death scene he had earlier fled: "So this is the strong sex."[38] Both Freud's subsequent letters to Fliess and his dreams find him attempting to respond to this taunt and to refute its implications of unmanning. Freud's sense of being feminized manifests itself in the homosexual overtones that colored his understanding of his friendship with Fliess. While Freud in theory distinguishes gender from sexuality, in (anxious) practice he often conflated the two. For example, in 1912 Freud would still speak of the ongoing effects of his broken relationship with the nose doctor as "some piece of unruly homosexual feeling."[39] Although according to Freud bisexuality is a universal, infantile characteristic, it is an orientation that must be worked through —as Freud claims that he had—or the patient risks severe psychoneurosis, if not psychosis.[40] As Freud writes in his "Fetishism" essay, the fetish "saves the fetishist from becoming homosexual" (21:154). Consequently, Freud's exemplary nose, which, again, substitutes for the maternal phallus, can serve as a substitute for Wilhelm Fliess, who wrote on the connection between the nose and female genitalia. The choice of this particular object as fetish thereby allows Freud to disavow his unmanning; it saves Freud from recognizing as well his own feminization and homosexualization.

In attempting to work through the episode of Eckstein's nose in the dream of Irma's injection and subsequent theoretical and epistolary writing, Freud sought to defend himself against both his own problematic gender identity and its generalization to include all male Jews. Freud, however, remained embedded in a matrix of social discourses that increasingly associated (male) Jews with women. For instance, fetishism had, in addition to its connection with *Judentum*, an association with the socially threatening feminine. It embodied "that [feminine] force of irrational passion for unregulated power and of instinctive mendaciousness and lubricity, which perverted all the institutions of legitimate authority."[41] Further, besides the fetishized nose and the fetid odor, already discussed, there was a third feminizing metonym of the Jewish body: circumcision. These three figures are interconnected. According to Gilman, the Jewish nose "represented that hidden sign of [the Jewish male's] sexual difference, his circumcised penis."[42] With the emphasis here on hidden, for the other marker of Jewish difference, odor, is—like the circumcised penis—invisible. Circumcision also had an impact on Freud's treatment of fetishism.

Bearing the Bared Glans—or, Don't Cry Wolf

Freud's notion of circumcision bears a most extraordinary relationship to his notion of fetishism. Although both represent absences—the foreskin and the maternal phallus—circumcision is both formally and substantively, even linguistically,[43] an inversion of fetishism. Circumcision is the "symbolic substitute" (*symbolische Ersatz*) for castration, for what is no longer there (23:122), whereas the fetish is the "substitutive symbol" (*Ersatzsym-*

bol) of the woman's penis, of what was never there (11:96). The circumcised penis both asserts the possible threat of castration (the foreskin has been removed) and denies it (the head of the penis is prominent as in an erection). Obversely, the fetish by definition both disavows the threat of castration (the mother has a penis) and affirms it ("the horror of castration has set up a memorial to itself in the creation of this substitute": the fetish; 21:154). Circumcision, for the uncircumcised,[44] calls forth the castration complex and elicits horror;[45] the fetish (for the fetishist) disavows that complex and generates pleasure.

This inverse structural relationship between circumcision and the fetish can be extended from these metonyms to what they represent: the circumcised Jew can be seen as the inverse of the fetishized woman. But this invert, the Jew, does not become male; rather, he seems to question gender difference and break the fetishistic compromise. Thus his attempted entry into the public sphere poses a grave threat to a society determined by the maintenance of definite gender roles and stereotypes as much as by ethnic and racial difference. The recognition of Jewish difference, like female difference, threatens Christian (and/or European) male bourgeois identity. That this threat inseminated the production of Freud's "Fetishism" essay becomes apparent when we consider one last manifestation of the inverse relationship between circumcision and fetishism: the act of circumcision bares the *glans*, the head of the penis,[46] while Freud's account of the fetishized nose hides it.

Freud's account hides something else. Unlike the Jewish nose, Freud's discussion of the nose fetish does not manifestly betray the identity of its possessor. Yet the patient's resort to "the language of the nose" led Nicolas Abraham and Maria Torok to conclude that the young man of Freud's example was in fact one of Freud's most famous patients, none other than the "Wolf-Man," the star of "From the History of an Infantile Neurosis," Sergei Pankejeff.[47] He is Freud's other oft-cited child victim of animal phobias—the complement to Little Hans, whose case will be taken up in the next chapter. They are paired together in *Inhibitions, Symptoms, and Anxiety* (which Freud had completed the year before "Fetishism"): with the Wolf-Man representing the negative Oedipal complex, and Little Hans the positive (20:107, 124).

The Wolf-Man, incidentally, is not a Jew but rather a Gentile Russian aristocrat. He came under Freud's care in 1910 when he arrived in Vienna "entirely incapacitated and completely dependent on other people" (17:7), as Freud put it. Pankejeff would leave therapy and Vienna in 1914.

Their engagement began with a bang as Freud confessed to Ferenczi about Pankejeff's transferential associations with Freud: not only did the young Russian identify Freud as a "Jewish swindler, he would like to use me [i.e., Freud] from behind and shit on my head."[48] The focus of the case study though was less Pankejeff's immediate condition than on its source in childhood neuroses that had been in abeyance for ten years. Eventually a tale unfurled of early sexual stimulation and sado-masochistic acts, of paralyzing animal anxieties and obsessional preoccupation with both religious practices (such as repetitive prayer recitation and icon kissing) and the story of Jesus (with whom he shared a birthday and with whom he consequently identified), and of screaming fits to provoke, to seduce, the object of his desire, his father, into beating him. The pivotal moment of the analysis comes to be a dream that Pankejeff had just before the age of four: He dreams that it is nighttime and he is in bed when the window at the foot of his bed suddenly opens on its own and he becomes terrified as he sees six or seven white wolves sitting in the branches of the old walnut tree outside. *"In great terror, evidently of being eaten up by the wolves, [he] screamed"* (7:29; emphasis in original) and awoke.

The patient generated a series of associations—many related to the illustrations in fairy tale books and to the stories themselves such as "Little Red Riding Hood," the "Wolf and the Seven Little Goats," and the tale of the wolf whose tail was pulled off by a tailor. These associations were rife with fears of castration and of desire for his father that converged on a generalized anxiety that he, little Sergei, would have to be castrated in order to satisfy his desire for his father. But the key for Freud is the open window: of a scene that was observed—the primal scene of the parents coupling *more ferarum, a tergo*, like animals, such that the genitalia of both are observed—which of course leads back to castration.

But the Wolf-Man in patient's guise who called attention to himself and his "shine on the nose" in Freud's essay is no longer the infantile neurotic. After all, as Freud claims in his 1918 case study, the Wolf-Man had successfully resolved his neurosis (7:100–101, 121–22n1).[49] He had returned to Vienna after the war—no longer the rich aristocrat, but rather the impoverished expatriate, who, with his wife, survived on the generosity of the members of the psychoanalytic movement. In October 1926 he attempts to return to analysis under Freud; Freud, however, sloughs him off to the care of his American pupil, Ruth Mack Brunswick. Freud does keep himself abreast of her patient's progress during the sessions of her ongoing training analysis with him. Pankejeff's analysis lasts five months, until shortly before Freud would write "Fetishism" in August 1927.

In her 1928 "A Supplement to Freud's 'History of an Infantile Neurosis,'" Brunswick describes her patient's condition when he recommenced treatment:[50]

> He was suffering from a hypochondriacal *idée fixe*. He complained that he was the victim of a nasal injury caused by electrolysis, which had been used in the treatment of obstructed sebaceous glands of the nose. According to him the injury consisted varyingly of a scar, a hole or a groove in the scar tissue. The contour of the nose was ruined. Let me state at once that nothing whatsoever was visible on the small, snub, typically Russian nose of the patient.

As is quite apparent, if Abraham and Torok's assumption is to be accepted, then Freud, to preserve the anonymity of his example, had displaced the object of fetishistic attention from his former patient's nose to the nose(s) of other people.[51] Freud also once again displaced the *glans*—or rather its absence, since the Wolf-Man draws upon the verbarium of castration phantasy to describe his condition—to the *Glanz*. Brunswick goes on to describe how the Wolf-Man played out the epistemic ambivalence characteristic of fetishism:[52]

> [H]e carried a pocket mirror which he took out to look at every few minutes. First he would powder his nose [give it a shine?]; a moment later he would inspect it and move the powder. He would then examine the pores, to see if they were enlarging, to catch the hole, as it were, in its moment of growth and development. Then he would again powder his nose, put away the mirror, and a moment later begin the process anew. His life was centered on the little mirror in his pocket, and his fate depended on what it revealed or was about to reveal.

Brunswick theorizes that the source of this particular obsession originated in his circle of acquaintances: "In the years following the war . . . he had even become rather proud (*I suspect because of his many Jewish contacts*) of his own nose. It now occurred to him that he was really exceptionally lucky to have a nose without a blemish."[53] It was his Russian nose that differentiated him from, and marked him as superior to, his cohort, both individually and ethnically. The nose was the mark of difference and of identity. Moreover, since for psychoanalysis the nose is a classic exemplar of displacement (*Verlegung/Verschiebung*; 5:387; 7:83) from lower to upper in dream symbols and neurotic symptoms, when the Wolf-Man saw these "hole[s]," these phantasms of castration staring back at him in the mirror, not only did he recall his earlier identifications with women (17:47, 64,

76–79, 81–82, 84, 100–101),[54] but he was unable to differentiate "his irreparably mutilated state" from that of the circumcised Jews.[55]

Brunswick clearly draws the connection between the Wolf-Man's altered nose and a circumcised penis in the analysis of one of Pankejeff's dreams where his father is a professor "resembling, however, a begging musician known to the patient. . . . His father's nose is long and hooked, causing the patient to wonder at its change." In her commentary, Brunswick notes that the musician "looks like Christ."[56] Generating associations with his dream, Pankejeff recalls an incident in which his father was termed a "*sale juif*" (dirty Jew)—which, Pankejeff quickly asserts, "of course he was not." Brunswick continues: "The begging musician who looks like Christ and the patient's father, and is at the same time a professor [whom Brunswick reads as Freud], is obviously according to his nose a Jew. Since the nose is throughout the symbol for the genital, the change in the father's [and the son's] nose making it Jewish denotes circumcision—castration."[57] Thus when Pankejeff looked in the mirror he recalled the early encounters with circumcision and identifications with the circumcised (Christ) that, according to Freud in "History," had convinced his patient of the reality both of castration and of his father as castrator.

In the original case study Freud had tied Pankejeff's obsessive religious practices to castration by way of circumcision: "He must have become acquainted, during the readings and discussions of the sacred story, with the ritual circumcision of Christ and of the Jews in general" (17:86). From there he moved to the "cruel God" who sacrifices his son and the sons of humanity, behind whom—of course—lay the father whom Pankejeff (and Freud?) identifies as the "castrator." With the identification of the castrator Freud appends a footnote whereby Gd the father is transformed into father, the tailor: "Among the most tormenting, though at the same time most grotesque, symptoms of his later illness was his relation to every tailor from whom he ordered a suit of clothes." Freud goes on to characterize this symptom as Pankejeff's "deference and timidity in the presence of this high functionary [*hohen Person*]" (17:87n2).

The German and the English editors intervene here to help clarify why Freud suddenly descends from father to tailor. For the German editor, "*man erinnere sich, daß es ein Schneider war, der dem Wolf den Schwanz ausriß*" ("one recalls, [that it] was a tailor who cut off the wolf's tail);[58] while the English adds, "The German word for 'tailor' is *Schneider* from the verb '*schneiden*' ('to cut'), a compound of which, '*beschneiden*' means 'to circumcise'" (17:87n2). But Freud is not done with his cutting connection. First, he ties Pankejeff's breathing ritual at the site of beggars and cripples to his younger self's sympathy for a former household retainer who could not speak "ostensibly because his tongue had been cut out [*abgeschnitten hatte*]" (17:87). Then the analysis moves to the recollection of other *sympathisch* servants, "about whom he emphasized the fact that they had either been either sickly or Jews (which implied circumcision).[59] The footman, too, who had helped to clean him after his accident at four and a half, had been a Jew . . ." (17:88).

So we have *Schneider . . . abgeschnitten . . . Beschneidung*, and, in the failure to resolve his castration complex, obsessional neurosis and—more pertinent—the assumption of a passive that is, a feminine, homosexual attitude. Clearly Freud is connecting the Wolf-Man's effeminate symptomology and initial sexual suggestions with circumcision, and such an association would not have been absent in the Wolf-Man's return in his analytic session with Ruth Mack Brunswick, and then, albeit in disguised form, in the "Fetishism" essay.

In sum, the fetishized nose as the substitute for the circumcised penis belies that feminine-coded Jewish difference. On the one hand, Freud's removal of odor and his failure to integrate his "*merkwürdigsten*" case into his argument may be an attempt to disavow the connection of Jews to the perverse sexuality and problematic gender identity constellated about the notion of fetishism. On the other hand, his gratuitous example, like all fetishes, "remains a token of triumph over the threat of castration and a protection against it" (21:154). But I would also add: it remains a token of triumph over the threat of Jewish difference and a protection against it. Freud's nose leaves a trace of the inscription of ethno-racial—as well as gender and sexual—difference on the male Jewish body, and thus of the role of ethnic or racial difference in the development of individual identity.

And what of the unmentioned circumcision? As its structural inversion, can circumcision provide the defense against homosexuality that Freud claims for the fetish? The next chapter examines the relationships inherent among circumcision, castration, and homosexuality.

CHAPTER 4

A Case of Conscience:
Clippings from Little Hans's Nursery

As discussed in the Introduction, studies of Sigmund Freud's Jewish identity trace a trajectory from the "ten- or twelve-year-old" son's shame over his father's submissive response to an antisemitic assault that Freud recalls in his first major work, *The Interpretation of Dreams* (4:197), to the opening filial gambit of his last completed work and only one devoted to an extensive analysis of *Judentum* and antisemitism, *Moses and Monotheism.* Often attempting to psychoanalyze the father of psychoanalysis, these works render that identity as symptomatic of a son dutifully acting out his own ambivalent Oedipal scenario whether with Jacob Freud, *Judentum*, or European modernity.[1]

Unlike that vast literature, this chapter examines the impact of Freud's Jewishness from his position as a father and not as a son. The focus of this analysis is one of Freud's classic case histories, "Analysis of a Phobia in a Five-Year-Old Boy," popularly known as the Case of Little Hans. This case, with one notable exception—a footnote in which Freud speculates on the origin of antisemitism in the castration fears aroused by circumcision—makes no explicit reference to either *Judentum* or to the Jewishness of all of the individuals involved. Yet, that exception is the synecdochal rule of the text; throughout "Analysis" Freud is working through the problematics of his Jewish identity. After examining the subtexts to the footnote, in particular the situation that led Freud to assume the paternal position in relationship to Little Hans, the chapter then analyzes how these contexts generated an ethical dilemma that not only may have conditioned how Freud (mis)read the case, but also shaped the later development of psychoanalysis. It shows how antisemitism as a living reality for Freud, on the one hand, and circumcision as a dispositive or apparatus of both knowledge-production about and identity-authorization for *Judentum*, on the other, combine with an assimilation-dictated homophobia to construct psychoanalysis's model of individual development and the ideal of the fighting Jew.

A Singular Footnote

Sigmund Freud inaugurated the first psychoanalytic journal, the *Jahrbuch für psychoanalytische und psychopathologische Forschungen* (Yearbook for Psychoanalytic and Psychopathological Researches), with a case study that he believed would provide the first compelling case for infantile sexuality as not just "the motive force of all the neurotic symptoms of later life" but as the "common property of all men" (10:6).[2] In "Analysis," Freud describes the onset, course, and apparent resolution of a young boy's pathological fear that a "*a horse will bite him in the street*" (10:22; emphasis in original). To explicate Little Hans's phobia Freud presents his first full elaboration of the castration complex and the consequences upon individual development of this phantasy that attributes the anatomical difference between the sexes to the penises of some children being cut off. The centerpiece of Freud's paper is the account of Little Hans's phobia and its treatment by his father, a member of Freud's circle; that section consists of the father's weekly reports of observations of and conversations with his son together with Freud's glosses.

Early in the case history Freud identifies the deferred threat of castration—"we are reminded of his mother's old threat that she should have [Hans's] widdler cut off if he went on playing with it" (10:35; cf. 10:7–8)—as a likely cause of Little Hans's symptoms. Freud suddenly appends to his commentary an extraordinary footnote (10:36n1):

> I cannot so far interrupt the discussion as to demonstrate the typical character of the unconscious train of thought which I think there is here reason for attributing to little Hans. The castration complex is the deepest unconscious root [*Wurzel*] of anti-Semitism; for even in the nursery [*Kinderstube*]

little boys hear that a Jew has something cut off his penis—a piece of his penis, they think—and this gives them the right to despise Jews. And there is no stronger unconscious root for the sense of superiority over women. Weininger (the young philosopher who, highly gifted but sexually deranged, committed suicide after producing his remarkable book, *Geschlecht und Charakter* [1903]), in a chapter that attracted much attention, treated Jews and women with equal hostility and overwhelmed them with the same insults. Being a neurotic, Weininger was completely under the sway of his infantile complexes; and from that standpoint what is common to Jews and women is their relation to the castration complex.

In sum, hatred of Jews arises as a reaction against "the dreaded castration" evoked by "its symbolic substitute" (23:91), circumcision. This correlation of castration and circumcision not only undergirds Freud's later elaboration of the causes of antisemitism in *Moses and Monotheism*, but it informs both some of the earliest psychoanalytic explorations of religious development[3] as well as the most recent psychoanalytic investigations of antisemitism.[4] More than stating a psychoanalytic truism about the symbolic relationship of circumcision and castration, the note condenses many of Freud's multiple identity and theory constructions by binding gender, sexuality, and ethnicity/religion/race to the workings of the unconscious, neurosis, and the castration complex. Not surprisingly, this footnote is perhaps the most cited of Freud's countless footnotes.

Yet, what is perhaps more extraordinary than this note's seminal role in psychoanalytic theory is that such a note appeared at all. The body of Freud's text bears no explicit sign of circumcision or other matters Jewish that could have motivated its inclusion. So why interrupt his discussion with what we may presume to be a demonstration of an *a*typical character of Little Hans's "unconscious train of thought"? Why the uncovering of what literally—after all, it is a footnote—lies under the body of the text? Is the footnote shod in a Freudian slipper? In which case, what has slipped out?

Since the late 1980s, such questions have spurred scholars of this footnote to traverse beyond the pages of psychoanalysis, such that Freud's supplemental remarks assume an increasing importance in the new historiography of European modernity and, especially, in analyses of the Jewish identity and identifications of Freud and his fellow Central Europeans. As earlier noted, analyses, notably by Gilman and D. Boyarin, find Freud's nonmention of the Jewishness of Little Hans, in actuality Herbert Graf, and, especially, of the convert to Protestantism and closeted homosexual

Weininger—as well as of Freud himself—particularly symptomatic of a Freud seeking either to deflect or to displace the implications of being Jewish in early-twentieth-century Vienna.[5] Moving beyond the brute facts of the political antisemitism of the Christian Social Party, which, under Karl Lueger, governed Vienna from 1897 to 1910, or the institutional antisemitism that limited Jewish professional advancement,[6] these works situate Freud and his writings negotiating the fin-de-siècle crises of gender, sexual, and ethno-religio-racial identities.[7] Freud himself is seen as more participant than prophet as he endeavors to work through his own situation, what this work has described as the "double bind" of the Central European Jew: the simultaneous demand for and the no-less assumed impossibility of assimilation. And as already noted, Freud, who identified himself with the values of the cultured bourgeoisie and the corollary objective universals of scientific positivism and Enlightenment rationality, was identified by many with the epitome of particularity: the Jew; and a fortiori, psychoanalysis, developed by Freud and pre-eminently practiced by Jews, was continuously attempting to deflect its identification as a "Jewish national affair."[8]

These personal and cultural subtexts intersect in the footnote. Yet, in erecting this footnote as a monument to an antisemitic,[9] misogynistic, and homophobic modernity and a perhaps "understandably" misogynistic and homophobic Freud,[10] these recent studies of Freud's Jewish identity have neglected the relationships of this footnote to Little Hans, to the stakes of Freud's analysis, and to one of the "deepest unconscious roots" for Freud's constructing his theoretical edifice upon the "bedrock" of the castration complex (23:252). Further, there are a number of riddles that also have not been satisfactorily addressed. Perhaps first and foremost, why does Freud allude to—and merely allude to—circumcision in the first place? But along with that comes another, perhaps as mysterious: only a year later Freud would undertake his first and most elaborate psychobiography in *Leonardo da Vinci and a Memory of His Childhood.* That essay contains an extended iteration of the adventures of our "youthful investigator" (11:95), to which is appended a footnote that connects castration, circumcision, and the roots of antisemitism; curiously, however, this footnote does not appear until 1919 when *Leonardo* is reissued. In order to unpack the condensations of Freud's original footnote and to resolve these anomalies, this chapter situates the note in relationship to Freud's avoidance of explicit Jewish (self-)reference in public writings during the period from 1905 to 1916; the arguments of the case history; Freud's relationship to the Graf family; the small matter of Herbert Graf's (non)circumcision;

Freud's earlier speculations about antisemitism; and several later writings, in particular, "Notes upon a Case of Obsessive Neurosis," *Leonardo*, and the 1919 essay in which Freud incorporates his analysis of his daughter Anna, " 'A Child Is Being Beaten.' "

Silence in the Judenschule

Perhaps the most immediately curious thing about this foonote is that it specifically mentions Jews. During the crucial years in his pursuit of public recognition and scientific legitimation for the psychoanalytic movement, 1905–16, Freud eschewed explicit public reference to matters Jewish in his analytic writings—with this one principal exception.[11] The Freud literature is replete with citations from his correspondence with his Jewish disciples about his concern that the movement's practitioners, patients, and objects of analysis were perceived as particularly Jewish. His quest for Gentile cover in the person of Carl Jung and other Gentile members of the Zurich school has also received much attention. While the virtual elision of any explicit mention of *Judentum* has been noted, little analysis has been devoted—with the possible exception of the anonymously published "The Moses of Michelangelo";[12] the publication of a de-Judaized version of his 1915 B'nai B'rith lecture "Death and Us [Jews]" (*Wir und der Tod*) as "Our Attitude toward Death," the second part of "Thoughts for the Times upon War and Death";[13] and Little Hans—to the apparent intentional omission of case material and the use of rhetorical misdirection to mask his or his patients' Jewish identities or to avoid the dissemination of anti-Jewish stereotypes. Even in a text that overflows with Jewish material like *Jokes*, Freud carefully avoids any identification of its author as Jewish.

The first fifty-one manuscript pages of the original case record of the "Rat Man" ("Notes upon a Case of Obsessional Neurosis"), now known to be Ernst Lanzer, have been preserved. While a partial translation was published in the *Standard Edition* in 1955, the complete German transcript was first published in France in 1974 and only included in the *Gesammelte Werke*, in the *Nachtragsband*, in 1987. The text is rife with Yiddish and German-Jewish expressions (for example, *Schügsenen* [Gentile girls], *Miessnick* [ugly creature], *gekoschiert* [koshered], *Parch* [futile person], and *chonte* [prostitute]; 10:276, 284, 291, 298, 312) as well as questions about conversion (10:301–2), considered as another way to kill his already-dead father who had faced up to antisemitism (10:305), and intermarriage (with explicit reference to the Jewishness of his then fiancée; 10:302). Yet it is clear from the case record that the patient remained Jewish.[14] The case study itself places some emphasis on his early religiosity and concern about the afterlife (for example, 10:235–36) without indicating that his religious inclinations were Jewish. Moreover, since virtually all Gentiles and many Jews did not realize that non-Reform Jewish traditions have developed notions of the afterlife,[15] the Rat Man's discussion of salvation would lead most readers to assume that the patient was not Jewish. A similar omission also occurs in his 1915 *judenrein* essay on attitudes toward death; the recognition "that different stances have been taken on the doctrine of immortality in popular Jewish religion and in the literature connected with the Holy Scriptures" is absent from the published revision.[16] One possible rationale for Freud's efforts to deflect attention from any connection between his patient and *Judentum* would be the fear that the numerous associations of Jews with money and rats, especially the depiction of Jewish capitalists as "golden rats,"[17] may have shifted the focus from psychoanalysis's ability to decipher symptoms to what is "typically Jewish." Another possible reason may have been that his patient, a former military officer (who would be killed in World War I),[18] rather than the exemplar of "the fighting Jew," was frequently beset by cowardice (*Feigheit*),[19] and considered by Freud from the outset of therapy as homosexual ("*ich erkenne ihn . . . als Homosexuellen*"),[20] or, as he comments in the third footnote of the case study (and only there; 10:160n), greatly influenced "in his life by homosexual object-choice," none of which Freud wished to associate with either *Judentum* or psychoanalysis.

Totem and Taboo (1912–13), too, strangely avoids reference to *Judentum*. When Freud presents his history of religious development from father-religion to son-religion here, in contrast to its reiteration in *Moses*, Christianity is shown to emerge out of cults of such youthful deities as Attis, Adonis, Tammuz, Orpheus, Dionysus-Zagreus, and in competition with the Persian Mithras;[21] there is no mention of *Judentum* or the Jewish community of Palestine. The one allusion to Jewish ritual practice occurs in an obfuscating footnote attached to the mention of Attis's death by castration. There, Freud paraphrases a portion of the Little Hans note. "When our children come to hear of ritual circumcision, they equate it with castration." Ritual circumcision, however, is not identified specifically as Jewish nor is the age of the operation directly indicated. Freud then draws the readers' attention further away from the Jews: "In primæval times and in primitive races, where circumcision is so frequent, it is performed at the age of initiation into manhood and it is at that age that its significance is to be found; it was only as a secondary development that it was shifted back to the early years of life." Circumcision as a customary practice and as a bearer of meaning is by no means to be sought among the (unnamed) Jews. He then continues to divert the reader from Jewish infant circumcision by shifting the emblematic "castration equivalent" from circumcision to "cutting the hair and knocking out teeth." Freud describes "these two operations," and not ritual circumcision, as the producers of castration anxiety in "our children" (13:153n1).

From Little Herbert to Little Hans

Before speculating on what may have led to the anomalous emergence of this conjunction of Jews and circumcision in the footnote to "Analysis," Freud's protagonist Little Hans need be introduced. In 1908, despite a favorable response by some sectors of the psychiatric community, especially Eugen Bleuler and Carl Jung of Zurich's famed Burghölzli Mental Hospital, psychoanalysis still lacked general acceptance and authority because of its dependence upon the reconstruction of the childhood sexual edifice out of the "débris" of adult pathology (10:6). Confronted by epistemological concerns and moralizing qualms about what Freud considered the incontrovertible hypotheses of his science, he conceded that "even a psychoanalyst may confess to the wish for a more direct and less roundabout proof" (10:6). When five-year-old Herbert Graf, the son of music critic Max Graf and one-time Freud patient Olga Hönig Graf,[22] suddenly developed a fear that "*a horse will bite him in the street*," Freud believed that he had found a case to provide such proof. Little Herbert, or as he came to be identified in "Analysis," Little Hans, would save the day.

Even before this analysis Little Herbert had already performed yeoman service for the cause of psychoanalysis. Thanks to the briefings his father, an early member of the Wednesday-evening group (*Mittwochsgesellschaft*) that would become the Vienna Psychoanalytic Society, had given to Professor Freud about his son's words and actions, Herbert had already made several contributions to the articulation of psychoanalytic theory. In the June 1907 essay "The Sexual Enlightenment of Children" the questions of this "delightful little boy" at age three demonstrated Freud's claim that children's "desire for sexual knowledge shows itself accordingly at an unexpectedly early age" (9:134). Such "intellectual interest in the riddles of sex" (9:134) was a crucial component of Freud's theory of universal infantile sexuality. Freud reassuringly adds that "I should like to say explicitly that little [Herbert] is not a sensual child or at all pathologically disposed"

(9:135).²³ The normality of Little Herbert helped legitimate Freud's theory.

A year later Freud would return to Little Herbert in "On the Sexual Theories of Children." In that essay Freud discusses the theoretical conclusion arrived at by the child from the data-gathering reported in the earlier piece. Herbert's "theory" of sexual difference, or rather his theory of the absence of the only difference that matters for Freud—Herbert's *"attributing to everyone, including females, the possession of a penis"* (9:215; emphasis in the original)—is represented as a normal stage of development.²⁴ In 1923 Freud would himself theorize Herbert's conclusion as the phallic stage, in which all children are acquainted with only one organ, the male one (10:110n2). In this context, however, Freud's source is no longer the delightful, nonpathologically disposed, then-four-year-old Little Herbert; rather it is an unnamed "five-year-old boy" undergoing analysis by his father. To explain this pathological situation—"the idea of a woman with a penis becomes 'fixated'" (*fixiert*; 9:216)—that arises from the contradiction between the dictates of Herbert's sexual theory and his perception of sexual difference, Freud introduces a new term, "the castration complex" (9:217). Freud also propounds the dangerous consequences of a boy fixating upon theory: "he is bound to become a homosexual" (9:216). Both complex and consequence would play major roles in Freud's working through "Analysis."

Although a number of researchers—among them Anzieu, Laplanche, and Green—have found adumbrations of the theory of the castration complex in the self-analysis that culminated in *Interpretation*,²⁵ Freud had not put it together in a publication until "Analysis."²⁶ Fixing upon Hans's "singular remark" (10:35)—"It's [i.e., his widdler (penis) is] fixed in" (*er ist ja angewachsen*; 10:34)—Freud proceeds to uncover "the typical character of the unconscious train of thought which I think is here reason for attributing to little Hans" (10:36n1); the thought is the castration complex. Freud follows that train of thought that, no longer repressed, had now through deferred action emerged with an accompanying animal phobia.²⁷ By the end of the analysis Freud intends to have demonstrated the fundamental role of the castration complex in the formation of a normal identity—that is, male heterosexuality—but at this point in his narrative the threat of castration is first identified as the likely cause of deferred pathological effects and phantasies in one five-year-old boy.

Now that he is on the trail of a solution to Hans's problems, Freud cannot "interrupt the discussion" (10:36n1); still, he does cut away for a moment and offers his readers that most extraordinary footnote in which he associates circumcision with castration. The next section examines the motivations behind this association.

A Complex Adoption

Little Herbert's (Hans's) father Max Graf writes in his 1942 sympathetic reminiscence of Professor Freud that:

> When my son was born [in 1903], I wondered whether it would not be better to have my son brought up in the Christian faith. Freud advised me not to do this. "If you do not let your son grow up as a Jew," he said, "you will deprive him of those sources of energy which cannot be replaced by anything else. He will have to struggle as a Jew, and you ought to develop in him all the energy he will need for the struggle. Do not deprive him of that advantage."[28]

Throughout his own life Freud characterized a Jew's fate as virile struggle; as he wrote in his autobiography, and repeated in his address to the B'nai B'rith Lodge of Vienna in the mid-1920s, being Jewish was "indispensable to me throughout my difficult life. . . . As a Jew I was prepared to be in the opposition and to renounce agreement with the 'compact majority'" (20:273–74).

His accounts of his earlier life characterize Jewishness as a test of masculinity presented by the antisemitic majority. The "unheroic conduct" of Freud's father, Jakob, when assaulted by the Christian lout as a young man, together with the son's embarrassed response to his father's submission, has become the classic instance of the gender stakes of Freud's Jewish identity. His letters to his fiancée, and later wife, Martha recount scenes in which he or other Jewish doctors successfully stand up to antisemitic slights and in the process preserve both their honor and the rightness of their position.[29] Perhaps the most graphic depiction of Jewish virility against Gentile cowardice appears in Freud's son Martin's memoir of a summer outing in 1901, some two years before the birth of Herbert Graf. He describes how his father confronted a crowd who blocked the way of Martin and his brother Oliver while heckling them with antisemitic abuse:

> Father, without the slightest hesitation, jumped out of the boat, and keeping to the middle of the road, marched towards the hostile crowd. . . . Ten men armed with sticks and umbrellas [and] the women remain[ing] in the background, but cheer[ing] on their men folk with shouts and gestures. In the meantime, father, swinging his stick, charged the hostile crowd, which

gave way before him and promptly dispersed allowing him a free passage."[30]

Martin could not have chosen a more "Freudian" account of Jewish gendered identity than Freud the Jew, brandishing his phallic masculinity, overcoming his castrated opponents.[31] Freud's charge to Herbert's father to raise his son as a Jew promised him a difficult, but ultimately successful, development into the early-twentieth-century bourgeois ideal of healthy, virile manhood.

Five years after Herbert's birth, however, Freud learns from the father that rather than the strong, self-determined child he had prophesied him to become, young Herbert is in the grips of a phobic neurosis. Initially Freud locates this turn of events as the deferred effect of the (maternal) threat of castration if Little Hans (Herbert) continues to masturbate. Yet in the footnote attending that first etiological deduction, Freud evokes circumcision and Otto Weininger, antisemitism and misogyny, none of which, again, appears either before or after the note.

Prompted by his own main text, Freud often inserts aperçus that bear the residue of his outside readings or other everyday encounters.[32] More, however, is attending this footnote than cognitive insight or the chance association of "here a cut, there a cut," the merely contingent fact of Herbert's (unmentioned) Jewish identity, or the remains of the Weininger case.[33] The first link in this note's particular chain of associations is less Hans's singular remark or his mother's recollected threat than an event that occurred five years earlier. While Graf does not date his conversation with Freud,[34] I, like everyone else,[35] presumed to take Graf at his word— "when my son was born"—and that as a consequence of the advice of his esteemed friend, Max had his son circumcised on the eighth day.[36] Unfortunately, instead of producing Herbert Graf, a "muscle Jew,"[37] a "fighting Jew,"[38] ready to take on the threats of an antisemitic world, the Freud-inspired circumcision had produced Little Hans, a neurotic *faygeleh* afraid to enter that threatening world.[39] Because of this possible misstep, the footnote signals that "Analysis" may be more about a "family romance" than it is about the history of a case.

This romance, however, is told from a different perspective than that discussed by Freud—but not testified to by Little Herbert—in the "Sexual Theories of Children."[40] This tale is not told from the perspective of the son who phantasizes that he has been adopted but by the father who, also in the realm of phantasy, has adopted him. In 1908 Freud believed that only a parent could analyze a child;[41] yet not only did Freud directly advise

Graf, but Graf's appropriation of Freud's theories mediated his own dealings with his son. Herbert was raised under (then-) Freudian principles:
little coercion, recording his dreams, listening to his chatter. His wife's
analysis with Freud may have had an effect as well. Further, Freud met
with Hans during the course of the analysis. "The Professor" was also
viewed by Hans as the ultimate arbiter (see 10:72). Finally, in the face of
Max Graf's rather incompetent interpretations of his son's behaviors and
phantasies Freud's glosses and discussion also provide analysis—so in a
number of ways he usurped the paternal role.

Still, Freud does not just assume the position of father figure in his role
as authority and analyst. Rather by advising Max Graf upon the birth of
his son, Freud had (god)fathered Herbert as a Jew; he acted like the *kvatter*
(godfather) who hands the child over to the *mohel* (ritual circumciser), if
indeed he did not assume the paternal role (which includes that of the
circumciser) and bound Herbert to the tradition. "Analysis" is a story that
seeks to hide Freud's adoption of Herbert and his responsibility for his
condition. Yet to determine the true nature of that condition it is necessary
to examine the ensuing connection between (the implicated) Little Hans
and Otto Weininger.

In the paragraph to which the footnote is appended, Freud describes a
"piece of [sexual] enlightenment" (10:36),[42] which supersedes Herbert's
earlier one: "women really do not possess a widdler" (10:36). Freud imagines that in the face of this information Little Hans concludes that "it
would no longer be so incredible that they could take his own widdler
away, and, as it were, make him into a woman!" (10:36). Gilman suggests
that the footnote is one of the stages for Freud's engagements both with
Weininger and with the representation of the diseased Jew that is figured
by circumcision.[43]

Admittedly Weininger's text was still a topic of discussion in 1908 and
1909,[44] although the significant responses of figures like Karl Kraus,[45] Otto
Rank,[46] and others were already several years in the past. Its immediate
relation to Freud at that moment appears to be incidental. Weininger's
name does not appear in Freud's now-extant letters of the time, and there
is but one mention of Weininger in the minutes of the Vienna Psychoanalytic Society during the period of the composition of "Analysis." That
one mention, however, did occur at a most opportune time: on 1 April
1908—that is, two days after Freud's one meeting with Herbert Graf during the course of the analysis, and therefore perhaps a week after Max
Graf's report that would in "Analysis" provoke the footnote on Weininger—the Wednesday-evening group met to discuss Nietzsche's "On

the Ascetic Ideal" (part three of the *Genealogy of Morals*). The minutes report that Paul Federn remarks, "It is worth mentioning that Otto Weininger also had to struggle with the suppression of sadism (ideas of lustful murder); his book shows him to be a highly ethical individual."[47] Although the content of Federn's comment is not reflected in Freud's note and while we cannot assume that the footnote and accompanying commentary originates with the receipt of Max Graf's report, the mention of Weininger may nonetheless be part of the day's residues, which would become attached to Freud's analysis. Despite this intriguing coincidence, and not to deny Gilman's train of thought, the appearance of Weininger in this note has more to do with the profound concerns that Little Hans's sexuality aroused in Freud.

Accessing Hans's Homosexuality

The trail of associations begins in the commonality of the characterization of Weininger and Little Hans: "highly gifted but sexually deranged."[48] Throughout "Analysis" Freud makes asides in the notes on Hans's insight: "Hans, with his usual acumen, had once more put his finger upon a most serious problem" (10:91n1). Earlier Freud speaks of how Hans "had worked out glosses upon the many difficulties involved in the stork hypothesis" (10:74n1); or when Hans sees through his father's rationalizations and argues for the value of a patient's thoughts for therapeutic understanding, Freud comments, "Well done, little Hans! I could wish for no better understanding of psycho-analysis from any grown-up" (10:72n1). But Hans is also "sexually precocious" (cf. 10:142). The agon of Hans's case for Freud lay not in the angst aroused in the young boy by the horse's penis but in Hans's sexual orientation. In "Sexual Theories" Freud would indicate the consequences of fixating on the existence of the maternal penis: the little boy was "bound to become a homosexual" (9:216). For Freud every child at a certain stage is homosexual (cf. 10:10); hence when Freud notes Hans's first trace of homosexuality, adding as well that "it will not be the last," he lightheartedly comments with paternal irony meant to tweak the noses of his Gentile readership that "Little Hans seems to be a positive paragon of all the vices" (10:20).

Yet it is important for Freud that this be a stage that is overcome. "In his subsequent development, however, it was not to homosexuality that our young libertine proceeded, but to an energetic masculinity with traits of polygamy" (10:110). He became a "true man" (*ein rechter Mann*; 10:17) and a "little Oedipus" (10:111). After this neurotic deviation Little Hans reassumed his destined role: heroic manhood characterized by virile heterosexuality.[49] As proof of Hans's polygamy Freud comments that "the sexual aim which he pursued with his girl playmates, of *sleeping* with them [*bei ihnen zu* schlafen; emphasis in original],[50] had originated in relation to his mother. It was expressed in words which might be retained in maturity though they would then bear a richer connotation" (10:110–11).

Unfortunately the case belies that conclusion. Little Hans does not employ this sexually connoted phrase, "sleeping with," or *schlafen bei*, with regard to his girl playmates during his "subsequent development." Rather, he uses it during that period prior to the onset of his phobia (cf. 10:16–17) when, as Freud had just put it, "Hans was a homosexual" (10:110; cf. 10:17: "accesses of homosexuality" [*homosexuellen Anwandlungen* = homosexual impulses]). The phrase ("sleeping with") only recurs near the conclusion of the case history, and then both boys and girls are sleeping with him. Hans is discussing "'his children'" (10:93; quotation marks in the original) with his father. When his father asks him what he did with the children, Hans replies that "I had them to sleep with me, the girls and the boys" (*Bei mir hab' ich sie schlafen lassen, Mädeln und Buben*; 10:94). And then in response to his father's questioning about where these children came from, Hans manifests his phantasy/desire of being a mother and giving birth (10:94–95):

> I: "But who did you think you'd got the children from?"
> HANS: "Why, from me."
> . . .
> I: When you sat on the chamber and lumf came, did you think to yourself you were having a baby?
> HANS (laughing): "Yes. . . ."

The day before this conversation Hans had already expressed his desire to be a mother: "And Daddy, until [*bis*] I'm married I'll only have one [baby] if [*wenn*] I want to, when [*wenn*] I'm married to Mummy, and if [*wenn*] I don't want a baby, God won't want it either, when [*wenn*] I'm married" (10:92). The translation in the *Standard Edition* effaces that desire by reading *bis* (until) as "when." By shifting the temporal reference and placing Hans in the position of the father the editors clear up Hans's somewhat convoluted statement and in the process echo Freud's subsequent (that is, in the text, not in the time of writing) dampening of any suggestion of Hans's effeminacy. In anticipation of the ensuing revelations of Hans's phantasy life, Freud felt compelled to offer in his footnotes the reassuring gloss that: "There is no necessity on this account to assume in Hans the presence of a feminine strain of desire for having children. It was with his mother that Hans had had his most blissful experience as a child, and he was now repeating them, and himself playing the active part [the masculine], which was thus necessarily that of mother" (10:93n1). If this preemptive commentary was not sufficient to distract the reader from "the presence of a feminine strain," then his discussion of Hans's expressions would complete the job. Thus, Freud takes Hans's claim that his children come from himself as signifying that "they were the children of his phantasy, that is to say of his masturbation" (10:94n2). With these glosses Freud sets up his readers to ignore Hans's own testimonies of desire and prepares them to accept the screen history of resolved neurosis and normal sexual development Freud would generate in his subsequent discussion of the case.[51]

Freud's ultimate denial of Hans's ongoing homosexuality occurs in (mis)interpreting Hans's second plumbing phantasy with which his father's report concludes: "The plumber [*Installateur*] came; and first he took away my behind with a pair of pincers, and then gave me another, and then the same with my widdler" (10:98). Hans had initially dreamed about the plumber several weeks earlier: "I was in the bath, and the plumber [*Schlosser*] came and unscrewed it [his widdler]. Then he took a big borer [*Bohrer*] and stuck it into my stomach" (10:65). As to the adequacy of the father's Oedipal translation of the initial phantasy—the big paternal penis kicking the son out of the maternal bed—Freud notes: "Let us suspend our judgment for the present" (10:65). With the return of the plumbing phantasy[52] Freud, too, seems to hold back. He allows Hans's father to interpret this second phantasy as Oedipal wish fulfillment: Hans wants to be like his Daddy. Freud then applies his own happy spin on the event: "With Hans's last phantasy the anxiety which arose from his castration complex was also overcome, and his painful expectations were given a happier turn" (10:100).

In the guise of mere scholarly speculation Freud offers some commentary on Hans's phantasies in a note (10:98n1):

Perhaps, too, the word "borer" ["*Bohrer*"] was not chosen without regard for its connection with "born" ["*geboren*"] and "birth" ["*Geburt*"]. If so, the child could have made no distinction between "bored" ["*gebohrt*"] and "born" ["*geboren*"]. I accept this suggestion, made by an experienced fellow-worker, but I am not in a position to say whether we have before us here a deep and universal connection between the two ideas or merely the employment of a verbal coincidence peculiar to German. Prometheus (Pra-mantha), the creator of man, is also etymologically "the borer." (Cf. Abra-ham, *Traum und Mythus*, 1909)

This word play would return in the discussion section; there it becomes the key to interpreting not only these phantasies but the entire network of Oedipal symptoms and phantasies. Freud deduces that "the big bath of water, in which Hans imagined himself, was his mother's womb; the 'borer,' which his father from the first recognized as a penis, owed its mention to its connection with 'being born.'" Consequently, Freud now recognizes that first plumbing phantasy as a *"phantasy of procreation*, dis-torted by anxiety" (*angstenstellte*) that requires what Freud qualifies as a "very curious" interpretation: "With your big penis you [his father] 'bored' me (i.e., gave birth to me [Freud's interpolation]) and put me in my mother's womb" (10:128). Armed with this combination of word asso-ciation and reconstructed thought, Freud traces Hans's phantasy back to the crisis precipitated by the birth of his sister: "He was faced with the great riddle of where babies come from, which is perhaps the first problem to engage a child's mental powers, and of which the riddle of the Theban Sphinx is probably no more than a distorted version" (*Entstellung*; 10:133). This riddle of where his sister comes from, and in particular the questions of the role of his father and his father's widdler in her production, as well as the matter of his mother's imagined widdler together precipitate the entire Oedipal scenario with its accompanying castration complex.

Yet Freud's trumpeting the phonic association between *bohrer* and *geb-oren* seems a "very curious" move when the manifest phantasy clearly por-trays a different scene of "passive-feminine identification" with his mother and desire for his father.[53] Little Hans is being penetrated by his father's penis. The refusal of Freud to draw this conclusion is all the more curious in light of Hans's father's interpretation of his conversation with his son just after learning of the plumber phantasy and of Freud's own comment on that interpretation.[54] Father and son talk about the sound of *lumf* fall-ing, after which Hans's father offers the interpretation that his (Hans's) "fear of defecation and his fear of heavily loaded carts is equivalent to the fear of a heavily loaded stomach." Freud comments that "in this round-about way Hans's father was beginning to get a glimmering of the true state of affairs" (10:66), namely, that the object of Hans's concern—and phantasy—was procreation. Freud would point out that Hans had made the connection between his mother's groans of pain (10:10; cf. 10:133) and the birth of his sister, that he had developed and had adopted the infantile excremental theory of childbirth (10:74–75), and that he desired to, and thought he could, have a child (10:86–87). Freud had already recognized the love that Hans felt for his father; Freud there contradicted Hans's father, who obdurately asserted Oedipal hostility in the face of his son's protestation: "Why did you tell me I'm fond of Mummy and that's why I'm frightened, when I'm fond of you?" (10:44). Yet Freud did not note the negative Oedipal situation then,[55] and neither did he recognize that in this phantasy of procreation Hans was phantasizing about replacing his mother and bearing his father's child.

This (mis)recognition of Hans's maternal identification is clearly indicated in a slip that the editors of the *Standard Edition* attempt to gloss over; it occurs during Freud's discussion of Hans's phantasy of the two giraffes, one big and the other crumpled. Initially Hans had argued that the former was his mother and the latter his baby sister; eventually, Hans accepts his father's interpretation that the big one is him (the father) and the crumpled one his mother (10:40). When deducing that the choice of the giraffes derives in part "perhaps, by an unconscious comparison based upon the giraffe's long, stiff neck" (10:122), Freud adds in a note that "Hans's admiration [*Bewunderung*] of his father's neck later on would fit in with this" (10:122n1). The only reference to a neck in the text is, however, to his mother's; in accepting his father's interpretation of the identity of the giraffes, Hans had demurred over his father's anatomical explanation. When his father suggests that the long neck (of the big giraffe) reminded him of a penis, Hans replied: "Mummy has a neck like a giraffe, too. I saw, when she was washing her white neck" (10:40). The editors suggest that Freud was condensing that scene with a later one in which Hans comments on how white and "lovely" his father's bared torso is (10:53).[56] Hans's original gloss on the giraffe scene can, however, more readily be read as expressing his continued belief in the maternal penis (and in his sister's "still quite small" one; 10:11).

Freud's slip with its reference to Hans's affect shifts the register from the cognitive to the sexual; the father becomes an object of desire. Consequently, rather than having resolved his castration complex and moved on to latency and "normal" psychosexual development, Little Hans had maintained his "homosexual accesses." Hence what Freud could not say in his text, but which the text more than testified to—namely, Little Hans's persistent homosexual or, more accurately, bisexual orientation—emerged with the footnote on antisemitism and Weininger. Whereas Hans's "fixed-in" penis had led Freud to recognize the deferred action of castration anxiety,[57] perhaps Hans's "fixation" on the maternal penis led Freud, because of its telos of homosexuality,[58] to associate him with the sexually deranged Weininger, who was under the "sway of his infantile complexes." Perhaps with this apposition of Little Hans and Weininger, Freud acknowledges what he would more explicitly state, albeit in the form of a general proposition, in the previously published, but apparently later composed, "Sexual Theories": namely, Herbert's inability to overcome his "infantile complexes" and the homosexual consequences of his fixation, perhaps because the condition that had generated his castration anxiety was still in effect—his circumcision.

I, like many others,[59] had suggested that Herbert's circumcision mediated either visually or ideationally the realizable threat of castration. Immediately before the "case history and analysis" proper in his text, Freud transcribes Max Graf's notes about a change in his son's behavior prior to the appearance of his phobic symptoms (10:19–20): "Yesterday, when I was helping Hans to do number one, he asked me for the first time to take him to the back of the house so that no one should see him. He added: 'Last year when I widdled, Berta and Olga watched me.' . . . I have repeatedly observed since then that he does not like to be seen widdling." Perhaps when he showed his widdler to his Gentile friends Berta and Olga at the *Sommerfrische* in Gmunden they had asked him, "Why is your widdler different from all other widdlers?"

Consequently, by advising Max Graf to raise his son Jewish, the authoritative Freud had, in effect, commanded Graf to circumcise his son and therefore had *condemned* Herbert not just to neurosis but to homosexuality. Hence, including the footnote may reflect Freud's concern about the general association of Jews with homosexuality.[60] For many, Weininger assumed an exemplary status of Jew as homosexual;[61] moreover, acknowledging the relationship between Herbert's (or Weininger's) homosexual impulses and the persistent castration anxiety generated by his own circumcision risks generalizing the phenomenon for all circumcised Jewish males and thereby confirming the stereotype. And yet, particular and personal matters may have been more pressing.[62] By interpolating Weininger and circumcision into his case study Freud-the-paternal-advisor (the paternal surrogate and circumciser) signals his sense of responsibility for Hans's neurosis and homosexuality, while Freud-the-circumcised-analyst, troubled over his own conflicted "homosexual accesses,"[63] indicates his identifications with Hans the investigator.[64]

The only problem with my earlier analysis, as I later learned in Vienna, was the fact that, according to the registration lists preserved by the Viennese Jewish community, Herbert Graf had not been circumcised. Should Freud have assumed that Herbert was circumcised? Probably not. Although Freud himself was circumcised,[65] according to those same lists, his registered-and-raised-as-Jewish sons were not.[66] As noted in chapter 1, neither the Viennese civil government nor the Jewish community authorities had required circumcision for Jewish registration since, at the latest, 1871. Apparently, it is not the sight of some little Jewish *Schmuck* that generates such anxiety. Rather, it is "a rumor about the Jews":[67] "even in the nursery little boys hear that a Jew has something cut off his penis."[68] No less than the stereotypical Jewish nose that Freud's Jewish colleagues attempted to fix as phantasy via a statistical rhinoplasty,[69] so, too, was that indelible mark of (male) Jewish identity a dangerous phantasy. Perhaps blinded by Freud's emphasis on the role of scopophilia in the potentially traumatic acquisition of knowledge about sexual difference,[70] by the ideological presumption that such difference is naturally signified by those genitalia, and by a positivist distrust—alas, on occasion shared by Freud—in the generative power of anything but a "real repetition of the event" (*reale Wiederholung des Ereignisses*; 23:101), as well as possibly by the need to secure a singular Jewish identity, previous readers—including at times myself—have overlooked the absence of a primal voyeuristic scene and misrecognized our own phantastic constructions for "how it actually was."[71]

As I have argued throughout this work, in Freud's long fin-de-siècle, a period of crises of individual and collective identity and difference, hegemony was legitimized and rendered visible by affixing natural differences to the bodies of the subjected others. And on the imagined Jewish body, the pre-eminent marker was the always already circumcised penis. In a text that analyzed the sexual identity of a young Jewish boy, all the while suppressing both his final sexual and his original racial identity, and that would thereby both provide conclusive proof of the then-assumed most provocative theory of psychoanalysis—childhood sexuality—and lay the no-less-controversial foundation for all psychological development with this first extensive articulation of the castration complex; in other words, in a work in which so much was invested, it is not surprising that the nodal point upon which all of these narratives converged—circumcision—would slip out. Throughout his corpus Freud would in part pathologize and in part transform into a universal characteristic this algorithm of Jewish difference, circumcision, or rather its symbolic substitute, castration; however, as we have observed in "Analysis," as also in works before and after, its repressed particularity, like all repressions, finds a way to return.

Still a few anomalous aspects of this note remain to be parsed.

The Roots of the Footnote

Prior to my earlier article the assumption had been that the note's speculation about antisemitism emerged out of the condensation of the thought
of castration and the displaced ethno-religio-racial and sexual identities of
Little Hans and Weininger. Freud had not in his earlier published writings
theorized a genetic (or any other beyond the empirical) understanding of
antisemitism. Yet among the *Nachlass* in the Sigmund Freud Collection at
the Library of Congress is a folder of notes on assorted subjects, the first
page of which bears the rubric *"Aus älteren Aufzeichnungen* von 1897 an"
(from older sketches from 1897 on; the first three words are underscored
in the original). Attached to the second page of the folder is a sheet containing a note entitled *"Eine Quelle des Antisemitismus"* (a source of antisemitism; underscored in the original). It reads: "The fact that anti-
S[emitism] is generated in the nursery [*Kinderstube*] is clear. Irma has a
physical horror of any Jew. When she was a child they said (in Ofen [=
Buda, Hungary]), if there was any trace of *Incontinentia alvi* [fecal inconti-
nence] on a child's vest: the Jew has wiped [*abgewischt*] his mouth on it
again."[72] Aspects of this earlier speculation share much in common with
the later theorization and its accompanying case study, and indeed may
have provided a template for Freud's later thoughts. Both theories share a
common origination for antisemitism in the nursery (*Kinderstube*) and are
a consequence of what was heard rather than seen. And each is generated
through the mediation of a famous patient of Freud's. Since Freud apparently had no patient by the name of Irma at that point in his career, the
"Irma" of this earlier note may very well be one of the women who together formed the Irma of the specimen dream (*Traummuster*): Ilona
Weiss, as I have argued in chapter 2.

   More significant are the remarkable parallels between the components
of *"Eine Quelle"* and the details of Hans's case history. The note from the
folder suggests that anti-Jewish sentiment is tied to the perception of the
Jew's deviant sexuality: specifically annilingus, but the note also implicates
other forms of oral sex, such as fellatio and cunnilingus, as well as olfactory
fetishism exemplarily enjoyed by the (Jewish) *renifleur*.[73] The association
of Jews with dirt and excrement is also clearly invoked. There is a third
field of anti-Jewish representation: the Jew as ass-licker, *Arschlecker*, or the
fawning flatterer, the *Schmeicheler*, of those in power. These elements have
all been picked up in later psychoanalytic and psychological interpretations of antisemitism,[74] and all three of these figures pervade "Analysis."

To English readers of the text the first two—deviant sexuality and excrement—are manifestly, even obsessively, represented.[75] The third is no
less pervasive and is heavily invested with sexual content. Hans manifested
his desire for his mother by "coaxing" with her; for example, "When I
was asleep I thought you [his mother] were gone and I had no Mummy to
coax with." A note adds that "coax" was his expression for "caress," and
the German word translated as "coax" is "*schmeicheln.*" Hans was a ready
Schmeicheler; forms of the term appear at least ten times during the course
of Freud's narrative. Shared by both the Jew figured in the earlier note and
Little Hans, these characteristics would transform Hans into "Itzig"—the
model of the clever, cheeky, and nosy Jewish boy who knows the facts of
life.[76] Given these correlations between the language of the notes, on the
one hand, and between the representations of the Jew and of Little Hans,
on the other, recollection of the earlier note or its accompanying ideas
may well have drawn Freud's attention to a connection between Herbert's
situation and antisemitism.[77]

Yet Freud does not trace the connection along the lines implied by the
note; rather, the nature of the case—like the history of Jewish representation—condenses the panoply of Jewish characteristics upon the circumcised penis. For Freud to have pointed out Hans's Jewishness would have
implicated him in Hans's dilemma because of his earlier counsel; hence
Freud needed to displace the attribution of Jewishness from a property of
the body of the concerned to the imagination of the non-Jew.

There were other factors at work not only in Freud's silence about the
Jewishness of the dramatis personae but also in the descriptive, yet nonetheless oblique, reference to circumcision. As already noted, during this
period in which he was working on "Analysis" Freud was concerned about
any associations between psychoanalysis and Jewishness. The day after
Hans's concluding plumber phantasy (3 May 1908), Freud writes to Karl
Abraham about the value of Jung's association with the Vienna Psychoanalytic Society: "I nearly said that it was only by his appearance on the scene
that psycho-analysis escaped the danger of becoming a Jewish national
affair."[78] Freud's concern is less the membership than the perception of a
particular Jewish character to psychoanalysis.[79] The importance of Jung as
a buffer against antisemitic judgments of psychoanalysis is reiterated in
another letter to Abraham that Freud sends later that year (26 December
1908) as he is about to publish his case history of Little Hans. Afraid that
"Analysis" will create an uproar, Freud wryly comments: "German ideals
threatened again! Our Aryan comrades are really completely indispensable
to us, otherwise psychoanalysis would succumb to anti-Semitism."[80] With

the "defensive din"—antisemitism—of his German readership Freud anticipates a confirmation of the scenario of castration threat and ensuing neurosis played out in the footnote in "Analysis."

Granted that his readership already identifies Freud as Jewish, would overt references to the Jewishness of his patient or an explicit reference to the Jew-associated circumcision (*Beschneidung*) have exacerbated the situation? Curiously, the term does not appear in Freud's published work until after the loss of his Gentile cover—that is, the breakup with Jung. Indeed, it then appears without any direct mention of *Judentum*, as we have seen, in the text that signaled that break, *Totem*.

The da Vinci coda

"Circumcision" does appear in a work written a year after "Analysis," *Leonardo da Vinci and a Memory of His Childhood*, but, as already has been mentioned, that passage was actually added in 1919. The opening sections of *Leonardo* extensively rehearse Freud's earlier arguments from "Sexual Theories" and "Analysis." Setting the stage for Freud's discussion is a notorious mistranslation. In naming the crucial figure in the memory of the essay's title the German translator of Mereschkovsky's biographical novel *Leonardo da Vinci*, Freud's primary source, employed *Geier* (German: vulture) for the *korshun* (Russian: kite) that "opened [baby Leonardo's] mouth with its tail and struck [him] many times with its tail against [his] lips" (11:82). Whereas a kite's tail is just a kite's tail, the mythological associations tied to the vulture proved more conducive to Freud's interpretation of Leonardo's fellatio-suggestive phantasy. Ancient natural historians believed the latter bird of prey only to exist as female; hence the Egyptians employed the figure to symbolize both motherhood and, more significant for Freud, the androgynous (that is, penis-bearing) mother goddess Mut.

Freud extrapolates from this mistranslation-driven phantasy of the maternal penis to an understanding of Leonardo's later development of "manifest, if ideal [sublimated] homosexuality" (11:98) by way of a long discussion of childhood curiosity about "the riddles of sexual life," the belief of the "youthful investigator" in the maternal penis, the obsession with his own penis, and the castration complex that directly and indirectly alludes to Little Hans's experience (11:95–96). When discussing the castration complex Freud brings up the misogyny that in "Analysis" he had relegated to a footnote: "Under the influence of the threat of castration he now sees the notion he has gained of the female genitals in a new light; henceforth he will tremble for his masculinity, but at the same time he will despise the unhappy creatures on whom the cruel punishment has, as he supposes, already fallen" (11:95). It is at this juncture that some nine years later Freud would append the footnote on circumcision and the unconscious roots of antisemitism. Freud then adds one more genetic factor into the mix of interpretations. His argument moves from viewing women as objects of contempt to a much different—yet complementary— relationship. In *Leonardo* Freud first recognizes what he pointedly ignores in "Analysis": the role of maternal identification in the development of homosexuality.

That juncture to which Freud does add the note is a pivotal one. With the following paragraph, Freud initiates his examination of the psychogenesis of "permanent homosexuality" (11:96). While that paragraph does indirectly refer to the case of Little Hans, the case of another patient whose Jewishness was disguised and who no less than da Vinci phantasized about that "familiar symbol and substitutive expression for the male organ" (11:85), the tail, is rather extensively alluded to as well: the Rat Man, Ernst Lanzer.

In the last chapter I suggested that Freud's work with Lanzer influenced his understanding of fetishism in *Leonardo* as well as in the footnote he added in late 1909 to his discussion of fetishism in *Three Essays*. Those allusions to the Rat Man entailed more than mere invocations of *"renifleurs"* and *"coupeurs de nattes"* whom Freud had treated. While I have already commented on the extensive lengths Freud appeared to have gone to in order to avoid any identification of the Rat Man as Jewish, there is a more significant discrepancy between Freud's notes and Freud's "Notes." While the case study of the Rat Man appeared after the recognition in "Analysis" of the significance of the castration complex in the formation of identity, and while the Rat Man's castration fears were discussed and indeed reconstructed by Freud in the extant case notes, which broke off on 20 January 1908,[81] or approximately when Freud received his first anxious report from Herbert's father, no mention of the castration complex makes its way into "Notes."

For example, to the discussion of the phrase "it would be the death of you," with which Lanzer's father's forbade masturbation when the patient was younger than six, Freud adds "and perhaps also threatening to cut off his penis" (10:263). In the case study, Freud reports that his patient had been "castigated" (*gezüchtigt*; 10:205), but makes no inference about a possible threat of castration. That silence is all the more curious, since Freud had just concluded an extended discursus on the relationship between masturbation, especially infant masturbation, and neurosis, in which he emphasized that "the injurious effects of onanism are only in a very small degree autonomous—that is to say, determined by its own nature" (10:202–3). Later in his notes, Freud reports that "the idea of his penis being cut off had tormented him to an extraordinary degree, and this had happened while he was in the thick of studying" (10:264) and suffering from the desire to masturbate (and to murder his already-dead father). Freud and Lanzer also discussed the meaning of the patient's tooth-extraction dream: their associative path moved from "a transposition from a lower to an upper part of the body," the tooth as a symbol for the penis,[82] through the analogy of pulling down (*abreißen*) a branch to the phrase "pulling one down" (*sich einen herunterreißen*), meaning to masturbate. Freud then led him to connect the pulling "down" back to the dentist's "pulling out" (*ausreißen*) the tooth, and from there to the operation of pulling out a rat's tail (*Schwanz*) that Freud then interprets as the desire to get revenge on the father by "pulling out" his penis (10: 315–18). In the margins of his notes Freud wrote "*Castration.*"[83] Incorporating Freud's evident analytic thread about masturbation and castration into the published case history would, one assumes, have provided ample support for his contention of the insufficiency of masturbation alone as a cause of pathology.

This *Operation des Schwanzausreißens* can also be situated in another string of associations in the case notes that Freud does not develop. The notes from several days earlier report, "His mother's hair [*Zopf*, or braid] is now very thin, and while she combs it he is in the habit of pulling it and calling it a rat's tail" ("*Rattenschweif*," in quotes and emphasized in the original; 10:313).[84] This present-day comment is then followed by a recollection, "When he was a child, while his mother was in bed once, happened to move about carelessly and showed him her behind [*Hintern*]; and he had the thought that marriage consisted in people showing each other their bottoms [*Popo*]. In the course of homosexual games with his brother he was horrified once when, while they were romping together in bed,[85] his brother's penis came into contact with his anus" (10:313). That the mention of pulling his mother's braid generated such a recollection may have led Freud a year later in *Leonardo* to articulate his theory of the fetish as a substitutive symbol for a woman's penis, because there Freud writes, "Without knowing it, '*coupeurs de nattes*' ['*Zopfabschneider*,' braid-cutters] play the part of people who carry out an act of castration on the female genital organ" (11:96). In other words, Lanzer is playing out the traumatic encounter with sexual difference that, Freud argues, initiates the castration complex.

Curiously, both Freud's case study and the formal therapy sessions with Lanzer open with the patient's encounters with his governesses' "genitals and lower part of [their] bod[ies], which struck [him] as very queer [*kurios*]" (10:160).[86] Lanzer also recalls observing one governess pressing out "abscesses on her buttocks" (10:161). These fingerings and sightings are accompanied by his account of his "burning and tormenting curiosity to see the female body" (10:160) without therapist's gloss or the usual self-congratulatory confirmation in an adult of what he reported in his recent essays on infantile sexuality.[87] This discussion also marks the only occasion in the case study whereupon Freud mentions homosexuality (specifically, "homosexual object-choices"), and then only in a note tied to the patient's social parapraxis and moment of forgetfulness rather than the subsequent foray into sexual epistemology that, as in the paragraph in *Leonardo* that I suggest above alludes to the Rat Man, threatens "permanent homosexuality" (11:96). Lanzer refers to the governess by her last name, one that happens to be identical to a masculine first name,[88] Peter,[89] rather than, as is customary, by her first name, which he claims to have forgotten. Thus, Freud opened his case study of the Rat Man by setting forth all of the dots, but neglects to draw the line that connects them: namely, the castration complex.

Why, then, does Freud not discuss the castration complex in "Notes"? According to the editors of the *Standard Edition*, "If there are occasional discrepancies between the record and the published case history, it must be borne in mind that the case continued for many months after the record ceased and that there was therefore every opportunity for the patient to correct his earlier accounts and for Freud himself to obtain a clearer view of the details" (10: 255–56). Several other possibilities, however, also suggest themselves. As a number of others have commented,[90] another glaring omission from Freud's case study is more-than-incidental discussion of Lanzer's mother, who does play a prominent role in the original record. A ready argument can also be made for the structural role of the missing mother.[91] Another possibility is that, perhaps not yet confident that he had found the philosopher's stone of human development, both normal and pathological, and not wanting to sound like Johnny One Note, Freud sought to focus on the particularity of each category of neurosis: hysteria, phobia, obsessive compulsion, and so forth.[92]

Then there are the other possibilities mentioned earlier in this chapter: recognizing that every negative quality exhibited by a member of a subjected group is viewed as representative of the group, whereas every positive quality is taken as exceptional, Freud may well have feared that a neurotically obsessive, less-than-virile Jewish man would be viewed as exemplary of every Jewish man. Moreover, Freud may have feared that any universal claims that he would make for his theories about obsessive neurosis or the castration complex could be dismissed as only applicable to Jews. Still, no one ever claimed Leonardo to have been a Jew.

Like Daughter, Like Son

If, as I have asserted, Freud was still concerned in 1910 with distracting his audience from Jewish associations with his work, then despite the extensive rehearsal of his arguments from "Sexual Theories" and "Analysis," the omission of circumcision as well as its relation to castration and antisemitism would be in order. Indeed, discussing the connection among these was as apparently extraneous to the argument in the main body of *Leonardo* as in "Analysis." Given that the addition of the footnote did not provide additional support for his argument, why, then, did Freud insist on appending a footnote about circumcision to the discussion of Little Hans's experience in the reissue of *Leonardo* in 1919? There were events that year such that, through some form of "deferred obedience" (10:35), Freud recognized again the pertinence of the footnote to Little Hans's narrative.

In 1919 Freud was working on his essay on the "Uncanny." His analysis revolves around a topic prominent in the case of Little Hans, namely, the castration complex,[93] as well as includes a long footnote on the male feminine attitude and the identification of a male self with a female (automaton or doll). It also examines two themes that played a role in the return of the footnote: repetition-compulsion and the *Doppelgänger*. More significant, Freud's own professional practice may have elicited from him his own experience of the uncanny, as he had recently taken on a patient whose case he would discuss in " 'Child' " and whose case has definitive echoes of Herbert Graf's. Although the rules of therapeutic practice had changed since 1908—the parent serving as his or her child's analyst, once normative (as witnessed by Max Graf's role in the analysis of his son Herbert), was by 1919 no longer sanctioned—Freud's new patient was his daughter Anna.

Freud's daughter had most likely played a minor role in the account related in "Analysis." Hans's father had successfully employed the mention of the Professor's "very pretty little girl" (10:33) to lure Hans to

Freud's office.[94] This gambit, which would attest to Hans's heterosexual "accesses," opens the section "Weekly Report from Hans's Father." Freud's commentary on the report culminates with the footnote on circumcision. Eleven years later Anna Freud was making her own visits to her father's office. She was troubled by her inability to decide among life options: should she adopt the more traditional female role of teacher, albeit one informed psychoanalytically, or should she follow in the footsteps of her father and become a psychoanalyst? During the course of her analysis she discussed her beating phantasies. In "'A Child Is Being Beaten'" Anna Freud is not mentioned by name; however, the "fifth patient, who had come to be analyzed merely on account of indecisiveness in life, would not have been classified at all by coarse clinical diagnosis, or would have been dismissed as 'psychasthenic'" (17:183), is generally considered to be Freud's daughter.[95] Several years later she would herself write of her own beating phantasies in "Beating Fantasies and Daydreams."

At the outset of his analysis Sigmund Freud describes the generic development of his patients' beating phantasies: "The phantasy has feelings of pleasure attached to it. . . . At the climax of the imaginary situation there is almost invariably a masturbatory satisfaction—carried out, that is to say, on the genitals. At first this takes place voluntarily, but later on it does so in spite of the patient's efforts, and with the characteristics of an obsession. . . . [T]he first phantasies of the kind were entertained very early in life: . . . not later than the fifth or sixth year" (17:179). While the obsessive masturbatory scene and age of the patient resonates with Hans's situation,[96] there are other aspects of her pathology that recall in particular the denials that had shaped Freud's analysis. Freud describes a "complication" that develops among girls who have beating phantasies: "When they turn away from their incestuous love for their father, with its genital significance, they easily abandon their feminine role. They spur their 'masculinity complex' . . . into activity, and from that time forward only want to be boys" (17:191). Despite this masculine identification, such a girl does not, Freud points out almost defensively, adopt either masculine behavior or homosexual object-choice. Indeed, she "escapes from the demands of the erotic side of her life altogether" (17:199) but not from her father (17:200).

The boy, by contrast, "who has tried to escape from a homosexual object-choice, and who has not changed his sex, nevertheless feels like a woman in his conscious phantasies, and endows the women who are beating him with masculine attributes and characteristics" (17:200); indeed, from its onset the boy's unconscious phantasy "is derived from a feminine attitude toward his father" (17:198). Freud emphasizes that *"in both cases, the beating-phantasy has its origin in an incestuous attachment to the father"* (17:198; emphasis in original).

The positions of Herbert Graf and Anna Freud at the time of analysis share much in common. Both are suffering from neurotic symptoms, both are caught in the throes of problems of judgment: in Herbert's case, the epistemic/narcissistic crisis over the existence of the maternal penis; in Anna's, the crisis over masculine or feminine career paths. That is, both were unable to resolve the castration complexes of their respective genders. Both are adopting nonnormative sexualities. And both are attached to their fathers.

In "'Child,'" as in earlier case studies from Leonardo to the Wolf-Man, Freud had recognized males adopting the feminine attitude (what he would later call the "negative Oedipus") that he did not—or could not—note in the case of Little Hans. Yet Freud's investment in Herbert Graf differed from that in his other patients. As with Anna's situation, Freud—as both adopted father and, through Max Graf's procuring, a prospective father-in-law—had to bear some responsibility for Herbert's pathology and sexuality. These pathological and relational parallels suggest that in analyzing his daughter Freud experienced the case of his adopted son *redivivus*. Through deferred action he recognized in Anna's passive masculine identification the passive feminine identification that he had denied observing in Hans (Herbert) in "Analysis."

Hans's return would be played out, however, on another stage. While writing "'Child,'"[97] Freud was also preparing "a second edition of *Leonardo*, the only truly beautiful thing I have ever written," as he relates to Lou Andreas-Salomé on 9 February.[98] To the third section of the *Leonardo* essay Freud makes a curious addition. In that chapter, as noted above, Freud discusses infantile sexual theories and the castration threat with extensive references to Hans's contributions, etiologies of male homosexuality—in particular, the revulsion toward the castrated woman, on the one hand, and identification with the mother, on the other hand—and the repudiation of sexuality. At the moment when enlightenment is achieved about the "uncanny and intolerable idea" of woman's castration, causing the boy to fear for his masculinity and despise those who have lost theirs, Freud adds in 1919 a footnote that offers an "inescapable" but also besides-the-point conclusion. It connects antisemitism to the unconscious equation of circumcision with castration and thereby hearkens back to the case of Little Hans and its no less anomalous footnote.

Deferred Action as Displaced Responsibility

When Freud concludes "Analysis" he argues that "strictly speaking, I learnt nothing new." He goes on, however, to indicate that the analysis has provided "a type and a model." Its typicality and exemplarity lay not in its symptoms but in their formation: "that the multiplicity of the phenomena of repression exhibited by neuroses and the abundance of their pathogenic material do not prevent their being derived from a very limited number of processes concerned with identical ideational complexes" (10:147). And the specific ideational complex addressed by the analysis is the castration complex, which by the end of Freud's career explicitly— but here implicitly—becomes the "bedrock," the foundation of all development.

At the time of the writing, the castration complex had a competitor for primacy: the primal scene in which the child observes parental intercourse. In 1909 Freud still desires the *realia* that had been lost with the virtual abandonment of the so-called seduction theory—that neuroses were the consequence of actual sexual assaults by parental figures during childhood—a decade earlier; he desired that objective, factual, external cause that would justify his science as science. There is contextual evidence for its existence in the Graf residence: Herbert did not leave the parental bedroom until after his sister was born. Explaining Little Hans's neurosis as a deferred effect of witnessing the primal scene would exculpate Freud from responsibility. On the other hand, to claim the primal scene would publicize the sexual indiscretions of a male colleague. In "Analysis" he both acknowledges his suspicion, but allows the colleague first denial: "Hans's father was unable to confirm my suspicion that there was some recollection stirring in the child's mind of having observed a scene of sexual intercourse between his parents in their bedroom. So let us be content with what we have discovered" (10:135–36).

The specific threat of castration does also offer that *realia*. Further, he is able to locate the inciting incident with the mother and not the ever-present, albeit never mentioned, reminder of Freud's advice: by being raised as a Jew, Herbert's identity was ineluctably bound to circumcision. Still, in his final discussion he universalizes the castration complex as a developmental structure; hence, it is not contingent on threat or chance observation. He can again thereby let himself off the hook.

Ultimately despite evidence to the contrary, Freud declares Hans normal: no harm done, no blame taken. Indeed, Hans's adventures in neurotica have been to his advantage. Culminating his analysis, Freud declares (10:143–44):

> I can therefore well imagine that it may have been to Hans's advantage [*heilsam*] to have produced this phobia. . . . It may be that Hans now enjoys an advantage [*hat . . . voraus*] over other children, in that he no longer carries within him that seed [*Keim*] in the shape of repressed complexes which must always be of some significance for a child's later life, and which undoubtedly brings within it a certain degree of deformity of character [*Charakterverbildung*] if not a predisposition to a subsequent neurosis.

In this concluding offer of restitution for the unintended consequences of Hans's unacknowledged "*jüdischen*,"[99] Freud returns to this case's primal scene. In describing the beneficial effects of overcoming neurosis he reiterates his earlier charge to Max Graf: "If you do not let your son grow up as a Jew . . . you will deprive him of those sources of energy which cannot be replaced by anything else. He will have to struggle as a Jew, and you ought to develop in him all the energy he will need for the struggle. Do not deprive him of that advantage." In this concluding narrative overcoming neurosis has accomplished what its genetic cause (that is, being Jewish, an identity mediated by the dispositive "circumcision") was supposed to have done. Freud has been vindicated. Thanks to his struggle (with neurosis) Hans—Herbert—could become a "fighting Jew." In the next chapter, there is no telltale footnote, the transfiguration of which marks the body of the text, to aid my analysis of the role of *Judentum* in Freud's case study of Judge Schreber, but Freud did leave behind something split off, relegated to the margins—marginalia, to be exact—that point to its catalyzing effects.

CHAPTER 5

Freud v. Freud:
Entmannte Readings on the Margins of
Daniel Paul Schreber's
Denkwürdigkeiten eines Nervenkranken

> . . . till near the nucleus [*Kern*] we come upon memories which the
> patient disavows even in reproducing them.
>
> —SIGMUND FREUD, "Psychotherapy of Hysteria"

Before beginning his analysis of Daniel Paul Schreber's memoir *Denkwür-digkeiten eines Nervenkranken/Memoirs of My Nervous Illness*, Sigmund Freud admonishes his "readers [first] to make themselves acquainted with the book" (12:11). Despite this advice, virtually all interpretations of Schreber's dementia over the subsequent seventy years (and most in the quarter-century thereafter) have been based upon Freud's selective citations in his "Psychoanalytic Notes on an Autobiographical Account of a Case of Paranoia (*Dementia Paranoides*)."[1] Displaced by Freud's case study, Schreber's text became thereby the "most-quoted unread book of the twentieth century."[2] This chapter, however, takes Freud's advice quite literally: it reads the markings and marginalia he made in his own copy of the *Denkwürdigkeiten* against the rhetorical strategies by which he constructed his case study. By analyzing the conflicts between those two narratives, I reconsider the methods and motivations of Freud's "Psychoanalytic Notes."

In his copy of the *Denkwürdigkeiten* Freud fixes upon a passage about which his marginalia, the case study, and Schreber's memoirs all pivot. After describing the series of events that led to his mental collapse, Schreber writes: "I must now discuss . . . what in my opinion is the tendency innate in the Order of the World, according to which under certain circumstances the '*Entmannung*' (transformation into a woman) of a human being . . . must result . . ."[3] Freud double-underlined this first appearance of "*Entmannung*" in the memoirs and wrote in the margins "*Kern der Sache*," "the heart of the matter."[4] The revelation of the *Kern der Sache* is the climax of a quest for sources, symptoms, and significance undertaken in the margins of Freud's copy. His comment also anticipates *Entmannung*'s central role in the case study. Finally this initial mention of *Entmannung* concluded Schreber's cosmological and biographical contextualization of his illness as well as heralded the central portion of his memoirs: the ensuing depiction of that "*Nervenkrankheit.*"

The matter of each of these three narratives hinges upon the core meaning of *Entmannung*—yet, as Freud had written of the etiology of hysteria, "It can happen that there is more than one nucleus" (*Kern*; 2:290). The contrasting strategies of the translators of the *Standard Edition* of Freud's works and of the translators of the *Memoirs* mark the opposing fields of meaning that converge on *Entmannung*. Strachey et al. read this term as "emasculation" and correlates it explicitly with both physical and figurative castration. "Emasculation" evokes the castration complex, the matrix of childhood phantasies and theories that leads to the recognition of sexual difference and the interpellation of the child into normative structures of symbolic differences. The "emasculated" Schreber is presented as a devirilized victim of phantasized sexual persecution. By contrast, Macalpine and Hunter, by opting for "unmanning," literalize a more figurative translation of the term in order, on the one hand, to emphasize *Entmannung*'s connection with Schreber's transformation into a reproductive woman and, on the other hand, to de-emphasize its connotation of "sterilization." The choice of "unmanning," by privileging women's necessary activity, here the female-specific capacity to reproduce, questioned the authority of castration as the determinant of difference. The "unmanned" Schreber, for Macalpine and Hunter, is a pregnant Redeemer.[5] "Emasculation" and "unmanning" converge on *Entmannung* in Schreber's text; so do the oppositions between universal theory and normative structures, male epistemology and the female body, homosexuality and heterosexuality, the hegemony of German Christian culture and Jewish identity. Schreber embraces these contradictory representations.[6]

But, as the heart of Freud's matter and possessed by such conflicting meanings, *Entmannung* threatens to undermine not only Freud's interpretation of the Schreber case but also the authority of psychoanalysis and even Freud's self-identity. His deployment of *Entmannung* in "Psychoanalytic Notes," particularly his separation of Schreber's "emasculation" from his pregnancy phantasies, endeavors both to constrain the overdetermination of the term and to elide the mixture of personal concerns and competing theories betrayed by that polysemy. When the divergent strands and curious silences that sometimes characterize Freud's marginal notes to Schreber's discussion of *Entmannung* are read against his emphasis in "Psychoanalytic Notes" upon "emasculation," more seems to be at work than the manifest motivations of the study: an interpretation of Schreber's delusion, an explanation of paranoia, and the promotion of psychoanalysis and its theory. Other matters that may have compromised either Freud's narrative or himself—the roles of bodies and women, homosexual and ethnic identifications—also occupy the margins of his copy.[7] Not unlike the original record of Freud's therapy sessions with Ernst Lanzer (the Rat Man), Freud's marginalia contested and conditioned a case study that sought to conceal its own heterogeneous origins.

After examining how Freud constructed "Psychological Notes" about the core of "emasculation," this chapter explores the alternative etiologies and troubling identifications that arose in Freud's annotations only later to be secreted in the case study. The last chapter examined how Freud sought to screen the Jewish identities of several of his patients and how circumcision and its complement, Freud's transferential phantasy of castration, betrayed those efforts. This chapter finds that the case of Schreber presents a variant on those efforts. Schreber, the former president or chief judge of Saxony's Royal Superior Court, was neither a patient nor a Jew; however, the *Denkwürdigkeiten* does confront its reader with several Jewish personae. The following exploration traces how the readings of one reader, Freud, tried to work through those confrontations. Particular focus is placed upon how Freud's neglect of Schreber's vision of the "unmanned" Eternal Jew (*der ewige Jude*),[8] both in print and in the margins, suggests a relationship between the "emasculated" Schreber's problems with his sexual identity and the circumcised Freud's own concerns about his ethnic identity. *Entmannung* reproduces a Jewish difference Freud would disavow, but that, like all disavowals, will not be dismissed.

Entmannung: *From the Court to Castration*

Freud first read the *Denkwürdigkeiten* in the wake of his discovery of the role of castration in psychosexual development.[9] He had concluded that castration, as little boy's theory and as paternal threat (although in his prime example—the case of Little Hans—the threat originated with the mother; 10:7–8, 35; see also the previous chapter),[10] was necessary to the recognition of sexual difference, the resolution of the Oedipus complex, and the formation of gender and sexual identity, both normal and pathological.[11] And an analysis of the *Denkwürdigkeiten*, since it explicitly discussed fathers, homosexuality, and castration/emasculation, offered him an ideal forum not just for explaining paranoia but also for presenting the truth and efficacy of psychoanalytic theory and method in general.[12]

In "Psychoanalytic Notes" Freud contours his narrative of Schreber's case about two foci: "emasculation" and its necessary concomitant, Schreber's father. Oriented by these topoi, Freud generates an interpretation of Schreber's delusional system in which "emasculation" represents both the key delusion and the key to the germ of his illness: "The enormous significance of homosexuality for paranoia is confirmed by the central emasculation fantasy."[13] Schreber's paranoia, he concludes, originated in the castration complex,[14] the consequent homosexual feelings toward his father, and their repression.

Freud opens his portrayal of Schreber's "Case History" (section 1) with a brief summary from the decision by the Royal Superior Court,[15] over which Schreber had presided at the time of his breakdown, acceding to Schreber's petition for release from Sonnenstein Asylum: "He believed he has a mission to redeem the world and to restore it to its lost state of bliss. This, however, he could only bring about if he were first transformed from a man into a woman" (12:16).[16] The soteriological and gender-crossing strands of the delusions delineated by the Court and echoed in the medical reports then become the guidelines for Freud's initial selection of citations. For the Court, Schreber's belief in his Redeemer role and not his transformation into a woman is primary; further, these delusional topoi are originally interconnected. But in his ensuing presentation of Schreber's system Freud shifts the Court's evaluations of the religious and gender components as well as its understanding of their relationship to one another. Once the initial depiction of Schreber's delusions is completed Freud asserts the opposite, "That the emasculation phantasy was of a primary nature and originally independent of the Redeemer idea" (12:20).[17] Freud's claim here also indicates a more important change in the meaning of Schreber's delusions. That is, his gender switch attains in Freud's presentation a more sexual significance: his delusion that he had been transformed into a woman becomes a phantasy of emasculation (*Entmannungsphantasie*).

Freud's preference for "emasculation" (*Entmannung*) over "transformed into a woman" follows from his recent determination of the castration complex. The consequent emphasis on "emasculation" determines

Schreber as a man who has been demeaned, who has lost his manliness, who has been overcome by homosexual affect. This choice all but obviates Schreber's avowed rationale for his transformation into a woman: the reproduction of the all-but-destroyed human race. Freud emphasizes, instead, an emasculated Schreber who is a resistant victim to a "sexual delusion of persecution" (12:18). This Schreber, reduced to playing the part of a prostitute or "female wanton" (*weiblichen Dirne*; 12:48), looks upon his transformation not as a blessing but as a "disgrace" (*Schmach, Schimpf*; 12:33, 48). This de-emphasis upon Schreber's acceptance of his gender transformation had already been implicit in Freud's selection of the Court excerpt as a summary statement; it omitted Schreber's claimed impregnation by Gd to repopulate the world. Further, in describing Schreber's situation almost solely in terms of *Entmannung* Freud ignores Schreber's use of the term. When he employs *Entmannung*, it is usually in conjunction with a parenthetical phrase that he added to clarify its meaning: "(transformed into a woman) [(*Verwandlung in ein Weib*)]."[18] Freud inverts that formulation: "the idea of being transformed into a woman (that is, of being emasculated)" (12:18). Schreber does not assume a new gender identity; rather in Freud's account normative sexual difference has been rendered problematic as Schreber becomes a feminized man.[19] *Entmannung* signifies his castration, not transformation (cf. 12:56).

The role of the Redeemer also undergoes a subtle shift of significance in Freud's depiction: from his saving relation with the world to his favored relation with Gd. This alteration allows Freud to emphasize the feminine aspect of the Redeemer's relation with the deity. Hence after Freud lays out the "Case History" he sets forth his project of elucidating Schreber's delusion: "In Schreber's system the two principal elements of his delusion (his transformation into a woman and his favored relation to God) are united in his assumption of a feminine attitude towards God. It will be a necessary part of our task to show that there is an essential *genetic* relation between these two elements" (12:34). In this formulation the relationship among the elements of Schreber's delusional system as determined by both the Court and the doctors has been transformed: the transformation into a woman is not just the formal cause for redemption, a mere albeit bizarre accident; rather, now understood as emasculation, it has become the final cause as well. Schreber becomes Redeemer in order to redeem his desire to be emasculated. And his emasculation is the realization of a wish: his assumption of a feminine attitude toward Gd.

In the next section of his case study Freud argues how Schreber's deluded emasculation, as the icon and index of the castration complex, would mediate the "essential genetic" relationship between Schreber's "transformation into a woman and his favored relation to God." Prior to concluding the "Case History," however, Freud proffers an image that exemplifies how "emasculation" dominates all aspects of his argument. Freud adds that either he demonstrates the nature of this relationship, "Or else our attempts at elucidating Schreber's delusions will leave us in the absurd position described in Kant's famous simile in the *Critique of Pure Reason*: we shall be like a man holding a sieve under a he-goat while someone else milks it" (12:34). By referring to this passage from Kant, Freud potentially identifies himself with an "incautious listener" who offers "absurd answers" to the propounder, here Schreber, of a question that "is absurd in itself and calls for an answer where none is required."[20] The logical implication, then, is that if Schreber's delusions are meaningless, Freud's interpretation is equally and embarrassingly so. But Freud is also evoking a rhetorical, if not strictly logical, implication. If Schreber's delusions have a meaning—and the meaningfulness of symptoms is presupposed by psychoanalysis—then the "essential genetic relation" theorized by Freud is the key to that meaning.[21] The context of Kant's simile further supports Freud's rhetorical intent: Kant is giving his "nominal definition of truth [as] the agreement of knowledge with its object." Freud, too, is making such claims about psychoanalytic theory and its objects: the neuroses and psychoses.

Yet for all of its desired rhetorical effects, Freud's choice of image is very curious. This gender-bending figure underscores the significance of understanding Schreber's gender transformation as emasculation. Thus in this simile Schreber assumes the position of one who cognitively mistakes the he-goat for a she-goat and—this is implicit to the notion of milking a male—physically emasculates him by pulling on his penis. The implications of this image for Freud and psychoanalysis are perhaps even more striking. On the one hand, it foregrounds emasculation as primary for his specific task of interpreting Schreber's delusions and for the general project of psychoanalysis: namely, the essential genetic role of the castration complex. On the other hand, it suggests that if Freud were unable to locate the etiology of Schreber's dementia, then Freud (and psychoanalytic theory), like the psychotic Schreber, would be unable to recognize appropriate sexual identities and their development. Rather than providing a theory that can explain all of the vicissitudes of sexual difference, psychoanalysis would fall victim to its own misrecognitions, and the alternative etiologies of his Leipzig psychiatric rivals, whether anatomy for Schreber's first psychiatrist, Paul Flechsig, or degeneration for the prolific author of pathographies and other monographs Paul Julius Möbius, would gain ascendancy.[22] Consequently, the significance of Freud's ensuing attempts at interpreting Schreber's delusional system extends beyond resolving his particular case or even generating a general theory of paranoia. What is at stake is the universality of the castration complex and the normative sexual difference that it maintains.

A Compelling Case for the Father

Having apparently milked the *Denkwürdigkeiten* of all the pertinent facts, Freud proceeds to secure their meaning. In his "Attempts at Interpretation" (section 2), Freud undertakes a series of brilliant rhetorical moves, among them the insertion of new material and the strategic omission of old material from Schreber's text. Finally, he reveals that Schreber's psychosis was an effect of his defense against the return of his repressed passive homosexual feelings toward his father. By the time Freud presents this conclusion, his compelling attempts render his interpretation—and the truth of psychoanalysis—seemingly self-evident.

First, Freud sets up the necessary conditions for his own efforts at interpretation. He had already undertaken a polemical differentiation of psychoanalysis from psychiatry with regard to the understanding of psychosis (12:17–18; cf. 12:43).[23] At the beginning of the second section Freud praises the previous interpreters of Schreber's delusional utterances—Jung and Schreber himself. The mention of Jung reinforces the authority of psychoanalytic interpretation over psychiatric. It was as the author of a treatise on psychosis—and Schreber—"Psychology of Dementia Praecox" (1907),[24] which Freud here describes as providing a "brilliant example" (12:35) in the interpretation of psychosis, that the psychiatrist Jung was so warmly brought into the fold in 1907.[25] Freud then proceeds to demonstrate the efficacy of the psychoanalytic method for interpreting such data. Satisfied that he can generate interpretations just as viable as those of the other practitioners, Freud wishes to distinguish himself (and psychoanalysis) from them. They are, according to Freud, caught up in Schreber's delusional effects without investigating the exciting causes. He also applies this diagnosis to a former member of his psychoanalytic circle: Alfred Adler. Schreber's feminization and his depictions of submission and domination evoked for Freud Adler's theory of the masculine protest.[26] Yet if the phenomenon of protest seems to confirm empirically Adler's theoretical counter to Freud's etiological primacy of sexuality, within Freud's case

study Adler's theory is subordinated to the role of footnote, and his conclusions are shown to invert the causal sequence. Schreber's protests
against his feminization come amid his dementia; they do not initiate it
(12:42 and note 2).

While bemoaning the absence of sufficient information on Schreber's
family to provide an explanation for his illness[27]—"In working upon the
case of Schreber I have had a policy of restraint forced on me by the
circumstance that the opposition to his publishing the *Denkwürdigkeiten*
was so far effective as to withhold a considerable portion of the material
from our knowledge—the portion, too, which would in all probability
have thrown the most important light upon the case . . ." (12:37; cf. 12:12,
45–46)—Freud returns to the case history to seek out those causes. He
asserts that he can base his interpretation almost exclusively on his reading
of the *Denkwürdigkeiten* because of the nature of paranoia. Since paranoi-
acs "possess the peculiarity of betraying (in a distorted form, it is true)
precisely those things which other neurotics keep hidden as a secret . . . it
follows that this is precisely a disorder in which a written report or a
printed case history can take the place of a personal acquaintance with the
patient" (12:9).

Yet, he returns neither to the wealth of Schreber citations he produced
in the first part of his paper nor to the medical reports, which he also
excerpted. Rather, to help determine the source of Schreber's dementia
Freud "now mention[s] a further element in the case history to which
sufficient weight is not given in the reports, although the patient himself
has done all he can to put it in the foreground. I refer to Schreber's relation to his first physician, Geheimrat Prof. Flechsig of Leipzig" (12:38).
Flechsig had been the presiding physician during Schreber's first breakdown and subsequent hospitalization that followed his unsuccessful run
for the Reichstag in 1884, and it was to Flechsig that Schreber returned
following the onset of the second attack.[28] With the emergence of Flechsig
into the foreground of his presentation, Freud prepares the way for Schreber's father. But first, after juxtaposing Schreber's persecution phantasies
about Flechsig both to a reiteration of his reverie of being a woman submitting to intercourse and to his statement of gratitude for Flechsig's earlier efforts, Freud boldly asserts: "The exciting cause [of his collapse],
then, was an outburst of homosexual libido; the object of this libido was
probably from the very first his physician, Flechsig; and his struggles
against this libidinal impulse produced the conflict which gave rise to the
pathological phenomenon" (12:43). Freud moves to quell the "storm of
[anticipated] remonstrances and objections" (12:43) to these claims with a

series of not-previously-cited passages from the *Denkwürdigkeiten*, including Schreber's fears of sexual abuse and his assertion that "what especially determined [his] mental breakdown"[29] was a night with six nocturnal emissions (12:45).

Amid this parrying with imagined interlocutors Freud addresses the issue of why at that particular moment Schreber became subject to a serious mental illness. Initially, Freud suggests that the fifty-one-year-old Schreber may have attained his "climacteric" and, by implication, the end of his capacity to reproduce (12:46). This curious resort to somatic rather than psychological causality will return in another guise once Schreber's concerns about reproduction can be safely nested in the father complex and separated from any necessary connection with his transformation into a woman (cf. 12:57–58). But at this juncture of Freud's narrative, discussion of Schreber's delusions of impregnation is avoided because of their connection to *Entmannung*, and Schreber's father has not yet assumed the central role he is destined for. Consequently, the matter is aborted.

Freud then returns to answer the doubts of his imagined opponents about the role of Flechsig in the sudden emergence of Schreber's paranoia. And here the father makes a brief, anticipatory appearance. While details from the *Denkwürdigkeiten* may quiet questions about the etiology of Schreber's personal pathology, Schreber's particular object of desire, his physician, presents a problem. His choice of Flechsig threatens to mark as potentially perverse one of the fundamental relationships in a masculinist society governed by a regime of (medical) expertise: that of the male patient with his doctor.[30] The transformation of Schreber's friendly relations with Flechsig into their opposite, Freud suggests, may be explained by the "transference" (12:47).[31] By invoking the transferential relationship between doctor and patient, Freud calls upon his own variant of the classic dramatic device deus ex machina: the *pater* ex machina. Flechsig thus becomes a surrogate for someone who is not there: the dead father. And here Freud quotes from Schreber's report to the Court: "The memory of my father and my brother . . . is as sacred [*heilig*] to me as . . ." (12:47).[32] The dead father silences all objections: "We shall therefore raise no further objections that the exciting cause of the illness was the appearance in him of a feminine (that is, a passive homosexual) wish-phantasy, which took as its object the figure of his physician" (12:47).

After this apparent conclusion Freud, rather than leaping to a discussion of the genetic mechanism of paranoia, makes a leap of faith; that is, he discusses the displacement of Schreber's affections from Flechsig to Gd. When the dead father returns, his irreplaceability must be secured.

Only after showing both that the particular characteristics of Schreber's Gd are compatible with the information Freud has available about Schreber's father (and fathers in general) and that another member of the series of Gd-identified figures, the sun, can, despite German grammar (*die Sonne*),[33] be a symbolic father substitute does Freud write: "Thus in the case of Schreber we find ourselves once again upon the familiar ground of the father complex" (12:55).

Once the father is firmly in place as the sun of Schreber's paranoid cosmology, the various strands of delusional material become accessories, like the ray-like ribbons with which Schreber used to adorn himself as he would prance half naked in front of the mirror,[34] to his relationship with his father. His father, Daniel Gottlob Moritz Schreber, was a leading nineteenth-century physician and pedagogue—he developed a series of appliances to teach and maintain, among other things, good posture.[35] He is perhaps best known from the so-called Schreber Gardens.[36] Consequently, the tie between Schreber's transformation into a woman and his being impregnated by Gd for the reproduction of the race arises from its earlier relegation to a footnote (12:32n1)[37] and submits to the law of the patronym: Schreber desires to continue the family name. Since Schreber's marriage had been childless and since he may have attained his climacteric, the "family line threatened to die out. . . . [Hence] Schreber may have formed a phantasy that if he had been a woman he would have managed the business of having children more successfully; and he may thus have found his way back into the feminine attitude towards his father" (12:58). Similarly, once both "'emasculation'" and the desire to reproduce are embraced by the father complex, Schreber's phantasies of world catastrophe, which in the *Denkwürdigkeiten* are tied to both unmanning and reproduction, can be disentangled from that particular knot and then positioned within the general theory of paranoia (12:68–71).

Freud provides a compelling argument; all of its threads, like so many Schreberian "sun's rays . . . nerve-fibers . . . spermatozoa" (*Sonnenstrahlen . . . Nervenfasern . . . und Samenfäden*; 12:78), seem to converge on the equation of Gd and father. Freud has apparently deflected all of the posed objections to his argument. And he has engaged his readers in a quest-narrative that requires a successful resolution. Moreover, Freud quotes so extensively from the *Denkwürdigkeiten*—he emphasizes that all of his interpretations are based upon verbatim quotations (12:11)—and expresses such apparent respect for Schreber's intelligence (cf. 12:35, 79),[38] that his Schreber and the Schreber of the *Denkwürdigkeiten* seem to be coextensive. Psychoanalytic theory and the facts of the case appear adequate to one another.

Freud's Ellipsis and Alternative Etiologies

The force of Freud's presentation is illustrated by an encounter I had with several colleagues, who had just completed reading Freud's paper. They expressed their anger toward Schreber over his virtual neglect of his wife in the *Memoirs*. In their conflation of Freud's quote-laden depiction of Schreber with the narrator of the *Denkwürdigkeiten*, Ottilie Sabine Schreber fell into Freud's ellipsis. That is, when, as discussed above, Freud prepares to shift from Schreber's relationship with Flechsig to that with Gd, and thereby to the identification of Gd with his father, he cites a passage from Schreber's appeal to the Court: "The memory of my father and my brother . . . is as sacred [*heilig*] to me as . . ." (12:47). Beyond providing rather weak evidence for Freud's hypothesis of the transference at work in Schreber's relationship with Flechsig, the passage associates the father with sacrality—with divinity. (Schreber never explicitly makes this connection in his published memoirs.) In addition to preparing the reader for the apotheosis of the father, Freud also omits a reference to Schreber's wife. The full passage reads: "The memory of my father and my brother *as well as the honor* [*die Ehre*] *of my wife* is as sacred to me as *to anyone in similar circumstances who has the reputation* [*der gute Ruf*] *of his near relatives at heart.*"[39]

Omission of Schreber's concern for his wife's honor and reputation is reasonable within the specific context in which Freud cited this passage. Within the larger contexts of his argument for the role of the father and the castration complex as well as homosexuality in paranoia the omission of Schreber's wife might also be understandable. Beyond responding to specific narrative and theoretical demands,[40] the restored ellipsis also suggests that like the Kantian simile even Freud's punctuation underscores the significance of "emasculation" by functioning as a performative symbol of castration: it cuts out the castrated one, woman.[41] But this ellipsis does not merely figure, in the words of Jacques Derrida, a "double invagination";[42] it acts as such. *Entmannung*, which, according to Schreber but not Freud, "consisted in the (external) male genitals (scrotum and penis) being retracted into the body,"[43] as it were folds back upon itself. That is, this hole in Freud's text, through which Schreber's own text appears, leads not only to the *Denkwürdigkeiten* but to Freud's marginalia as well. In order to understand the role of the ellipsis, it becomes necessary to draw on more than the elided passage. Freud's other text on Schreber, his marginalia to the *Denkwürdigkeiten*, offers another interpretive perspective both on the ellipsis and the passage that frames it. Beyond insight into Freud's strategy of citation, pursuing the implications of this ellipsis and its frame provides access to the myriad concerns that constellate about Freud's preoccupation with *Entmannung*.[44] Bringing the *Denkwürdigkeiten* and Freud's accompanying marginalia to bear on Freud's discourse of "emasculation" unmans it.

JEALOUSY

Specifically, by omitting Schreber's wife, Freud also effaces alternative etiologies of Schreber's psychosis. Although "emasculation" and its implications—father complex, homosexual wish-phantasies and their repression, delusions of persecution, narcissism—dominate the construction of Freud's narrative, his marginalia call attention to other possible etiological factors and/or symptoms of Schreber's paranoia that are largely ignored in the case study. At the top of the page in which Schreber records his reverie about being a woman enjoying intercourse,[45] Freud writes: "*Aetiologie d[er] Erkrank[un]g* [etiology of the illness]." Such a comment is consistent with the case study; however, this reverie is not the only passage on the page that caught Freud's attention. He doubly emphasizes the first few lines of that page, which read: "My wife felt even more sincere gratitude and worshipped Professor Flechsig as the man who had restored her husband to her; for this reason she kept his picture on her desk for many years." In the case study Freud cites this passage initially to demonstrate that Schreber had long been married (12:12) and later to exemplify "the original cordiality of [Schreber's] feelings towards the physician who had treated him so successfully" (12:42). But in the margins of the *Denkwürdigkeiten* Freud writes "*Eifersucht* [jealousy]." Jealousy certainly plays a significant role in the initial interpretation of the Schreber case that he communicated to Jung:[46]

> I have fathomed the secret. The case is easily reduced to its nuclear complex. His wife falls in love with the doctor and keeps his picture on her writing-desk for years. He, too, of course, but in the woman's case there are disappointments, attempts to have children are unsuccessful; a conflict develops; he ought to hate Flechsig as his rival, but loves him thanks to his predisposition and the transference from his first illness. The infantile situation is now complete, and soon his father emerges behind Flechsig.

Although the presence of Schreber's wife is not obscured in this letter by an ellipsis, even here the manner in which Freud presents this material certainly detracts from any possible role for Schreber's relationship with his wife in the etiology of his illness. Nonetheless, Freud apparently did not wish to give fodder to his opponents or even broach the possibility of a nonmale mediator between Schreber and his father by even discussing the wife's catalytic role.[47]

SYPHILIS

Schreber's relationship with his wife may have provided still another contributing cause of his dementia, and the key to this alternative also appeared on the page that Freud crowned with *"Aetiologie d[er] Erkran-k[un]g."* On that page Freud jots down *"kinderlos* [childless]" next to Schreber's regret about "the repeated disappointment of our hope of being blessed with children."[48] Both in the marginalia and in the case study Schreber's childlessness is emphasized. While Freud did not have access to the medical reports of Schreber's first institutionalization that connect his wife's miscarriages with possible syphilitic infection,[49] it was a truism of the time to suspect syphilis in cases of repeated miscarriages or stillbirths.[50] Did Freud surmise that Schreber may have suffered from some organic ailment like syphilis?

Freud quotes Dr. Weber's testimony (12:13) that Schreber complained of *Hirnerweichung* (softening of the brain) when he committed himself the second time. At the time softening of the brain was a frequent euphemism for syphilis-caused progressive paralysis.[51] Similarly many of the "miracles" that Schreber's body underwent find themselves described in the medical textbooks of the time as indications of constitutional syphilis.[52] What Freud considers to be Schreber's identification with a prostitute—he writes *"Prostitut[ion]"* in the margin next to Schreber's fear that his "body, after the intended transformation into a female being, was to suffer some sexual abuse, particularly as there had even been some talk for some time of my being thrown to the Asylum attendants for this purpose"[53]—could be just as much a reaction to the acquisition of syphilis from a prostitute as to his own reputed and repudiated homosexuality. Freud also emphasizes in the margin Schreber's account of how he built a wall to protect Gd's realms against "an advancing yellow tide: I related this to the peril of a syphilitic epidemic."[54] Schreber's syphilis or his fear of having syphilis could both elucidate Schreber's insistence on the connection between "emasculation" and reproduction as well as undercut Freud's theory of

Schreber's climacteric. While neither an organic complaint nor a phobic reaction would necessarily contradict Freud's interpretation, they would not support it either. Is Freud fearful of history repeating itself? Just as a family history of syphilis placed a shadow over his exemplary case of psychoneurotic hysteria, namely that of Dora,[55] syphilis, or the fear of syphilis,[56] may have colored the etiology and symptomology of Freud's paradigmatic paranoid psychotic. This question cannot be definitively answered. None of Freud's letters of the time even broaches the possibility. Still some fifteen years later in *Inhibitions*, Freud connects syphilis—or rather syphilophobia—with castration in such a way as to recall the case of Daniel Paul Schreber: "Thus, for instance, a man may retain his fear of castration in the guise of a syphilophobia, after he has come to know that it is no longer customary to castrate people for indulging their sexual lusts, but that, on the other hand, severe diseases may overtake anyone who thus gives way to his instincts" (20:148).[57]

INCEST

It is not only the ellipsis that secretes an alternative cause for Schreber's dementia; its frame does as well. The "passage in which the patient sets these doubts [about Flechsig's surrogacy] at rest: 'The memory of my father and brother . . .'" (12:47) seems self-evidently to anticipate Freud's eventual conclusion of the importance of the father complex—and to foreclose Schreber's possible incest with a sister as a possible etiological factor. But first, to follow the intrepid Freud's "prolonged search through the pages of the *Denkwürdigkeiten* [until he] came at last upon" this passage restores those doubts—if not necessarily about the transferential relationship or the father complex,[58] then certainly about Freud's selection of quotes. The *Denkwürdigkeiten* seemed to provide for Freud clear confirmation of the truth of psychoanalysis's discoveries about the father and castration complexes. Thus, as soon as the sun is mentioned Freud connects it with the father by remarking, "*Sonne als Symbol[isierung] Gottes Vaters* [sun as symbol of Gd the Father]."[59] And adjoining Schreber's discussion of the state of blessedness achieved after death, Freud writes, "*die Seligkeit (Todter Vater)* [bliss (dead father)]."[60] The latter annotation would seem to be the product of Freud's second reading of the text at the earliest, however, since Freud claims to have had no knowledge of Schreber's family prior to reading the *Denkwürdigkeiten*. Moreover, the first suggestion that Schreber's father was in fact dead at the time of his son's illness occurs some eighty-four pages later. There Schreber refers to "his father's soul."[61] This passage also happens to be the first time in the published memoirs that Schreber mentions his father—as Freud himself noted in the margin: "*erstes Auftreten* [first appearance]." Freud, however, does not comment upon, or even cite, this passage in "Psychoanalytic Notes."

Freud's clear awareness of the earlier appearance of the dead father in the *Denkwürdigkeiten* renders dubious his claim to have had to undertake a prolonged search to discover the dead father.[62] Consequently, Freud's selection of the later passage about the "memory of his father *and brother*" (emphasis added) suggests that it was as important to introduce the brother as it was the father. The emergence of the brother manifestly served at least two functions; less evident is a third. First, his appearance allowed Flechsig to be positioned within the family constellation as the brother (cf. 12:50) after Schreber breaks off his (transferential) identification of Flechsig with Gd in order to allow his father alone to assume that position.[63] Second, it allowed Freud to evoke once again the connection of Schreber and homosexuality by implying Schreber's possible homosexual feelings toward his brother. The latter rationale for resurrecting the dead brother may have had an added motivation: it also "breaks off" the pursuit of the role of incest in the etiology of Schreber's illness. That is, just before Freud begins the discussion in which Schreber's father and brother make their first appearance, he attempts to understand Schreber's feminine attitude toward Gd. To that end he pursues the "thread" of soul murder to Schreber's invocation of Byron's *Manfred*.[64] When Schreber mentions *Manfred* in the *Denkwürdigkeiten*,[65] Freud queries in the margin "*Schwesterinzest?* [sister incest?]"; however, in the case study Freud remarks that the "essence" (*der Kern*) of the poem is *Geschwisterinzest*, which is translated as "incestuous relation between a brother and a sister" (12:44).[66] By opting for the more general term (lit. "sibling incest"), Freud chose a more sexually ambivalent term, since *Geschwisterinzest* need not be exclusively heterosexual. Although Schreber had four sisters, Freud does not pursue the possibility—cannot, because, as he remarks in a phrase evocative of castration: "And here our thread breaks off short" (*reißt . . . ab*; 12:44)—at which point Freud follows another line that takes him to Schreber's brother and homosexuality. The lack of biographical data may be responsible for the abrupt end of his speculations. How much family information Dr. Stegmann made available to Freud is unknown, although it is reasonable to assume that the issue of *Der Freund der Schreber-Vereine*, celebrating the centenary of Schreber *père*'s birth, that Freud received (12:51n1) would have mentioned all of his children. Freud may be both resisting brother-sister incest as a competing explanation as well as reinforcing the importance of Schreber's homosexuality, because for Freud the *Kern* lies elsewhere—in "emasculation."

Der Kern der Sache

Freud explored alternative etiologies or contributing causes of Schreber's paranoia—jealousy, syphilis, incest—in the margins of the *Denkwürdig-keiten*. Women's acts, their bodies, and "their" diseases threaten the explanatory authority of the castration complex in all cases, not just Schreber's. But these alternatives never surface as such in the case study. In "Psychoanalytic Notes," "emasculation" remained the primary delusion and the key to Freud's understanding of the causes of Schreber's dementia. Yet when Freud's response to Schreber's discussion of *"Entmannung"* is pursued along the margins of his copy, certain aporia appear that may affect the understanding of his study. Freud's marginalia respond to an *Entmannung* whose conflicting meanings threaten to undermine its own central role. The "heart," the "nucleus" (*Kern*) of Schreber's case and of psychoanalysis seems to be split. Unwritten annotations that appear like cracks in his commentary—empty margins amid the plethora of notation—signal a shift in the significance of "emasculation." The object of analysis begins to incite Freud's subjective identifications and evoke his social situation. *Entmannung* divides the analyst from himself,[67] and Freud emerges as an emasculated Jew.

When *Entmannung* first appears in the *Denkwürdigkeiten*,[68] Freud, as already mentioned, double-underlines the term and writes *"Kern der Sache"* in the margin. But placed against this assertion and the narrative trajectory in which it is situated, his later responses to Schreber's discussion of *Entmannung* appear aporetic. The *Kern der Sache* had emerged as the climax of a narrative seeking sources and sexual references. In lieu of the excised biographical detail, Freud sought possible sources of Schreber's delusions in his literary references. When Schreber mentions a work of literature, the margins of Freud's copy read *"Quelle* [source],"[69] and occasionally *"Reaktion auf Lektüre* [reaction to reading]."[70] When the middle name Fürchtegott repeatedly appears in Schreber's genealogy of his and Flechsig's families, Freud queries: *"Leipzig? (Christian Fürchtegott) Gellert? Hinweis auf Quelle* [indication of source]."[71] In these literary allusions Freud also sought clues to reconstruct the psychosexual source of Schreber's illness. Thus, as noted above, Freud queries *"Schwesterinzest?"* following the mention of *Manfred*.

Freud also attended to more explicitly sexual references. Anticipating the revelation of the *Kern der Sache* Freud had underlined, emphasized in the margins, and/or annotated all suggestions of sexuality or phantasies of feminization (*"w. Ph."*[= *"weibliche Phantasie"*]).[72] Thus he heavily emphasizes Schreber's self-comparison with the Virgin Mary and underlines his comparison of male sperm with divine nerves. After Schreber describes divine nerves, Freud notes *"Ursprüngl[iche] sexuelle Natur der Nerven* [original sexual nature of the nerves]."[73] Freud exclaims *"Secret! Sexuell,"* next to the censored passage "on the essential nature of soul murder or, so to speak, its technique."[74] Schreber's reverie about how nice it would be "to be a woman submitting to the act of copulation" is doubly emphasized and marked *"fem[inine] Ph[antasie]."*[75] And just prior to the first mention of *Entmannung*, Freud doubly emphasizes Schreber's description of his night of six emissions. Freud also notes in the margin and at the top of the page, *"Homosex[uell]!"* and *"Beweis f[ür] Homosex[uell]* [proof for homosexuality]," respectively.[76]

All of these passages are cited in the case study; yet all are deformed by the requirements of the soon to be revealed *Kern der Sache*: *Entmannung* and its consequential homosexuality. Thus, for example, when Freud invokes Schreber's self-comparison with the Virgin Mary, Freud refers to her as "God's wife" (12:32) and not, as Schreber describes her, the mother of Jesus Christ. Where Schreber's designation clearly emphasizes her reproductive capacity, Freud's terminology privileges (conjugal) sexuality. In other words, Freud again severs the connection between Schreber's transformation into a woman and reproduction in order to maintain the authority of castration.

"It can happen that there is more than one nucleus"

Just as the narrative of Freud's marginalia reaches a climax with the revelation of the *Kern der Sache*, the emergence of " *'Entmannung' (Verwandlung in ein Weib)"* at the end of Schreber's fourth chapter both concludes Schreber's own history of his illness up to his collapse and heralds the central portion of his memoirs. The recognition of this "tendency innate to the Order of the World," that is, of being " 'unmanned' (transformed into a woman)"—as well as the other symptoms he mentions here, inner voices and compulsive thinking—marks a shift in the narrative.[77] All that had preceded provided a frame and a series of contexts for the depiction of his *"Nervenkrankheit."* Chapter 5 begins the account of that nervous illness. Schreber describes voices from outside, obsessive thinking, and the struggle for domination among nationalist-religious groupings of souls, consisting of Catholics and Germans, (baptized) Jews and Slavs. He then proceeds with his vision of the end of the world and in its wake the necessary transformation of the last man into a woman in order to save the order of the world. According to this vision (*Vision*):[78]

> Perhaps God was also able to withdraw partially or totally the warmth of the sun from a star doomed to perish . . . ; this would throw new light on the problem of the Ice Age. . . . In such an event, in order to maintain the species, one single human being was spared—perhaps the relatively most moral—called by the voices that talk to me the *"Eternal Jew."* This appellation has therefore a somewhat different sense from that underlying the legend of the same name of the Jew Ahasver; one is automatically reminded of the legends of Noah, Deucalion and Pyrrha, etc. Perhaps the legend of the founding of Rome belongs here also. . . . The Eternal Jew (in the sense described) had to be *unmanned* (transformed into a woman) to be able to bear children. The process of unmanning consisted in the (external) male genitals (scrotum and penis) being retracted into the body and the internal sexual organs being at the same time transformed into the corresponding female sexual organs, a process which might have been completed in a sleep lasting hundreds of years. . . . A regression occurred therefore, or a reversal of that developmental process which occurs in the human embryo in the fourth or fifth month of pregnancy, according to whether nature intends the future child to be of male or female sex. It is well known that in the first months of pregnancy the rudiments of both sexes are laid down and the characteristics of the sex which is not developed remain as rudimentary organs at a lower stage of development. . . . I have myself twice experienced (for a short time) the miracle of unmanning on my own body, as already mentioned in footnote 1 . . .

Most curiously, in this first, and indeed most extensive, discussion of the rationale for and technique of *Entmannung* to follow its revelation as the *Kern der Sache*, Freud's copy is unmarked. Freud does underline the tie of "moral decay" (*sittliche Fäulnis*) and "nervousness" (*Nervosität*) to the destruction of the world.[79] This connection reappears in the case study to confirm Freud's notion that moral repugnance toward homosexuality is one of the motors for repression (12:30–31 and note). Freud also marks the appearance of the gods Ariman and Ormuzd as sort of gender toggles: the former "emasculating" the Eternal Jew and Schreber, the latter restoring his masculinity.[80] And Freud notes how those miraculously created human forms that Schreber calls "fleeting-improvised-men" (*flüchtig hingemachte Männer*) take care of the Eternal Jew.[81] Both the gods and the "fleeting-improvised-men" are also discussed in the case study—although Freud only cites from among their other appearances in the *Denkwürdigkeiten*. Thus, while the rationales and delusions that frame the vision are noted, the entire discussion of the Eternal Jew—his "emasculation," its purpose, the procedure, the tie to embryology—is ignored both in the margins and in the case study. Instead when Freud focuses upon Schreber's phantasies of world catastrophe, Freud invokes (12:68–69) other mentions of world destruction.[82] He does mention the glaciation of the world, but without providing a page reference.

Why would Freud, who up until this chapter had been anything but reluctant to mark up his copy of the *Denkwürdigkeiten*, ignore what appeared to confirm the significance of *Entmannung*? Several possibilities suggest themselves.[83] For instance, *Entmannung* is not identified with *Kastration*, an act of cutting or loss—according to Schreber the penis is, as it were, preserved, only invaginated. Second, Freud may have found the embryological argument of innate androgeny or bisexuality (asexuality) problematic on several grounds. Freud had repudiated heredity as the sole determinant of sexuality.[84] In a development related to this theoretical concern, Freud is beginning to argue at this time against theories of repression (and psychosis is at this point an effect of repression) based on bisexuality, whether by his former colleague Adler, who does appear in the case study, or by his former friend and confidante Wilhelm Fliess.[85] Fliess, in particular, had adopted the embryological argument in order to ground bisexuality in biology.[86]

The Fliess connection suggests a third, and perhaps more significant, rationale for the empty margins: Freud was disavowing his lingering homosexual affect for Fliess,[87] as well as his consequent fear that he, too, had been "emasculated." Although Fliess is never explicitly mentioned in the case study or in the marginalia, the editors of the *Standard Edition* note the continuing influence of Fliess's theory of periodicity (12:46n1) when Freud curiously emphasizes Schreber's age. More pertinent, Fliess had embodied for Freud the connection between paranoia and homosexuality. In a 1908 letter to Jung, Freud wrote "My one-time friend Fliess developed a dreadful case of paranoia after throwing off his affection for me, which was undoubtedly considerable. I owe this idea [of paranoia caused by the repression of homosexuality] to him, that is, to his behavior."[88] Hence it is not surprising that while engaged on the Schreber case Freud would re-encounter his allegedly worked-through homosexual affect toward Fliess. After returning from the trip during which he read the *Denkwürdigkeiten* Freud wrote to Ferenczi that "this need [for intimacy with colleagues like Ferenczi] has been extinguished in me since Fliess's case, with the overcoming [of which] you just saw me occupied. A piece of homosexual investment has been withdrawn and utilized for the enlargement of my own ego. I have succeeded where the paranoiac fails."[89] Fliess returns in the letter announcing the completion of the "Psychoanalytic Notes": "I have now overcome Fliess, which you [Ferenczi] were so curious about. Adler is a little Fliess *redivivus*, just as paranoid."[90]

Although the earlier letter to Ferenczi suggests that Freud's homosexual affect toward Fliess had been "overcome" prior to preparing his "Psychological Notes," a letter to Jung written two days after the later letter questions that impression. The Jung letter also puts in doubt whether that affect was indeed ever overcome.[91] Speaking of his "fleetingly improvised" (*flüchtig hingemacht*) work—an intentional reference to Schreber—Freud comments: "I am unable to judge its objective worth as was possible with earlier papers, because in working on it I have had to fight off complexes within myself (Fliess)."[92] Perhaps the fear that the allegedly worked-through affect was merely repressed and that the distinction between his own work and that of the paranoiac may not be so clear-cut motivated the silent margins just as it seemed to motivate his famous conclusion to "Psychoanalytic Notes." After asserting that he arrived at his theory of projection prior to reading the *Denkwürdigkeiten*, Freud half facetiously poses a question to those who come after: "It remains for the future to decide whether there is more delusion in my theory than I should like to admit, or whether there is more truth in Schreber's delusion than other people are as yet prepared to believe" (12:79). Concerns about his interchangeability or identification with paranoid, repressed homosexuals are clearly evident in Freud's encounter with Schreber.

The necessary connection between impregnation and "emasculation" in Schreber's "vision" presented another problem for Freud. As discussed above, Freud severs reproduction from its context in the *Denkwürdigkeiten* and delays the mention of this wish-phantasy until the conclusion of his explication of the causes of Schreber's delusions. There he ties the childless Schreber's phantasy of becoming a childbearing woman to his desire, as the apparently only surviving son, to extend the family line despite having reached his purported climacteric. Hence the desire to reproduce, to provide a (grand)son for his father, becomes yet another expression of his feminine attitude toward his father. Opponents might argue instead that the delusion of "emasculation" is a logical outgrowth of the necessity for the last man to reproduce humanity: how else could it be reborn? More pointed, to have cited this passage may have undercut both the genetic role of "emasculation" and its indexical relationship to castration; it may have undercut the castration complex, the function of which is to produce subjects, not *re*produce them.

In addition to the theoretical, personal, and rhetorical reasons for avoiding this passage, ethnic and political reasons may also be at play. Schreber's vision of the Eternal Jew suggests an antisemitic dimension to his delusions. The figure of the Eternal Jew has obvious negative connotations for Schreber; hence to justify the moral stature of his visionary creation, as well as to maintain his vision of redemptive life rather than death,[93] Schreber adds that "this appellation has therefore a somewhat different sense from that underlying the legend of the same name of the Jew Ahasver." Freud is quite aware of this aspect of Schreber. In Schreber's earlier discussion of the chosenness of the Germans,[94] Freud writes in the margin "*chauvin[istisch]*." And bearing perhaps additional testimony of Freud's sensitivity to antisemitism and antisemitic representations, the only nonexplicitly castration-like hypochondriacal symptom that Freud underlines in Schreber's chapter about "bodily integrity damaged by miracles" is the "Jew's stomach" (*Judenmagen*),[95] which replaced Schreber's "healthy, natural" one.[96] Calling attention to Schreber's tendency toward antisemitism would have confirmed the role of the castration complex in Schreber's dementia that Freud had noted less than two years earlier in the footnote to "Analysis" (discussed in the last chapter). For the neurotic (and the psychotic) antisemite the imagined-as-circumcised Jew is "emasculated."

Yet to assert any connection between antisemitism and Schreber's paranoia would have had a number of negative consequences. First, Freud desires to construct a universal theory, and to tie psychosis to the particularities of German politics rather than to universal human development would undercut his intentions. Second, for the Jewish Freud to call attention to Schreber's antisemitism might be perceived as special pleading and would undermine his authority as a spokesperson for universal science. Combining these first two concerns is a third feared consequence: that discussion of this passage would confirm the allegation that psychoanalysis was a "Jewish national affair,"[97] not a universal science. Finally, for Freud to call attention to an "emasculated" Eternal Jew would have recalled the phantasized "emasculation" of all male Jews—their assumed circumcision. Any discussion would have contributed to the regnant associations of Jews with effeminacy and deviant sexuality, on the one hand, and with mental illness, on the other, that have been noted throughout this volume. It might also have reinforced an identification with the emasculated that the Jewish Freud had been endeavoring to disavow.

Freud's inability—refusal?—to recognize Schreber's identification with the Eternal Jew further substantiates this contention. Although in the *Denkwürdigkeiten* Schreber never explicitly identifies himself as the un-manned Eternal Jew, his account suggests otherwise.[98] Schreber records a delusion that he, like the Eternal Jew, was the last human alive:[99] "During the latter part of my stay in Flechsig's Asylum [early 1894] I thought this period [the last 212 years allotted the earth] had already expired, and therefore thought I was the last real human being left, and that the few human shapes whom I saw apart from myself . . . were only 'fleeting-improvised-men' created by miracle." Similarly, Schreber describes his body in the process of being transformed into a female body at this same time. Later,[100]

> I could see beyond doubt that the Order of the World imperiously de-manded my unmanning, whether I personally like it or not, and that there-fore it was common sense that nothing was left to me but to reconcile myself to the thought of being transformed into a woman. Nothing of course could be envisaged as a further consequence of unmanning but fer-tilization by divine rays for the purpose of creating new human beings. My change of will was facilitated by my not believing at that time that apart from myself a real mankind existed; on the contrary I thought all the human shapes I saw were only "fleeting and improvised."

Freud's marginalia distances Schreber from such an identification by situ-ating his assumption of a redemptive role, his "*Größe* [megalomania]" in a later passage. There Schreber wears a Christ-like *Strahlenkron* (crown of rays) and is called the *Geisterseher* (seer of spirits, which Freud under-lines).[101] Finally, when in the "Psychoanalytic Notes" Freud allows Schreber's text to testify to the connection between unmanning and repro-duction, he draws from a much later passage and situates it in a footnote (12:48n1).[102] Since, as suggested above, Freud was concerned about a cer-tain affinity with Schreber, Schreber's identification with a non-Jewish Eternal Jew may have drawn him and Freud, who also identified himself with a variety of Jewish and non-Jewish cultural heroes, concluding late in his life with Ahasuerus, the Wandering Jew,[103] closer together. Ultimately, by refusing to recognize Schreber's identification with the Eternal Jew, Freud substitutes an "emasculated" Schreber for an "unmanned" Jew.

Charles Bernheimer has shown how castration not only provided a the-ory for Freud's understanding of fetishism, but for how castration had also become a fetish for Freud's understanding of theory.[104] As discussed in chapter 3, above, in Freud's final theorization of fetishism, the fetish is described as an overvalued symbolic substitute that simultaneously disavows and acknowledges the sexual difference instituted by the resolution of the castration complex. If castration is a fetish, for what does it symbolically substitute? This chapter has shown how the "heart of the matter," *Entmannung*, which Freud reads as an icon and index for the castration complex, dominated both Freud's narrative construction of "Psychoanalytic Notes" and his reading practices of the *Denkwürdigkeiten*. As Bernheimer suggests, Freud's fetishized theory of castration might well be, in its allegedly shared phantasy of an originary universal maleness that half of humanity lose and the other half fear to lose, a male "bastion" against the gender difference it would purportedly acknowledge, a "fortress" erected to supervise and orient all within its purview.[105] The polyvalence of *Entmannung*, however, undercut Freud's rhetoric of "emasculation." By situating Freud's case study against both Schreber's text and Freud's marginalia, this chapter has examined how alternative etiologies and threatening identifications along the margins of Freud's copy often contested the authority of "emasculation" (castration) as an explanatory principle of individual development and a structuring principle of social relations. The most striking of these contestations—Freud's silence about the "unmanning" of the Eternal Jew—may indeed reflect a certain fetishistic logic. Whereas Freud's jottings elsewhere in the *Denkwürdigkeiten* demonstrate a cognizance of a certain antisemitic tendency in Schreber's delusions, Freud ignores the site where castration and a Jewish referent converge. While in his case study of the Rat Man, Freud elided—disavowed—the explanatory value of castration, by the time of the Schreber essay, castration was becoming fixed as what Freud would later call the "bedrock" of psychoanalysis. Consequently, theorizing the phantasy of castration might be a symbolic substitute for his disavowal and acknowledgment of not just gender difference but of an ethnic/racial difference that in early-twentieth-century Europe would have questioned the scientific claims of psychoanalytic theory and jeopardized the professional status of the psychoanalytic movement. This phantasmatic construction of a universal complex that interpellated the (male) subject into society transfigured circumcision, the dispositive that mediated the institutional and discursive antisemitism that would deny his own claims to subjecthood.

CHAPTER 6

From *Männerbund* to *Urhorde*:
Freud, Blüher, and the *Secessio Inversa*

In *Totem and Taboo* Sigmund Freud endeavored not only to reconstruct the origins of religion but also those of socio-political life. Out of threads of British colonial ethnography (Atkinson, Darwin, Lang, Robertson Smith, Spencer and Gillen, Westermarck) and their French interpretations (Durkheim, Reinach), Freud manifestly wove together his narrative of the primal horde (*Urhorde*), the murder of the father by the band of brothers, and its consequences.[1] Upon this evolutionary patchwork *Totem* would read the Oedipus complex and its uncanny companion, the castration complex—Freud's double algorithm of individual development and desire within the nuclear family—into the origin of human culture.

This chapter argues that the warp and woof that structures Freud's tapestry of human history is less the confluence of British imperialism, French theory-production, and Austrian bourgeois social norms than the entanglement of the gendered, sexed, and ethnic position of this son of *Ostjuden* living and writing in the metropole with a particular strand of argument that emerged out of the enthusiasm and *Männerphantasien* (male fantasies) surrounding Germany's late-nineteenth-century colonial adventures:[2] Hans Blüher's sexualizing of the ethnographer Heinrich Schurtz's theories about the foundation and governance of the state by male associations.[3]

Despite devastating critiques by anthropologists of his "just-so story" (18:122),[4] Freud remained until the last stubbornly convinced of its truth.[5] Yet as the tale traversed his corpus from *Totem* to *Moses*, Freud would continually tinker with the relationships within the band of brothers, especially with the role played by homosexuality. The changes in Freud's depiction of homosexuality in his accounts of social origins—the increasingly sharp distinction between homosociality and homosexuality,[6] which ultimately culminated in the foreclosure of homosexuality from Freud's narrative of origins—may be connected with the antisemitic, *völkisch* turn of *Männerbund* (male-band) theories as well as the racialization of homosexual identities. In the wake of both Blüher's writings and the loss of Germany's overseas colonies, some postwar German ideologues and ethnographers recolonized their tribal past with homogeneous communities led by cultic bands of male warriors, while others endeavored—far too successfully—to restore those idealized *Männerbünde* (male bands) in the present. Moreover, Blüher's work facilitated the public dissemination of a racial typology of homosexualities: the opposition between the healthy inversion characteristic of manly Germanic men and the decadent homosexuality of effeminate Jews.

Overdetermined Origins

Writing *Totem*, like so many other psychical acts, was overdetermined. For Freud this story of beginnings was meant also to signify an end—and indeed ensured one. He wrote to his colleague Karl Abraham that his study would "cut us off cleanly [*reinliche abzuschneiden*] from all Aryan religiousness [*arisch-religiös*]" associated with what he refers to as the *Abfall*—politely translated as "secession," although either "apostasy" or "offal" would have been more accurate—of Zurich, namely, of C. G. Jung.[7] By this public performance, this removal of (as well as from) useless leavings rather than that other allegedly dirty cutting off, circumcision (*Beschneidung*), would distinguish psychoanalysis—and its unsaid qualifiers, Jewish and scientific—from Aryan-religious analytic psychology. It did. Further, as some have noted, Freud's account of the primal horde with its violent and jealous father, with its band of parricidal sons, with its guilt-motivated apotheosis of the paternal *imago*, may well be said to characterize the psychoanalytic movement of the time.[8] Others have taken a different biographical tack and posited Freud's own ambivalent relationship to his father.[9] Still others have also indicated that rather than tracing the origin of social life, he was backdating the bourgeois family of his own day.[10] In this last endeavor Freud joined with the vast majority of ethnographers and social thinkers who viewed kinship ties—and naturalized familial roles—as the crucial form of social organization of tribal societies (*Naturvölker*).[11] They further considered the paternalistic family as both the culmination of those societies' evolutionary development and the foundation of modern European (*Kulturvölker*) civil life.

Freud's exercise in genealogical construction was, however, perhaps less the blind bourgeois tendency to universalize its historical norms than the no-less-unconscious attempt to legitimize both his own position as a postcolonial subject and that institution of socialization and identity formation,[12] as well as of refuge,[13] the family, which was under siege.[14]

Faulting the Feminizing Family

In discursively acting out his position within the dominant order, Freud sought to defend not only his place there, but that order itself. As Freud was preparing his first major foray into societal origins, the bourgeois family was going largely unchallenged in ethnographic and historical discourses; however, its political significance was being contested throughout Central Europe. The contradictory changes that this region experienced as the long nineteenth century was coming to an end—industrialization, bureaucratization, urbanization, increasing commodification, technological change (especially in transportation and communication), women's emancipation, nationalism, the decline of liberalism amid the rise of mass politics, as well as the perception of demographic decline, feminization,[15] syphilization,[16] and enervation—led to a revolt of sons (and daughters) against the fathers,[17] against the old order. In crepuscular Vienna not only was the legitimacy of the family in question, so was that of the paternalistic state: because "the family is the germ-cell [*Keimzelle*] of the state."[18] In a society in which conventional identities were emptied of their assumed essences and values, in which traditional elites were countered by mass politics, and in which rational morality competed with nonrational violence, the state was viewed as nothing but sterile convention, hierarchy, and constraint.[19] Critiques proliferated. Alternatives were propounded.

In *Totem* Freud was not just responding to the crisis by anchoring the family in the origin of human society, he was also responding to an alternative notion of the political that emerged amid the confluence of the newly self-conscious youth culture and several other new powerful male-exclusive social formations in Germanophone Central Europe:[20] the friendship circle about Kaiser Wilhelm II, the homosexual orientation of which was a public secret until Maximilian Harden's articles transformed it into a public scandal;[21] that other friendship circle about Benedict Fried-laender, the self-proclaimed elite of manly men who pursued *eros uranios* and formed the Greek-miming *Gemeinschaft der Eigenen* (community of the special);[22] the circle of poets, critics, and idolizers surrounding Stefan Georg; and the ultra-virile community of colonial entrepreneurs (who after World War I and the loss of the colonies was matched by the *Frei-korps*, who shared frontline experience of trench warfare).[23] Within these romanticized communities of male comrades organized about charismatic leaders, perhaps best exemplified by Hans Blüher's admittedly tendentious history of the individual circles (*Horden*) of the *Wandervogelbewegung* (the German youth movement),[24] the (antibourgeois and antifeminist) notion of the male band as the foundation of the political began to be theorized as the counter to the woman- and Jewish-coded family held responsible for both the bureaucratic anonymity of modern public life and the "feminization" of social life.[25] In particular, the development of the (homo)sexualized, and later racialized, version of the *Männerbund* initially disseminated by *Wandervogel* (member of the youth movement) Hans Blüher, may help explain the persistent return of Freud's construct of the primal horde throughout the rest of his writing life.

Correspondences

While writing *Totem* Freud was engaged in an extensive epistolary debate and an exchange of writings with Blüher over the nature of homosexuality and its role, in particular, in the German youth movement and, by extension, in social formation.[26] The then twenty-three-year-old Blüher was one of the leading thinkers of the German youth movement and theoretician of the role of homoeroticism in male groups; he would soon add philosopher, psychiatrist, and author of a series of anti-Jewish (and antifeminist) tracts, including *Secessio Judaica*, which argued for the severing of the Jews and their corruptive and carnal modes of thinking from Germans, Germany, and German culture,[27] to his list of credits. During their exchange, Blüher moved from effusive paeans to Freud in public article as well as private letter, to contributions to several Freud-aligned—and non-aligned—psychoanalytic journals, to the publication of an open letter detailing his dissent from Freud's understanding of homosexuality, and finally, after contact between the two men had been severed, to the denunciation of the "decadent," "Jewish-liberal conception (*Kulturanschauung*)" of inversion that, to his mind,[28] psychoanalysis had come to exemplify.[29]

In his initial contact with the father of psychoanalysis, Blüher notes that his recent encounter with Freud's writings was for him a "true illumination."[30] He was particularly moved by "'Civilized' Sexual Morality and Modern Nervous Illness," in which Freud first speculates on the relationship between sexual life and stage of cultural development, specifically on "progressive [instinctual] renunciation in the course of the evolution of civilization" (9:187). Both Blüher and Freud would continue to examine this relationship, but what most struck Blüher about Freud's essay was how he determined, and then distinguished between, two forms of "developmental" displacement of the reproductive function, two nondegenerate deviations from the cultural norm: perversion and inversion (or homosexuality). As he had in the first of his *Three Essays*, Freud argued in "'Civilized' Sexual Morality" that neither perverts nor inverts form a degenerate group of individuals separated from the rest of humanity, but rather represent a variant of sexual aim or object that all human beings at some point in their development, consciously or unconsciously, desire (7:55–56n1; note added in 1915).[31] Just as significant for Blüher, by distinguishing inversion from perversion Freud relieved homosexuality from the medico-moral onus that still clung to the term "perversion." Moreover, while Freud argues that psychoneurosis is the negative form of perversion, he makes—at this juncture—no corresponding neurotic determination of inversion. Rather than a degeneration from the evolutionary pinnacle that is modern civilization, homosexuals are "often distinguished by their . . . special aptitude for cultural sublimation" (9:190).[32] Not only do they creatively contribute to the progressive development of society, but homosexual behavior may itself be a consequence of the development of "civilized" sexual morality. Modern European society supports the suppression of all forms of the sexual instinct except for the purpose of reproduction and then it is only permitted within the confines of a legal marriage; consequently, "a blocking of the main stream of libido has caused a widening in the side-channel of homosexuality" (9:201).

Not only does Blüher commend Freud's refusal to classify inversion as either a perversion or a sign of degeneration, but also adds that he understands why Freud's writing on inversion vacillates between pathological and nonpathological, negative and positive, categories—Freud speaks of "people suffering from inversion" and of inversion as a developmental stage that is overcome: as a physician Freud was more concerned with disturbed individuals, more concerned with discerning causes of the disturbance and viewing manifest behaviors as symptoms of something else. Nonetheless, Blüher's own experience of nonsublimated inversion in its culture-promoting role suggested that Freud's theory could no doubt think through that, too. To that end he also sought to enlist Freud in helping him secure the publication of the third volume of his history of the *Wandervogel*, *The German Youth Movement as an Erotic Phenomenon*, which specifically addressed the sexual structure of this "clearly inverted social complex."[33]

In response Freud was rather guarded with respect to Blüher's judgment of homosexuality. He notes that the negative side is more worthy of attention. Freud defines that negative aspect as impotence with women. Blüher makes the point in his subsequent letter to Freud that for non-neurotic inverts, impotence with women is unimportant since their psychosexual orientation is exclusively toward men. It is only when they despise and attempt to suppress their orientation that neurosis arises. More significantly, although Freud did recommend Blüher's work to another psychoanalysis-friendly publisher, he informed Blüher that any word from him (Freud) to his publisher Deuticke about printing a volume addressing the theme of homosexuality would meet without success.[34] The sexual inquisition unleashed by the Harden-Eulenburg-Moltke *contretemps* continued to ripple throughout German and German-speaking society.

Freud became the first outside Blüher's immediate circle to receive the third volume. In the letter accompanying the manuscript, Blüher hopes that it will overcome the differences in judgment between himself and Freud and that Freud would realize that Blüher's work would fill a gap in his (Freud's) theory of sexuality. And as in his first letter, Blüher adorns his supplements to Freud's theory with the most effusive praise of the "honored master," whom Blüher credits with crystallizing his own work.[35]

Freud returns the compliment by extending his respect for Blüher's work on the youth movement.[36] Blüher's contention that the German male youth movement entailed a revolution against the rule of the fathers (*Väterkultur*) appeared to comport with Freud's own working-out of the once-and-future social conflict between generations in the writing with which he was then engaged: *Totem*. Freud strenuously disagreed, however, with aspects of the second component of Blüher's analysis of the youth movement: his particular characterization of the movement as an "erotic phenomenon." While Freud described what he had read as "much more intelligent than most of all the literature from the homosexual community and more correct than most of the medical literature"—outside of Freud himself—he takes issue with Blüher's argument that the persecutors of homosexuals in the German youth movement are neurotic, repressed homosexuals who project their own struggles with their sexual inclinations by attacking the openly homosexual members of the movement. Repressed they may be, but they are not neurotics, returns Freud, who reserves this honor for those who are among the persecuted. He sends Blüher a copy of the Schreber case study to demonstrate his point.[37] Freud does express relief when Blüher confides to him that he (Blüher) does not consider himself an invert: "By the way it pleases me to hear that you no longer count yourself among the inverts, because I have seen little good from them."[38] Yet while the same letter reveals bourgeois homophobia or, echoing "'Civilized' Sexual Morality," Freud's pragmatic recognition that prospects for an open homosexual in 1912 were very limited and that his (Blüher's) life would be extremely difficult,[39] Blüher's evangel of inversion was ground for debate and not for either dismissal or derision. Freud was usually willing to admit into his circle an initially errant acolyte who represented fields and groups previously indifferent or resistant to psychoanalysis, confident that he could guide the would-be convert to adopt the true line, and thereby allow psychoanalysis to colonize these new regions.[40] In his 1933 lecture "Explanations, Applications, and Orientations," Freud confides, "In every [disciplinary] region there is a growing number of people who study psycho-analysis in order to make use of it in their special subject, and in order, as colonists to replace the pioneers [*als Kolonisten die Pionere abzulösen*]" (22:145).[41]

Versions of Inversion

While homosexuality at this point in Freud's theorization was held to be conditioned by fixation at an earlier stage of development,[42] for Blüher inversion was inborn. Unlike the *Zwischenstufentheorie*, or theory of intermediate (sexual) types (that is, the Third Sex), propounded by Magnus Hirschfeld and his supporters, whose Jewishness Blüher would in later writings readily note as if to imply some connection among effeminacy, decadence, and Jewishness,[43] the authentic invert was not the often physiologically hermaphroditic effeminate male (*invertierten Weibling*) depicted by Hirschfeld (in Blüher's terms, the "homosexual"),[44] but the manly man (*der Männerheld*, or hero of men).[45] These heroic men are socially and sexually oriented toward other men; concurrently, these charismatic inverts are the idealized object of male desire. In this characterization Blüher was following the lead of Benedict Friedlaender and, before him, Gustav Jaeger and his notion of the "supervirile man."[46]

Blüher also posited a third type, the latent homosexual, who unconsciously struggled against this tendency with the consequential neurotic reaction of becoming a persecutor of inverts—or, conversely, as in the case of Judge Schreber, of becoming a paranoiac. Blüher would designate both latent and feminine homosexuality as pathological conditions; "normal [homosexuality] in the ancient sense" is by contrast "thoroughly healthy."[47] By 1913 in the conclusion to his "Three Fundamental Forms of Homosexuality" (a copy of which he had sent to Freud),[48] effeminacy is ultimately delineated as less an inborn possibility than an effect of decadence. Blüher would argue that effeminacy—as the characteristic form of inversion in the Roman Empire—is a form of decadent homosexuality that grows out of racial mixing (*Rassenmischung*), inbreeding (*Engzucht*), and misery (*Verelendung*).[49] Hirschfeld, the editor of the *Yearbook for Sexual Intermediate Types* (*Jahrbuch für sexuelle Zwischenstufen*), in which Blüher's long essay was slated to be published, insisted that this passage and the concluding two pages in which it appeared, be expunged. Later this characteristic sexual life of a society in decline would come to be qualified as Jewish—"the 'decadent portion' of the Jewish race."[50]

Unlike the Third-Sex theorists, Blüher does not propose a multitude of genders, but instead a spectrum of sexual practices and relationships from friendship to genital sex engaged in by manly men. More to the point, inversion is not about genitality but about love and respect, "the affirmation of a man based upon his worth."[51] Inversion is about the relations among authentic, responsible, idealistic men. It is a universal (male) disposition, not an extravagance of nature. For Blüher inversion (as opposed to homosexuality) is not a sign of degeneration; rather, it is a manifestation of men's sexual-social talent for socializing and state building. Erotic relationships (as opposed to either kinship or mechanical [for example, economic and/or political] ties) determine male alliances. Inversion is not effeminization; it is neither an identification with the mother nor an assumption of a passive attitude, as Freud sometimes theorized.[52] The invert is a virile agent. The space of his activity is the only "productive social form": masculine society (*männliche Gesellschaft*) or the male band (*Männerbund*). According to Blüher, all previous theoreticians of the state who derive the monarchy, and hence the state, from the institution of the family are making superficial analogies.[53] The sole purpose of the family, that product of the heterosexual drive component of men's fundamental bisexual nature,[54] is the reproduction of the species.[55]

While Freud, for his part, recognized that homosexual desire—which he modeled after heterosexual desire—is a component of human bisexuality, homosexuality remained a stage to be worked through, overcome, avoided via fetishism, or sublimated. Homosexuality is derivative and not original, but neither was it to be ignored. Further, where Freud located the reproduction both of the species and of individual identity in the family, Blüher separated these two processes: male identity forms in masculine society largely through identification with the nonpaternal *Männerheld.*[56] In sum, Blüher biologizes gender and sexual difference rather than, according to Freud, effecting it as either a developmental process or a product of the economy of desire: male libido turned toward men in the absence of women. Rather than a force for individual development, homosexuality for Freud disrupts or closes off advancement—unless it is sublimated. These disagreements between Freud and Blüher were irreconcilable.[57] To accept Blüher's theory would have forced Freud to abandon (or at least seriously modify) his construction of both homosexuality and the dynamics of the primal horde/brother band (*Brüderband*): Oedipus would be dethroned and perhaps replaced by his father, Laius,[58] or worse.[59]

So against Blüher's implicit alternative narrative of homosexual social development Freud endeavors to isolate any necessary role for homosexuality—it becomes epiphenomenal not generative. Although in his initial discussion of the primal horde in *Totem*, Freud suggests that the band of *expelled* brothers may have been held together by homosexual feelings and acts, ultimately he distinguishes their homosocial bonds from homosexual attraction when he reminds the reader not to forget that it was hate of the father, not affection, that led to the parricide; they share a fraternal tie based on not treating one another as the father. Homosexual desires are not as powerful as potentially fratricidal heterosexual ones; Freud posits the institution of the law of incest to prevent heterosexual rivalry and preserve the brother band after the murder of the father because "[hetero]sexual desires do not unite men but divide them" (13:144). Then, as his genealogy of religious development progresses, the formation of the family in patriarchal society restores the fundamental structure of the primal horde.

Freud next discusses the primal horde in the once-lost metapsychological paper, "The Overview of the Transference Neuroses." In the surviving draft, Freud attempted to tie the development of particular neuroses phylogenetically with particular stages in the historical development of humanity. He elaborated further on the homosexual relationship among the excluded sons. Unlike *Totem*, the later work explicitly connects social feelings with sublimated homosexuality: living together had to bring the brothers' social feelings to the fore and could have been built upon homosexual sexual satisfaction. Further, Freud contends, "it is very possible that the long-sought hereditary disposition for homosexuality can be glimpsed in the inheritance of this phase of the human condition. The social feelings that originated here, sublimated from homosexuality, became mankind's lasting possession, however, and the basis for every later society."[60]

Of course, Freud does recognize a few problems with his theory, and in order to resolve them he once again boxes out any generative role for homosexual desire. For example, unless they have triumphed over the father and gained possession of the women, "the psychological condition of the banished sons, bound together in homosexuality, cannot influence the next generations, for they die out as infertile branches of the family. . . . But if they do achieve this triumph, then it is one generation's experience that must be denied the necessary unlimited reproduction."[61] In other words, that generation of brothers, once having renounced women and found their sexual satisfaction with each other, remain fixated in their homosexual stage of development and, as a consequence, remain impotent with women. Freud gets around this reproductive bottleneck through the youngest son, who, thanks to the protection of his mother, avoids castration; he, too, suffers the vicissitudes of the male sex, is tempted to renounce women and leave the horde, but does not. Although at that stage he was disposed toward homosexuality, he neither realized this possibility nor remained fixated at that stage; homosexuality as an inherited disposition then is propagated through his descendants. Thus, while Freud can explain how humanity survived, he still begs the question of how these dispositions were genetically passed on.[62]

Sources

When Freud read Blüher's *Youth Movement*, he was no doubt struck by the extensive use the author made of his theories.[63] He was the source for many of Blüher's psychological assumptions; in particular Freud's theories of bisexuality, repression, and neurosis provided Blüher with a way of understanding the persecutors as repressed homosexuals.[64] His employment of Freud indeed led several reviewers in Austrian *Wandervogel* journals to attack Blüher and contributed to others questioning his German identity. Such remarks as "Hey, is Blüher a Jew?" and "Blüher's book is sick. There is something like a struggle between the German race and another! This one may not forget," were printed.[65]

These responses to Blüher's work were not surprising since the youth movement had become increasingly racially polarized. Perhaps leading the way were the groups in Austria: they included an Aryan paragraph in their Krems convention of 1913: "We do not want the Slavs, Jews, or French [*Wälsche*] in our ranks." Karl Fischer, the former leader of the *Wandervogel* in whose defense Blüher was most vociferous, argued for a separate Jewish organization that expressed "Semitic culture." Other prewar symptoms include the 1912 Zittau case, in which a Jewish girl was refused membership because, it was argued, the *Wandervogel* was a "German movement" that had no use for Jews; another was the 1913 publication of Friedrich Wilhelm Fulda's *German or Nationalist: A Contribution from the Youth Movement to the Race Question*. Siegfried Copalle, one of the founders of the movement, later wrote that even when not so manifestly antisemitic, the youth movements were very much influenced by the radical right, antisemitic media of the time. For example, the recommended reading list of the youth movement paper, *Deutsche Zeitung*, excluded Jewish and Catholic writers as well as those cosmopolitans Goethe and Schiller, but included Theodor Fritsch's *Catechism for Antisemites*.[66] The antisemitic works of Paul de Lagarde, Paul Langbehn, and Houston Stewart Chamberlain were standard reading among *Wandervogel*.[67] Another *Wandervogel* journal, *Führer Zeitung*, asserted that "the *Wandervogel* is neither a depository for old boots formerly worn by flat-footed [Jews] and stinking of garlic nor is it an object of speculation for Jewish enterprises."[68] In the second volume of his history of the *Wandervogel*, Blüher remarks how many members identified themselves with the values embodied in Langbehn's *Rembrandt as Educator* and figured themselves as Rembrandt-Germans. Blüher also notes Fischer's desire to separate German and "Semitic" youth movements.[69]

While these and other racial discourses would eventually have a greater influence on Blüher's writing, they were not absent from *Youth Movement*—for Freud was not the only source for Blüher's conception of inversion. While writing that work Blüher was distilling the fruits of his own experience of the youth culture as embodied by the *Wandervogel*, of the rampant homophobia generated by the Harden-Eulenberg-Moltke scandal, of the subsequent purge of any suspected homosexual members of the *Wandervogel* (which Blüher chronicled in his history of the movement),[70]

and of discipleship under Benedict Friedlaender as well as continued reading of his works, especially *The Renaissance of Eros Uranios*, after his mentor's early death at age forty-four in 1908.

Friedlaender's influence on Blüher's early work is clear—as the accusation of plagiarism by Friedlaender's intellectual heirs might attest.[71] Similar to the later elaboration by Blüher,[72] Friedlaender distinguished
between the female family sphere and the exclusively male socio-political
sphere founded upon male-male sociality. Friedlaender sought validation
of his theories of innate male-male attraction in the practices of both ancient Greece and tribal groups (*Naturvölker*):[73] that is, societies that did
not suppress the male's natural instinct for friendship with other males.
Friedlaender explained the presence of this in a tropismatic characteristic
of human physiology that Gustav Jaeger before him proposed as grounded
in the perception of aromas, or what Friedlaender preferred to call "chemotaxis."[74] Friedlaender asserted that not only are homosexuals attracted
to the olfactive emissions of other homosexuals and are repulsed by the
scent of women but that male-to-male chemotaxis occurs in all men; it
is only his repulsion from women that distinguishes the invert from the
heterosexual. Still following Jaeger, Friedlaender considered the natural
repulsion of Europeans toward those internally and externally colonized
peoples, the Jews and the Africans, as the exemplary instance of chemotaxis.[75] Thus the stereotype of the *foetor Judaicus*, or Jewish stench, is
grounded in physiological truth; Jews smell different because they are different. Beyond the descriptive level, Friedlaender also followed Jaeger in
his antipathy toward Jews, although the extremely misogynistic Friedlaender justified his aversion on what he perceived as the Jewish feminizing
influence on society as well as his belief that the inflated status of women
and the prohibition against male-male love were racially Jewish institutions. Moreover, for Friedlaender the Jewish family sense reinforced that
bourgeois institution.

Friedlaender also transformed Jaeger's notion of the supervirile male
into the homosexual *Männerheld*, the hero of men. Thus, in contrast to
Hirschfeld's depiction of the homosexual as an effeminate male, Friedlaender's determination of the invert was a manly man, the most exemplary of
which was that *Männerheld*, the charismatic leader about whom the group
of men, both inverted and not, were oriented. When detailing his understanding of the role of inversion in male groups Blüher readily appropriated Friedlaender's conception of the manly hero of men. Further
echoing Friedlaender, Blüher argued that the family (as the product of the
heterosexual drive) was in no way the basis for state formation; rather, the

state was founded on homosexual drives.[76] He concluded that inversion, attraction toward the charismatic *Männerheld*, is the organizing principle of society.

In "Three Basic Forms of Homosexuality," published with an open letter publicizing his disagreements with Freud over homosexuality just prior to the appearance of the latter's *Totem*, Blüher elaborates further on the sources for his understanding of the role of male associations in the formation of the state. That essay, among other provocations, acknowledges Otto Weininger—who, since the 1903 publication of his misogynistic and antisemitic *Sex and Character* and subsequent suicide, had been, as discussed earlier,[77] a problematic figure for Freud—along with the aforementioned antisemites, Jaeger and Friedlaender, as contributors to that understanding. At this juncture Freud discontinued their correspondence.

Soon thereafter the anti-Jewish implications of Blüher's theories (already suggested by his references to those three predecessors) became manifest. Even in the earlier *Youth Movement* Blüher noted that the membership of the youth circles (*Horden*) "strongly emphasized German racial type."[78] As new editions of Blüher's work appeared during the 1910s, his depiction of the healthy inversion of the *Männerbund* increasingly borrowed from the rhetoric of German racialism and *völkisch* ideology. Thus, as opposed to Germanic inversion Blüher would pejoratively categorize the homosexuality of so-called *weibliche Männer* (effeminate men) as the decadent-Jewish type; eventually the evaluation of psychoanalysis shifted from a form of enlightenment to the Jewish mimetic translation of Christian confession and penitence—and mimesis was far from a favorable quality for Blüher.[79]

Blüher's sources for his "Three Basic Forms" were not limited to Freud or various acknowledged and unacknowledged anti-Jewish writers; he also cites, most notably, Heinrich Schurtz.[80] This primacy accorded Schurtz also reveals how Germany's colonial experience affected the theorizing of new societal origins and forms. Schurtz had been the primary research assistant at Bremen's Übersee-Museum (Overseas Museum) and the beneficiary of the flood of colonial artifacts deposited there, especially after Germany entered into colonial competition in 1884.[81] Schurtz's first major distillation of his work at the Übersee-Museum, the 1900 *Early History of Culture*, provided intimations of the theory of the formation and development of society,[82] which he would elaborate two years later in *Age Classes and Male Bands* (*Altersklassen und Männerbünde*).[83] Schurtz argued that the sib-obsession of ethnographic predecessors had blinded them to a phenomenon that was not derivative from the family but intrinsic to itself: the existence of age-classes and men's houses. He also argued that all attempts to found society and the state on the family were retrojections. Schurtz grounded the development of the major social institutions of culture in two fundamental natural differentiations: first are the opposed psychologies of men and women; second is the antagonism between younger and older generations. The social instinct of men, as opposed to the familial instinct of women, led to the formation of men's houses, which were often distinguished by age.

Just as the perception of the important role of kinship may be tied to the tendency of bourgeois thinkers to view the institution of the bourgeois family as both the culmination of an evolutionary trajectory and the universal standard, Schurtz may well have been drawing upon those social tendencies out of which the *Wandervogel* and the various antibourgeois male movements noted above emerged in Germany and other German-speaking lands. Schurtz's title captured these alternatives to the bourgeois family: age-classes and male associations. His theorizing of a natural difference, gender,[84] resonated in a world in which capitalism and modernization had collapsed traditional identities and differences into so much exchange value, in which bureaucracy had rendered the individual anonymous; the *Gesellschaft* (society) now recognized as feminine, had eviscerated, unmanned, the masculine *Gemeinschaft* (community). Blüher took Schurtz's work and sexualized it; and description paved the way for action.

The Erotics of Race

Already planning it while still corresponding with Freud in 1913,[85] Blüher published the first volume of *The Role of the Erotic in Masculine Society* in 1917; the second volume appeared a year later. He felt this work provided both the biological and the empirical bases for his earlier claim that the youth movement was an erotic phenomenon; it also demonstrated that the youth groups were not the exception but the rule. To these ends Blüher embraced Schurtz's data and valuation of the bipolar gendered nature of human society.[86] While noting that Schurtz skirts the sexual content of these male associations, Blüher, as his mentor Friedlaender had before him, drew upon the ethnographic studies of Ferdinand Karsch-Haack, particularly his *Gleichgeschlechtliches Liebesleben* (same-sex love life), as supplemental evidence for the "strong inclination toward inversion" in tribal societies.[87] Blüher then argues that Schurtz's own speculation about a male social instinct proves more tautological than sociological, and offers instead his own more dynamic—psychosexual—theory: the existence of male-male (*mannmännliche*) attraction and of the invert type (*typus inversus*) as explanation.

In *Role of the Erotic* Blüher writes that *"beyond the socializing principle of the family that feeds off the Eros of male and female, a second principle is at work in mankind, 'masculine society,' that owes its existence to male-male Eros and finds its expression in male-bonding."* But unlike in Schurtz's work, this second principle is neither supplementary nor complementary to the first; it is, to a considerable extent, its adversary:

> In all species where the familial urge is the sole determinant . . . the construction of a collective is impossible. The family can function as a constitutive element of the State, but not more. And *wherever nature has produced species capable of developing a viable state, this has been made possible only by smashing the role of the family and the male-female sexual urges as sole social determinants.*[88]

The *Männerbund* bound together by male-male Eros embodies the second principle that overcomes the claims of the family and heterosexuality.

For Blüher, the inverse of the inverted type is neither the heterosexual nor the effeminate male, but the Jew:[89]

> With the Jews it is as follows: they suffer at one and the same time from a weakness in male-bonding and a hypertrophy of the family. They are submerged in the family and familial relations. . . . Loyalty, unity, and bonding are no concern of the Jew. Consequently, where other peoples profit from a fruitful interaction of the two forms of socialization [that is, the family and the *Männerbund*], with the Jews there is a sterile division. Nature has visited this fate upon them and thus they wander through history, cursed never to be a people [*Volk*], always to remain a mere race. They have lost their state.
>
> There are people who are simply exterminated as peoples and who therefore disappear, but this cannot be the case with the Jews, for a secret process internal to their being as a people constantly displaces the energies typically directed toward male bonding onto the family. . . . Consequently the Jews maintain themselves as *race* through this overemphasis of the family.

Here Blüher touches upon the political mediation of the riddle and scandal that Jewish persistence presented to European modernity. The riddle is, how have the Jews persisted without a state? And the scandal, that they have persisted without a state. Since the state was understood as the objectification of a "civilized" people (a *Kulturvolk* as opposed to a *Naturvolk*) the survival of the stateless Jews threatened the legitimacy of the colonizer state. Jewish persistence presented intimations of its (the colonizer state's) mortality. Against these threats the accusation that the Jews form a state within a state was propounded, thereby both denying the paradox and concretizing the threat.

Other thinkers from Spinoza, in the *Tractatus Theologico-Politicus*, to Freud, in *Moses*, have made other efforts to solve this scandalous conundrum.[90] To his primary explanation for Jewish persistence, circumcision, Spinoza juxtaposed his proffered explanation for continued Jewish statelessness, the feminization of the Jews,[91] an apparent conjunction, as will be discussed in the next chapter, that Freud sought to suppress, if not disavow.

Blüher, too, saw Jewish survival and statelessness as connected to their effeminacy. That is, the Jews have devoted themselves exclusively to the woman's realm of the family and have focused upon the woman-associated reproductive instinct. The importance placed on circumcision confirms this since this sign fetishizes that instinct. In *Secessio Judaica* Blüher explicitly ascribes effeminacy to the Jews: "The correlation of masculine nature with German essence and a feminine and servile nature with the Jewish essence is an unmediated intuition of the German people, which from day to day becomes more certain."[92]

But the Jews pose an even greater peril to modern society. Not only do they threaten the formation of the state, but they also portend the subversion of the *völkisch* family: "There are men so burdened by the incestuous drives of the Penelope type [that is, woman as wife and mother] that they are driven to marry into a foreign race. This is particularly characteristic of the Jews and, notably, even among the Zionist Jews, who consciously promote their own racial type for both sexes while being unconsciously driven toward foreign races."[93] By so characterizing the Jews Blüher has depicted them as the pathographic homosexual whom Freudian theory argues is motivated by a primal fear of incest and hence avoids sex with all women.[94] The Jews represent the kind of homosexual, the inverted *Weibling*, from whom Blüher sought to distinguish his *Männerheld*.

Blüher's exemplar of the inverted *Männerheld* who forms the *Männerbund* is Carl Peters. In his *The Founding of German East Africa* Peters describes the colonial community of males bound to one another without the presence of women. Blüher in turn describes Peters as an inexhaustible conqueror, organizer, man of action, a politico who will have nothing to do with women.[95] This designation of the colonialist self-construction as exemplary demonstrates that the experience of German colonialism led writers to draw upon a different reservoir of fantasies than those generated prior to Germany's entry into the colonial venture.[96] No longer either the representative of a familial, kinder, gentler colonialism or the lone investigator opening up virgin territory, the German male colonialist became the vanguard of the *Herrenvolk* (master race). With the loss of those colonies after World War I, the German ethnographic analysis of tribal societies turned to another idealized vanguard: the ecstatic-warrior male cultic bands that led the ancient Germanic tribes. Posited as a source and foundation of the religious, ethical, and political life of the German *Volk*, this construct provided a counter to the cultural claims of the Western colonial powers.

The scientific and popular image of those original Germans had been that of the peasant during the nineteenth century.[97] As a pure racial image, it was embraced by the "conservative-German cultural wing." Such blood-and-soil romanticism was denounced by Blüher, however: explicitly as nonheroic, retrograde kitsch, and implicitly for valorizing the family as the foundation of Germanness.[98] Other models would follow, including the idyllic vision drawn from the Icelandic sagas of a noble clan who trusts in the gods, who in turn vouchsafe their paradisiacal situation. In the 1920s, however, another model emerged among the students of the Viennese scholar of Ancient Germanic Studies Rudolf Much that drew from Schurtz's and Blüher's writings on *Männerbünde*. It posited an ecstatic-warrior male cultic group as most characteristic of the ancient Germans. These secret societies were responsible for warring against human and demonic enemies and thereby protecting the tribe on both the material and spiritual levels. Weiser's 1927 *Ancient Germanic Youth Initiation Rites and Male Bands* and Höfler's 1934 *Secret Cultic Groups of the Germans* in particular emphasized not only that these groups lorded over the tribe but also that they bore within themselves state-forming power. They held that these secret male societies were a source and foundation of the religious, ethical, and political: in sum, of the cultural life of the German *Volk* to the present—the national socialist present.[99]

Anthropologists also revisited the phenomenon of *Männerbünde* after the loss of Germany's colonial possessions; however, unlike Schurtz, whose inventory of colonial appropriations was conditioned by the crises gripping Wilhelmine Germany, these researchers took a proactive stance in their ethnographic comparisons and exemplars. Wilhelm E. Mühlmann—a student of Eugen Fischer, who had developed his theories of racial eugenics and miscegenation while working in German Southwest

Africa—focused on cultures with state-forming, militaristic-ascetic male bands. He considered such culling of heroic types to form elite *Männerbünde* as typical of racial groups, like the Polynesian Arioi and the ancient Germans, that are born both to expand their hegemony and to dominate other populations.[100] These identifications were then picked up by both postwar youth groups and the right-wing paramilitary *Freikorps*, and then by Nazi ideologues like Alfred Baeumler, the author of *Männerbund and Science*, who already in the 1920s directed students to call to mind the *Männerbünde* of earlier times, out of whom the original state emerged. Ultimately Himmler embraced the *Männerbund* in his vision of the SS.[101] These racial, and finally antisemitic, reconstructions and realizations of the *Männerbund* idea diverged from Blüher's conception by both de-emphasizing the erotic dimension and, since race was their fundamental proposition, fusing the male socializing and state-forming drives with the reproductive instinct. They did, however, retain Blüher's positioning of Jewry as the antithetical enemy of masculine society.

Disavowing Homosexuality

This positioning of the Jew as effeminate homosexual and social threat could not have appealed to Freud, that "manly" postcolonial Jewish subject. In the cases that preceded his encounter with Blüher, cases in which he was working through his theory of homosexuality, Freud made every effort to sever the connection between homosexuality and male Jewry. As argued in chapter 4, above, in "Analysis" Freud made every rhetorical effort to disavow the continuation of Little Hans's homosexual "accesses" (9:17) after the resolution of his anxiety neurosis and, by never acknowledging his patient's Jewishness, to deny the relationship between Hans's imagined-as-circumcised identity and the castration complex at the root of both those "accesses" and that neurosis. Even when Freud returns to this case in the 1926 *Inhibitions* (20:101–10), he pointedly refuses to explain Little Hans's neurosis in terms of the negative Oedipal complex, whereby the boy assumes a passive, feminine attitude toward the father; instead that "little Oedipus" (9:111), as Freud had originally referred to Little Hans, continued to be characterized by an "energetic masculinity" (9:110). Similarly, as discussed in the last chapter, Freud avoids, in his study of the relationship between Judge Schreber's repressed homosexuality and his paranoia, any suggestion of Schreber's identification with the Wandering Jew; Freud also further distanced this Jewish-identified psychotic from effeminacy by reading Schreber's feminizing emasculation as castration. The singular status Freud accorded Schreber—making his case paradigmatic for the psychological effects of repressed homosexuality—became, as noted above, a major point of contention between Freud and Blüher. Another instance of Freud's efforts to screen this connection between Jewishness and homosexuality is apparent in his publication of "History" in 1918, the year the second volume of *Role of the Erotic* appeared. The infantile neurosis belonged to Sergei Pankejeff, also known as the "Wolf-Man," whom Freud was seeing during the period leading up to his first communication with Blüher. As discussed in chapter 3, above, when assaying the factors that contributed to the Wolf-Man's latent homosexuality (that is, his negative Oedipus complex, as Freud would eventually describe it), Freud includes circumcision; however, he specifies that it is the circumcision of Christ that the young Sergei would have learned "during the readings and discussions of the sacred story" (17:86).

The association of effeminate homosexuality and the Jews was not the only aspect of Blüher's text that would have been of concern to Freud. Exacerbating its problematic reception by Freud would have been the prominent place Freud's *Dämonie* and the object of his homosexual affect, Wilhelm Fliess, assumes in Blüher's volumes.[102] Upon opening the work, Freud would have discovered that, in addition to discussing the blatantly antisemitic activist for masculinist homosexuality Friedlaender as precursor and devoting once again considerable attention to the, for Freud, ever problematic homosexual Otto Weininger, Blüher immediately addresses Fliess's work. Blüher argues that Fliess's "valuable" research on male and female periodicity and on the relationship between smell and sexuality—the two major research areas that preoccupy the Freud-Fliess correspondence—grounds his (Blüher's) own conclusions about the biological basis of marriage.[103] Upon completing reading of Blüher's work, Freud would again have Fliess's presence rubbed into his nose. Not only did Fliess and Blüher share the same publisher, Verlag Eugen Diederichs, the leading disseminator of writings from the German masculinist counterculture, but advertisements for Fliess's works also covered the back page of Blüher's tome.

In Freud's works that appear after the publication of *The Role of the Erotic* and its elaboration of the universal (homo)erotic character of masculine society and of male identity formation, homosexuality becomes more and more marginal to Freud's theory of social origins. Thus, when he brings up the primal horde and its successors in his work *Group Psychology*, homosexuality is relegated to a footnote that elaborates upon what he

means by emotional ties forced upon (that is, they are extrinsic) the brothers by the inhibition of their sexual aims (toward their mothers). This
footnote does make an interesting addition by suggesting that only
through this reorientation—that is, by displacing their love and desire
from the father as well as the mother—could they kill him (18:105–6 and
note). Freud further equivocates on the role of homosexual ties in the
relationship between sublimated libido and sociality; as Diana Fuss also
suggests, here Freud conceptualizes "homosexuality and homosociality as
absolutely distinct categories."[104] The former is a matter of desire and
object-choice, where the latter is created by identification.

Soon after the publication of *Group Psychology* Blüher's widely read antisemitic pamphlet *Secessio Judaica* appeared.[105] In that text the work of the
"Jew Sigmund Freud" is presented as exemplary of corrupt Jewish ways of
thinking due to its "pure materialism" and "insidious presuppositions."[106]
More significant than the specifics of Blüher's latest mad ravings was, as
discussed above, the appropriation of his work by racialist theoreticians
and streetfighters.[107] Freud describes Blüher at this time as one of the
"prophets of these out-of-joint times." While Freud argues that such "collective psychoses" of the Germans are beyond reason,[108] nevertheless his
two later discussions of the primal horde, in *Civilization and its Discontents*
and "The Acquisition and Control of Fire," appear to reflect an additional
distancing or recharacterizing of the *Männerbund*. In these texts homosexuality among the brothers has shifted its locus from sociality to rivalry.
Both these discussions emphasize the importance of renouncing homosexuality for cultural and technological progress to take place.

> Putting out fire by micturation . . . was therefore a kind of sexual act with
> a male, an enjoyment of sexual potency in homosexual competition. The
> first person to renounce this desire and spare the fire was able to carry it
> off with him and subdue it to his own use. By damping down the fire of his
> own sexual excitation, he had tamed the natural force of fire. This great
> cultural conquest was thus the reward for his renunciation of instinct.
> (21:90n)

Where Freud invokes homosociality it does not serve a genetic function;
rather, it emerges as an external happenstance. Any sexual content to these
relations derives from displaced heterosexual libido:

> The work of civilization has become increasingly the business of men, it
> confronts them with ever more difficult tasks and compels them to carry
> out instinctual sublimations. . . . [H]e has to accomplish his task by making
> an expedient distribution of his libido. What he employs for cultural aims

he to a great extent withdraws from women's sexual life. His constant association with men, and his dependence on his relations with them, even
estrange him from his duties as a husband and father. (21:103–4)

The communal life of humanity, Freud argues, is founded upon "the
power of love, which made the man unwilling to be deprived of his sexual
object—the woman—and made the woman unwilling to be deprived of
the part of herself which had been separated from her—her child"
(21:101). The family is "the germ-cell of civilization" (21:114).[109] The
diminution of the role of homosexuality and the shift in its tenor suggest
that Freud may well be motivated by the specific threat that *Männerbund*
theory and practice presents to him and his fellow Jews.

Finally, when Freud transfers his consideration of the primal horde to
the deserts of Midian in *Moses*, any suggestion of homosexuality in the
relationships and rivalries among the brothers are avoided. Instead, he
writes that the brothers clubbed together and stole wives. While such
avoidance behavior accords with Freud's desire to silence the association
of male Jews with effeminate homosexuals as well as his desire to maintain
the truth of his theory, he may also be distancing himself and the Jewish
people from the now Aryan-identified—and Germany-and-Austria ruling—*Männerbund*.

Yet Freud implicates homosexual rivalry when addressing the origins of
antisemitism. One of the "deeper motives" he proposes posits Christian
peoples jealous of their elder brother ("the first-born favorite child of God
the Father"), the Jews. This unconscious motive is conjoined with another:
the "disagreeable, uncanny impression" created by that "custom by which
the Jews marked off their aloof position": circumcision. The attempt to
foreclose the "dreaded castration idea" that Freud considers as a primary
root of antisemitism (23:91) is also one of the sources of adult homosexuality. Indeed, in his 1922 essay, "Some Neurotic Mechanisms," Freud
suggests that two primary factors that lead to the development of homosexuality are the fear of castration—whether manifest in a horror of
women as a consequence of the discovery that they do not have a penis or
in a renunciation of women in order to avoid the potentially dangerous
rivalry with the father and father-figures—and the repression and transformation of the hostile and jealous rivalry with an older brother (18:230–
32). Antisemitism hence arises, in part, as a substitute for, displacement of,
or other defense against emasculation and homosexuality, and Freud, even
as he has sustained the internalized heterosexual norms and his own theory, here engaged in postcolonial mimicry and in the process reversed

the stereotypical roles of the nonvirile, homosexual Jews and the virile, heterosexual non-Jews.[110] But all was for naught as the *Männerbund* drove the father of psychoanalysis from his home.

The End of a Rivalry

As Freud's primal horde, with its internalized bourgeois European norms, traveled from *Totem* to *Moses*, so the notion of the *Männerbund* transferred from a fund of colonial knowledge to a metropole viewed as alienated from its own colonizing force to an unmanned state colonizing its past to a masculine society colonizing the colonizers. During this period Freud engaged and disengaged Blüher who drew upon that fund to generate theories about the foundational role of Eros in the formation of masculine societies and states. As this chapter has shown, the conflict of social-ontological visions of identity and state formation—between the paternalistic family represented by Freud and the distinct homosocial masculine society professed by Blüher, between the postcolonial's mimicry of the colonizer (with its potential for subverting the latter) and the colonialist's phantastic appropriation and transmogrification of the colonized (with its potential for erasing the latter)—was mediated by rival conceptions of homosexuality and of these notions' relationships to the Jews. Thus Blüher in *Role of the Erotic* ties the psychoanalytic notion of curing inversion to a most profound agreement with the "norms of the bourgeois order," and contends that the physician "perceives only the family and is blind to masculine society."[111]

Beyond the texts discussed above, Freud, for his part, is simply dismissive of Blüher personally. Commenting to Werner Achelis in 1927 about Achelis's manuscript "The Problem of Dreams: A Philosophical Essay," Freud wrote, "I several times felt that the essay contained quite 'brilliant' thoughts. At other times, for instance when you invite the reader to admire Blüher's genius, I had the impression of being faced with two worlds separated by an unbridgeable gulf."[112]

Yet Freud, dying in exile, like many of his "people" after the *Männerbund* called National Socialism had extended its rule to Vienna, offered his last word—last completed work—*Moses*, which chronicles how the children of Israel, acting like the *noninverted* band of brothers who had been exiled from the primal horde, murdered "the greatest of [Jewry's] sons" (23:7). The next chapter takes up that last work and its attempts to subvert the compulsive force that was threatening both Freud and *Judentum*.

CHAPTER 7

A Paleontological View of Freud's Study of *Judentum*: Unearthing the *Leitfossil* of an Unlaid Ghost

In his final study of religion, *Moses and Monotheism*, Freud writes: "Moses did not only give the Jews a new religion; it can be stated with equal certainty that he introduced the custom of circumcision to them. The fact is of decisive importance for our problem and has scarcely ever been considered" (*ist kaum je gewürdigt worden*; 23:26).[1] But before this deficit can be remedied the problem is, what is Freud's problem? In a letter to Arnold Zweig, Freud clearly states that his purpose is to understand the development of both the Jewish people and antisemitism, "how the Jews have come to be what they are and why they have attracted this undying hatred."[2] No mere intellectual exercise, these questions arose for him "in view of the new persecutions."[3] Nor was this a new concern, as he wrote to Lou Andreas-Salomé: the problem "has pursued me throughout the whole of my life."[4]

Readers of *Moses* have a more difficult task of answering that question.[5] They are confronted by a text that consists of three essays (the third in two parts), three embedded prefaces, and a mixture of genres; it is filled with instances of "if" and "let us suppose," false starts, deferred conclusions, repetitions, rationalizations, defensive self-justifications, questionable methods, and weak arguments that are readily acknowledged as such by Freud (cf. 23:27n2).[6] And even if the readers were to pick their way through this stylistic chaff and isolate "the kernel of my hypothesis—the dependence of Jewish monotheism on the monotheist episode in Egyptian history" (23:31), they would discover in the first two essays of *Moses* what biblical scholars consider manifestly problematic propositions:

1. Moses was an Egyptian,[7] probably a member of the nobility and a follower of Pharaoh Amenhotep IV, also known as Akhenaten, and his monotheistic cult of Aten.

2. Moses, following the death of the Pharaoh and the overthrow of his cult, led the Jews out of Egypt, converted them to the Aten cult, and obliged them to accept the Egyptian practice of circumcision.

3. Burdened by the demands of Moses and his religion, the people murdered him.

4. Two generations after this traumatic event, the followers of the Mosaic religion merged with the Midianite followers of the volcano god-demon Yahweh and their leader, whom Freud calls the "second Moses." The nonmonotheistic Yahwist religion was retained by the people, but Yahweh was identified with the god of the exodus, and the allegedly Egyptian custom of circumcision was also kept. This "compromise at Kadesh" helped the Jews to deal with the trauma of Moses' murder: it aided and abetted the repression of virtually all traces both of the murder and of Moses' Egyptian origins.

5. Many centuries later Jewish prophets drew upon the oral tradition of the Mosaic religion kept by the priests and engineered the return of its god.

Although Freud repeats this account in the third essay, the problem shifts. He supplements his historical reconstruction of Jewish monotheism's origin by drawing an analogy with psychopathology. He compares the development of religious phenomena with that of neurotic symptoms: "Early trauma—defense—latency—outbreak of neurotic illness—partial return of the repressed" (23:80). During the course of this essay the original "kernel of our hypothesis" becomes the "kernel of historical truth" (23:16; cf. 23:58, 85). The latter, the material cause for psychopathological development in the individual, initiates on the collective level cultural development, in general, and religious phenomena, in particular. However, whereas for an individual the original trauma happens to him or her, for a group the original trauma appears to have been secreted by unconscious memory-traces of the archaic heritage of humanity, which includes the "countless times repeated" (23:81) actual murder of the primal father by his sons.[8]

When *Moses* concludes, however, it appears that the text had been addressing yet another problem. Apparently, the ultimate focus of Freud's work was neither the Egyptian origin of Moses and his religion nor the origin of religion and its relation to neurotic development, neither the origin of *Judentum* nor that of antisemitism; rather, at the crux of his peripatetic reflections was how the Jews "have been able to retain their individuality till the present day" (23:136–37)—a problem, he concedes, that he was unable to solve. He is very defensive about his failure: "But exhaustive answers to such riddles cannot in fairness be either demanded or expected" (23:137). That an inquiry into the persistence of the Jews is at stake is only first mentioned in the second part of the concluding essay. And when the topic does arise it is tucked within the "problem of how the special character of the Jewish people arose" (23:103),[9] and cloaked in psychoanalytic terminology: the Jewish people "ha[ve] met misfortunes and ill-treatment with an unexampled capacity for *resistance* [*Widerstand*]. . . . We should be glad to understand" this (23:105; emphasis added). Freud himself appears to be resisting the solution to this problem.

In the "Summary and Recapitulation" that begins part two of the third essay Freud confesses that there is something about this project galvanizing his resistance: "Actually [*Moses*] has been written twice: For the first time a few years ago in Vienna, where I did not think it would be possible to publish it. I determined to give it up; but it tormented me like an unlaid ghost, and I found a way out by making two pieces of it independent and publishing them . . ." (23:103).[10] Freud continues, "I had scarcely arrived in England before I found the temptation irresistible to make the knowledge I had held back accessible to the world" (23:103). Further, the work's "irresistible claim" (23:85) upon him is adduced by his admission that he published the work, although the text exceeded his attempted revising; in his prefatory remarks Freud himself refers to the repetitions and contradictions (see 23:69, 103–4) of his text and confesses that he was "unable to wipe out the traces of the history of the work's origin" (23:103). Indeed, Freud confesses, "the work proceeds as it can, and often presents itself to the author as something independent or even alien" (23:104). While, Freud offers, the stylistic problems such as these as well as the encrypted language, self-censorship, and abundant references to untold "secrets" were all a part of a strategy to avoid the hostility of the Catholic Church, this explanation appears insufficient (cf. 23:55–57).[11] The ceaseless suffering that accompanied old age (*Moses* was begun in Freud's late seventies) and incurable mouth cancer does not provide sufficient illumination either. His other writings during this period do not share comparable expository or editorial problems.[12] Rather, these passages and their accompanying explanations portray avoidance and compulsive behaviors like those Freud describes as neurotic responses to trauma and as the effects of repression (cf. 23:75ff.). Further, Freud has taught us to attend to the "noticeable gaps, disturbing repetitions, and obvious contradictions—indications which reveal things to us which [a text] was not intended to communicate" (23:43)—in other words, to the distortions that, as Freud readily concedes (cf. 23:54–58, 103–4), obviously mark this text. And such "distortions . . . testify to the influence of the *resistance* (not entirely overcome) [*des nicht ganz überwundenen Widerstandes*]" (23:95; emphasis added).

Finally, by embedding this symptomatic story of the origin of his work within his story of the origin of *Judentum*, Freud seems to have let slip the existence of another scene—not Kadesh but Vienna—where Freud, Freud the Jew, substitutes for Moses the non-Jew. Perhaps the inquiry into the "secret intention" (23:14; cf. 23:27n2), which according to Freud lay behind the Moses myth, is but a screen (cf. 23:74) for Freud's true motives.[13]

From Motive to Leitmotif

As already reviewed in the Introduction, a number of commentators have attempted to assay the motives behind the composition of *Moses*. Until recently these readings, after calling attention to Freud's longtime identification with Moses, as evinced in his 17 January 1909 letter to Jung,[14] would read the work, the only extended treatment of *Judentum* written by the "Gdless Jew," if not on his "mattress grave,"[15] then at least at the close of his time on the couch, as an autobiographical testament. In particular, triangulating *Moses* with the other primal scene,[16] described by Freud in *Interpretation* (his father's shameful submission to an antisemitic lout), these analysts saw Freud playing out his relationship to his Jewish identity: apologetic,[17] ambivalent,[18] or negative.[19] Others, picking up on Freud's discussion of the "family romance" (*Familienroman*) in the first essay of *Moses*,[20] placed more emphasis on Freud's working-through his relationship with his father,[21] or on his failing to work through his relationship with his mother.[22] Many, notably Grubrich-Simitis, also move beyond Freud's personal issues in the text to his broader concern not only with the sources of the "new persecutions," but with possible means to combat them: whether negatively, by debunking their rationales, or positively, by, in the words of the racial anthropologist and fellow Viennese Jew Ignaz

Zollschan, "employ[ing] the same weapons as our opponents—that is to say, the weapons of anthropology, sociology, and natural science [Freud would add, of course, psychoanalysis]—to investigate the social value of the Jews."[23]

Yet what all of the interpretations had "scarcely considered" (cf. 23:26), what they were still sidestepping when I presented the first version of this chapter in 1987, was not Jewish identity per se, but its stumbling block: namely, circumcision (cf. Galatians 5:11). In the interim, circumcision did gain the attention of such readers as Sander Gilman, Daniel Boyarin, and Jacques Derrida. More recently, however, the attention afforded circumcision has yielded to other prominent topics: *Geistigkeit*, on the one hand,[24] and the nexus of memory, tradition, and Lamarckism, on the other.[25]

This chapter examines how, initially, circumcision in Freud's text marks the place of the "kernel of historical truth" necessary to legitimate his theories of religion as well as of gendered-identity construction. Further, it demonstrates how circumcision bears the trace of the "shameful fact" (23:70) no less needed to motivate the processes of repression and the return of the repressed in addition to those of splitting and acting out. Then the analysis moves to the increasing marginalization of that Jewish-identified, Egypt-originating practice in Freud's argument. After unearthing the *Leitfossil* circumcision—and then observing its attempted reburial by Freud—this analysis reconstructs the traumatic "knowledge" that Freud seeks to disavow, a source of the antisemitism that had long jeopardized his situation as a Jew. I argue that Freud's resisted solution to the resisting problem of Jewish persistence, of the Jew as the unlaid ghost who haunts European modernity, is not Jewish religion per se, but the Jews' race- and gender-inflected[26] collective identity that was mediated by the dispositive circumcision. While the preceding chapters have examined how Freud's discourse emerged out of the everyday trauma of antisemitism, the present one explores how the "recent events" in Germany and, eventually, Austria disrupted the modus vivendi (the compromise of Vienna that helped construct as well as became integral to psychoanalytic discourse) and unceasingly confronted Freud with the need to defend against that which would nihilate his self, his movement, and *Judentum*.

On the Trail of the *Leitfossil*

When discussing the compromise at Kadesh, Freud writes: "We may once again call on the evidence afforded by circumcision, which has repeatedly been of help to us, like, as it were, a key-fossil" (*Leitfossil*, 23:39). It is necessary to gather up all the fossil remains in order to reconstruct the function of circumcision within this text. Throughout his text Freud employs a rhetoric of signs (*Zeichen, Anzeichen, Abzeichen*) to describe it. It both identifies the Jewish people and makes them a people apart (cf. 23:30). However, "As a mark [*Abzeichen*] that is to distinguish one person from others . . . one would choose something that is not to be found in other people" (23:45). Unfortunately, this necessary precondition for the effective functioning of this sign seems not to be the case. Freud draws upon Herodotus (23:26–27; cf. 23:30n2) and biblical scholars such as Eduard Meyer (23:34–35) to testify that circumcision was indigenous only to Egypt and that "no other people of the Eastern Mediterranean . . . practised this custom" (23:27) until taught by the Egyptians. Freud discovers that the manifest sign of the Jewish people has latent meaning. This "truth about circumcision" (23:30) is a fundamental link in his deduction of *Judentum*'s Egyptian roots. Freud questions why Moses, if he were a Jew who had just liberated his "compatriots" in order to help them "develop an independent and self-conscious national existence in another country," would simultaneously "impose on them a troublesome custom which even, to some extent, made them into Egyptians and which must keep permanently alive their memory of Egypt" (23:27). Freud holds that the fact of circumcision's Egyptian origin falsifies the hypothesis of Moses' Hebrew origins—and not vice versa, although "no attempts were spared [in the Hebrew Bible] to detach the custom from Egypt" (23:44). This fact "had to be disavowed at any price" (23:45). The attempts to backdate circumcision to the patriarchal period (for example, Genesis 17:34) and thereby to control the interpretation of this sign are "distortions which should not lead us astray" (23:26) and "clumsy invention[s]" (23:45). Freud describes the "quite particularly obscure passage" (23:26) in which Gd seeks to kill Moses for neglecting the custom (Exodus 4:24–26) as "a deliberate denial of the betraying fact" (23:44) of its Egyptian origin. All of these efforts to cover up the "truth about circumcision" become the prime examples of the distorting effects of repression. Freud argues how circumcision serves in the biblical text to connect the Jewish people with Yahweh *ab origine* and thereby to elide both its and its practitioners' Egyptian origin. It is "the token [*Zeichen*] of the covenant between [Yahweh] and Abraham" (23:45) and therefore no longer the "most suspicious indication [*Anzeichen*] of dependence on Egypt" (23:44). By tracking the distorted trail circumcision cuts through the *Hexateuch*—and *Moses*' second essay—Freud reveals how circumcision betrays the Jewish claim to having originated monotheism.

For Freud, "the distortions of a text resemble a murder: [that is,] the difficulty is not in perpetrating the deed, but in getting rid of its traces" (23:43). As Freud, like some paleontological detective, follows the trail of the *Leitfossil* circumcision through the biblical text, he discovers that the scene of the crime is not Egypt but Kadesh: "the retention of circumcision [is] evidence [*Beweis*] for the fact that the founding of the religion at Kadesh involved a compromise" (23:40). The origin of circumcision alone no longer holds significance for Freud; rather, its meaning and value lie in its persistence. Like monotheism, circumcision may have originated in Egypt, but it only became significant as a consequence of the compromise at Kadesh and the guilt-ridden necessity for that compromise. The adoption of the custom, this "concession to the followers of Moses" (23:39), marked the inability of *Judentum* to efface totally its origin with the Egyptian Moses, which is also to say, the inability to repress completely the memory of Moses' murder. The *Leitfossil* becomes, like the biblical narratives in which it is also embedded, the "mausoleum [*Grabbau*] . . . beneath which, withdrawn from the knowledge of later generations, the true account of those early things . . . was, as it were, to find its eternal rest" (23:62).

Of course, there are a few instances of circumcision in the biblical text that Freud curiously omits to mention. Perhaps the most significant oversight occurs when Freud notes: "Moses is said to have been 'slow of speech'" (*schwer von Sprache*; 23:33). Moses' "defective speech" offers Freud another possible confirmation of Moses' Egyptian origins:[27] "It may recall, slightly distorted, the fact that Moses could not communicate with his Semitic non-Egyptians without an interpreter" (23:33). The editors reference Exodus 4:10 for Moses' confessing difficulties speaking; neither they nor Freud call attention to another passage where Moses twice more attempts to avoid being a spokesperson because of his speech problem. In Exodus 6:12 and 30, Moses protests that, in the words of the Freud family's Philippson Bible, "Ich bin je unbeschnitten an Lippen . . . Ich bin unbeschnitten an Lippen" (I have *uncircumcised* lips). To describe Moses in any way as "uncircumcised" might question Freud's claim for Moses' Egyptian origins.

Freud's resistance to this passage is further indicated by several other curious actions. Although the Torah does not explain Moses' speech defect, Jewish tradition does in both Midrash (exegetical narrative or legend) and Josephus (*Jewish Antiquities*). Freud is familiar with both sources and had, in the paragraph preceding the noting of Moses' vocal impairment, recounted the (first half of the) background story; however, he does not indicate the relationship between the anecdote's events and their consequences. Instead as an illustration of Moses' precocious ambitiousness, Freud relates the tale in "a slightly different form" (23:32n1) than does Josephus. Both begin, "Once when Pharaoh had taken him in his arms and playfully lifted him high in the air, the little three-year-old boy snatched the crown from the king's head" (23:32). Josephus has Pharaoh place the crown on the crown-grabbing child and explains that Moses' motivation for playing with it was childishness, not ambition. This version contradicts the character-revealing function that Freud desires; consequently, he extends the shared narrative with the midrashic account: the child put the crown "on his own [head]. This portent alarmed the king, who did not fail to consult his wise men about it" (23:32). The legend, but not Freud, continues: they advise the Pharaoh to have the child Moses choose between a jewel and a flaming coal. When Moses—through angelic intervention—opts for the coal and then sticks his burnt fingers into his mouth, he burns his mouth, resulting in his lifelong speech impediment. This traditional etiology does nothing to support Freud's claim.

In the third essay circumcision retains its sign function. Circumcision is the "external mark [*Zeichen*] of the religion of Moses" (23:62) and later becomes the "visible mark" (*Anzeichen*) of their chosenness (23:88), but as will be discussed below, the sign appears to be pointing otherwise. With the shift to the psychoanalytic register in this essay circumcision can be seen as not only iconic of the compromise at Kadesh, but as the sign of compromise characteristic of all neurotic symptoms and of repression—including Freud's text. As circumcision is the "symbolic substitute" for castration (23:122) and as the threat of castration is the paradigm of all trauma (cf. 23:79), circumcision is the paradigm of all symptomatic signs of and distortions effected by repression and other defenses against trauma. It is the remainder and the reminder—both ontogenetically and phylogenetically. Circumcision makes "a disagreeable, uncanny impression, which is to be explained, no doubt, by its recalling the dreaded castration and along with it a portion of the primæval past which is gladly forgotten" (23:91). Thus circumcision is the figure for the effects of trauma upon ego development, since "alterations of the ego, comparable to *scars* [*Narbenbildungen*], are left behind" (23:77, emphasis added; cf. 23:127, "the scar of repression" [*Verdrängungsnarbe*]). Circumcision is the sign that marks the place of the "kernel of historical truth" necessary both to legitimate Freud's reconstruction and to motivate the processes of defense and the return of the repressed (cf. 23:101).

This discussion of circumcision offers some insight into the displacement of Freud's alleged aim in writing *Moses* as he moves from essay to essay: from inquiring whether Moses was a Jew to examining why there are still Jews. As in his treatment of the Jewish people, what concerns Freud in his treatment of circumcision is not its origin but its persistence. Moreover, there is another congruency between circumcision and the Jewish people: circumcision is the fossilized sign of a fossil. From the triumph of Christianity on, "the Jewish religion was to some extent a fossil" (*Fossil*, 23:88). Circumcision is hopelessly intertwined with the fate of *Judentum* (cf. 23:47, 63, 88). Thus the relationship between circumcision and the Jewish people is more than one of sign to referent. Indeed, the referent appears to have become a sign. It would seem that Freud is reiterating in a psychoanalytic register the traditional Jewish self-identification as a "sign unto all of the nations." The "neurotic Jew" becomes the sign of the psychopathological processes that underlie civilization.[28]

Of Fossils, Fetishes, and Cultural Psychoses

By designating both circumcision and the Jews as "fossils" Freud may also be indicating that something else is at stake than the repetition of antisemitic characterizations.[29] During the period in which *Moses* was written, Freud was supplementing his theories of neurotic compromise and repression in order to address the problems of trauma, fetishism, and psychosis.[30] He was exploring what he called the "splitting of the ego" as a defense against trauma, against the primal and paradigmatic trauma of castration. Signaled in *Moses* by the phrases "'fixations' to the trauma" and "compulsion to repeat" (23:75) and the analogy—although apparently not "The Analogy" in the eponymous subsection of the first part of the third essay in which it is found—to a state within a state, Freud theorized a piece of the psyche (other than either the id or the super-ego) that emerges with the traumatic encounter and remains coexistent with but inaccessible to the ego (that itself developed out of the reworking and integrating of the other earlier experiences). In contrast to the reality-responsive ego, this psychic fellow traveler obeys the paradoxical logic of reality-disavowal and, when possible, substitutes a representation for that disavowed reality. There is neither compromise nor dialectical relationship between these attitudes, but instead a supplemental one. The products of the latter piece of psyche are acted out, even if resisted, by the former. Classic examples are the fetish, a representation generated by the desire to disavow the castration of the mother's (nonexistent) penis, and therefore the threat to the fetishist's own as well, and the mausoleum (recall Freud's comparison of the J and E biblical narrative strands to mausoleums; 23:62), which is an apotropaic monument that both asserts and denies the loss of the loved one as well as protects us from "unlaid ghosts" (23:103).

The figure of the fossil opens upon this entire problematic. A fossil is the animate turned to stone. This process immediately recalls the effects of the Medusa. In the posthumously published note "Medusa's Head" Freud equates the terror of Medusa with the terror of castration aroused by the sight of the mother's genitals (18:273–74). Yet the head of Medusa doubly mitigates that terror. First, like a fetish Medusa's decapitated head when borne represents both the penis and its absence or castration. Second, the effect of viewing the head upon the male spectator, that is, turning to stone with terror—in effect, becoming erect—both asserts the horror of castration and the preservation of the penis (albeit that of the male spectator).[31] Moreover, this symbol of castration, this shield-adorning emblem, repels threatening enemies; that is, this symbol of death turns away death. In sum, displaying the head of Medusa is an apotropaic act. The implications of the designation "fossil," like Freud's brief sketch, echo his work on trauma, fetishism, and psychosis and they suggest a connection between the "circumcised" Jew and the "castrated" woman.

Also suggestive of Freud's rethinking of defense mechanisms in terms of the splitting of the ego is the text's pervasive rhetoric of doubles. Freud's historical reconstruction hinges on dualities:

> Jewish history is familiar to us for its dualities: two groups of people who come together to form the nation, two kingdoms into which this nation fell apart, two gods' names in the documentary sources of the Bible. To these we add two fresh ones: the foundation of two religions—the first repressed by the second but nevertheless later emerging victoriously behind it, and two religious founders, who are both called by the same name of Moses and whose personalities we have to distinguish from each other. All of these dualities are the necessary consequences of the first one: the fact that one portion of the people [the Hebrews] had an experience which must be regarded as traumatic and which the other portion [the Midianites] escaped. (23:52)

Even the original German title betrays the duality. The phrase "der Mann Moses" ("der Mann Moscheh"—the man Moses—in the Philippson

Bible) appears twice in Torah. In Exodus 11:4 (3), Moses is viewed as a great man in Egypt in the eyes of the Pharaoh's courtiers and of the people. By contrast, Numbers 12:3 reads: "Moses was a man of great humility, the most humble man on earth." Freud finds that "these last qualities would evidently have fitted in badly with the Egyptian Moses . . . ; they might have belonged to the character of the other Moses, the Midianite" (23:41),[32] and thus feels justified in his assertion of the existence of two Moses.

More indicative of the influence of trauma theory upon Freud's considerations in *Moses* is a passage in which he discusses the compulsive quality of neurotic phenomena. They "exhibit a far-reaching independence [and] are insufficiently or not at all influenced by external reality . . . or its psychical representatives, so that they may easily come into active opposition to both of them. They are, one might say, a *State within a State* . . . which may succeed in overcoming what is known as the normal party and forcing it into its service. If this happens . . . the path to a psychosis lies open" (23:76; emphasis added). Freud has characterized neurotic phenomena by one of the foremost antisemitic accusations, one, interestingly, initially coined about women: namely, that the Jews constitute a "State within a State."[33] By implicitly connecting the Jew with the splitting process, Freud has perhaps shed additional light on his own solutions or nonsolutions to the problems of antisemitism and of the persistence of the Jews.

When he first announces to Arnold Zweig that he has completed his manuscript "Der Mann Moses: Ein historischer Roman" (the man Moses: a historical novel), Freud writes: "The starting point of my work is familiar to you—it was the same as your *Bilanz*."[34] In his 1927 *German Jewry: An Attempt at a Balance Sheet* [*Bilanz der deutschen Judenheit: Ein Versuch*], Zweig had explained as psychotic the contradictory and unsuccessful efforts of post–World War I Germany to assert, in particular, its masculinity. "If this is not the depiction of a divided soul [*in sich zerrissenen Seele*], in which delusion and reality horrifyingly career into one another, if such a people do not convey the impression of having fallen mentally ill, then the phenomenon of mass delusion, sweet self-deception, and compulsive self-destruction has never appeared." He then, in the chapters "The 'Other'" and "Why the Jews?", analogized the German situation to Freud's most famous case of paranoia, that of Judge Schreber, and his projection onto others what he could not justify in himself.[35] Similarly, Freud's text seeks to understand the irrational intensity of antisemitism (23:90–92);[36] the text also seeks to understand the linear development of religious phenomena and particular groups by extrapolating from "the pattern of individual neurotic symptoms" (23:58). In *Moses*, however, Freud is also theorizing the conditions for psychopathology that move beyond what he had written in his Schreber case study. By making reference to the "State within a State" Freud suggests an extrapolation of splitting phenomena onto the collective level, such that relations between groups may be potentially psychotic, and therefore returns to the problem that, as I argued in chapter 1, was already a primary concern in his much earlier *Psychopathology of Everyday Life*. And in the case of the Jewish people, circumcision, the custom that keeps the Jews "apart from the foreign peoples among whom their wanderings would lead them" (23:30),[37] is the foremost source for generating such a state of affairs. The reason is not just, as Freud argues, because circumcision is a "symbolic substitute" for castration (23:91) and thus motivates Christianity's efforts at disavowal; rather, both circumcision and the circumcised embody the disavowal because circumcision is apotropaic. As noted earlier, circumcision both asserts the possibility of castration, insofar as the foreskin has been removed, and yet denies it, insofar as the glans is prominent, as in an erection. Consequently, while Freud identifies *Judentum* with the advance in *Geistigkeit* over sensuality, and which therefore is identified with the law of paternity (cf. 23:114, 118) over and against maternity's dependence upon the senses, its paradigmatic sign places that "juridical revolution" (23:114; cf. 23:83) in question. Circumcision calls forth the castration complex, which is the crux of sexual difference. Yet even as circumcision asserts the truth of the threat of castration, it disavows it—the circumcised Jew seems to question sexual difference.

Men among the Man—Maybe

As was extensively analyzed in chapter 4, above, Freud had already drawn the connections among circumcision, the castration complex, women, and Jews in the famous footnote in his Little Hans case history more than twenty-five years earlier. In *Moses* circumcision binds the (male) Jew to woman all the more closely, even as Freud endeavors to dissociate any identity between the "circumcised" and (the "castrated") woman. Throughout this work Freud characterizes *Judentum* as masculine. Jewish monotheism itself represents the culmination of the "religious revolution" (23:46) against mother goddesses. The belief in one (father) god epitomizes the advance in intellectuality over sensuality and is founded upon the law of paternity (cf. 23:114, 118)—the deduction of conception and, hence, of the genitor—over and against maternity's dependence upon the senses. Coeval with monotheism and equally essential to Freud's understanding of Jewish religiosity is *Judentum*'s prophetic ethics of instinctual renunciation that Freud traces back to the triumphant sons (23:118–19).

This hypermasculinization is accompanied by the omission of any explicit association of the Jews with the feminine.[38] This is already evident in the different ways Freud characterizes the association of circumcision with castration. A cut-off "piece [*Stück*] of [a Jew's] penis" (10:36n1) in the famous footnote is replaced by a "gladly forgotten . . . portion [*Stück*] of the primæval past" (23:91) in *Moses*. The designation of the person missing a *Stück* has shifted from the circumcised to the spectator/phantasist. Nor is castration-anxiety-induced antisemitism here, in contrast to the earlier discussions in "Analysis" and *Leonardo*, tied to misogyny. More directly, by valuing thought-process over sense perception, *Judentum*, the people chosen by no mere *Mensch* (human being), but rather by "*dem Mann*" (the man) Moses, form a masculine *Volk*. They are not the effeminate race (*Geschlecht*) that Central Europeans imagine they see when they view *Judentum* through the dispositive of the unseen "secret treasure" (23:115), the "external mark" screened by discretion (*Bescheidenheit*), circumcision. In order to circumvent the accusation of Jewish nonvirility, as exemplified by Jochanan ben Zakkai's decision to open a Torah school rather than fight to the death (23:115), Freud bifurcates the definition of masculinity into the intellectual, at which the Jews excel, and the "less worthy" brutal, violent, muscular aspect that is the "popular ideal" (23:115).[39]

By way of contrast, the enemies of the Jews and of psychoanalysis have shown themselves to be less than virile. The church "proved, to use the words of the Bible, 'a broken reed'" (or staff, *schwankes Rohr*; 23:57) and thus embodied the emasculated phallic symbol that traditionally had adorned the female icon of the Synagogue, that is, of *Judentum*.[40] The monotheistic religion of the Jews, unlike that of other pretenders, had staying power due to its masculine origins. Not only is its compulsive force generated by the recollection of the sons' murder of and guilt over the death of the father, but also "there constantly arose from the Jewish people men [*Männer*] who revived the fading tradition, who renewed the admonitions and demands made by Moses, and who did not rest till what was lost had been established once again" (23:111).

Such is not the case with the appearance of monotheism in Egypt. Initially, Freud offers a threadbare reflection theory—Egypt's "imperialism was reflected in religion as universalism and monotheism" (23:21)—but then adds: "some of the royal wives were Asiatic princesses, and it is possible that direct incitements to monotheism even made their way in from Syria" (23:21–22). Finally, in his discussion of "The Great Man," when he again admits that "the great religious idea for which the man Moses stood was . . . not his own property; he had taken it over from King Akhenaten," Freud, following his sources,[41] comments that the Pharaoh "may perhaps have been following hints which had reached him . . . through the medium of his mother" (23:110). To this conditionally qualified detail Freud appends, perhaps to avoid the taint of the feminine attaching to Moses and his followers,[42] "or by other paths" (23:110). Moreover, in contrast to the "man Moses," the "mighty prototype of a father" whose "image . . . was probably not easy for [the 'poor Jewish bondsmen'] to distinguish . . . from that of God" (23:110), the surviving artistic renderings of Akhenaten's "distended skull, protruding abdomen, and almost feminine build,"[43] belied the image of the Great Man. Freud was familiar with these images, but left them unmentioned.

More than a reaction-formation, Freud's express association of *Judentum* with *Männlichkeit* may have sought to screen the more common gendered representations associated with circumcision that have been examined in this work from the outset. Yet beyond the ambient associations of the dispositive, a powerful portrayal of a feminizing circumcision had recently been widely disseminated. At least a year prior to Freud's work on Moses, the gender-inverting effects upon Jews of the Egyptian practice of circumcision had been highlighted in the first volume of a historical novel avidly read and praised by Freud,[44] one written by the foremost émigré German novelist. In *Joseph and His Brothers*, Thomas Mann wrote:[45]

> We must remember that the rite of circumcision, taken over as outward practice from the Egyptians, had in Joseph's family and tribe long ago acquired a peculiar mystic significance. It was the marriage commanded and appointed by God between man and the deity. . . . Many a man bore the name of God on his organ of generation, or wrote it there before he possessed a woman. The bond of faith with God was sexual in its nature, and thus, contracted with a jealous creator and lord insistent upon sole possession, it inflicted upon the human male a kind of civilizing weakening into the female. The bloody sacrifice of circumcision has more than a physical connection with emasculation. The sanctifying of the flesh signified both being made chaste and the offering up of chastity as a sacrifice; in other words, a female significance . . .

The primary source for Mann's passage was a work by one of Freud's favorite authors and that Freud also possessed: *The Secrets of the East* by

Dmitri Mereschkovsky,[46] whose novel about Leonardo da Vinci provided the childhood memory crucial to Freud's own analysis in *Leonardo*. Mann appropriates Mereschkovsky's reading of Ezekiel's marriage allegory of the bloody consummation of Gd's entering into covenant with Jerusalem (Ezekiel 16:6–8) through Exodus 4:25. By means of the "puzzling and incomprehensibly worded passage" (23:44) where Zipporah circumcises her and Moses' son while uttering, "You are my blood-bridegroom," and which for Freud betrays "the most suspicious [*gravierendste*] indication of [*Judentum's*] dependence on Egypt" (23:44), Mereschkovsky is able to see in Ezekiel's figure what others have not, namely,[47] "God's marriage-tie with Israel—this is the meaning of the words 'You are my blood-bridegroom.'"

Mereschkovsky had earlier drawn two conclusions from Exodus's account of Moses' nighttime encounter while returning to Egypt: not only does it designate the moment where Moses "found circumcision,"[48] but it also reveals circumcision as the "strange and horrible . . . 'betrothal of man with God' in flesh and blood, a marriage-union, a sexual tie of man with God."[49] In the Mann-appropriated passage, Mereschkovsky clarifies the gender distribution of this marriage.

> God is the bridegroom; Israel is the bride. The empirically given male genital [*Geschlecht*] is circumcised (Circumcision—'Castration' [*Beschneidung—'Verschneidung'*]), and the transcendent, female genital [*Geschlecht*] comes to light: according to Weininger all of Israel is an absolute 'W' [Weininger's symbol for the ideal type Woman].[50]

Mereschkovsky here explicitly connects circumcision with feminization.

In the oft-cited 30 September 1934 letter to Arnold Zweig, Freud writes: "Faced with the new persecutions, one asks oneself again . . . why they should have attracted this undying hatred."[51] Is the source of the revulsion the narcissistic immodesty, the arrogance of the chosen, of those who have achieved new heights of ethical *Geistigkeit*, that consumes the second part of the third essay or do these ties among fetishism, circumcision, feminization, and sexual difference find another site where psychosis emerges?[52]

A Spinozan Prooftext

The trail from the *Leitfossil* to the "fossil" to woman leads to "My fellow unbeliever Spinoza" (8:77). Spinoza, who like Freud entered and dispossessed the biblical text of its manifest inerrancy and who as a consequence was rendered anathema by his fellow Jews,[53] provides a prooftext against which to read *Moses*. In the third chapter of Spinoza's *Tractatus Theologico-Politicus*, "Of the Election of the Jews . . . ," Spinoza makes what Leo Strauss refers to as his "Testament":[54]

> As for the fact that [the Jews] have survived their dispersion and the loss of their state for so many years, there is nothing miraculous in that, since they have incurred universal hatred by cutting themselves off completely from all other peoples; and not only by practicing a form of worship opposed to that of the rest, but also by preserving the mark of circumcision with such devoutness. That their survival is largely due to the hatred of the Gentiles has already been shown by experience. . . . The mark of circumcision is also, I think, of great importance in this connection [that is, Jewish persistence]; so much so that in my view it alone will preserve the Jewish people for all time; indeed, did not the principles of their religion make them effeminate [*effoeminarent*] I should be quite convinced that some day when the opportunity arises [so changeable are human affairs] they will establish their state once more, and that God will choose them afresh.[55]

This passage evokes many of the major manifest themes of *Moses*: the mark of circumcision, the importance of antisemitism, and the Jewish claim of chosenness with its associated qualities of self-confidence and aloofness. But there is one factor in Spinoza's passage denied explicit mention in Freud's work: the Jews as "effeminate."[56] More important for this discussion, the solution to the problem of Jewish persistence that so eluded Freud is given a definitive answer: circumcision. By tying together circumcision, the persistence of the Jews, and effeminacy, Spinoza alerts us to a hidden link in many of the "network[s] of causes" that produced Freud's text (cf. 23:108). The traumatic knowledge that Freud seeks to repress and a primary source of the antisemitism that so problematizes his situation as a Jew is an identification secreted behind the ever-present, never-acknowledged solution to his problem, namely, circumcision: In the imagination of Central Europe, a society in which I have argued individual identity and social cohesion are principally (but by no means exclusively) determined by the sexual division of labor and its gender-coded spheres, "circumcised" male Jews are identified *with* (not *as*) men without penises, that is, *with* (not *as*) women.[57]

The connection of Jew and woman also had an empirical correlate. The Jews' presence in professions and the public sphere—but always as others, as non-Germans—became associated with another excluded group endeavoring to enter and feminize the public sphere, German feminists.[58] The Jew, above all the male Jew, endeavored to enter the *Männerbund*, thereby transgressing the male sphere and threatening the underlying structure of that society. As a consequence of these identifications and transgressions, sexual difference, so necessary to both Freud's theory and to his society, was jeopardized.[59] Thus, to acknowledge this cultural fact, this historical truth that Jews were neither male nor female, both male and female,[60] would entail the repudiation of psychoanalysis and its algorithm for the production of normatively gendered and sexed identities: Oedipus. Rather than face the implications of circumcision upon the fates of psychoanalysis and of the Jewish people, as Freud says with regard to the Jews and their knowledge of the Egyptian origin of circumcision, "the truth about circumcision must also be contradicted" (23:30). The "circumcised" Jew, who like the castrated (phallic) woman is a "State within a State" threatening the "normal party" (23:76), sets up a chain of disavowals that threaten the disavowal upon which Central European bourgeois society is founded: that of the necessity of woman (and other others) for individual (male) development and social cohesion.

The (Re)Construction of Moses

Having followed the lead of the *Leitfossil*, we can now reconstruct how the distortions in *Moses* represent the effort to disavow the traumatic knowledge of the identification that underlies his work. The construction of Freud's text appears to be motivated by a repetition compulsion (cf. 23:75–76), a repetition of the original that would create a new origin. This is what Freud does in the four divisions of the text. The first essay is an example of armchair or belle-lettristic theorizing that, while suppressing "any further implications," concludes with the "view that Moses was an Egyptian" (23:16). When the second essay begins "If Moses was an Egyptian," Freud is being neither inconsistent nor contradictory; rather, he is commencing a rewrite, in a historical-critical mode, of the first essay. His purpose here is to draw forth some of those implications. Part 1 of the third essay is yet another rewrite, the history of a group becomes a case history of group psychology that seeks less to reveal what *Judentum*—and Freud's argument—have resisted than to analogize this process to the return of the repressed.

However, once Freud switched from a historical to a psychoanalytical register, from a happenstance particular to *Judentum* to the inevitabilities of interaction within individual and group development, the threatened return of the disavowed connection of Jew with woman necessitated the continuous rewriting of the text. Since the sign of *Judentum*'s "hidden sources," circumcision, referred to this identification as much as it did to the identity and death of Moses, the sign itself needed to be repressed—or split off, disavowed.[61]

Freud begins the marginalization of circumcision in the third essay. First, the *Leitfossil* is reduced in Freud's narrative to a mere sign: "the external mark of the religion of Moses." Its reference is then further delimited to the "visible mark" of chosenness at the same time as its abandonment by Paul to ensure the success of Christianity is noted. The announcement of the latter coincides with the fossilization of the "Jewish religion" in Freud's text (23:88). Then, when inventorying the "disagreeable, uncanny impression" that circumcision makes among the "deeper motives for the hatred of the Jews," Freud indicates that the practice is but one "among the customs by which the Jews made themselves separate" (23:91). The first part of the third essay culminates with the discussion of the difficulties of applying his analogy between individual and group psychology; in that discussion the role of circumcision as an agent in *Judentum*'s development is expropriated by the repressed, unconscious memory-trace: "if we assume the survival of these memory-traces in the archaic heritage, we have bridged the gulf between individual and group psychology" (23:100).

Excuses, Excuses: An Excursus

Before discussing the epispasm, the restoration of the severed *Stück*, that is the second part of the third essay, a few comments need be made about Freud's suture between the two parts, the "extensive explanations and apologies" (23:103) for the state of his text that he makes at the outset of the last part. Unlike the two brief eponymous "Prefatory Notes" (*Vorbemerkungen*) that precede the first part, this prefatory note is entitled "Summary and Recapitulation" (*Zusammenfassung und Wiederholung*). This heading, rather than describing the form of the subsection—offering a summary and repetition of what has gone before as background for what is to follow—glosses its content.[62] The "Summary and Recapitulation" subsection announces that what is to follow is but a summary and a repetition of the first part of the third essay.[63]

This emblematic doubling (of doubling—both summaries and repetitions represent copies that often substitute for the original) is rife with a discourse of doubles that, as noted above, also characterizes Freud's recon-

struction of the origins of both Moses and monotheism. Freud provides
what appear to be two different accounts of the genesis of this second part.
He initially describes the subsequent text as "nothing other than a faithful
(and often word-for-word) repetition [*Wiederholung*] of the first part [of
the third essay], abbreviated in some of its critical enquiries and aug-
mented by additions relating to the problem of how the special character
of the Jewish people arose" (23:103). Although the reader assumes Freud
is describing a process of secondary elaboration (*sekundäre Bearbeitung*)
such that the second part was written after the first, Freud soon apologetically announces that in fact the first part was a "second version" (*zweite
Bearbeitung*; 23:103) written in London of an earlier revision of the third
essay that he had written but dared not publish in Vienna, and that the
second part is but an "unchanged" addition of "a whole piece [yet another
Stück] of the first presentation to the second" (23:104). Freud then concludes his remarks by repeatedly repeating defenses of and from repetition
in general and in this work that "actually . . . had been written twice"
(*zweimal*; 23:103).[64] Not only is he endlessly enacting that of which he
writes, but he is also reproducing structurally the supplement to his theory
of repression discussed above. This "unchanged" piece of earlier experience that splits off from the ego is reproduced by Freud's inability to relin-
quish what becomes the nonintegrated and unworked-through second
part of the third essay.

In the "Summary and Recapitulation" subsection Freud also remarks
that he had returned to his manuscript while still in Vienna because, as
already noted, "it haunted [him] like an unlaid ghost" (*unerlöster Geist*;
23:103). He tried to break the spell of this spectral visitor by way of a
"compromise": the publication in his house journal *Imago* of the first two
essays that make up *Moses*. He then describes another haunting compulsion—"I had scarcely arrived in England before I found the temptation
irresistible to make the knowledge I had held back accessible to the world"
(23:103) that also is resolved through the "compromise" of adding the
"unchanged" second part. The excessive apologetics, the compulsive supplementing of his "secondary revising" with text that makes the entire
work into an "independent, even an alien creation," and the spectral sight-
ing all lead readers to ascribe unusual value to the second part of the third
essay. That Freud chose "The Progress in *Geistigkeit*," a subsection of the
supplemental *unerlösten Geist*, to be read by his daughter Anna at the last
International Psychoanalytic Congress during his lifetime in Paris (2 August 1938), and that he published it as its own self-contained article[65] fur-

ther gives the second part in general, and that subsection in particular, a testamentary quality.[66]

Geistigkeit has become the *Geist* that haunts many of the most recent readings of *Moses*,[67] as it had many nineteenth- and early-twentieth-century Jewish apologetics.[68] I by no means wish to gainsay the importance of *Geistigkeit* or of that subsection or, for that matter, of the second part of the third essay; however, readers should be wary about ascribing primacy to the *Geistigkeit* that is trumpeted by the prohibition against making an image of the divine.[69] The *Geistigkeit* that is made in the image of *Geist* (cf. 23:114) may indeed attempt to lay that ghost to rest, but it should not be confused with that spirit.

Rather than anticipating its own redemption (*Erlösung*), Freud's phrase should be seen as yet another double, another repetition. This was actually the second time that Freud had used this uncanny image in his corpus.[70] The first instance was at a crucial moment in the discussion of "Analysis": immediately following Freud's parapraxis in a note glossing Hans's "phantasy of the two giraffes" (10:122n1). As discussed in chapter 4, above, the note acknowledged what the body of the text sought so hard to screen; rather than resolving his castration complex, working through the narcissistic crisis of sexual difference, and continuing with "normal" heterosexual development, Hans had remained fixated at that stage and retained his "homosexual accesses" (10:17). "Immediately after the giraffe story" (10:122)—both in Hans's chronology and Freud's later discussion—Hans produced two minor phantasies that his father "failed to interpret." At this point, Freud intervenes: "In an analysis, however, a thing which has not been understood inevitably reappears; like an unlaid ghost [*unerlöster Geist*], it cannot rest until the mystery has been solved and the spell broken" (10:122). Freud's ready solution is Oedipal, desire for the mother.

Freud's apparent ghostbusting—overcoming the crises of (gender, sexual, ethnic) difference and of Jewish persistence through the erection of Oedipus—had not been successful, for here in his last completed work, in this sublated *Stück* of text, the "unlaid ghost" has returned.

Spiriting away the Leitfossil

In part two of the third essay, circumcision, the "visible mark," becomes immaterial. The practice becomes but one among the many burdens of instinctual renunciation (see 23:122), of renouncing the satisfaction of drive-motivated urges, required by monotheism. In its place is an overwhelming emphasis on Jewish aniconism. Although Freud's initial discussion of the monotheistic cult of Aten focused on Akhenaten's iconoclasm and effacing of the old divine names, their import for Freud's argument for the Egyptian origins of *Judentum* are quickly superseded by circumcision; however, after re-emerging in the first part of the third essay as a possible second bargaining chip with circumcision at the compromise at Kadesh— "and possibly in establishing certain restrictions on the use of the name of the new god" (23:62)—the "Mosaic prohibition" (23:114) is triumphant in the second part. More significantly, where Spinoza would have circumcision and not divine election as the principal reason for Jewish persistence—and, as I have argued throughout, persistence rather than chosenness as more responsible for antisemitism and more of a threat to Jewish survival—in the second part of the third essay, those feelings of pride, exaltedness, ennoblement, consecration, and contempt for others for which he earlier held the custom of circumcision responsible (23:29– 30), now find their source in being Gd's chosen people.[71] Ironically, it is in the second part that Freud finally broaches the questions of Jewish persistence as well as of what qualities might be responsible for it; yet, these issues appear in such an offhanded, unemphasized way as to pass unnoticed (cf. 23:103–5). Thus, at the same time the Spinozan problematic underlying Freud's text finally emerges, the problematic itself as well as Spinoza's primary explanation are thoroughly screened.

This last section that predates the first part proves to be the ultimate rewrite. It reads as a revisionist routinization of the "secret ownership of some precious possession" (23:105) of the preceding discussions. In this final chapter the super-ego,[72] like some deus ex machina, surprisingly materializes and the historical dynamics of repression or of his underdeveloped theory of sublimation become subservient to the law of renunciation and to the super-ego's chosen *telos* of ethical and intellectual advancement, *Geistigkeit*.[73] Less the apologetic, messianic, or redemptive positivism that many commentators ascribe to Freud, as if he were proclaiming "look, neither the ethical demands of monotheism nor its Mosaic distinction[74] are inherent to the Jewish race (it is all that gentile Moses' fault),"[75] or "look, the Jews are as *geistig*, Protestant, and masculine as the Teutons,"[76] Freud's "unaltered" paean to *Geistigkeit* is more a screen of what portended the demise of *Judentum*. The primacy Freud grants the deity with "neither a name nor a countenance" (23:113) overshadows the inscription, following Thomas Mann, of "the name of God on his organ of generation" via circumcision,[77] via that Hebrew practice named *milah*, a homophone of the Hebrew word for name, *mila*, during which Jewish males receive their names. With the elision of circumcision comes the elision of the connection of women and Jews. By according circumcision the "decisive importance" Freud stated it was due, this analysis has generated insight into *Moses*'s style and rhetoric, its metapsychological concerns and apologetic ploys, and, above all, its Jewish problem.

Forgotten Connections of Women and Jews—Excursus

In addition to a new understanding of the motives and means behind the construction of *Moses*, the recognition of the disavowed identification reveals a text riddled with secret associations and omissions. Connections between woman and Jew are seen to traverse the text. For instance, the textual site upon which "the Christian scholar" Ernst Sellin—and following him, Freud—mined his murder (martyrdom) of Moses is in Hosea (12:13–13:1).[78] The initiating trope of Hosea is the prophet's prostitute-wife, Gomer, who is the figure for Israel/the Jewish people; indeed, the image of Israel as (unfaithful) woman permeates the text of Hosea.

The association of woman and Jew also arises in Freud's discussion of the patriarch Jacob (cf. 23:27, 44). This reference recalls Freud's father, who shares the patriarch's name. As Freud's father's "shameful submission" to, his "unheroic conduct" (4:217–20) in the face of, an antisemitic assault perhaps embodies the emasculated Jew, so the patriarch evokes the repressed identification. In Genesis Jacob wove his son Joseph a coat of many colors, and Freud, in his lecture "Femininity," credits women with but one contribution to the history of civilization: the invention of weaving (22:132). That lecture also signals another confluence of woman and Jew as it knocks its head against the "riddle" of woman; yet, Freud writes, "In conformity with its peculiar nature, psychoanalysis does not try to describe what a woman is—that would be a task it could scarcely perform—but sets about enquiring," however inadequately, "how she comes into being" (22:132). Similarly, while *Moses* resolves, inadequately, how the Jew came to be, the enigma of the Jew is the persistence of the Jews, their "isness." Moreover, the relationship described in "Femininity" between "the lack of a penis" and the "configuration of femininity" is both similar and similarly significant to the relationship described in *Moses* between the lack of a penis tip and the nature of *Judentum*.

Still another secret reserve of the feminine can be found in Freud's figuration of doubles. In addition to the dualities cited above, there are two families in the family romance that appears in Freud's discussion of

Rank's *The Myth of the Birth of the Hero*. Curiously, Freud chooses to employ this text rather than, in the face of all these doubles, Rank's 1914 "The Double" (*Der Doppelgänger*).⁷⁹ The importance of "The Double" for this analysis is Rank's association of the phenomenon of the double with narcissism:⁸⁰ the individual's direction of the libido inward toward the ego and not outward toward objects. Narcissists separate themselves from the outside world, keep themselves aloof, and feel self-important; they are characterized in much the same way as a circumcised (or a chosen) Jew is in *Moses*. Moreover, Freud's "On Narcissism," another work of 1914, describes "the purest and truest feminine type" of object-love as the complete narcissistic type (14:88). In sum, Freud's rhetoric of doubles leads to narcissism that in turn leads both to Jews and to women.

The Missing Link, or the Seventh Degree of Separation

This chain has another link that leads back to Spinoza and thus to the prooftext upon which *Moses* may well rest like a palimpsest. Freud's model for the complete narcissistic type was Lou Andreas-Salomé. As recounted in the Introduction, while I was thunderstruck over the remarkable thematic correspondences of the two testaments—Spinoza's and Freud's— such a coincidence could not argue on its own for claims of Spinoza's influence, or rather of Spinoza providing an optic for that which Freud would disavow. Was Freud familiar with the passage? The question presents a bit of a problem, insofar as according to the concordances to both the *Standard Edition* and the *Gesammelte Werke*, Spinoza only appears twice in Freud's corpus.⁸¹ While Theodor Reik claimed that the painting "Spinoza Being Stoned by the Jews" that hung in his office is a copy of a painting that had hung in Freud's, there is no other record to confirm Reik's assertion.⁸² Further, the extant holdings of Freud's library do not contain a copy of the *Tractatus*. There is, however, one record of his possessing a work that contained the Spinoza citation in its entirety: Siegfried Hessing's *Spinoza-Festschrift*, a collection to which Freud had been invited to submit a chapter but in which only his gracious letter of refusal appears.⁸³ The citation appears in Joseph Klausner's contribution, "The Jewish Character of Spinoza's Teaching,"⁸⁴ and based on Freud's letter expressing gratitude to Hessing for having sent him a copy of the published volume, Freud had at least skimmed it: "It produces an impression by its rich content and by the many sided points of feeling."⁸⁵

Yet as I come to a close of what had been the preliminary and is now my latest investigation I recognize that Freud's familiarity with the passage is no more necessary for the construction of *Moses* than Herbert Graf actually having been circumcised for the construction of "Analysis." The workings of the dispositive circumcision in Central European modernity that were examined in the Introduction are sufficient to suggest these discursive effects of Freud's engagement with matters *jüdisch*. Nevertheless, Spinoza and Freud did intersect at a number of significant moments that may be worth noting, in particular as they relate to the woman who served as Anna Freud's mentor and second mother: Lou Andreas-Salomé. Just prior to the appearance of Freud's "Moses of Michelangelo" and the narcissism piece, as well as *Totem*, Freud was involved in a triangle with Andreas-Salomé and Viktor Tausk. This relationship may have had a number of consequences for the construction of *Moses*. First, both Andreas-Salomé and Tausk were Spinozaphiles. Indeed, in the journal she kept when she was, as she puts it, "in Freud's School," Andreas-Salomé wrote in a section headed "Spinoza":[86] "It delights me that the one thinker I approached in my childhood and almost adored now meets me once again, and as the philosopher of psychoanalysis. Think far enough, correctly enough on any point at all and you hit upon him; you meet him waiting for you, standing ready at the side of the road." Second, the rivalry between Freud and Tausk was not over a common love object, Andreas-Salomé; rather, the "love object" was merely the object of exchange in a relationship between two men.[87] Freud and Tausk were rivalrous doubles:[88]

> Only now do I perceive the whole tragedy of Tausk's relation with Freud: that is, I realize now that he will always tackle the same problems, the same attempts at solution, that Freud is engaged in. . . . As if by a thought transference he will always be busy with the same thing as Freud, never taking one step aside to make room for himself. . . .
>
> There is no doubt about it that Freud acts with complete conviction when he proceeds so sharply against Tausk. But along with this "psychoanalytic" fact [that is, bearing in mind Tausk's original neurotic disposition], it is also clear that any independence around Freud, especially when it is marked by aggression and display of temperament, worries him and wounds him quite automatically in his noble egoism as investigator. . . .

Their rivalry recapitulated the structure of gender relations of the society at large. In sum, the conglomeration of allusions in *Moses* to texts and events of the period 1912–14 suggests that "deferred action," perhaps occasioned by the death of Andreas-Salomé during the revision of *Moses*,[89] may also have provided a lens by which Freud was able to recognize, even as he disavowed, the identification of Jew with feminization.

As his life and the world he had known were also coming to an end, Freud found himself still haunted by an uncanny, unredeemed Spirit (*unerlöster Geist*): *Judentum*. He sought to foreclose its threatened Wagnerian redemption (*Erlösung*), its going under (*der Untergang*),[90] by means of another indeterminate hybrid of the living and the dead, the *Leitfossil* circumcision. As this fossilized, hybridized, indeterminate figuration of feminizing circumcision converged upon the figuration of persisting *Judentum*, Freud found that once unearthed this reconstructed device could not lay the ghost to rest without further jeopardizing *Judentum*. In his earlier work the persistent encounter with the dispositive by which the dominant culture constructed *Judentum*, as well as itself, circumcision, had led to the transferential phantasy of castration that would come to animate his corpus and render meaningful the life-narratives of all as well as provide "the *a priori* condition governing interhuman exchange in the form of exchange of sexual objects."[91] Both the individual and society were founded on difference, but an indeterminable difference is very dangerous to the powers that (would) be unless channeled, so lame-footed Oedipus emerged to maintain the norm and neurosis, reinforced by a new topography of the three fates: id, ego, and super-ego. But as the times and Freud's theory achieved new configurations—the Third Reich and the splitting of the ego—Freud's engagement with *Judentum* was working at cross-purposes. The psychic and social conditions mediated by the dispositive circumcision were overflowing the channels and tending toward the psychotic. And Freud, despite his efforts at secondary revision, and like many faced with such a crisis, generated a supplementary fetish or two, like *Geistigkeit*.[92]

As *Moses*, enacting Freud's disavowal of the identification of *Judentum* with the dispositive circumcision, increasingly found few traces of the sign of the compromise at Kadesh, a similar marginalization was perfomed on his transferential phantasy, his fetishized substitute, generated by the cumulating traumas of being ascribed a Jew in Vienna that so shaped psychoanalytic discourse. Castration, whether simple or complex, received its last mention in the phylogenetic discussion of memory-traces (23:99), and there, as was done to circumcision by the writers of the Pentateuch, it was backdated to screen its disruptive force as the disavowal of a difference that may not be channeled by Oedipus. As Freud wrote in "Dostoevsky and Parricide" (21:184):

> What makes hatred of the father unacceptable is *fear* of the father; castration is terrible, whether as a punishment or as the price of love. Of the two

factors which repress hatred of the father, the first, the direct fear of punishment and castration, may be called the normal one; its pathogenic intensification seems to come only with the addition of the second factor, the fear of the feminine attitude.

Yet, as is always the case with psychical hydraulics, castration will surface elsewhere. In the Afterword I will detail how in "Analysis: Terminable and Interminable," as in Freud's other last writings, such as *Outline* and "Splitting," castration as the "repudiation of femininity" (23:250, 252) is key, a key that will open onto another closed door in *Moses* and in Freud's engagement with *Judentum*.

A Forensic Analysis of Sigmund's Rod, or Cracking Open the *gewachsene Fels* of Psychoanalysis

> One defends oneself in every way against the fear of castration. Here
> a piece [*Stückchen*] of opposition [*Opposition*] to one's own Jewishness
> [*Judentum*] may still be hiding cunningly. Our great Moses was, after
> all, a strong anti-Semite and made no secret [*Geheimnis*] of it. Perhaps
> he really was an Egyptian.
>
> —Letter from Sigmund Freud to Arnold Zweig, 18 August 1933

> Above all, I found that I was expected to feel myself inferior
> [*minderwertig*] and an alien [*nicht volkszugehörig*] because I was a
> Jew. . . . These first impressions at the university, however, had one
> consequence which was afterwards to prove important; for at an early
> age I was made familiar with the fate of being in the Opposition
> [*Opposition*] and of being put under the ban [*Bann*] of the "compact
> majority" [*kompakten Majorität*].
>
> —SIGMUND FREUD, *An Autobiographical Study* (20:9)

As I come to the end of this work and look back on the arguments and
analyses that I have strewn before the reader, I see less pieces of a mosaic
than the links in a chain—a chain such as Homer described in the *Iliad*
and as Freud may have re-encountered in reading Mereschkovsky's *Geheimnis des Ostens/Mystery of the East*. In this passage Zeus gives the advantage to the Trojans by forbidding heavenly intervention:[1]

> let a golden chain [*Kette*] hang down from heaven . . .
> I could haul you up, with earth and sea too,
> and tie the chain to some Olympian peak [*Felsenhaupt*]
> so everything would dangle in midair . . .

For Mereschkovsky each link is a severed foreskin consecrated to Gd, a
circumcision ring that binds the human and the divine. Analogously, I
would argue that each is the "piece of a penis" that ties Freud to *Judentum*.

First it is necessary to move from this "Olympian peak," not to the
"Infernal Regions" (5:647), but to the last section of one of the last psy-

choanalytic works that Freud completed and published in his lifetime, that
he was writing as he was wrestling with the "unlaid ghost," the manuscript
of *Moses*: namely, the 1937 study "Analysis: Terminable and Interminable," and his invocation of the "bedrock" that marks the limit and the
limen of psychoanalysis, the interface of the psychological and the
biological.

Freud there comes to a final reckoning with some old ghosts, his three
primary, all now deceased, alter-egos—Wilhelm Fliess, Alfred Adler, and
Sandor Ferenczi—over what he holds to be the stumbling block of both
therapeutic and character analyses: sexual difference and its role in "the
psychical life of human beings" (*menschlichen Seelenlebens*; 23:250).[2] Freud
will remedy their lacks and remove their excesses by condensing the dispositions toward penis envy in women and the masculine protest in men into
the shared "repudiation of femininity" (23:250, 252). In the last instance
this "remarkable feature [*merkwürdigen Stückes*]" (23:250) proves to be the
castration complex:[3] "What they reject is not passivity in general ['what
might be called the social aspect of femininity'], but passivity towards a
male. In other words, the 'masculine protest' [and the 'wish for a penis'] is
in fact nothing else than castration anxiety" (23:252–53n1).

Freud's phrase translated in the *Standard Edition* as "bedrock" is *gewachsene Fels* and the two iterations of the idiom in successive sentences
are the only two occasions in Freud's collected works that he employs it.
Gewachsene Fels literally (and figuratively) signifies growing or living rock.
Its description as the unplumbable point of an analysis, where analyst and
analysand can penetrate no further, harkens back to the Irma dream's
navel,[4] and the specific figuration evokes its inverse, petrified life, the fossil
that emerges in Freud's discussions of fetishism, circumcision, and *Judentum*. Such living rock may also be contrasted with that source of living
water, Jesus in the Gospel of John (4:10, 7:38), itself an allusion to (and
fulfillment of) Psalm 78:15–16, in which Gd brings water out of rocks and
crags—in Luther's translation, both are *Felsen*—that in turn is a revisionist
allusion to Numbers 20:7–11, where to stem a rebellion at Kadesh Moses
strikes the rock (*Fels*) with Aaron's rod, bringing forth water to stem the
revolt and to incur Gd's wrath by suggesting that the miracle was Moses'
and not Gd's.[5] As punishment, Gd condemns Moses to die before he
reaches the Promised Land.

In *Moses* Freud obliquely addresses the biblical explanation of Moses'
death: "Indeed God himself punished him in the end for an impatient
deed, but we are not told what it was" (23:32).[6] He obscures the allusion to
Numbers 20 all the more by situating it in a discussion of Moses' "irascible

nature" that may "correspond to a historical truth" (23:32), rather than among the biblical attempts to screen the historical truth of Moses' murder at Kadesh (cf. 23:47–50).

More curious is Freud's claim to ignorance of the deed. The passage had emerged in the 1919 edition of *Interpretation*. Freud appended to his section "Representation by Symbols" Hanns Sachs's analysis of an 1863 dream of a great man that his colleague read through Numbers 20. The Iron Chancellor Otto von Bismarck's dream is rife with rocks, with "*Fels-*":

> I dreamt . . . that I was riding on a narrow Alpine path, precipice on the right, rocks [*Felsen*] on the left. The path grew narrower, so that the horse refused to proceed, and it was impossible to turn round or dismount, owing to lack of space. Then, with my whip in my left hand, I struck the smooth rock [*glatte Felswand*] and called on God. The whip grew to an endless length, the rocky wall [*Felswand*] dropped like a piece of stage scenery [*Kulisse*] and opened out a broad path . . . (5:378)

Sachs's comments that "the whole episode of a miraculous liberation from need by striking a rock [*Fels*] and at the same time calling on God as a helper bears a remarkable resemblance to the biblical scene in which Moses struck water from a rock [*Felsen*] for the thirsting Children of Israel" (5:380). When Sachs continues he not only notes the consequences of Moses' action, but he also brings forth themes that were very much circulating in Freudian circles at the time of his writing in 1913: the rebellion of ungrateful followers as well as Freud's own engagement with Moses (the writing of "The Moses of Michelangelo"): "It should not be unlikely that in this time of conflict Bismarck should compare himself with Moses, the leader, whom the people he sought to free rewarded with rebellion, hatred and ingratitude. . . . Moses seized the rod [*Stock*] in the face of God's command and the Lord punished him for this transgression by telling him that he must die without entering the Promised Land" (5:380).[7] What then should be made of Freud's ingenuousness in *Moses*? Can it be struck and release living water?

I am struck by a chain of signifiers that connects these texts from the Bible to *Interpretation* to "Analysis: Terminable and Interminable" to *Moses*, and points in between: in particular, "*Fels-*" and "*Stück*" (rock and piece)—those trace remains of castration and circumcision as well as of Freud's repressions and disavowals. To mix and match my allegorical signifiers and referents, and following Daniel Boyarin, this afterword's first epigraph conjoins castration and circumcision and opens a door upon

Freud's Jewish body and his body of work, but rather than read Freud's corpus as an elaborate and elaborated "masculine protest" against circumcision-induced inferiority,[8] I would rather juxtapose that confession to Zweig with another, more public testimonial to Jewish identification, that of the second epigraph. In that passage from *An Autobiographical Study* (echoed before the more restricted audience of the B'nai B'rith the following year), the sense of inferiority, and the protest thereof, implicit in the first citation are explicitly conjoined to a stance and a signifier shared by both: "Opposition." What characterizes that "Opposition" differs in these two instances. In the letter to Zweig, being in the "Opposition" renders Freud divided against himself, whereas in his self-presentation that position splits him from the "'compact majority.'" Not to deny Freud's ambivalence—such is *la condition humaine*—but I would rather follow the other allusion in the second epigraph, for it leads to another relationship between the *Fels* and the *Stück*: Moses' rod.

I do not wish to wave that phallic symbol against that which would humble it—whether castration or circumcision—but rather see it as that which conditions the synechdochal relationship between not only *Fels* and *Stück* (when the stick strikes the rock, little pieces are generated), but also castration and circumcision. The phrase "'compact majority'" that Freud twice brandishes (20:9, 274), like that umbrella his son Martin recalled,[9] is a citation from Henrik Ibsen's play (*Theaterstück*), *The Enemy of the People*. The phrase is uttered by Dr. Stockmann, (the man of the rod; *Stock* = rod) as he sacrifices his livelihood by pointing out inconvenient truths: the medicinal springs that are the lifeblood of the community are contaminated. He refuses to compromise and, despite being ostracized, opts "to sharpen my pen till they can feel its point."[10] Freud greatly admired Ibsen; his plays have cameos in one of the dreams analyzed in *Interpretation* ("*Norekdal*"; 4:296), and Freud several times commented on Ibsen's insights into the relationships between fathers and sons (for example, 4:257). Such was not the only crucial filial relationship in *Enemy*. Stockmann had a daughter, whose name Petra etymologically returns us to the *Fels* (as does her opposite, her compromising and compromised uncle Peter).[11] At the end, Stockmann bemoans his fate; there is no one to succeed him— that is, there is no son old enough. While he recognizes that his daughter Petra is a chip off the old block, he is unable to appreciate that she is both willing and able to fill that role of liberal- and high-minded tribune. Instead, she is to be a helpmeet in his school for "street urchins" and "ragamuffins" whom he will raise to *Geistigkeit*.[12] While the parallels to Freud's Moses narrative—to Freud's life, as well?—are self-evident,[13] my interest in Freud's allusion is rather to emphasize how Freud's engagements with *Judentum* and the development of psychoanalysis constantly intersected at these "nodal points" (5:340–41), "*Fels-*" and "*Stück*," which, like "switch-points" (5:410), sought to mitigate "castration" and "circumcision" and, as this work has shown, thereby helped generate his discourse.

INTRODUCTION: FREUD'S JEWISH QUESTION AND MINE

Several texts have converged upon this introduction, including the review essay "Identifying 'someone who is himself one of them': Recent Studies of Freud's Jewish Identity," *Religious Studies Review* 23, 4 (1997): 323–31, and my March 2001 lecture at the Freud Museum in Vienna, "*Atheist* Jew or Atheist *Jew*: Freud's Jewish Question and Ours," that later appeared in a revised version in *Modern Judaism* 26 (February 2006): 1–14.

1. Freud/Pfister, *Letters*, 63.

2. That is, vol. 8, p. 177, in Freud's *Standard Edition* (SE). All further citations from the SE appear in this format. The particular work and its standard dating are listed in the bibliography of references to Freud, below.

3. Freud/Martha Bernays, *The Letters of Sigmund Freud*, 203 (2 February 1886).

4. Graf, "Reminiscences," 473.

5. In this and every subsequent quote from the *Standard Edition* in which the word "Judaism" appears, I have substituted the German original (usually *Judentum*). The use of "Judaism" in English and "*Judäismus*" in German refer exclusively to Jewish religious belief and practice. The term "*Judäismus*" does not appear in Freud's *Gesammelte Werke*, as was normative in all pre-1945 German texts with the occasional exception of theological works. Hence its use as a translation of *Judentum*, whose field of meanings is discussed above, is at best too narrow and often misleading. Similarly, throughout this text I regularly employ the German *Judentum*.

6. "[F]or at an early age I was made familiar with the fate of being in the Opposition and of being put under the ban of the 'compact majority.' The foundations were thus laid for a certain degree of independence of judgment."

7. Klein, *Jewish Origins*, esp. chap. 3, "The Prefiguring of the Psychoanalytic Movement: Freud and the B'nai B'rith."

8. Freud/Abraham, *Letters*, 34; *Briefe*, 47 (3 May 1908); hereafter, the bracketed number will refer to the letter's placement in the *Briefe*, as in note 10, below.

9. Freud/Ferenczi, *Correspondence*, 491 (8 June 1913).

10. See the last of Freud's *New Introductory Lectures* (1933), "The Question of a *Weltanschauung*."

11. Freud/Abraham, *Letters*, 46 [57] (23 July 1908).

12. Ibid., 34 [47] (3 May 1908).

13. Ibid., 64 [73] (26 December 1908).

14. Freud/A. Zweig, *Letters*, 91 (30 September 1934).

15. Cf. Herzog, *Intimacy*.

16. Cf. Fabian, *Time*.

17. Cheyette and Marcus, "Introduction," 3. Cf. Stephen Frosh's more explicitly psychoanalytic description of the paradoxical necessity for, and repudiation of, the Jews in modern Western society (*Hate*, 196): "Through its historically derived cultural pervasiveness [the figure of the Jew] is perpetuated as a representation of that which is needed yet despised, that which holds in place the otherwise potentially intolerable destructiveness of a social system founded on inequality and alienation. Such systems create their own psychic structures and psychological disturbances; thus, given the organization of Western society, anti-Semitism is as much an element in the unconscious of every subject as is any other psychosocial state—love, loneliness, or loss, for example. The Jew, and more generally the figure of the 'other', is a constitutive feature of Western consciousness, an element out of which subjectivity is made." Jonathan M. Hess's brilliant textual analyses of leading late-eighteenth-century Jewish and Gentile discussions of *Judentum* in *Germans, Jews* demonstrates both how "reflections on Jews and Judaism played in constructing modernity as a normative category" (20), as well as the "provocation to modernity and its emancipatory project" (23) presented by *Judentum*.

18. Even as it incorporated, especially through the post-1848 convergence of aristocratic and bourgeois student associations, certain ritually reinforced aristocratic values: hierarchy (among alleged equals, friends/rivals who ritually contest among themselves for rank within the organization); membership by descent (with the rise of political and academic antisemitism in 1879–82, the return of the *völkisch* exclusion of Jews [and, more generally, non-Germans] that marked the first bourgeois student associations [*Burschenschaften*] of the Wars of Liberation); and honor as the *Schibboleth* by which group boundaries were negotiated. See Frevert, *Ehrenmänner*, and Kurth, *Männer*.

19. See Frevert, "Bürgerliche Meisterdenker"; Hull, *Sexuality*; and Geller, "Contact."

20. Baeumler, *Männerbund*; Blüher, *Die Rolle*; Brunotte, *Zwischen*; Bruns, "Homosexueller Staatsfreund"; Kreisky, "Stoff"; Mayer, *Outsiders*, 103; Mosse, "Friendship," *Nationalism and Sexuality*, and *Image*; Rosenberg, *Mythus*; Thalmann, *Être femme*, esp. chap. 2; the essays collected in Völgler and

Welck, *Männerbande*; Sombart, *Deutsche Männer*; Widdig, *Männerbünde*. See also Geller, "Hegel's," and especially chap. 6, below. This is not to suggest that the public sphere formed either simultaneously or uniformly among the various populations of Europe; on the public sphere, see Landes, *Women*, following Habermas, *Strukturwandel*.

21. Butler, *Gender Trouble* and *Bodies*; Connell, *Masculinities*; Hewitt, *Political*.

22. See Karin Hausen's classic essay, "Family and Role-Division"; the German 1976 original, "Polarisierung," is perhaps the most influential essay in Germanophone gender analysis. Also see Poovey, *Uneven Developments*, esp. chap. 1, "The Ideological Work of Gender," 79–80, 199, and passim; Nicholson, *Gender and History*; Connell, *Gender and Power*; Brittan, *Masculinity*; Stratton, *Virgin*; and Frevert, "Einleitung," 4ff., who draws on Carl Welcker's 1847 lexicon article as paradigmatic of the bourgeois understanding of the intimate connection among male-female relationships and the legitimation of the bourgeoisie's separate gender-specific spheres of activity: "the most universal and important relationship of human society," "a fundamental relationship upon whose just and wise regulation the beneficial development of society totally depends." For Frevert and Ute Gerhard, "Andere," who provides some conclusions at the end of Frevert, *Bürgerinnen und Bürger*, sexual inequality is a necessary part of bourgeois society since its articulation; it represents the hidden obverse of the formal equality of rights that the bourgeoisie proclaim as the fundamental principle of society.

23. Cf. Brown, *Manhood*, 5: "the quest for manhood as freedom from constraint, as domination of men and the environment, and as thought and action liberated from sensual and emotional aspects of being, results in a bureaucratic and capitalist machinery in which man is utterly ensnared, unfree, and by Weber's own account, inhuman"; such contradictions, especially between male phantasies of autonomy and male dependence upon women, as well as the monkey wrench that market machinery places in masculine ideals, are also addressed by Brenkman, *Straight*, esp. 236–41; Santner, *My Own*, examines the rage generated because the "central values of Enlightenment ideology and culture, above all a sense of individual moral agency . . . the autonomy of even the most masculine of men is stained by heteronomy" (89, 142); also see Maugue, *L'Identité*.

24. Aschheim, *Brothers and Strangers*.

25. Verdery, "Internal Colonialism," drawing upon Hechter, *Internal Colonialism*.

26. Coextensive with the center-periphery imperial division was the inside-outside distinction between the homogeneous *Volk* and the others.

27. Cf. Berman, *All*, unpacking Marx's figure in *The Communist Manifesto*. Santner, *My Own*, brilliantly describes this black hole of values as the crisis of

symbolic investiture: "the social and political stability of a society as well as the psychological 'health' of its members would appear to be correlated to the efficacy of these symbolic operations . . . whereby individuals 'become who they are,' assume the social essence assigned to them by way of names, titles, degrees, posts, honors, and the like [I would, at the very least, include gender among the 'like']. We cross the threshold of modernity when the attenuation of these performatively effectuated social bonds becomes chronic, when they are no longer capable of seizing the subject in his or her self-understanding" (xii).

28. See Foucault, *Order*, esp. part 2, and *Sexuality*; Gallagher and Laqueur, *Making*; Poovey, *Uneven Developments*, 6, and chap. 2; Laqueur, *Making Sex*; Schibinger, *Nature's Body*. Foucault's and Laqueur's work, in particular, spurred a remarkable series of German publications, including Duden, *Geschichte*; Honegger, *Ordnung*; Frevert, *Mann und Weib*; Schmiersahl, *Medizin*; Bublitz, Seier, and Henke, *Gesellschaftskörper*; and Planert, "Dreifacher Körper." Micheler, *Selbstbilder*, esp. 23–44, discusses the modification of Laqueur's influential conclusion that in the late eighteenth century the earlier one-sex model (woman as a lesser man that is also reflected in anatomy) was replaced by a two-sex model of natural biological difference, in which heterosexuality was also inscribed as natural (like magnetism: that opposites attract is a natural law), and thus for a man to desire a man or a woman a woman indicated, respectively, femininization or masculinization. Rather than a paradigm shift, Micheler draws upon early modern historians to argue that the two-sex theory was not a new invention but one of a variety of theories and notions, but that during the eighteenth and early nineteenth century it became hegemonic.

29. Schäfer, *Vermessen*, 150.

30. In addition to the texts already cited, see, among many others, Turner, *Body*; Weeks, *Sex*; Stoler, *Race*.

31. Möbius, *Schwachsinn*, 77; cit. Omran, *Frauenbewegung*, 101.

32. See Armstrong, "Occidental"; Brickman, *Aboriginal*; Efron, *Medicine*; Gilman, *Jew's Body*; Hartsock, *Money*; Hödl, *Pathologisierung*; Lane, *Psychoanalysis*; Nandy, *Intimate*.

33. See Vogt, *Lectures*.

34. See Gilman, "Struggle," 300–301, and Haller, *Outcasts*.

35. Schmiersahl, *Medizin*, 86, cites the sexologist Albert Moll's best-selling 1898 treatise *Untersuchungen über die Libido sexualis*.

36. Riehl, *Naturgeschichte*, 5, 8 (emphasis in original); cit. Schmiersahl, *Medizin*, 23, 21–22. At least seventeen editions of Riehl's prescriptive as well as descriptive work were published through 1935.

37. Buschan, "Die beiden Geschlechter," 3:444; cit. Schmiersahl, *Medizin*, 91. The body parts characterized as sexual (*sexuell*) determine the sex (*Geschlecht*)—that is, the gender, as a whole.

38. On the gender division of labor, see the classic article by Gayle Rubin, "The Traffic in Women."

39. Hauser, "Jüdische Rassedivergenzen"; cit. Feder, "Judenfrage," 61. See also, Günther, *Rassenkunde*, 421.

40. Nordmann, *Juden*, 76.

41. Cf. Dijkstra, *Idols*. These Jewish "idols" are not to be confused with the figure of the "beautiful Jewess"; from Shylock's Jessica and Nathan's Recha through Ivanhoe's Rebecca and Cesar's Delphine (in Gutzkow's *Wally die Zweiflerin*) to Schleiermacher's Henriette Herz and Eliot's Mirah, and, like the "tragic mulatto," the staple of bordello fantasy offerings, these exotic embodiments of pure vegetal sensuality who had the potential to crossover from the Jewish to the Christian camp were during the course of the nineteenth century largely replaced by the Jewess as diseased sexual animal. See Bergman-Carton, "Negotiating"; Gilman, "Salome"; Kohlbauer-Fritz, "'La belle juive'"; Krobb, *Schöne Judin*.

42. See O'Brien, *Politics*, and Jay, "Sacrifice."

43. See Planert, "Dreifacher Körper."

44. See Hull "Bourgeoisie."

45. See *Meyers Konversations-Lexikon*. That this was also a concern of the Jewish community is evident from the prominent Jewish dermatologist and sociologist Felix Theilhaber's apocalyptic 1911 treatise, *The Downfall of German Jewry*: "The consequences of *Zweikinder*-marriage [for Jews] are therefore the quantitative diminishing and the qualitative worsening of the race" (*Untergang*, 61).

46. Weiss, "Discussion," 1758.

47. Ellis, *Sexual Selection*, 45; cf. Horkheimer and Adorno, *Dialectic*, 184; Berillon, "Psychologie," 264; Lowe, *History*; and Stoddart, *Scented*.

48. Cf. Ellis, *Sexual Selection*, 59–61; Corbin, *Foul*; Stallybrass and White, *Politics*, 139–40; Classen, Howes, and Synott, *Aroma*.

49. Hauser, *Geschichte*, 96.

50. Ibid., 387, 96, 322; his earlier discussion of the origins of Christianity and its separation from *Judentum* emphasizes circumcision (197ff.)—as does Freud in *Moses*, 23:88; see chap. 7, below.

51. Fischer and Kittel, *Antikes Weltjudentum*, 168.

52. On the representation of the gender, sexual, ethnic, racial, colonial, class other as a fetish—the substitute that disavows difference—rather than the synecdochal argument I am making, see, inter alia, Stratton, *Virgin*; Bhabha, "Other Question"; and McClintock, *Imperial*. No invocation of fetishism can be made without acknowledgment of the remarkable and influential work of William Pietz (see the bibliography). See also Geller, "Fetishism."

53. Rathenau, "Höre Israel," 456. The importance of Rathenau's characterization of the feminized Jewish body is testified to by his remarks being

explicitly invoked by Günther in his influential (and notorious) *Rassenkunde*, 150–51.

54. An impossibility rendered absurd by George Eliot in *Daniel Deronda* (see discussion, below), the discretion-demanded elision of circumcision is exemplified by the changes made with the publication of the correspondence between Carl Friedrich Zelter, the director of Berlin's Singakademie and composition teacher of Giacomo Meyerbeer, and Johann Wolfgang Goethe. When Zelter's 26 October 1821 letter expressing skepticism about the artistic potential of "the son of a Jew, [but] no Jew himself," Felix Mendelssohn, appeared in print some twelve years later, his explanation of the distinction, that Mendelssohn's "father at significant personal cost had not allowed his sons to be circumcised and educated them as is proper," was altered to read "at significant personal cost had allowed his sons to learn some things . . ."; see Bilski and Braun, "Power," 46, and note 40.

55. Cf. Lupton, "*Ethnos*," 194: "Physical yet not physiological, genealogical but not genetic, circumcision marks the Jews off as a distinct people without being a 'racial' indicator in the modern sense of an inherited trait. . . . In European Christendom, increasingly distanced from the Jewish grounds of Paul's life and thought, the *ethnos* flagged by circumcision increasingly came to denote a preserve of atavistic, dangerously literalist rites whose resistance to sublation challenged the dialectical narrative of Western history."

56. Bar Amitai, *Beschneidung*, 12.

57. On the return of the foreskin to the resurrected Jesus, see Steinberg, *Sexuality of Christ*; conversely, on Jesus's foreskin as relic, see Shell, "Holy."

58. On the notion of dispositive, see Foucault, "Le Jeu"; Deleuze, "Dispositif"; Bührmann, "Normalisierung"; Heiden, *Der Jude*, esp. 225–27; and Walter, *La Shoah*.

59. *Mohels* were also referred to as *Schochets*.

60. See Fanon, *Black Skins*; his analyses of the dilemma of the colonial or postcolonial in the metropole have become a regular counterpoint in studies of Freud's Jewishness. Cf. D. Boyarin, *Unheroic*, 248, and "What?" and Pellegrini, *Performance*. On the representations of Jews as black, see Gilman, *Difference*, esp. 29–35.

61. Cf. Fuss, *Identification*, 35–36.

62. See Efron, *Medicine*, esp. chap. 5 ("The Psychopathology of Everyday Jewish Life").

63. Discussions of the postcolonial subject as a negotiator of the interface of local experience and practice with imperial (read: universal) culture, language, and representation can be found in Williams and Chrisman, *Colonial Discourse*. For the analogous situation in India, see Nandy, *Intimate*; Mufti, *Enlightenment*. As these analyses are specifically applied to Freud, see D. Boyarin, *Unheroic*, and Brickman, *Aboriginal*.

64. And not just writers: see Soussloff, *Jewish*; Bland, *Artless*; and Kozloff, *New York*, on Jewish artists.

65. "Corporeal," 448; for earlier formative discussions, see Eilberg-Schwartz, "People," and Seidman, "Carnal."

66. A variant was "Ob Jud, ob Christ ist einerlei, in der Rasse liegt die Schweinerei" (Whether Jew or Christian doesn't matter, [his] race is the source of [his] chicanery [or of this disgusting mess]).

67. See Botz, Oxaal, and Pollak, *Zerstörte Kultur*.

68. On Billroth's lecture, *Über das Lehren und Lernen der medizinischen Wissenschaften an der Universitäten der deutschen Nation*, see Klein, *Jewish Origins*, and Wistrich, *Jews*. On the extensive anti-Jewish content of German scientific discourse, see, in addition to the prolific work of Sander Gilman, Efron, *Defenders* and *Medicine*, and Hödl, *Pathologisierung*.

69. Whether these traces were unconscious or split off from the ego was a question Freud was debating to the very end; see chap. 7, below.

70. On Benjamin's discussion of Freud and the relationship between (*Schock)Erlebniß* and *Erfahrung* (reflected experience), see Benjamin, "Some Motifs," esp. 160–65, 174–77.

71. On Freud's theorizing of the cumulative effect of trauma, see Grubrich-Simitis, *Early Freud*; a historically, theoretically, and exegetically inadequate attempt to understand Freud's development of psychoanalytic theory as a byproduct of the need to overcome the cumulative "social trauma" of racial antisemitism was essayed in Lehman, "Impact."

72. Freud/Schnitzler (24 May 1926), in H. Schnitzler, "Briefe," 100. In an earlier letter (14 May 1922), Freud confessed that he had avoided meeting and engaging him in conversation out of "a sort fear of doubles" (*aus einer Art von Doppelgängerscheu*; ibid., 96–97).

73. *My Youth*, 6–7.

74. On homeopathy and repetition compulsion, see, respectively, Santner, *Stranded* and *My Own*.

75. Perhaps most phantastic of all is Freud's reenvisioning of castration as the removal of the penis rather than what the term had conventionally referred to prior to Freud's corpus: the removal of the testicles (or ovaries); see Taylor, *Castration*.

76. Laplanche and Pontalis, *Language*, 59 (s.v. "Castration Complex").

77. Stratton, *Coming Out*, 65, drawing upon my article "*Judenzopf*."

78. Hence for all of his affirmations of Jewish identity and despite all of his equally strong disparagements of religious ritual as well as of living in a society in which circumcision was always already assumed of the male Jew, that he chose not to have his sons circumcised cannot but suggest some level of ambivalence; cf. Beit-Hallahmi, "Political," 33.

79. A more scrupulous and less tendentious early reading of Freud's gender rhetoric, especially in his investigations of Christianity and *Judentum*, is provided by Van Herik, *Freud*.

80. Yerushalmi, *Freud's Moses*, 116n25.

81. Wittels, *Freud*; Maylan, *Freuds*; Sadger, *Freud*; Simon, "Freud"; Bakan, *Freud*; Klein, *Jewish Origins*; Schorske, "Politics"; Le Rider, *Modernité*; Cuddihy, *Ordeal*; Roith, *Riddle*; Robert, *D'Oedipe*; Krüll, *Vater*; Gay, *Godless*; Yerushalmi, *Freud's Moses*; Derrida, *Mal* and *Archive*; and Bernstein, *Freud*. An extensive bibliography of the literature on Freud's Jewish identity up to early 1992 can be found in Gilman, *Case*, 229–32n22.

82. Schäfer, "Triumph"; Wistrich, "Last Testament"; Jan Assman, "Sigmund Freud," "Monotheismus," and "Return." In the preface to his *Moses* Assman cites Yerushalmi's book as the catalyst for his study of Moses and the Mosaic distinction (ix); see also Santner, "Ethics." Among many recent engagements by scholars not normally associated with Jewish Studies are those of the psychoanalysts and Freud scholars Ilse Grubrich-Simitis (*Freuds Moses-Studie*) and Wolfgang Hegener (*Wege*); that of the Lacanian political psychologist Thanos Lipowitz (*Fortschritt*); that of the psychoanalytic anthropologist Robert A. Paul (*Moses*); that of the cultural critic Edward W. Said (*Freud*); and that included in the special issue of the Protestant journal of pastoral psychology *Wege zum Menschen*.

83. For example, D. Boyarin and J. Boyarin, in *Powers*, chronicle how even a term associated with Jewish historical experience like "diaspora" has been expropriated by such analyses and indeed resituated in an explicitly antisemitic context.

84. Cf. Gates, "Writing," 4, 6.

85. The classic rejoinder is Plaskow, "Blaming."

86. Gilman, *Freud*, 36–48; cf. Jonte-Pace, *Speaking*, 77–81. Other recent works adopt this claim and extend Freud's displacement to include the (non-Jewish, nonwhite) racialized other, among them Brickman, *Aboriginal*, 165–67, and Frosh, *Hate*, 41–42.

87. D. Boyarin and J. Boyarin, "Diaspora"; see also Shapiro, "Écriture," and Stratton, *Coming Out*.

88. Slezkine, *Jewish*.

89. Cf. Mendes-Flohr, *Divided Passions*.

90. Cf. Crews, *Memory* and *Unauthorized*. More recently, France has witnessed a similar spree of Freud-debunking initiated by the so-called black book of psychoanalysis, Meyer, *Livre noir*; see also the follow-up by Borch-Jacobsen and Shamdasani, *Dossier*.

91. Lincoln, *Theorizing*, xiii; Marks, "Juifemme," 344–45; and (on Gardiner and Auerbach) Gubar, "Eating," 20.

92. Cf. Assmann, *Moses*.

93. Cf. Gay, "Freud verstehen," who saw in the work of Rice (e.g., *Freud and Moses*) and Yerushalmi (e.g., *Freud's Moses*) as well as in the reception of their work "symptoms of a post-Hitler anxiety, which to be sure has nothing to do with Freud, but rather solely with the burden of being an American Jew in this terrible century" (979; the translation is from R. H. Armstrong, "Contrapuntal," 255n11).

94. Novick, *Holocaust*.

95. A number of others have made similar arguments; Jack Neusner had already noted this in *Stranger*.

96. To provide another example: Professor Amy-Jill Levine of Vanderbilt was invited to address a gathering of Baptist campus ministers and their students at a December 2001 Washington D.C. conference whose goal was "challenging [Christian college students] to engage the world's diverse peoples." As a part of this event, the students were scheduled to visit "places such as the Holocaust Museum, the Islamic Center, the Hindu Center, the Buddhist Congregational Church, and others." In other words, by situating the Holocaust Museum in this series, the conveners were identifying it as a center of Jewish religious observance.

97. Novick, *Holocaust*, 2.

98. In addition to the works already cited, see, inter alia, Rainey, *Freud*, and Roazen, *Meeting*.

99. Freud/Eitingon, *Briefwechsel*, 1:85, 85. The poignancy of the moment is enhanced by Freud, confronted with the defection of Jung and thereby the frustration of his "ideal wishes" for the movement not to be limited to "our people," asserts that he feels empowered to be able again to rely on "our indestructible national consciousness."

100. *Letters of Sigmund Freud*, 261 (21 September 1907).

101. Also see Blumenberg, "Jude."

102. In the original edition of *Interpretation*, Freud made one of his most famous parapraxes—perhaps the primal Freudian slip. Instead of the name of the father, Freud wrote that of Hannibal's brother, Hasdrubal. This slip, which Freud rather inadequately analyzes in *Psychopathology*, his next major work, signaled to later interpreters the heavily overdetermined nature of the recollection.

103. Yerushalmi, *Freud's Moses*, 73.

104. See Rice, *Freud and Moses*; Gresser, *Dual*; and Ostow, "Sigmund."

105. See Gay, *Godless*, 127; Gay, however, lacks a corresponding skepticism about Freud's claims to scientificity.

106. Yerushalmi, *Freud's Moses*, 77.

107. For example, Shengold, "Parapraxis," and Roith, *Riddle*, 170–74.

108. Rieff, *Freud*.

109. Rice, *Freud and Moses*, and Gresser, *Dual*, would locate a more religious character to Freud's Jewishness; for example, as characterized by Stern ("Ego," 46) Rice plots Freud's trajectory from the inscription to *Moses* as "the old and sentimental tale, beloved by so many uneasy American Jews, of the prodigal Jewish son who eventually repents and comes home, reconciled to his father and to his father's faith."

110. Yerushalmi, *Freud's Moses*, 112. Yerushalmi, however, does not go as far as Gresser—who would found his argument upon these cups and whose argument instead founders upon them (cf. my review of Gresser's work ["Review"]).

111. I agree with Bernstein's observation that the author of *Zakhor* overplays Freud's Lamarckism while he oddly underplays the role of the Jewish commandment of *Zakhor*, remember, in *Moses*. Freud, they would argue, in writing his work, provides a model for the way Jews (and non-Jews, too) can and do work through their tradition, their cultural memory, and their archival history. Freud's analogy of the ontogeny of traumatic experience with the role of tradition in Jewish history has paved the way for thinking about all forms of experience, traumatic or otherwise. Freud viewed trauma not as an event with inevitable (if variable) consequences, but as a process that is not unlike dream-work (see Santner, "Nomological"). He proposes an analogy between this process of trauma and the development of *Judentum* as a way of understanding the gap, described by the biblical scholars he consulted, between Moses' original ethical monotheism and its return centuries after its abandonment by the people of Israel. The past event (for example, the murder of Moses that Freud alleges occurred) is, however, less the precipitating cause of *Judentum* than is that past's relationship to the present as it unfolds in the event of writing or narrating or redacting. More significant, I believe, is Freud's suggestion in *Moses*—even if he ultimately disavows its importance— that unintegrated or otherwise-integrated fragments of the Mosaic traditions ("like gravestones") had been passed down before the production of the canon. Drawing upon his insights into the temporality of *Nachträglichkeit*, deferred action, Freud recognized that the individual—that matrix of habit and hope, discourse and desire, affect and narrative, social relationships and impersonal structures—is confronted by the remains of a past event. Whether due to the inadequacy of our categories of understanding or the category-shattering character—the violence, shame, or dehumanization of what occurred—the event could not be given meaning or integrated into ongoing self-narratives. The engagement with such memory-traces is an affect-laden, transferential relationship. That transferential relationship can be one of acting-out, of un-

consciously repeating the earlier practices and assumptions, but it can also be an ongoing working-through of that event and its remains: giving them meaning by integrating them into the interminable series of self-narratives. In sum, in dealing with such events that individuals and/or their communities either could not or did not desire to remember, Freud brought both new insight into how we obey the commandment to remember, and added confirmation of its centrality. Freud has placed such an ongoing engagement with the past, with the tradition of pasts, at the center of his and our endeavors. Thus, to recall again that long passage from *Moses*, the present of, on the one hand, that "pious" repetition and, on the other, that (technically speaking) "distorted" meaning-production is the text—whether the *Torah* or rabbinic responsa or *Moses*. Although Freud did not see his interpretive and anamnestic practice of psychoanalysis as guided by religious intentions, that does not preclude us from recognizing that in the end they have come to embody for us a viable form of Jewish practice. Chapter 7, below, approaches Freud's discussion of trauma from a different, more pessimistic perspective.

112. And subsequently reiterated in the second 1919 edition of *Leonardo da Vinci and a Memory of His Childhood*. See chap. 3, below, on Freud's curious decision to omit this footnote from the 1910 edition of *Leonardo* (i.e., in the immediate wake of his Little Hans case study), yet to include the note some nine years later when he re-edited it.

113. In addition to Gilman and D. Boyarin, who are discussed below, the seminal work of George Mosse, such as *Nationalism* and *Image*, needs to be cited. The catalytic role of his winter 1984–85 lecture at the University of North Carolina, Chapel Hill, on this project is recognized below.

114. D. Boyarin, "*Épater*," 36.

115. See also Eilberg-Schwartz, *Phallus*.

116. Weininger, *Sex*, 278; emphasis in original.

117. Gilman, *Freud*, 80, 87, 87, 46.

118. D. Boyarin, *Unheroic*, 239, 239, 215, 273.

119. Gilman, *Case*, 226.

120. My own analysis of Little Hans and penis spectation is in chapter 4, below. Although my rhetoric in some earlier publications (and still employed in chaps. 3 and 7, below)—such that the relationship of circumcision to the uncircumcised parallels that of the fetish to the fetishist—might have conveyed the impression that I intended "to maintain that Freud intended this disagreeable, uncanny impression to be only the province of Gentiles" (D. Boyarin, "Homophobia," 166), my discussion throughout this work demonstrates that my phrasing did not preclude the circumcised from suffering castration anxiety.

121. See Cohen, *Why?*; Mark, *Covenant*; and Levitt, "Correcting."

122. This includes (post-)Christian American society. Although the rate of circumcision in the United States is still much higher than in European nations, the practice of infant circumcision, once nearly universal among those of European descent, has declined by about one-third over the last two decades; see Glick, *Marked*, and Silverman, *Abraham*.

123. On circumcision as cultural diacritical mark, see Boon, "Foreskins."

124. Yerushalmi, *Freud's Moses*, 10, 35.

125. This apparent resistance to, or discomfort over, the significance of circumcision is not limited to those seeking a religious identity for Freud; it is repeated in reviews of Gilman's *Freud* and *Case*, such as that by the noted historian of psychoanalysis John Forrester, "Triumph," for whom circumcision serves an exemplary role in demonstrating Gilman's "absence of evidence" for his claims. By contrast, Gilman's show-stopping retrieval from *Anthropophyteia*, that the clitoris was known in the Viennese slang of the time as the *Jud* or Jew, "clinches the argument" for others, such as Cheyette, "Jew," 9. See also Porter, "Fear"; Malchow, "Review"; and Berman, "Review." The only other document that I have been able to find that shares a similar comparison with the "argument clincher" appears in Neugebauer, "17 Fälle," 235, where the "penislike clitoris" of a hermaphrodite is seen as similar to the circumcised "penis of a Jewish kid"; cit. Hödl, *Pathologisierung*, 218.

126. Yerushalmi, *Freud's Moses*, 3, 54. Bernstein, *Freud*, 12, also notes this curious de-emphasis of circumcision's significance in Freud's text.

127. Robert, *D'Oedipe*, 251.

128. Schur, *Freud*, 468; cit. Yerushalmi, *Freud's Moses*, 7 (emphasis added).

129. Yerushalmi, *Freud's Moses*, 7.

130. Derrida, "Circonfession."

131. Derrida, *Archive*, 12.

132. Ibid., 23.

133. Here *précision* combines, in good Derridean form, *pré*puce (foreskin) and circon*cision* (circumcision).

134. Derrida, *Archive*, 22n3.

135. Ibid., 38; cf. ibid., 42. Since circumcision is the sign of the covenant or *brit* (the Hebrew is usually transliterated as *brith*) the ritual ceremony in which the circumcision is performed is called *brit mila* (covenant of circumcision) or, in Yiddish, *bris*.

136. Ibid. 42; cf. ibid., 26.

137. Ibid., 42. While Derrida's discussion of circumcision and Freud in *Mal/Archive* did not rise above foreplay, it appears that circumcision is more than merely a trope for the identity/difference of the Jew (whether of Derrida or of Freud) and joins the proper name, the signature, the date, the passion of Christ, and other "singularities" that Derrida has deployed. Because they ap-

pear to cut through the play of differences and the necessity of iteration (hence of self-estrangement), such signs—including circumcision—would thereby testify to a transcendental, totalized order or its complement, a "really existing social fact" (Santner, *My Own*, 43); however, they instead betray themselves as performative practices—even when not performed!—that institute that order, produce that fact, and thereby insinuate the other into identity. Discussions of Derrida's rhetoric of circumcision include Caputo, *Prayers*; Cixous, *Portrait*; and Ofrat, *Jewish*.

138. Maciejewski, *Psychoanalytisches Archiv*, 309; citations are from Freud's letters to Abraham on 3 May and 23 July 1908, in Freud/Abraham, *Letters*, 34 (condensation of "you are closer to my intellectual constitution because of racial kinship"), 46,

139. Again Lupton quite rightly contrasts the performative function of circumcision for the Jewish community with the signifying role it serves in the dominant (for Christians) Pauline tradition; however, even as the practice of circumcision became less common among Jews in nineteenth-and early-twentieth-century Central Europe, the enunciation of "circumcision," whether by Jew or Gentile, became all the more performative; see Lupton, *"Ethnos,"* 193–210.

140. Wasserman, *Life*, 150; cit. Judd, "German," 279. Note that this situation is the inverse of the Wolf-Man's; see chap. 3, below.

141. Maciejewski, *Psychoanalytisches Archiv*, 312. For a more extensive discussion of Maciejewski's claims see chap. 4, below.

142. Or whichever gender within the discursive system is most negatively valued; hence in Georg Groddeck's system, Jewish circumcision overmasculinized the Jewish male at the cost of innate human bisexuality; see Groddeck, "Le double," and Lewinter, "Groddeck."

143. For example, Grau, *Semiten*, or, more positively, Jellinek, *Studien*.

144. Geller, "Contact."

145. In his 1879 speech that helped initiate political antisemitism in Wilhelmine Germany, court chaplain Adolf Stoecker's first demand upon modern Jewry is "please be a bit more modest" (*ein klein wenig bescheidener*); "Unsre Forderungen," 146.

146. For example, women's reproductive capacity is necessary to the maintenance and reproduction of the state, the nation, and the *Volk*; cf. Planert, "Dreifacher Körper," 567 and note 109. On the soteriological necessity of the Jews, see below.

147. Corollary to this, I realized that, in order for individuals from those other groups to participate in these exchanges they, too, must internalize and trade in the coin of the realm—their ascribed identities, as classically described by Fanon, *Black Skins*, and Nandy, *Intimate*. These negotiations are not quite

as monolithic as they may seem since there is space for disguise and counterfeit: thus, if the dominated sufficiently mime their role they can become invisible or employ dominant discourse to subvert itself. For example, Freud's psychoanalysis endeavored to transvalue the discourses and identifications by which Jews had been categorized and marginalized; see, e.g., Gilman, "Struggle." Unfortunately, this mimetic ability came to be seen as one of the most threatening aspects of the Jews and the other others. See Geller, "Mice," and Horkheimer and Adorno, *Dialectics*. Consider, too, the explorations of colonial and gender mimesis in Bhabha, *Location*; Butler, *Bodies*; and Taussig, *Mimesis*.

148. Mayer, *Outsiders*, and Carlebach, "Forgotten."

149. See chap. 7, below.

150. Spinoza, *Traité*, 665 (*Tractatus*, 63).

151. On the social-pathological consequences of this double bind, see Mehlman's suggestive "Suture."

152. See Geller, "Blood Sin."

153. Only later did I learn that the late, great comparativist, Charles Bernheimer, had also drawn attention to it several years earlier in an essay on Flaubert's *Bouvard et Pécuchet*; see Geller, "Fetishism," 165–66.

154. Including Stratton, *Coming Out*, whose discussion of fetishism, circumcision, and Jewish difference (esp. 53–58) seems to be unaware of my 1993 article in *American Imago*, about which this chapter is constructed.

155. While checking Herbert's records, I also confirmed the absence of notation that any of Freud's sons were ritually circumcised by a *mohel*; see Rice, "Jewish," 251–52 and the accompanying note, where a lecture by Peter Swales, an interview with Elliott Philipp (Martha Freud's first cousin, once removed), and Albrecht Hirschmüller's testimony are cited. This does not preclude the highly unlikely possibility that any of the four was nonritually circumcised at birth by the attending physician.

156. The current title has recently been redubbed by Professor Michael Rose of Vanderbilt (perhaps with a nod to Leo Baeck, if not to Lenny Bruce), *Judentumessence*.

157. Cf. Eilberg-Schwartz, *People*.

158. Marcus, "Human Nature," 41. As will be noted below, whether Eliot conveniently forgot to have Deronda turn his gaze down or imagined that Deronda's Jewish mother, like Felix Mendelssohn's father (see note 54 above), chose not to circumcise him, Eliot's innumerable allusions to circumcision or non-circumcision (e.g., Eliot implies the latter when she has Deronda's mother, Princess Leonora Halm Eberstein, tell her son: "I rid myself of the Jewish tatters and gibberish that make people nudge each other at sight of us, as if we were tattooed under our clothes, though our faces are as whole as theirs. I delivered you from the pelting contempt that pursues Jewish separate-

ness"; *Deronda*, 698) indicate that the dispositive circumcision was for her the "hidden" signifier of Jewish identity. Perhaps more stunning at the time of its publication than the richly consequential comment itself is that an eminent scholar (of Victorian literature) gave the credit to a graduate student.

159. Eliot, *Deronda*, 35.

160. And before him Certeau, *L'écriture*.

161. Yerushalmi, *Freud's Moses*, 29–30, 87.

162. Ibid., 31. Bernstein, *Freud*, argues for a weaker reading of Freud's Lamarckianism.

163. Eliot, *Deronda*, 49.

164. Cf. J. Boyarin, *Thinking*.

CHAPTER 1: THE PSYCHOPATHOLOGY OF EVERYDAY VIENNA: FAMILIARITY BREEDS PSYCHOANALYSIS

This chapter began its existence as a lecture to my "Freud und das Judentum" class at the Universität-Wien, Summer Semester 2001. Its next avatar was "The Psychopathology of Everyday Vienna: Psychoanalysis and Freud's Familiars," in *The International Journal of Psychoanalysis* 85, 5 (2004): 1–14, before this exercise in differential doubling.

1. See, e.g., Gilman, *Freud*, and Efron, *Medicine*.

2. Although *Gast* is usually translated as "guest," in several German compounds *Gast* signifies host; e.g., *eine Gastfamilie* is "a host family." Hence, *unheimlich* and *Gast* are formal inverses of one another: where two opposing signifiers (*un/heimlich*) converge on the same referent, so two opposing referents converge on the same signifier (*Gast*). In both instances clear distinctions are undermined, threatening the extant order.

3. Pinsker, "Auto-Emancipation," 77.

4. Newman, "Death."

5. Pinsker, "Auto-Emancipation," 77, 77–78.

6. Erikson, "Pseudospeciation," and Volkan, "Need."

7. Freud continues, sardonically, yet perhaps with the hope that he is providing what is merely a historical example: "but unfortunately all the massacres of the Jews in the Middle Ages did not suffice to make that period more peaceful and secure for their Christian fellows."

8. Harrison, "Cultural," 345.

9. Cf. Heer, *Glaube*, esp. 102–12 on Christian-Socialist deputy of the Austrian Imperial Parliament and antisemitic polemicist, Monsigneur Joseph Schleicher.

10. On the history of Viennese Jewry, see Wistrich, *Jews*, esp. chap. 1, and Grunwald's classic, *Vienna*.

11. See Hess, *Claims of Modernity*.

12. Rozenblit, "Jewish," 235.

13. Philipson, *Reform*, esp. 291–320, cit. 320.

14. On Abraham a Sancta Clara, see Heer, *Glaube*, 79–80.

15. Volkov, "Antisemitism." On the use and abuse of Volkov's work, see Heiden, *Der Jude*, esp. 222–24 and nn.

16. This is not a new story—it goes back at least as far as Plato and the sophists; or from another perspective, to our own infancy.

17. Theilhaber, *Untergang*, 127–46.

18. Rozenblit, *Jews*.

19. Cf. Botz, "Ausgliederung." Stourzh, "Age," 21–22, describes a curious memorial in Vienna's Neue jüdische Friedhof am Tor 4 (New Jewish Cemetery at Gate 4), a series of tombstones and monuments bearing crosses or crosses and Stars of David: these were the graves of those Nuremburg Law Jews, whether Catholic, Protestant, or *Confessionslos*, who were denied burial elsewhere.

20. The French is in the original. One should be wary when an author resorts to foreign terms, especially an author such as Freud, who broke away from the medical tradition of employing Latin when referring to indelicate matters, and one such as Freud, who devoted a chapter to parapraxes involving foreign words.

21. The translation of "race" is somewhat misleading. "Ethnic group" would now be a less tendentious translation of the German *Volksstamm* and would better reflect the Jews' legal status in the empire. The German word *Volksstamm* refers to an ethnic group, such as the Czechs, Ruthenians, Hungarians, and the Jews, and was employed in Article 19 of the 1867 State Constitution to characterize all groups claiming common descent and language, whether or not their nationality status and consequent political rights were officially recognized.

22. Cf. Smith, *Butcher's*.

23. Wistrich, *Jews*, 6–7. The specific accusation was desecration of the Host; such libels were homologous to the ritual killing of children since the Host (as the transubstantiated body of Christ) was said to bleed.

24. In *Interpretation* Freud analyzes one of his own dreams that, he writes, was provoked by his attendance at Herzl's play *The New Ghetto* and manifestly addresses the "Jewish Problem" (*Judenfrage*). Known as "My Son, the Myops," it has aroused interest in analyses of Freud's Jewish identity (e.g., D. Boyarin, *Unheroic*, 221–31), in particular, the dream-phrases that also "aroused [Freud's] interest": "*Auf Geseres*" and "*Auf Ungeseres*." Not only does Freud generate a series of associations with Passover through the phonological similarity to "*gesäuert/ungesäuert*" (leavened/unleavened), but he also draws upon

information from philologists as well as his recollection of the use of the term in "*Jargon*." With regard to the last, the *Standard Edition* translates this term as "slang," which occludes that *Jargon* was jargon for Yiddish. While attention has been placed on the dream as Freud's ambivalent mediation of Rome (cf. note 26, below) and Jerusalem, of his possible ambivalences toward assimilation, what should also be noted is its Viennese provenance (see oewb.retti. info/oewb-public/show.cgi), and that the "weeping and wailing" referred to by *Geseres*, pronounced "Gezeres," was initially in response to the *Wiener gezerah*.

25. Kleinpaul, *Menschenopfer*. While accepting the historicity of some Israelite engagement with the child sacrificial cult of the Semitic deity Moloch (see Lev. 18:21, Jer. 32:35, and 2 Kings 23:10)—which such antisemitic polemicists as Georg Friedrich Daumer (*Feuer- und Molochdienst*), Friedrich Wilhelm Ghillaney (*Menschenopfer*), and Gustav Tridon (*Molochisme*) asserted still persisted in the form of the ritual murder of Christian children by Jews— Kleinpaul devotes his second chapter to how circumcision (and the paschal lamb sacrifice) substituted for child sacrifice. Kleinpaul extensively describes the entire ritual procedure, both in the synagogue and, as he has personally witnessed in Rome's ghetto, in a home, including the implements employed to perform circumcision. Freud may have found particularly fascinating the description of one cutting tool that Kleinpaul says "aussieht wie ein Zigarrenabschneider" ("looks like a cigar clipper"; 12). He also compares the Italian Jewish mother of the circumcised child to the portrait of a noble (hence non-Jewish) Florentine women by a sixteenth-century painter such as Andrea del Sarto or Ghirlandaio.

26. Freud also connected his identification with Hannibal to his self-diagnosed Rome neurosis, his seeming inability to reach Rome during any of his many trips to Italy. This neurosis was resolved the year of *Psychopathology*'s publication. That visit to Rome would also mark his acquaintance, and eventual obsession, with Michelangelo's *Moses*, specifically, and identification— perhaps substituting for that other non-Jewish, non-European Hannibal— with the person of Moses; cf. 4:196–98.

27. Gruman, "Freud's 'Forgetting,'" 131 and 145.

28. Also cf. Schnitzler, *Road*, in which the tauntingly hopeless plight of the postliberal Jewish generation and their circle is symbolized by the death, after a single breath, by strangulation with his umbilical cord of the protagonist Georg von Wergenthin's out-of-wedlock son with Anna Rosner.

29. See Lichtblau, "Chiffre," and Bajohr, *Unser Hotel*.

30. See Beller, *Vienna*, 34, 45–46.

31. Cf. Hitler, *Mein Kampf*, 247: ". . . since every department store Jewess is considered fit to augment the offspring of His Highness."

32. Nordau and Nordau, *Max Nordau*, 117.
33. The story was added to the fifth edition of *Psychopathology* (1919).
34. Wortis, *Fragments*, 144.
35. Cf. Gilman, "Max," esp. 59–61, on Freud's analysis of his correspondence with an American doctor who returned to Christianity and subsequently attempted to proselytize Freud in "A Religious Experience" (21:170–71). Grossman, "Some Sources," discusses possibly significant differences between Freud's German translation of the American's letter and the English original. While the question of Freud's views on conversion and Jewish identity are not discussed in relation to the slips, Grossman does draw extensively upon two items that are frequently addressed in studies of Freud and *Judentum*: the illustrations of the family Philippson Bible and Freud's father's inscription in that Bible on the occasion of his son's thirty-fifth birthday.
36. Schnitzler, *Youth*, 6–7.
37. Cf. Gilman, *Self-Hatred*.
38. Henseler, "Einige Gedanken"; cit. Hirschmüller, "Psychoanalyse," 43.

CHAPTER 2: NOT "IS PSYCHOANALYSIS A JEWISH SCIENCE?" BUT "IS IT *UNE HISTOIRE JUIVE?*"

This chapter began its existence as "(G)nos(e)ology: The Cultural Construction of the Other," a presentation at a session of the Religion and the Social Sciences Section devoted to Psychosocial Construction of the Body during the 1989 American Academy of Religion annual meeting. Its next avatar bore the same title as a chapter in *The People of the Body*, ed. Howard Eilberg-Schwartz (Albany: State University of New York Press, 1992), 243–82. It has since undergone several rhinoplasties and other grafts, including portions of "Some More Additional 'Day Residues': The First Review of *Studien über Hysterie*, Ilona Weiss, and the Dream of Irma's Injection," *Psychoanalysis and History* 2, 1 (2000): 61–75.

1. Such nuances would have escaped the famous biblical scholar and infamous antisemite Gerhard Kittel, who in his *Judenfrage/The Jewish Question* argued that the sign that among the ranks of the intellectual and social leaders of the German bourgeoisie antisemitism played a harmless role during the supposedly peak years of pre–World War I German antisemitism (the 1880s) was that they easily (*mit einem gewissen Behagen*) told jokes about those especially grotesque particularities of Jews, "the foreskin and circumcision." The harmlessness of such jokes was confirmed by their being repeated "with particular delight (*mit besonderer vorliebe*) by the modern assimilated Jew" (*Assimilationsjude*; 34).
2. Sander Gilman discusses Freud's use of Jewish jokes and their both expiatory and exemplary role in Jewish self-hatred in *Self-Hatred*, 261–69.

3. Hers is the first of five case histories that Freud and Breuer published together in *Studies*.

4. Hers is the last of the cases; see below.

5. Freud, *Complete*, 417. Six days later Freud reaffirms the dating to Fliess: "I have authenticated the date of July 24, 1895, however. The dream is dated the same way in the book, July 23–24, and I know that it was the first time I grasped the general principle, just as I know that I analyzed the dream the following day" (ibid., 419 [letter of 18 June 1900]). While Freud's claim that he analyzed the dream and grasped the principle on that date has come into question (Wilcocks, *Maelzel's*)—his failure to mention his discovery in his letter of 24 July 1895 has long been noted—that he dreamt the dream around that time is not in question. Freud discusses a portion of the dream in his 1895 "Project for a Scientific Psychology" (Freud, *Origins*, 403). Ironically, all that remains today of that villa is an identically worded marble tablet that later adorned the grounds.

6. This rather triumphalist statement was actually added to the second edition of *Interpretation* in 1909 at the end of the penultimate section on "repression" and prior to the last section on "reality." The possible dual referents of the phrase are also indicated by its placement immediately after the citation from the *Aeneid* (7.312) that also functioned as the epigraph of the entire work: *"Flectere si nequeo superos, Acheronta movebo."*

7. This dream only assumed its central role in *Interpretation* because Fliess advised against Freud's employing his only completely analyzed dream—Irma was merely "thoroughly" analyzed—as a frame upon which he would construct his text. See Freud, *Complete*, 315, 316n1, 317 (letters of 9 and 20 June 1898). That original dream has never turned up, but cf. Mautner, "Freud's."

8. See Anspaugh, "Repression"; Anzieu, *Self-Analysis*; Eissler, "Farewell"; Elms, "Freud, Irma"; Erikson, "Dream"; Gay, *Freud*, 80–86; Greenberg and Pearlman, "If"; Hartman, "Reappraisal"; Kuper and Stone, "Dream"; Lacan, *Ego*; Mahony, "Towards," "Friendship," and "Le jeu"; Masson, *Assault*, 57, 60, 213n1, 213–14n4; Schur, "Some"; Sprengnether, "Mouth"; Swan, "Mater"; and Van Vetzen, "Irma." For example, in PsychInfo, the literature database of the American Psychological Association from 1887 to January 2006, the string (Irma AND Freud) or (Irma's AND Freud) finds sixty-four citations for works. The second most discussed dream, "The Dream of the Botanical Monograph," has only seven citations.

9. See, respectively, Kuper and Stone, "Dream"; Erikson, "Dream"; Van Vetzen, "Irma"; Schur, "Some"; Sprengnether, "Mouth"; and Davis, *Dreaming*.

10. Anzieu, *Self-Analysis*, 155.

11. Mahony, "Towards," 93; cf. "Le jeu," 87–88.

12. On the propensity of dreams to take advantage of the ambiguity of the pronunciation as well as of the meaning of words, also see Mahony, "Towards." Freud, *Complete*, 295 (letter of 22 January 1898), also punned with other of Fliess's nose-related terms when awake; for instance he jokingly refers to the "reflex new-roses" (*Reflexneu–rosen*), a play on the nasal reflex neuroses (*Reflexneurosen*).

13. Showalter, *Little Man*, 61; also see Fuchs, *Juden*, esp.161–65. Fischer and Kittel argued that caricatures of the Jewish nose can be traced back to at least the third and fourth centuries c.e.; *Antikes Weltjudentum*, 167–72.

14. Cf. Habermas, *Strukturwandel*.

15. Lavater, *Essays*, 1:17; cf. Gilman, "What," 56.

16. See Erb, "Wahrnehmung."

17. Fuchs, *Juden*, 161–62; cf. Schäfer, *Vermessen*, esp. 219–29.

18. *The Jewish Encyclopedia*, 9:338–39 (s.v. "nose"), citing Jacobs "Racial." On Jacobs, see Efron, *Defenders*, esp. chap. 4, "Joseph Jacobs and the Birth of Jewish Race Science."

19. Horkheimer and Adorno, *Dialectic*, 184.

20. Fuchs, *Juden*, 163.

21. Lavater, *Essays*, 3:363.

22. Fliess, *Les relations*, 17.

23. Küpper, *Illustriertes*, s.v. "Nase," lists more idioms under *Nase* than under either *Auge* (eye), *Ohr* (ear), or *Mund/Maul* (mouth). On the influence of proverbs on Freud's thought, see his 14 November 1897 letter to Fliess (Freud, *Complete*, 279): "(. . . the notion [of organic repression] was linked to the changed part played by sensations of smell: upright walking, nose raised from the ground, at the same time a number of formerly interesting sensations attached to the earth becoming repulsive—by a process still unknown to me.) (He turns up his nose = he regards himself as something particularly noble)."

24. Cf. Hoffman-Krayer and Bächtold-Stäubli, *Handwörterbuch*, 6: 970; Ellis, *Sexual Selection*, 67.

25. Chamberlain, *Foundations*, 1:375–76. Conversely its presence/absence is an indication of Jews as mongrel race, see ibid., 1:389. Antisemitic assumptions are nonfalsifiable.

26. Freytag, *Soll*, 40. Curiously the English translation (Freytag, *Debit*) omits this passage.

27. Hubrich, *Gustav*, 91.

28. Burckhardt, *Letters*, 169 (letter of 24 July 1875); cit. Mosse, *Germans*, 58–59.

29. Hess, *Revival*, 58–59.

30. See Gilman, *Making*, 130–37.

31. Heine, *Börne*, 270, 271; cf. Rainey, *Freud*, 61, on Freud's cherishing of Börne's works and Börne as a possible model for the young Freud.

32. Heine, *Rabbi*, 50 (translation altered), 55, 56, 76; cf. Rainey, *Freud*, 22, on similarities between Freud's adolescent epistolary imagery and Heine's work.

33. This "regression to a very early interchangeability of the container and the contents, in other words to a mechanism of primary thought" (Anzieu, *Self-Analysis*, 153), may also reflect the psychopathology of a dominant group that seeks to deny its dependence on the other for its own self-determination.

34. On the medieval origin of the notion of a *foetor Judaicus*, see Trachtenberg, *Devil*, 47–50; Fishberg, *Jews*, 314–16; cf. Poliakov, *From the Time*, 142–43 and note 14.

35. Andree, *Volkskunde*, 68–69.

36. *Res Gestae* (22.5.5): "For Marcus [Aurelius], as he was passing through Palestine on his way to Egypt, being often disgusted with the malodorous and rebellious Jews, is reported to have cried with sorrow: O Marcomanni, O Quadi, O Sarmatians, at last I have found a people more unruly than you"; cit. M. Stern, *Greek*, 2:605–6.

37. See Jaeger, *Entdeckung*, 1:113; he recounts how a certain Dr. M., when allowed to kiss the slipper of Pius IX during a papal audience, immediately perceived by the odor that the pope was of Jewish origin (1:246–48).

38. Andree, *Volkskunde*, 68.

39. "Knoblich, Knoblich, toffes Gwarz / Stärkst dien Jüden Sinn unn Harz, / Unn giebst ihn die ganze Wuch / Aechten, koschern, Jüdeng'ruch"; cit. Fuchs, *Juden*, 282; cf. Hödl, *Pathologisierung*.

40. Nietzsche, *Ecce Homo*, 233. Despite Nietzsche's olfactory sensitivity and his alleged antisemitism, Nietzsche does not contribute significantly to the dissemination of the *foetor Judaicus*; however, he does remark in the *Anti-Christ* (161): "One would no more choose to associate with 'first Christians' than one would with Polish Jews. . . . Neither of them smell very pleasant." Also see Bloch, *Odoratus*, 10–11: "In the act of olfaction it seems that a real contact of the psyche with the material world has taken place, a penetration into the sensed matter and an immediate perception of its essence . . . the sublimated thing-in-itself."

41. Others vying for this honor include Richard Wagner (see Weiner, "Wagner's Nose"); Jaeger (*Entdeckung*, 6–7, 10, 64, 113 [citing Andrée, "Völkergeruch," 246–47]); Berillon ("Psychologie," 266); Günther (*Rassenkunde*, 260–68, esp. the chapter entitled "Geruchliche Eigenart"); and Hitler (*Mein Kampf*, 57), who writes: "The cleanliness of [the Jews], moral and otherwise, I must say, is a point in itself. By their very exterior you could tell that these were no lovers of water, and, to your distress, you often knew it with your eyes closed. Later I often grew sick to my stomach from the smell of these caftan wearers." This last passage in retrospect perversely evokes the depiction of

the Davidic Messiah in B. Sanhedrin 93b—"And further it is written, And He will let him have delight in [lit., 'will let him scent'] the fear of the Lord [*Isaiah* 11: 3; Luther's *Bibel* reads 'mein Riechen wird sein bei der Furcht des Herrn']. R. Alexandri said: 'This teaches us that they burdened him with commandments and sufferings like millstones' [assuming *hariho*, which literally means 'he will let him scent,' derives from *rehayim*, millstones]. Rava said: '[This teaches us that] he will scent [the truth] and will adjudicate, as it is written, and he shall not judge after the sight of his eyes, neither reprove after the hearing of his ears, yet with righteousness shall he judge the poor' [Isa. 11:3–4]"; cf. Patai, *Messiah*.

42. Schopenhauer, *Parerga*, 1:73.

43. Schopenhauer, *World*, 2:645.

44. Schopenhauer, *Parerga*, 2:375; cf. *Grundprobleme*, 4:240.

45. Horkheimer and Adorno are perhaps referring to Schopenhauer when they write in their "Elements of Anti-Semitism" (*Dialectic*, 184): "The multifarious nuances of the sense of smell embody the archetypal longing for the lower forms of existence, for direct unification with circumambient nature, with the earth and mud. Of all the senses, that of smell—which is attracted without objectifying—bears clearest witness to the urge to lose oneself in and become the 'other.' As perception and the perceived—both are united—smell is more expressive than the other senses. When we see we remain what we are; but when we smell we are taken over by otherness. Hence the sense of smell is considered a disgrace in civilization, the sign of lower social strata, lesser races and base animals. The civilized individual may only indulge in such pleasure if the prohibition is suspended by rationalization in the service of real or apparent practical ends. The prohibited impulse may be tolerated if there is no doubt that the final aim is its elimination—this is the case with jokes or fun, the miserable parody of fulfillment. As a despised and despising characteristic, the mimetic function is enjoyed craftily. Anyone who seeks out 'bad' smells, in order to destroy them, may imitate sniffing to his heart's content, taking unrationalized pleasure in the experience. The civilized man 'disinfects' the forbidden impulse by his unconditional identification with the authority which prohibited it; in this way the action is made acceptable. If he goes beyond the permitted bounds, laughter ensues. This is the schema of the antisemitic reaction. Antisemites gather together to celebrate the moment when authority permits what is usually forbidden. . . ."

46. See Corbin, *Foul*.

47. On the primitiveness of language that does not distinguish between objective and subjective perspectives, see Jaeger, *Entdeckung*, 1:108.

48. See Howes, "Olfaction." Or as any fifth-grader knows: "Who smellt it, dealt it."

49. Cit. Ellis, *Sexual Selection*, 46.
50. Ibid., 55.
51. Nordau, *Degeneration*, 14.
52. See ibid., 541ff.; Corbin, *Foul*, 198–99, 205–6; Ellis, *Sexual Selection*, 73.
53. Nordau, *Degeneration*, 209, cites the antisemites' fascination with the work of Jaeger (*Entdeckung*), which identified the individuality of each soul with the totality of odors released in the breakdown of protein molecules and the natural differences between the race with the correspondingly different—and incompatible—scents.
54. Ellis, *Sexual Selection*, 46, 55, 67–70.
55. Ibid., 64.
56. Bloch, *Odoratus*, 74.
57. Gilman, "Struggle," 300.
58. Haeckel, *Anthropogenie*, 656–57; cit. Sulloway, *Freud*, 150.
59. See Sulloway, *Freud*, 150; Bloch, *Sexual*, 15.
60. Bloch, *Odoratus*, 24–25.
61. *Revue de l'hypnotisme*, "Etude," 124.
62. Sulloway, *Freud*, 148–49; cit. from Mackenzie, "Physiological," 117–18.
63. Freud, *Complete*, 223; cf. Bloch, *Odoratus*, 120; Koestenbaum, "Privileging"; Ellis, *Sexual Selection*; Iribane, "Névropathies"; Krafft-Ebing, *Psychopathia*; Mackenzie, "Pathological."
64. Ellis, *Sexual Selection*, 64. Bloch, *Odoratus*, 70, cites a different odor, that of trimethylamin, which appears in the dream of Irma's injection and which Freud associates with Fliess.
65. Bloch, *Odoratus*, 69–70, citing Jaeger, *Entdeckung*.
66. On the other hand, Bloch, *Odoratus*, 74, notes: "In strong, vigorous men this *odeur de l'homme* is considerably sharper than among effeminate and weak ones."
67. The association between chloroform and questions of gender identity also played a role in Freud's early career; the Viennese psychiatrist, former teacher of Freud, and chloroform addict Theodor Meynert, objected strenuously to Freud's contention that men can suffer from the archetypical woman's neurosis, hysteria. In *Interpretation* Freud reports on Meynert's death-bed confession that he was a male hysteric (5:438). This conflict, which was implicitly about gender identity, led to Freud's foreclosure from the neurological institute at the University of Vienna and severely limited his opportunities within Viennese medical circles; cf. Kris, "Introduction," 20. On Meynert's addiction to drinking chloroform, see Freud, *Complete*, 293 (letter of 4 January 1898).

68. See Poovey, *Uneven Developments*, esp. chap. 2.

69. See, inter alia, Gilman, *Case*, 96–99, 155; Beusterien, "Jewish"; Katz, "Shylock's."

70. Verein zur Abwehr des Antisemitismus, *Antisemiten-Spiegel*, 435. On Jewish male menstruation and the blood libel, see also Trachtenberg, *Devil*, 50–51, 149, and Hsia, *Myth*, esp. his discussions of Johannes Eck and Andreas Osiander (4, 134, 138). Interestingly, *Gerücht*, which incensed many Gentiles against the Jews, has an olfactive popular etymology. The word is said to derive from "in gutem (schlechtem) Geruch stehen" (to have a good (bad) reputation), which literally means "to stand in good (bad) odor."

71. Gilman, "Struggle," 302–3.

72. Fliess, *Les relations*, 26, cf. 19.

73. Ibid., 242 (case 147, Dr. L . . . n).

74. Freud, *Complete*, 256.

75. Fliess, *Les relations*, 10; trans. in Kris, "Introduction," 7.

76. Freud, *Complete*, 212 (letter of 6 December 1896).

77. Kristeva, *Powers*, 71.

78. Foucault, "Introduction," viii; cf. Turner, "Body," 21.

79. Freud, *Complete*, 464 (letter of 23 July 1904).

80. Cf. Gilman, "Struggle," 304: "Jews show their inherent difference through their damaged sexuality [that is, their implicit bisexuality], and the sign of that is, in the popular mind, the fact that males menstruate. . . . The hidden sign, the link between the homosexual, the woman, and the Jew is the menstruation of the Jewish male."

81. Fliess, *Les relations*, 135–36, had theorized that there were "stomach ache spots" adjacent to the nasal genital spots (the *Nasenmuscheln*). The cocainization, cauterization, and extirpation of the offending parts were among the operative procedures to which Fliess would subject his patients who suffered from any number of possible nasal reflex neuroses.

82. Greenberg and Pearlman, "If," table 1, list some twenty correlations—some of which are rather tenuous—between elements in the dream and those in Freud's letters to Fliess.

83. See Jones, *Life*, 1:252; Gay, *Freud*, 72–73; David-Menard, *Hysteria*, 67–70.

84. Freud, *Complete*, 280 (letter of 14 November 1897); cf. 10:247–48; 21:100n., 106n.; and chapter 3 in the present volume, below. For Sulloway, *Freud*, 359, Freud's theory of organic "repression and the sense of smell were to become paradigmatic for all of his subsequent attempts to resolve the problem of repression in phylogenetic terms." Indeed, the tie of smell and repression, " 'the corner-stone' in Freud's theory of psychoneurosis" (ibid., 368), is the corner-stone of Sulloway's claims of both Freud's continued biologism

and his extensive theoretical dependence upon Fliess. Perhaps not surprisingly, Schopenhauer (*World*, 2:31) refers to smell as "the sense of memory."

85. Gilman, "Struggle," 299–305.

86. "Without such an audience I cannot work"; Freud, *Complete*, 243 (letter of 16 May 1897).

87. Freud, *Complete*, 374 (letter of 21 September 1899); cf. ibid., 73 (letter of 21 May 1894): "you are the only other, the alter."

88. Schur, *Freud*, 77 and ff.; Mahony, "Friendship," 68.

89. In addition to the operation that occurred during the same period as the botched operation on Eckstein, Freud regularly consulted him on his cardiac condition and cigar addiction. See Freud, *Complete*, 129 (letter of 25 May 1895): "I hope to bring enough with me to Berlin so that I can amuse you and hold your interest for the entire time I am your patient."

90. See esp. Swan, "Mater," 24; Koestenbaum, "Privileging"; D. Boyarin, *Unheroic*, chap. 5 ("Freud's Baby, Fliess's Maybe").

91. Freud, *Complete*, 134.

92. Freud/Ferenczi, 6 October 1910, in Freud/Ferenczi, *Correspondence*, 221; cf. Freud to Ernest Jones, 8 December 1912, in Freud/Jones, *Correspondence*, 182 ("some piece of unruly homosexual feeling"); also see Gay, *Freud*, 274–83; Heller, "Quarrel."

93. Cf. Baeumler, *Männerbund*, 6–9, 30–42, 166–67; Mosse, "Friendship"; Steakley, "Iconography"; J. Jones, "*We*"; Oosterhuis and Kennedy, *Homosexuality*; Micheler, *Selbstbilder*.

94. See McGrath, *Discovery*; Koestenbaum, "Privileging"; Davis, *Drawing*; D. Boyarin, *Unheroic*; Toews, "Fashioning" and "Refashioning."

95. See Planert, "Dreifacher Körper."

96. See, for example, Freud, *Complete*, 57–58, 90–91, 92–94, 98, 101–2 (letters of 6 October 1893; 18 August 1894 [Draft F]; 23 August 1894; and 7 January 1895 [Draft G]). Hartman, "Reappraisal," 578, sees Irma's dream as possibly sheathed with a condom: "While the first latex condom was commercially introduced in England in 1890, most condoms were still made from fish bladders that had to be preserved in salt, or sheep intestines that had to be kept moist in a preservative solution of denatured (mixed with propyl) alcohol or isopropyl alcohol. . . . Trimethylamin's smell of rotting fish should be remembered." For the most recent discussion, see Sprengnether, "Mouth." At this juncture in his career Freud more or less accepts the general hysteria about the dangers of masturbation. Combining both is the depiction of contraception use as "conjugal onanism" in the British medical journal *Lancet*; cit. Mosse, "Nationalism." 226. Fliess, *Les relations*, 238, also remarks that "the sexually mature man, who to the extent that he can satisfy entirely the reproductive instinct, does not have anxiety. The excitation finds its normal expression and thereby its equilibrium."

97. See Gay, *Freud*, 66–67. Summarizing the skepticism surrounding her pregnancy and subsequent pseudocyesis is Borch-Jacobsen, *Remembering*, chap. 4 ("Constructions"); however, that Freud felt compelled to relate such anecdotes rather than their veracity is what matters for my argument.

98. Freud, *Complete*, 131. The manner in which the ideology of reproduction channels Freud's desire into the desire to sublate woman's reproductive power finds its most blatant expression in his ode to celebrate the birth of Fliess's second son and his father's calculation of the exact birthdate: "Hail / To the valiant son who at the behest of his father appeared at the right time, / . . . / But hail to the father, too, who just prior to the event found in his calculations / the key to restraining the power of the female sex / And to shouldering his burden of lawful succession; / . . . / He calls upon the higher powers to claim his right, conclusion, belief, and doubt; / . . . / May the calculation be correct and, as the legacy of labor, be transferred from father to son . . ." (Freud, *Complete*, 393–94 [letter of 29 December 1899]); cf. Koestenbaum, "Privileging," 73–74.

99. Freud, *Complete*, 129.

100. Ibid., 113–14.

101. Ibid., 116.

102. Ibid., 116–17.

103. Fliess, *Les relations*, 111, 69.

104. Schur, "Some," 57n13, comments: "There is hardly a more sickeningly foetid odor than that of iodoform gauze left in a wound for fourteen days."

105. "Some," 59.

106. Rainey, *Freud*, 109, reported that during his eight years at gymnasium Freud, as was required of all gymnasium students, had accumulated fifty class hours (per week) of Latin studies; this averages to 6.25 per week each year.

107. Freud, *Complete*, 117.

108. The identity of the individual is unknown. Professional women were extremely rare in 1895 Vienna—women were not yet allowed to matriculate to the University of Vienna's medical school—and *"Doktorin"* (lit., female doctor), was also used as the title assigned a physician's spouse.

109. All preceding citations are from Freud, *Complete*, 117, except for "child of sorrows," which appears on 118.

110. Ibid., 118.

111. In "Draft K. The Neuroses of Defense"—is this perhaps the fully matured "six-month-old fetus" of 12 June 1895?—enclosed in the letter of 1 January 1896, Freud writes, "Where there is no shame (as in a male person) . . ." (ibid., 163).

112. Ibid., 118.

113. Ibid., 134.

114. Cf. Anzieu, *Self-Analysis*, 134; Eissler, "Farewell"; and others. Anzieu, *Self-Analysis*, 134, 140, also suggests that Anna O. is one of the individuals condensed into the figure of Irma. Surprisingly, although Masson makes much of the significance of Emma Eckstein for both Freud's seduction theory and his relationship with Fliess, he accepts the Anna Lichtheim hypothesis; *Assault*, 57, 60, 213n1, 213–14n4.

115. Thus Eissler, "Farewell," like Elms, "Freud, Irma," before him, focuses on Freud's relationship with and the pregnancy of Martha. Anzieu, *Self-Analysis*, 153, does tie Anna in with the motif of smell: "Ananas is pronounced in German in exactly the same way as Anna *nass* (wet Anna); so she stinks."

116. Freud/Abraham, *Letters*, 20.

117. See Gay, *Freud*, 83–87.

118. Freud, n.d.; cit. Grubrich-Simitis, *Back*, 111–12.

119. "The mother says to her and her friends: Well, now each of you will make a dessert remark (bonbon—bon mot); cit. Grubrich-Simitis, *Back*, 103.

120. Freud, *Complete*, 230.

121. Michael Molnar, the senior researcher at the Freud Museum, private electronic correspondence. The book is currently in the Sigmund Freud Collection at the Library of Congress. I am unable to confirm the absence of Irma since Sigmund Freud Copyrights had placed this once-available document back on the restricted list at the time of my visit in 1998.

122. Ibid., 140–41.

123. Despite limits on access to material under the jurisdiction of Sigmund Freud Copyrights, a number of scholars have drawn from Freud's letters, articles, and contextual material to reconstruct the identities of his early patients. Most persistent of these researchers is Peter Swales (see, for example, Swales, "Freud," on Anna von Lieben, a.k.a. Frau Cäcilie M.); see also Appignanesi and Forrester, *Freud's Women*.

124. Gay, *Freud*, 71.

125. Freud, *Complete*, 130 (letter of 25 May 1895), on Emma E.'s "weakness in walking."

126. Although, by employing the pronoun "this" the English translation conveys the impression that she accepted his conclusion, the German original is somewhat more ambiguous: "sie widersprach mir nicht" (she did not contradict me). One happy marriage and three daughters later, she did dispute Freud's conclusion; she confided to her youngest daughter that Freud had tried "to persuade me that I was in love with my brother-in-law, but that wasn't really so" (Gay, *Freud*, 71).

127. Ibid., 72.

128. Cf. Freud, *Complete*, 8 (letter of 18 September 1892), and Anzieu, *Self-Analysis*, 64–65.

129. That is, Freud applied pressure to the patient's forehead with his hand as the patient closed her eyes and concentrated on the symptoms; this procedure brought forth associated memories and thoughts.

130. Jones, *Life*, 1:243. Jones actually makes more of the case than perhaps is its due. He writes: "On one historic occasion, however, the patient, Frl. Elisabeth, reproved [Freud] for interrupting her flow of thought by his questions. He took the hint, and thus made another step towards free association" (243–44). Yet the footnote in *Studies* that Jones cites as the source for this scene associated with the origin of free association is from the case of Frau Emmy von N. (2:62n1); it is clear from the case study of Elisabeth von R. that free association is already assumed (2:145). Jones also adds that this was "one of the countless examples of a patient's furthering the physician's work"; he compares it to Anna O.'s "discovery" of the cathartic method. Ilona and Anna O. or Bertha Pappenheim share another characteristic. The onset of their hysterical symptoms followed exhaustion caused by taking care of their respective fathers during their last fatal illnesses. Pappenheim also figures prominently, according to Anzieu, *Self-Analysis*, 134–35, among those whom are condensed in the figure of Irma.

131. Schur, "Some," 48; emphasis in original.

132. Jones, *Life*, 1:354.

133. See Hirschmüller, *Life*, 153–54, 171.

134. Grubrich-Simitis, *Early Freud*, 39.

135. The editors of the *Standard Edition* remark that "this is the first mention of the important clinical fact of 'resistance'" (2:154n1).

136. Of the last association Wilcocks, *Maezel's*, argues for a provenance later than 1895. Freud does not discuss this section in his first account of the dream in his Scientific Project of September 1895; Freud, *Origins*, 403.

137. Another element shared by the case of Elisabeth von R. and the dream is the locus of the symptoms: the throat (*Hals*). While Elisabeth does not complain per se of pain in her throat, Freud interpolates into her case history the case of Fräulein Rosalie H., whose throat is suffering severe distress. Rosalie H.'s story serves to illustrate (both substantively and performatively) how new symptoms can emerge in the middle of an analysis that are generated by association with, and recollection of, the affect that caused the original illness (2:169–73).

138. Cf. Gay, *Freud*, 72, 83.

139. This was the anticipated date of publication; it is assumed by the editors of the *Standard Edition*, who concede that no exact date appears on the volume (2:xv). Freud wrote to Fliess on 11 April that the book "will be ready in about three weeks," and on 20 April he writes that he will send the second half of the galleys to him (Freud, *Complete*, 124–25). Curiously his extant let-

ters of May and June make no mention of the volume's appearance. Its inclusion on the 26 May 1895 list of books received for review by the *Wiener medizinsiche Presse* confirms the May date.

140. As well as the author of the rather antisemitic 1885 tract, *Das Judentum in Gegenwart und Zukunft.*

141. W., "Studien," 1094.

142. Another possible candidate for W. is Dr. Windscheid of Leipzig, who during 1893 and 1894 reviewed a number of books on neurasthenia and hysteria for the *Wiener medizinische Presse*, including the *Handbuch der Neurasthenie* (Handbook of Neurasthenia) and *Die Hysterie nach der Lehre der Salpêtrière* (Salpêtrière's Theory of Hysteria). Two factors, however, make his candidacy unlikely. First, Windscheid has a byline for his reviews. Authors of reviews and feuilletons in the *Wiener medizinische Presse* are either cited with their name or with their initial; an apparent member of their board of contributing editors, Dr. Professor R. von Basch, of the University of Vienna Medical Faculty, has a byline for his articles but signs reviews, feuilletons, and reports of medical meetings with Ba; cf. Basch, "Suggestionsexperiment," which speaks very favorably of Breuer and Freud. Second, in an 1896 lecture reported by the *Wiener medizinische Presse*, Windscheid focuses upon the ovarian-uterine origin of hysteria; this is not the position of W. in his feuilleton. I extensively discuss the internal evidence that leads to my arguing for Heinrich Weiss as W. in "Some More."

143. Summary from Ellenberger, *Discovery*, 764, of Benedikt, "Neuralgien."

144. Cf., inter alia, Erikson, "Dream," 33; Van Velzen, "Irma"; D. Boyarin, *Unheroic.*

145. Jones, *Life*, 1:166.

146. Ibid., 1:199. Anzieu, *Self-Analysis*, 37, recounts how, "when working under Scholz [in the neurology department of Vienna's General Hospital (from January 1884 to February 1885)], Freud succeeded in producing a brilliant diagnosis, corroborated by autopsy, of several cerebral lesions (cerebral hæmorrhage, syringomyelia, and endocarditis with acute multiple neuritis . . .)—thus confirming the wisdom of his decision after Nathan Weiss's suicide and a talk with Breuer, to specialize in neurology."

147. Erikson, "Dream," 33.

148. Both Erikson, "Dream," and Swan, "Mater," focus on the male medical confraternity, the *Männerbund*, formed by Freud's colleagues in his dream and on Freud's in/exclusion from this group as a consequence of his shifting relationship to Irma. Erikson's model is, in Swan's formulation, "the religious brotherhood [which] forms and perpetuates itself through rites in which a group of men assimilate for themselves symbolically the powers of feared, envied and excluded women. That is, the model adopted by Erikson is the

social institution which, historically, has offered a patriarchal and homosexual resolution to masculine anxiety about weakness and passivity" ("Mater," 28–29). Swan's model is historically specific to late-nineteenth-century European bourgeois society that was marked by separate gender-coded spheres.

149. Just as here at the beginning of his career Freud worries over his identification with a female figure and loss of male authority, so too at the end. He compares his last work, *Moses*, with a female "dancer [*Tänzerin*], balancing on one toe," who would have collapsed in a heap were it not for Rank's work on the myth of the birth of the hero and Sellin's on Moses' murder. Cf. Weber, "Doing Away."

150. Swan, "Mater," 34.

151. Gilman, "Struggle," 299. And by relinquishing medical authority to his colleagues, he is no longer the *Partieführer*, the foreman of the medical examination team.

152. Writing in response to Freud's explanation of his latest in a series of fainting spells as a "bit of neurosis that I ought to really look into" (29 November 1912; Freud/Jung, *Letters*, 524 [#329 F]), Jung proposes: "May I draw your attention to the fact that you open *The Interpretation of Dreams* with the mournful admission of your own neurosis—the dream of Irma's injection—identification with the neurotic in need of treatment. Very significant" (3 December 1912; in ibid., 526 [#330 J]). Freud apparently recognized the significance. Soon after the receipt of Jung's missive, on 8 December, Freud wrote to Jones. He first discusses his recent fainting spell in terms of "some piece of unruly homosexual feeling"—which Jones surmises relates to Fliess (cf. Schur *Freud*, 264–72)—and then describes how he deflected Jung's parry, when "in [Jung's] last letter [he] again hinted at my 'neurosis'" (Freud/Jones, *Correspondence*, 182). Freud, who seven years earlier had written of "the necessary universality of the tendency to inversion in psychoneurotics," hints at his own feminization (7:166n; Freud concedes here that Fliess had first drawn his attention to this universal). Jung rubbed Freud's nose in this "hint." His letter of 3 December 1912 opens with, "My very best thanks for one passage in your letter, where you speak of a 'bit of neurosis' you haven't got rid of. This 'bit' should, in my opinion, be taken very seriously indeed because, as experience shows, it leads 'usque ad instar voluntariae mortis.' I have suffered from this bit in my dealings with you . . ." (Freud/Jung, *Letters*, 525 [#330J]).

153. I will return to this particular "spot" of male passivity in the Afterword.

154. Herzl, "Mauschel," 165. Gilman, *Self-Hatred*, undertakes an extensive analysis of the role of *mauscheln* as both the *langue* and the *parole* of Central European Jewry.

155. Nordau, "II Kongressrede," 74, 75 (cf. 72).

156. "Muskeljudentum," 380. At the Colloque International Max Nordau, 9 July 1992, Maison des Sciences de l'Homme, Paris, John Hoberman, "Max Nordau and the *Fin-de-Siècle* Critique of the Jewish Male," and Ingrid Spörk, "Das Bild von Juden in Texten Nordaus" (= "L'image") provided fine analyses of the concerns about Jewish masculinity that mark Nordau's speeches to the Turnvereine and elsewhere.

157. "Höre Israel," 458.

158. Fliess, *Les relations*, 17.

159. The toxin [*Gift*] is also a sign of the (anticipated) consummation of a marriage, the dowry [*Mitgift*].

160. Freud, *Complete*, 288 (letter of 22 December 1897).

161. Thus in a later letter to Fliess (7 August 1901) Freud wrote: "I do not share your contempt for friendship between men, probably because I am to a high degree party to it. In my life, as you know, woman has never replaced the comrade, the friend. If Breuer's male inclination were not so odd, so timid, so contradictory . . . it would provide a nice example of the accomplishments into which the androphilic current in men can be sublimated." In this letter Freud finally realizes that "there is no concealing the fact that the two of us have drawn apart to some extent" (Freud, *Complete*, 447).

162. Swan, "Mater," 5, writes: "In Freud's work, the contradictions of late-nineteenth-century bourgeois society appear in the form of unresolved conflicts about masculine and feminine identification." I would amend Swan's formulation to read "entail" rather than "appear in the form of."

163. On the implications of the merger of "viraginous woman and the effeminate Jew," see Djikstra, *Idols*, esp. the last paragraph, 401.

164. Freud also would later recode certain dream-symbols mentioned in the first edition as castration symbols: for example, "a tooth being pulled out by someone else" (5:387 and note 1).

165. Kofman, *Enigma*, 31; cf. 32: "The intimate, shameful secrets that Freud fears to expose to the public, because of the horror they are very likely to arouse, are thus inseparably linked with his Jewishness and with femininity, with castration anxiety. In this sense *The Interpretation of Dreams* is another Medusa's head." Also see Anzieu, *Self-Analysis*, chap. 5; Laplanche, *Problématiques*; and Green, *Le complexe*.

166. Although this chapter has de-emphasized the relationship between the repudiation of femininity and homophobia in favor the connection of that self-denial and the fear of identification with woman—as male individual and as Jew—it by no means precludes such a relationship: quite to the contrary, as can be seen in the next chapter and subsequent ones. I do, however, resist any reduction of the repudiation to sexuality alone.

CHAPTER 3: "'A GLANCE AT THE NOSE'": FREUD'S DISPLACED FETISHES

This chapter began its existence as "'A *glance* at the nose': The Inscription of Jewish Difference," presented at a session devoted to Representations of the Jewish Body during the 1989 Association for Jewish Studies annual meeting. Its next avatar was under the same title in *American Imago* 49, 4 (1992): 427–44. It has subsequently undergone several hybridizations.

1. Pietz, "Problem I," 8. Pietz's three-plus-part essay on fetishism, "Problem I–IIIA," is a brilliant, self-proclaimed historical dialectic exploration of the term. He demonstrates its origin as an effect of cultural contact and its career as a negative critical force. See also Geller, "Fetishism."

2. In *Three Essays*, 7:151, Freud discussed "chance experiences as an explanatory principle" in Binet's theory. Binet's work shifted the object of study from the religious life of the "primitives" to the love life of the civilized, and the methodological perspective from nosological observation of perverse behavior to psychological analysis of normal sexuality: "everyone is more or less fetishistic in love" (Binet, "Le Fétichisme," 144 [cf. 272]; cf. 7:154). Freud comments that Binet was the first to recognize that the choice of fetish object is the "after-effect of some sexual impression" (7:154).

3. Cf. Hirschfeld, *Sexual*, 73.

4. Ibid.

5. In "Fetishism" Freud recognizes how he is popularly associated with omnipresent phallic symbols. Thus he writes: "When now I announce that the fetish is a substitute for the penis I shall certainly create disappointment" (*Enttäuschung*). So what else is new? But he continues: "so I hasten to add that it is not a substitute for any chance penis . . ." (21:152).

6. Nor does Freud connect the opening example to the other motivation for the particular choice of fetish: "the last impression before the uncanny and traumatic one" (that is, before the perception of woman's lack; 21:155).

7. Bernheimer, "Fetishism," 165–66, also calls attention to this extraordinary omission. He draws on the insight of Rosolato, "Le Fétichisme."

8. Bernheimer continues: "The absence of *glans*, where the real meaning lies, promotes the movement of translation between languages, while it retains the hidden fantasy of the ultimate inclusion of all semantic differences in one universal language" ("Fetishism," 165–66).

9. Just as the absent *glans* recalls the absent maternal phallus, the presence of *übrigens* evokes a number of the material characteristics of the fetish itself: it is "*nebenbei*," or in some contiguous relationship with the mother's genitals, and it leaves a remainder (*übrigbleiben*), a reminder of castration.

10. There is a fourth option: psychosis. If the boy chooses to foreclose rather than disavow (which leaves a remainder, and thus is analogous to neu-

rotic repression; cf. 21:153–56) maternal difference, he follows the fourth path. This particular theorizing of psychosis, one that presupposes Freud's working through of narcissism in his 1914 metapsychological essay "On Narcissism," therefore postdates his classic analysis of psychosis, the Schreber case. Consequently, as will be examined in chapter 5, below, Freud's attention was directed toward the representation of the father-son relationship; this, of course, does not preclude other motivations for the absence of the mother in that analysis; cf. Jonte-Pace, *Speaking*; Kofman, *Enigma*; and Sprengnether, *Spectral*.

11. Freud's choice of example is once again very curious; the imperial authority of his youth, the Habsburg monarchy, had been dissolved nine years earlier and had been replaced by a republican form of government. On the other hand, it could be argued that at the beginning of August 1927, when Freud was writing this essay, the smoke from the July burning of the Palace of Justice had not yet cleared and the blood of the massacred workers still stained the streets; hence the threat was from a particular class—from an often racially marked class difference. The mention of the nonexistent throne is also yet another remainder of the repression of (coprophilic) smell that marks this essay (see below). That is, the pervasive sign of royal rule was the adjectival phrase *kaiserlich-königlich*, or, more frequently, the initials *k.k.*; these initials were pronounced *Kaka* (= feces); cf. Robert Musil's characterization of the Austro-Hungarian empire as the State of Kakania in his *The Man without Qualities*.

12. My argument in this chapter initially focuses on the role of gender difference in social formation, because that is the manifest focus—on the individual level—of Freud's essay; however, just as this chapter goes on to show that the crisis generated by ethnic or racial difference is no less at play, albeit screened by Freud's apparent emphases, so, too, the earlier discussions of the comparable roles that the ascription of other differences played in the formation of European hegemony are not here precluded and should not be forgotten.

13. On the difference that makes no difference, also see Bernheimer, "'Castration.'"

14. See Mannoni, "Je sais," and Kofman, *Enigma*, 84–89.

15. Bloch, *Sexual*, 622.

16. He had previewed this analysis in his 18 February 1909 letter to Karl Abraham; see Freud/Abraham, *Letters*, 73.

17. While Freud would expand upon these comments in *Civilization* (21:99–100n1), he had already speculated about the phylogenetic causes of atrophy of the sense of smell in normal adults as well as the heightened sensitivity to odors among neurotics in a 14 November 1897 letter to Fliess; Freud, *Complete*, 279; see also the 11 January 1897 letter in ibid., 233.

18. This "other factor" is evident not just in Freud's "On the Sexual Theories of Children" and "Analysis of a Phobia in a Five-Year-Old Boy" but also when the Rat Man discusses his habit of pulling his mother's braid (10:313) in Freud's preserved case notes to his study. Such discussion, however, is absent from the published case history itself, nor does Freud offer any explicit gloss within the notes themselves. An analysis of this and other curious exclusions from "Notes" is discussed in the next chapter.

19. Curiously, in a letter written to Abraham while he was working on *Leonardo* (24 February 1910), Freud expands upon the role of smell as the "chief factor" in foot fetishism to which he adds, not as "another factor" but as what "must be emphasized," "the female foot is apparently a substitute for the painfully missed, prehistorically postulated, female penis." He then includes the "plait" (*Zopf*) as another such substitute, the cutting off of which "stands for castration of the female"; Freud/Abraham, *Letters*, 87. These phallic supplements, severed from their connection with smell, surface in the discussion of fetishism in *Leonardo* (11:96).

20. The scopophilic component of foot fetishism was already mentioned in a 1915 addition (7:155n2) to the 1910 footnote discussed above.

21. Binet, "Le Fétichisme," 144 (cf. 272), 147 and note 1.

22. Ibid., 155–58.

23. Ibid., 148, 145.

24. Ibid., 160; Binet suggests later on that Schopenhauer may have had his own fetishistic predilections (261).

25. Ibid., 159.

26. Ibid., 164.

27. See, for example, Hartmann, *Judentum*. The pertinence of such traits to contemporaneous French antisemitic characterizations of Jews is examined in Birnbaum, *Les fous*.

28. Binet, "Le Fétichisme," 266–67.

29. Ibid., 271. On *Judentum* as the embodiment of abstraction, see Chamberlain, *Foundations*, among many others.

30. Binet, "Le Fétichisme," 274.

31. Ibid., 143.

32. Pietz, "Problem IIIa," 121, 120.

33. For example, in his 1793 treatise *Religion within the Limits of Reason Alone*, Immanuel Kant analogized clericalism to fetishism in order to distinguish between true moral religion and false religion, between autonomy and heteronomy. Such labeling allowed Kant to discredit his opponents, render them "irrational," without ascribing either evil intent or demonism to them. "Now the man who does make use of actions, as means, which in themselves contain nothing pleasing to God (that is, nothing moral), in order to earn

thereby immediate divine approval of himself and there with the attainment of his desires, labors under the illusion that he possesses an art of bringing about a supernatural effect through wholly natural means. Such attempts are wont to entitle sorcery. But (since this term carries with it the attendant concept of commerce with the evil principle, whereas the above mentioned attempt can be conceived to be undertaken, through misunderstanding, with good moral intent) we desire to use in place of it the word fetishism, familiar in other connections" (*Religion*, 165). By extending materiality from particular objects to all means, fetishism or "fetish-faith," came to extend beyond the borders of Africa to encompass everything in the realm of religion—including, in a clear allusion to Moses Mendelssohn's *Jerusalem*, the Jews—except for "purely moral" religion (ibid., 181–82).

34. On commodity fetishism, see the opening chapter of Marx, *Capital*, and Pietz, "Fetishism." On the tie between Jews and capitalism, see Marx, "Jewish Question." For Marx, the Jews personify civil society, which is characterized by self-interest, continuous bargaining, and money; indeed, the practice of Christian economic society has become Jewish. Another reading of the relationship between the representations of Jewry and of the commodity is provided by Postone, "Anti-Semitism"; Postone postulates that the anticapitalistic and antimodern antisemitic movement identified the Jews with the same fetishized characteristics as the commodity: on the one hand, abstract, intangible, universal, mobile, and, on the other hand, destructive, immensely powerful, and international.

35. See Fliess, *Beziehungen/Les relations*.

36. Gilman, "Struggle" and *Jew's Body*, and chap. 2 above.

37. Freud, *Complete*, 183 (26 April 1896; Freud dates the particular passage 28 April).

38. Ibid., 117 (8 March 1895).

39. Freud to Ernest Jones, Freud/Jones, *Correspondence*, 182 (8 December 1912).

40. Gay, *Freud*, 274–77, offers a concise summary of the homosexual overcoding of Freud's relationship with Fliess. Also see, inter alia, D. Boyarin, *Unheroic*; Davis, *Drawing*; Heller, "Quarrel"; Koestenbaum, "Privileging."

41. Pietz, "Problem, IIIa," 120.

42. Gilman, "Who Won?" 301.

43. Even epidemiologically. In his 1923 *Der Fetischismus dargestellt für Ärzte und Kriminalogen*, longtime Freudian renegade Wilhelm Stekel states that fetishism is almost exclusively a Christian male problem. He argues that this psychopathology arises from a dual identification with Jesus and with Jesus' phallus, the latter mediated by the fetishists' uncircumcised penises: "The circumspection of the penis by the tightened prepuce [that is, phimosis]

and, furthermore, the compulsive attitude which these enuretics had to take towards their bladders, may well have been the basis for the development of the fetishistic compulsion itself" (*Sexual Aberrations*, 341).

44. And the circumcised as well; however, Freud's imagined readers are either uncircumcised, such as the European bourgeois *gentilhomme* (of science), or the "passing" Jew whose knowledge of circumcision *should* shield him from, as well as allow him to revel in, *Schadenfreude* at any distress suffered by the *Goyim*.

45. Cf. Freud, "Analysis," 10:36n1: "The castration complex is the deepest unconscious root of anti-Semitism." The next chapter analyzes the emergence of this footnote into Freud's discourse.

46. Interestingly, the first appearance of the term *glans* in the *Standard Edition* (in *Three Essays*, 7:187) refers to the head of an uncircumcised penis.

47. Abraham and Torok, *Wolf*, 9–12, 50–52. Professor Ned Lukacher of UIC called my attention to Abraham and Torok's identification of Freud's exemplary patient as the Wolf-Man.

48. Freud/Ferenczi, *Correspondence*, 138 (13 February 1910).

49. The first claim reflected Freud's conviction at the termination of the analysis in 1914 that Pankejeff was cured; the latter, appended in 1923, notes that his recovery needed to be reconsolidated after the war and that the effort met with success. Fourteen years later, in "Analysis Terminable and Unterminable," Freud would remark about the Wolf-Man's recurrent illnesses in an image that nos(e)talgically recalls Freud's own possible primal scene discussed in this and the preceding chapter, the near fatal nasal hemorrhaging of Emma Eckstein: "In other attacks [of illness], however, the pathogenic material consisted of the patient's childhood history, which . . . now came away—the comparison is unavoidable—like sutures after an operation, or small fragments of necrotic bone" (23:218).

50. Brunswick, "Supplement," 264.

51. Abraham and Torok, *Wolf*, 32, draw their conclusion not only from the nasal symptomology but also from the references to the English nursery—the Wolf-Man's English governess plays a significant role in the original case history—and to the relationship between words and symptoms.

52. Brunswick, "Supplement," 265.

53. Ibid., 269; emphasis added. One cannot avoid the impression that Freud's WASP princess was not herself free of antisemitic prejudice.

54. Brunswick describes how her patient re-enacted his youthful desire to put himself in the woman's place when he "borrowed first his wife's mirror, in order to examine his nose, as it were, her feminine habit of frequently looking at herself in it" (ibid., 281).

55. Ibid., 265.

56. In the original case history, Freud notes on several occasions the young Pankejeff's identification with Christ; 17:63, 66, 115, 117.

57. Brunswick, "Supplement," 286.

58. Freud, *Studienausgabe*, 8:201n2.

59. The German original does not mince words. In the parentheses Freud emphatically writes *"Beschneidung!"* The "which implied" was gratuitously added by the translators of the *Standard Edition*; they apparently sought to mitigate the implications of Freud's exclamation.

CHAPTER 4: A CASE OF CONSCIENCE: CLIPPINGS FROM LITTLE HANS'S NURSERY

This chapter began its existence as a lecture, "The *Kvatter* of Psychoanalysis: Circumcision, Antisemitism, Homosexuality, and Freud's 'Fighting Jew,'" delivered as the Samuel Rosenthal Center for Judaic Studies Lecture, Case-Western Reserve University, in September 1998. Its next avatar was "The Godfather of Psychoanalysis: Circumcision, Antisemitism, Homosexuality, and Freud's 'Fighting Jew,'" *Journal of the American Academy of Religion* 67, 2 (1999): 355–85. Sections underwent further revisions as "Little Hans: A Footnote in the History of Circumcision," a part of the jointly delivered Joy Gottesman Ungerleider Lecture, "Freud's Foreskin," at the New York Public Library, May 2006.

1. "To deny a people the man whom it praises as the greatest of its sons is not a deed to be undertaken lightheartedly—especially by one belonging to that people" (23:7).

2. For example, by 1911–12 the writer and philosopher of the German youth movement Hans Blüher (*Wandervogelbewegung*, 125–26) would employ the case of Little Hans as a proof-text of the sexual etiology of neurosis (as well as of infantile sexuality). On Blüher, see chap. 6, below.

3. Reik, *Der eigene*.

4. Frosh, *Hate*; Glenn, "Circumcision."

5. See also Rudnytsky, "Does."

6. Freud, for example, held that it was antisemitism that delayed his appointment as a Professor Extraordinarius at the University of Vienna (Gay, *Freud*, 136–39). The roles of political and institutional antisemitism in Vienna have been explored by many; see, especially, Wistrich, *Jews*; Katz, *Prejudice*; and Pulzer, *Rise*.

7. See also Le Rider, *Modernity*.

8. Freud/Abraham, *Letters*, 34 (3 May 1908).

9. Again, in "Fetishism" Freud writes: "[T]he horror of castration sets up a sort of permanent memorial to itself by creating this substitute" (i.e., the fetish; 21:154).

10. That is, not only has the East-European-born Jew Sigmund Freud introjected the misogynistic and homophobic norms of the Viennese bourgeoisie in the process of assimilation, but perhaps he has even overcompensated in order to ensure that he passes as a virile and therefore acceptable male member of his society. On the psychology of the colonized male (or the postcolonized such as Freud), cf. D. Boyarin, "*Épater*" and "Homophobia"; Nandy, *Intimate*; and Sinha, *Colonial*.

11. There is a brief note, "'Great is Diana of the Ephesians,'" signed "Freud" that appears under the rubric "Varia" in the house organ, *Zentralblatt für Psychoanalyse*, in 1911, in which there is reference to Jews. There is also a patient's embarrassed second-hand reporting of another's recollection of a religious instructor's statement that "Jonah was a Jew and that Jews would squeeze in anywhere" in "An Evidential Dream" (12:270); it appeared with other contributed dream interpretations by several psychoanalysts in the *Internationale Zeitschrift für ärztliche Psychoanalyse* in 1913. The "Jew" returns in the *Introductory Lectures* he began to publish in 1916 (15:161, 186, 188, 189).

12. See, inter alia, Robert, *D'Oedipe*, and Goldstein, *Reinscribing*. In 2003 *American Imago* (60, 1) devoted a special issue to "Freud's Michelangelo," although minimal attention was addressed to its relationship to Freud's Jewish identity or identification with Moses.

13. "Death and Us," after its oral delivery, was originally published in the B'nai B'rith's bimonthly. See Jonte-Pace's marvelous discussion of the original lecture and its transformations in terms of the relationship among *Judentum*, the uncanny, and the maternal body in "Jewishness and the (Un)Canny: 'Death and Us Jews,'" chap. 3 of *Speaking*.

14. Brenkman, *Straight*, draws upon those notes and other sources to construct a Jewish Rat Man, Paul Lorenz [*sic*], who mirrors the Jewish Freud. He employs these parallel lives in order to illuminate psychoanalysis's blindness to the role, in its Oedipal construction of the "real man" (121), of socialization into particular "structures of feeling" and "dominant fictions," by which heterosexuality and male dominance are rendered both natural and compulsory. While Brenkman concludes at one point that "the castration complex is the key to each moment of this ideal progress" (121), he develops this insight neither into the role of castration nor of the relationship of castration to Jewish identity (aside from bare citation of the usual Freudian passages that relate circumcision and castration), but instead focuses on the work of, respectively, Raymond Williams (e.g., *Marxism*) and Kaja Silverman (e.g., *Male*) to supplement the gaps in Freud's theories.

15. As Freud indicates in his B'nai B'rith lecture "Death and Us," there is no mention of an afterlife in the *Torah* (27). For Christians, the omission of reference in the Pentateuch combined with the encounter between Jesus and

the Sadducees on the question of resurrection in Mark 12:18–27 confirmed the assumption of the absence of any such Jewish doctrine. Both the rabbinic de-emphasis and the Christian denial of Jewish belief in an afterlife, in contradistinction to its prominence in Christian doctrine, emerged during the process of both Jewish and Christian self-definition that occurred over the first four to five centuries of the common era. The Christian denial may also have been a reaction formation or served as a screen against the threat presented by Jewish persistence to Christian supersessionism and truth claims. Removal of reference to resurrection in Reform prayer books also contributed to a similar assumption by Reform, or liberal, Jews.

16. Freud, "Death," 27.

17. Cf. Marr, *Goldene Ratten*, and Geller, "Mice."

18. In 1923 Freud appended a concluding footnote: "Like so many other young men of value and promise, he perished in the Great War" (10:249n1).

19. In the case study, see 10:185, 206; the last entry preserved in the case record recounts a scene from his first year at the university: "He was suspected by a friend of 'funking' ['*Kneifen*']. Because he had allowed himself to have his ears boxed [*Ohr*feige] by a fellow student, had challenged him to a duel. . . , and then done nothing further" (10:318).

20. See Freud, *L'Homme*, 38.

21. In setting forth this particular genealogy, Freud may well have been following the lead of Solomon Reinach, a Jewish classicist and historian of religions, who classified both *Judentum* and *Christentum* as barbaric, viewed the *Talmud* and those backward Jews who followed it with disdain, but who nonetheless played leading roles in both the Alliance Israélite universal and the Societé des études juives. To make his case in *Totem* Freud extensively drew upon several of the studies collected in Reinach's *Cultes*. For example, the competition between Christianity and Mithras is discussed by Reinach in his essay "Morality," 72–73. In another study, *Orpheus* (1909), 228, Reinach writes that "Christianity belongs to a group of religions quite different from the official creeds of Judæa, Greece and Rome. . . . Such were the religions of Osiris, Dionysos, Orpheus, Adonis, Attis and the like. . . ."

22. See Fleming, *Freud*, 53.

23. All German editions since 1924 and the *Standard Edition* (but not the Collier edition of *The Collected Papers of Sigmund Freud*; see Freud, *Sexual*, 20, 21) have substituted Little Hans/der kleine Hans; see editors' addition, 7:135n1. While Freud's emendation provides consistency and continuity between this account and the account in "Analysis" (10:11 and note 3), it also helps conceal Herbert's identity.

24. As many others have commented, Freud's privileging of the penis is already evident in his identification of Hans's term "Wiwimacher" (lit., pee-

maker) with the penis. Cf. Silverman, "Fresh," and Glenn, "Freud's Advice" and "Integrative."

25. Also, among the notes collected in the folder *"Aus älteren Aufzeich-nungen* von 1897 an" (from older sketches from 1897 on; the first three words are underscored in the original). Freud writes "Angstfall bei Lektüre *Caesar* im *Gymnasium* wegen *castra*. Kastration. Einengen—Ausschweifen. Keusch u. 'Keusch'?" (Case of anxiety while reading *Caesar* [Shakespeare's play or Cae-sar's writings?] in school because of castra[tion]. Castration. Constricting— dissipating. Chaste and "discreet").

26. As is discussed below, Freud's surviving original notes of the Rat Man case report that as early as a 12 October 1907 session, the threat of castration was a primary motif of the doctor-patient exchange (10:263). Nonetheless, no mention of castration, complex or simple, made its way into the published account.

27. Following Laplanche and Pontalis, *Language*, 111, "deferred action," or *Nachträglickeit*, is the "term frequently used by Freud in connection with his view of psychical temporality and causality: experiences, impressions and memory-traces may be revised at a later date to fit in with fresh experiences or with the attainment of a new stage of development. They may in that event be endowed not only with a new meaning but also with psychical effective-ness." The "deferred obedience" discussed below is a form of this psychical process.

28. Graf, *Reminiscences*, 473. See *Letters of Sigmund Freud*, 92–94 (28 Janu-ary 1884), 143–44 (12 May 1885).

29. M. Freud, *Sigmund*, 70–71. Elsewhere (Fraenkel, "Professor," 16), Martin recalled that afterward his father told them: "We are Jews. You will often have such experiences. Prepare yourself for it in time."

30. According to Freud (18:273), multiple phalli or phallic images symbol-ize castration.

31. See, for example, 10:98n1 (discussed below), 113n1 (in which he quotes the poet Conrad Ferdinand Meyer), and 131n1 (where he recalls drawings by T. T. Heine).

32. Although the controversy over Weininger's alleged plagiarism via Freud and his patient, Weininger's confidante Hermann Swoboda, of Fliess's theory of bisexuality had peaked in 1906, Little Hans's castration anxiety allows Freud to deliver the final salvo in the cycle of recrimination and accusa-tion. See Heller, "Quarrel," and Le Rider, *Le Cas*.

33. *Pace* Gilman, *Case*, 88, who refers to a question of baptism and suggests that this discussion was epistolary.

34. Most recently, Maciejewski, "'Dichter Beschreibung,'" argues that ul-timately all of Herbert's psychological plaints arose from the trauma of his

circumcision. Clearly his thick description was built upon the thinnest of evidence. Indeed, Maciejewski builds the grandest theoretical edifices upon the *realia* of circumcision and its consequent trauma in his *Psychoanalytisches Archiv*.

35. In my original article I had inserted here a note that queried whether raising his son as a Jew would require Graf to circumcise his son. Since, as already noted (and see below), Herbert Graf was not circumcised, my aside shifts from the conditional to the very conditions for the analysis of both Freud's note and case study. I had then concluded that if Graf did not have his son circumcised, the allusion to circumcision in this case of a young Jewish boy would only confirm that circumcision is the *leit*-signifier of Jewishness even in the absence of any empirical sign. Below I will expand upon that assertion.

36. See the discussion of Max Nordau and *Muskeljudentum* in chap. 2, above.

37. M. Freud, "Who?" 201.

38. *Faygeleh*: Yiddish: lit., a little bird. Though used as a term of endearment toward a little child, *faygeleh* has the connotation of effeminate homosexual.

39. Although not specifically mentioned in that essay's account of children's (including Herbert Graf's) phantasies about their parents and where they (the children) come from, Freud had already labeled the phantasy of adoption as a family romance (*Familienroman*) in a 20 June 1898 letter to Fliess (*Complete*, 317) and would elaborate on that romance in a supplemental note, written roughly contemporaneously with "Sexual Theories," to Otto Rank's 1909 *The Myth of the Birth of the Hero* ("Family Romances")—although Little Hans (or Herbert) is not mentioned by name in this brief essay, one might assume that, given his prominence in the earlier and immediately subsequent works on childhood sexuality, that he was a source here as well. Freud returns to the family romance in his initial attempt to leverage open Moses's Egyptian origins in the opening salvo of *Moses and Monotheism*. There are several other curious connections among that 1898 letter, Herbert Graf, and *Moses*. One such is "Meyer." Freud draws upon the authority of the biblical scholar *Eduard* Meyer to justify his questioning the scriptural account of Moses' birth in order to have it conform, albeit inversely, to the form of the family romance (23:13). It is the analysis of the novella *Die Richterin* by one of his favorite authors, Meyer—although in this case, *Conrad Ferdinand* Meyer—that motivates Freud's initial comments on the family romance to Fliess. It is also a verse from that same Meyer's poem, "Huttens letzte Tage," that Freud employs as a gloss on Hans's ambivalent, albeit strong (and desexualized), feelings toward his father (10:113n1). In this particular instance, Freud emphasizes

Hans's demurral of his manifest aggression toward his father, even as Freud ultimately seeks to underplay Hans's desire for his father. Another curious overlap is the treatment of beating phantasies that appears in the 1898 letter (*Complete*, 318) as well as in the discussion that Freud would gloss with Meyer's verse. To compound this connection, it is a particular patient and her beating phantasies, as I argue below, that may have led to the return of the repressed footnote in the second, 1919 edition of Freud's *Leonardo* essay.

40. Glenn, "Integrative," 131.

41. As if rhetorically to reinforce the importance of castration, the translators have here appended the "piece"; the original merely reads "Die Aufklärung," or the Enlightenment.

42. Gilman, *Freud*, 77. The particulars of this analysis are discussed more fully in the introduction.

43. See Harrowtiz and Hyams, *Jews*, and Steuer, "Book."

44. Kraus, "Weib," 5.

45. Rank, "Essence."

46. Nunberg and Federn, *Minutes*, 1:359.

47. This characteristic was also shared by the subject of another case history, Judge Schreber ("Psychoanalytic Notes"). On Freud's positive valuation of (and possible identification with) Schreber, see, inter alia, Freud 12:79; Santner, *My Own*; and chap. 5, below.

48. In *Leonardo* Freud writes: "Indeed it almost seems as though the presence of a strong father would ensure that the son made the correct decision in his choice of object, namely, someone of the opposite sex" (11:99).

49. Interestingly, when Hans employs the phrase, the love objects are always "sleeping with him" (*bei mir schlafen*), not he with them. Little Oedipus remains more Little Narcissus.

50. Rudnytsky, "'Mother."

51. Although Hans calls the "plumber" "*der Schlosser*" in the first phantasy and "*der Installateur*" in the second, in his gloss on the second Freud paraphrases the first, substituting the *Installateur* for the *Schlosser* and then comments that "the two phantasies are identical" (10:98). Further, when he later returns to discussing the phantasies what the *Standard Edition* refers to as "the plumber" (10:127) reads "*Der Schlosser oder Installateur*" in the original.

52. M. Silverman, "Fresh," 109, 115; Frankiel, "Note" and "Analysed"; Carvalho Ribeiro, "Oedipe"; and Cornut-Janin and Cournut, "La castration," esp. 1374–81.

53. More curious still, the language of "*bohr-*" makes several significant appearances in the case study and notes of the Rat Man. Lanzer's first mention of rats is of their reported use as a punishment: a pot filled with rats was placed upside down on the criminal's buttocks and they "bored their way in" (*die sich*

... *einbohrten*; 10:166). And in both cases, Freud has no qualms about supplementing his patient's account with "into his anus." The original record is explicit about the meaning of the completed narrative: "I indeed recognized the homosexual component after the utterances of the first session" (Freud, *L'Homme*, 44); see Mahoney, *Freud*, 104–6 (trans. on 106). Such recognition is explicitly disavowed in the case of Little Hans with Freud's distortion of Hans's second plumber phantasy.

54. Nor later. In his reconsideration of the case in *Inhibitions*, Freud contrasts Little Hans's "'positive' Oedipus complex" with the Wolf-Man's inverted one (20:107, 124); *pace* Freud, see Garrison, "New Look," on Little Hans's "'negative' Oedipus complex." In the interim (1922) Freud had met the grown-up Herbert Graf, "a strapping youth of nineteen [who] declared that he was perfectly well, and suffered from no troubles or inhibitions" (10:148). Graf would later marry (twice), have a child, and become a leading opera director in both Europe and the United States; see Strauss and Röder, *International*, 411.

55. Rather than rationalizing Freud's parapraxis, the editor of the Collier edition of Freud's collected papers, Philip Rieff, completely occludes it by substituting "mother" for "father"; Rieff, *Sexual Enlightenment*, 158n15.

56. Hans's choice of language—"It's fixed in" (*er ist ja angewachsen*), the "singular (*sonderbare*) remark" that Freud fixes upon, repeating it twice after reporting Hans's father's account of it—might also have contributed to the appearance of the footnote. Freud may have associated uncovering the significance of the penis that has "taken root" (i.e., *angewachsen*; the term translated as "fixed in" is defined in the *Wahrig Deutsches Wörterbuch* as "Wurzel geschlagen") with uncovering the "deepest unconscious root [*Wurzel*]" of antisemitism and misogyny.

57. Cf. 9:216. Or conversely, since "Sexual Theories" was written while "Analysis" was probably in page proofs (cf. editor's note, 9:207), perhaps this ascription of a homosexual telos was Freud's after-the-fact recognition of Hans's persistent homosexual accesses.

58. See, e.g., Gilman, *Freud*, 72, and D. Boyarin, *Unheroic*.

59. See, inter alia, Mosse, *Image*, esp. 68–70.

60. Although for some reviewers Weininger's Viennese soil as much as his Jewish roots led him to his conclusions; Sengoopta, *Otto*, 140, cites an anonymous reviewer in Munich's *Beilage zur Allgemeinen Zeitung* who states that it was no surprise that the Viennese Weininger had written *Sex and Character* since Vienna was "universally known for its innumerable effeminate men."

61. The move from castration to circumcision, the sign of Jewish difference, might also betray Freud's attempt to universalize Jewish particularity.

62. A significant literature has grown up around Freud's homosexuality/homophobia; see, for example, Koestenbaum, "Privileging"; D. Boyarin, *Unheroic*; and Davis, *Drawing*.

63. On this identification, see my discussion, above.

64. His *bris* on 13 May 1856 is recorded in the Freud Family Bible.

65. This confirms Rice's assertion in "Jewish," 251–52 and accompanying note, that Freud's three sons were not circumcised. Rice cites a lecture by Peter Swales, an interview with Elliott Philipp (Martha Freud's first cousin, once removed), and Albrecht Hirschmüller's testimony that the records in the Israelitische Kultusgemeinde of Vienna note neither the date of circumcision nor the name of the *mohel*, the ritual circumciser, for Freud's three sons. Also see Ferris, *Dr. Freud*, 379, and Gilman, *Freud*, 86. The latter notes that "Freud did not have his sons *ritually* circumcised" (emphasis added); that they may have been *non*ritually circumcised is extremely unlikely.

66. Cf. Bronner, *Rumor about the Jews*, regarding the Jewish world conspiracy alleged by the forged *Protocols of the Elders of Zion*.

67. Cf. the footnote in *Totem* that invokes circumcision: "When our children come to *hear* of ritual circumcision . . ." (13:153n1).

68. Jewish physical anthropologists and other "defenders of the race" determined that the distribution among Jews of that nefarious nasal index was comparable to that of their Gentile neighbors; see the *Jewish Encyclopedia*, s.v. "nose."; and *Jüdisches Lexikon*, s.v. "Nase." See also Efron, *Defenders*.

69. This is most glaringly displayed in *Leonardo*, 11:95–96.

70. I would here like to thank Anne Golomb Hoffman, whose 18 December 2005 presentation before the Association for Jewish Studies on perspectives of Jewish Studies on the life and work of Sigmund Freud and subsequent manuscript "Archival Bodies" for helping me keep my eyes open to the nursery conversations reported by Freud.

71. Cit. Grubrich-Simitis, *Back*, 111–12.

72. Cf. 10:295, on the Rat Man as *renifleur* and preceding chapter. In his preserved case notes (but again not in the case study), Freud reports on some transferences to a dream made by the Rat Man that echo *"Eine Quelle"*: "A number of children were lying on the ground, and he went up to each of them and did something into their mouths. One of them, my [Freud's] son (his brother who had eaten excrement when he was two years old), still had brown marks round his mouth and was licking his lips as though it were something nice" (10:286).

73. Among many others, see Horkheimer and Adorno, *Dialectic*, esp. the chapter entitled "Elements of Antisemitism"; Rubenstein, "Religion"; and Grosser and Halperin, *Anti-Semitism*.

74. I intend here not just deviations with regard to object, such as homosexuality, but also those with regard to aim, such as is characteristic of oral sexuality. Although in his analysis Freud focuses upon penile penetration of

the lower body, oral sexuality plays a prominent role. When Freud first introduces Hans's widdler, he makes a curious association in order to, in effect, sustain his never-questioned identification of *Wiwimacher* with penis and thus to maintain his claim for the existence of the castration complex. He cites Hans's "innocent" question, "Mummy, have you got a widdler too?" and her fateful answer, "Of course"—fateful because this initiates the chain of misunderstandings that make viable the castration threat. Then he notes Hans's identification of a cow's udder as its widdler. Yet to adduce Hans's typicality Freud adds as evidence: "I once put forward the view that there was no need to be too much horrified at finding in a woman the idea of sucking at a male organ. This repellent impulse, I argued, has a most innocent origin, since it was derived from sucking at the mother's breast" (10:7). Of course, Hans's primary phobic representation is the horse biting off Hans's widdler. One might also locate here another remainder of Freud's repression of Hans's homosexual reserve. During this period Freud would draw upon "udders," whether goat or cow, to signal the connection between castration and deviant sexuality. For example, in his analysis of Schreber (12:34) Freud employs Kant's simile of milking a he-goat; see chap. 5, below. Freud's non-necessary resort to the everyday with his bovine example suggests to Sprengnether, *Spectral*, 62–63, Freud's utter failure to efface the traces of another repression, that of the important role of the preoedipal mother.

75. Around the time Freud was writing up the case history of Little Hans, Freud told the following joke to Theodor Reik: "The boy Itzig is asked in grammar school: 'Who was Moses?' and answers, 'Moses was the son of an Egyptian princess.' 'That's not true,' says the teacher. 'Moses was the son of a Hebrew mother. The Egyptian princess found the baby in a casket.' But Itzig answers: 'Says she!'" (cit. Yerushalmi, *Freud's Moses*, 1, who deduces 1908 as the time of its telling from Reik's account in "Freud," 18).

76. One other overlap between the earlier note (i.e., "*Eine Quelle*") and the case study leads to a further speculation about the connection between Hans's situation and antisemitism. The last message that Hans wishes to share with the Professor (Freud) is how that morning (1 May) he had wiped (*aus*gewischt; emphasis added) the behinds of his phantasy children. He had done this, he informs his father and the Professor, because he would like to have children and when they came he would clean (ab*putzen*; emphasis added) their behinds. He also wanted the Professor to know that when he did lumf and widdled in the W.C., the children had looked on (*zugeschaut*; 10:97); Hans had earlier described how Berta, the Gmunden landlord's child, had always watched him widdle (*zugeschaut*, 10:60–61; cf. 10:21, where Olga, Berta's sister, joined in the audience, and 10:32, where Grete, another Gmunden friend, also is re-

ported to have been shown Hans's widdler). The juxtaposition of Hans's wiping lumf with the public uncovering of his Jewishness recalls the scene of the earlier note within a new situation in which circumcision is the foremost Jewish trait. This construction of Hans's message suggests that the earlier note had come to mind when Freud had perhaps been informed that Hans (Herbert Graf) had been the object of antisemitic taunts from his Gentile friends and perhaps imagined, out of habit, that Herbert's Jewish difference had been pointed out to him during his public urinations while staying at Gmunden.

77. Freud/Abraham, *Letters*, 34.

78. Freud's concern here is double. Not only is he wary of the repudiation of an antisemitic public, but the judgment of particularity would disqualify psychoanalysis from making any universal—that is, scientific—claims.

79. Freud/Abraham, *Letters*, 64. Freud is referring to the discussion of sexuality in general, and childhood sexuality in particular. Six weeks earlier (10 November 1908) Abraham had written to Freud describing the reaction to his interventions at a meeting of the Berliner Gesellschaft für Psychiatrie und Nervenkrankheiten: "I had, inter alia, mentioned Conrad Ferdinand Meyer . . . as an example of love for the mother. That was unheard of. German ideals were at stake. Sexuality was now even attributed to German fairy tales, etc." (ibid., 56). Konrad Ferdinand Meyer seems to hover about "Analysis."

80. Ernst Lanzer's therapy that began 1 October 1907 would extend almost a year (i.e., beyond the course of Herbert Graf's).

81. In the ensuing bizarre exchange, Freud states that "linguistic usage likens the face to the genitals," to which Lanzer ingenuously responds, "But there are no teeth down below" (10:316). While Freud is trying to get Lanzer to think penis, an alternative response might be, "Yes, a vagina dentata."

82. Freud, *L'Homme*, 246.

83. Ibid., 234.

84. Ibid., 234–35n517, reads *Bad*/bath instead of *Bett*/bed,

85. Freud here Germanizes Lanzer's use of the French "curios" recorded with quotation marks in the original case notes (ibid., 34). When Freud then goes on to talk about his patient's sexual "curiosity" he employs the usual German word *Neugierde*. As noted in the first chapter's discussion of *Psychopathology*, and as would be revealed in any brief purview of nineteenth-century medical textbooks (such as Krafft-Ebing's *Psychopathia Sexualis*), the use of foreign words often betrays content that one normally should not speak about or desire.

86. See, for example, the long footnote 10:206–8n.

87. In a perhaps telling slip, the original English translation of *Vornamen* read "Christian name" according to Mahony, *Freud*, 22.

88. In the original case notes Lanzer refers to her as Fräulein Rudolf and Freud parenthetically comments, "the name strikes him" (Freud, *L'Homme*,

34). Perhaps what struck him was not just its masculinity, but its very specific-ity. Not unlike what unleashed the sensational scandal and the torrent of ho-mophobic and antisemitic responses by, respectively, accusers and defenders that filled the German-language papers of record, and not just the tabloids—namely, the Jewish-born, leading journalist Maximilian Harden's accusations of homosexuality in the Liebenberger circle that surrounded Kaiser Wilhelm II (see, inter alia, Hull, "Kaiser Wilhelm"; Steakley, "Iconography"; Bruns, "Skandale"; and the discussion in chap. 6, below)—similar scurrilous rumors were emerging from the histories of the notorious late-sixteenth-, early-seven-teenth-century Habsburg Emperor Rudolf II. In his 1891 *Die conträre Sexual-empfindung*, one of the founders of modern sexology and lifelong rival of Freud's Albert Moll discusses Rudolf's infamous surrender of authority to a circle of beautiful male favorites. He compares his collecting of beautiful young men with his other hobby (*Liebhaberei*): "thus he collected in his mu-seum at Hradschin all manner of curiosities [*Curiositäten*] of nature and art. . . ." (43). Moll then draws upon Ireland's *Herrschermacht und Geisteskrank-heit* in describing Rudolf as a great misogynist (*großer Weiberfeind*) in order to bring up the possibility that there was a sexual basis to his relationship with his favorites. (Then again, Rudolf may have recalled Crown Prince Rudolf, the only son of Emperor Franz Josef I, who purportedly committed double suicide with his mistress at Mayerling in 1889.) That Freud would displace Rudolf onto Peter in this scene of ambiguous sexual difference and castration/phallic symbols is also *kurios*. The fluent English-speaker Freud may have been familiar with the English equivalent of the German phrase "*ein Loch mit dem anderen zustopfen*" (plugging up one hole with another) as "robbing Peter to pay Paul"; cf. the discussion in chapter 1 of the role of *Rudolf* Klein*paul* in the "forgetting of foreign words" chapter of *Psychopathology*. A "peter" is also slang for penis; to "peter out" is to diminish slowly and come to an end. Another association is with the *Peterkarte* (Peter card) in the game of *Schwar-zer Peter* (Black Peter); the player who is stuck with that card at the end of the game gets his nose blackened (i.e., is slugged in the nose); consequently some-one who is, as one says, "left holding the baby" is said to be "*den schwarzen Peter zugeschoben*." And as is discussed in the Afterword, below, Peter is de-rived etymologically from the Latin for "stone" or "rock"; a German equiva-lent is "*Fels*," a word that is thoroughly embedded in Freud's discourse of castration.

89. See the discussion in Mahony, *Freud*, 32–36 and nn.

90. Again see, for example, Jonte-Pace, *Speaking*; Kofman, *Enigma*; and Springnether, *Spectral*.

91. By 1918, when he publishes his case study of the Wolf-Man, anal eroti-cism and the primal scene, together with the castration complex, play the pri-

mary roles in the development of his patient's neurosis. In his masterful reading of the Rat Man case study against the case notes, Mahony, *Freud*, largely reads the disjunctions in light of Freud's later theorization of obsessive neurosis, in general, and the case of the Wolf-Man, in particular. Consequently, he overlooks the more immediate relationship with the case of Little Hans (and of Lanzer and Freud's shared *Judentum*). Verhaeghe, "Riddle," notes that as late as 1914, in "On Narcissism," Freud considers the castration complex too "narrow a foundation" (14:93) on which to base all neuroses and states that there are neuroses in which it does not appear at all.

92. Although not cross-referenced in Freud's 1919 essay, the Rat Man in both Freud's notes and his "Notes" employs the qualifier "uncanny" (*unheimliches*) to describe the feeling that accompanied his erection-arousing wish "to see [girls] naked" (10:162; cf. Freud, *L'Homme*, 38). He specifically felt that "something must happen," something he had to prevent, when the wish arose. When asked by Freud, Lanzer responds that the exemplary fear is that "his father might die" (10:162), a possibility that (although already realized eight years prior to the analysis and four years prior to the intensification of his neurosis) he paired with his compulsive impulse "to cut his [own] throat with a razor" (10:158). The relationship to the castration complex is unmistakable, if also unremarked upon by Freud.

93. Anna had been the lure, the (withheld) gift, in several psychoanalytic transactions at the time: Otto Rank and Sandor Ferenczi all imagined that they were being groomed to become Anna's husband, and thus Freud's son-in-law and heir apparent (see Roustang, *Dire*,10). Ernest Jones, too, was later (1914) tempted by such phantasies (see Gay, *Life*, 433). Whether or not Freud tacitly indulged these phantasies of his disciples, he was already well aware of the consequences for the daughter of a father "handing her over" to another man—even if the requirements of theory led him to look beyond such venal maneuvers; cf. the Dora case ("Fragments"). The then-twelve-year-old Anna also appeared in a couple of the Rat Man's transferential phantasies (10:276, 307–8).

94. Anna Freud's biographer, Elizabeth Young-Bruehl, does note that the "sixth patient is not directly described at all, and this may signal that Freud protected his daughter's privacy with silence" (*Anna*, 104).

95. They also share sadistic components that are not addressed here.

96. Freud informed Ferenczi on 24 January 1919 that he was working on the paper that would bear the title "'A Child Is Being Beaten,'" when completed in mid-March of that year. See editor's note to Freud's paper (17:177).

97. Freud/Andreas-Salomé, *Letters*, 90.

98. Cf. Bar Amitai, *Beschneidung*, 12.

CHAPTER 5: FREUD V. FREUD: *ENTMANNTE* READINGS ON THE MARGINS
OF DANIEL PAUL SCHREBER'S *DENKWÜRDIGKEITEN EINES
NERVENKRANKEN*

This chapter began its existence as a presentation to the 1991 National Endowment for the Humanities Summer Seminar "Freud and the Culture of His Time," led by Professor Sander Gilman at the Freud Museum, London. Its next avatar was as "Freud v. Freud: Freud's Readings of the *Denkwürdigkeiten eines Nervenkranken*," in *Reading Freud's Reading*, that I co-edited with Jutta Birmele, Sander Gilman, and Valerie Greenberg, 180–210 (New York: New York University Press, 1994), before this transformation.

1. The early work of Baumeyer, "Fall"; Niederland, *Schreber* (includes articles from 1951 to 1972); and Schatzman, *Soul*, as well as the appearance of Han Israëls's 1980 University of Amsterdam thesis, *Schreber, vader en zoon* (English ed., *Father and Son*), which drew on then–East German archive material, Schreber family mementos, and a close reading of the *Denkwürdigkeiten*, marked the turning point. A brief survey of Schreber interpretation in the wake of Freud appears in the editors' introduction to Allison, Prado de Oliveira, Roberts, and Weiss, *Psychosis*. In the wake of Israëls and Allison et al., a number of monographs on Schreber have appeared, most notably those of Busse, *Schreber*; Lothane, *Defense*; and Santner, *My Own*.

2. Kendrick, "God," 33.

3. Schreber, *Denkwürdigkeiten*—S, 45; *Memoirs*—MH, 68–69. Hereafter pagination from Schreber's edition of the *Denkwürdigkeiten*—S will be preceded by S and the corresponding pages from Macalpine and Hunter's translation, *Memoirs*—MH, will be preceded by MH.

4. I employed my transcriptions of Freud's marginalia in the earlier version of this chapter. In the interim, Gerhard Fichtner has published his transcription as Appendix 7 in the cd-rom that accompanies Fichtner and Davies, *Katalog*, cd 567–73. All citations of marginalia in this chapter conform to Fichtner's version. I am grateful to Professor Fichtner, both in the *Katalog* and in personal correspondence, for correcting my occasionally errant decipherings.

5. Cf. Macalpine and Hunter, "Notes," 361.

6. On the role of these oppositions in the *Denkwürdigkeiten*, see Geller, "Unmanning."

7. See Gay, *Freud*, 267, 277–84.

8. In this chapter I retain Macalpine and Hunter's literal translation of the German designation of the figure who is traditionally referred to in English as the Wandering Jew.

9. Freud mentions possessing a copy of the *Denkwürdigkeiten* in his 22 April 1910 letter to Jung; Freud/Jung, *Letters*, 188 (#187F). He began to read it while traveling in Italy during the summer of 1910 with Ferenczi.

10. And, again, as redefined (by Freud as the loss of the penis rather than the removal of the testicles or ovaries).

11. As I discussed in the previous chapter, Freud worked out the implications for psychoanalysis of his recognition of the importance of castration in "Original Record"; "Sexual Theories"; "Analysis"; and *Leonardo*. See also Freud's letters to Jung of 21 June 1908 and 21 November 1909; Freud/Jung, *Letters*, 159 (#158F), 265–66 (#163F); Bernheimer, "'Castration'"; Green, *Le complexe*; Laplanche, *Problématique*; and Schatzman, *Soul*.

12. After working on his analysis of Schreber's paranoia throughout the fall of 1910, Freud announced on 16 December in letters to two of his closest junior colleagues, Ferenczi and Abraham, that he had completed the case study. The following summer Freud published it in *Jahrbuch für psychoanalytische und psychopathologische Forschungen* 3, 1; "Editor's Note" to "Psychoanalytic Notes," 12:3.

13. Freud to Jung, 31 October 1910; Freud/Jung, *Letters*, 369 (#218F).

14. Although in the case study Freud does not explicitly make this connection, the castration complex is implicit to Freud's discussion of the relationship between Schreber's wish-phantasy of becoming a woman and his infantile resistance toward, and eventual acceptance of, the father's threat of castration (12:56). While working on his analysis of Schreber, Freud wrote to Jung that "the castration complex is only too evident"; Freud/Jung, *Letters*, 369 (#218F; 31 October 1910).

15. Schreber included in his *Denkwürdigkeiten* the medical and legal documentation generated by the court hearing that allowed him to return home after a nine-year institutionalization.

16. Citation is from S475/MH330.

17. While the case study decenters the role of religion in Schreber's delusion, Freud took great delight in Schreber's implicit skepticism of normative Christianity. For example, in his introduction Schreber broaches the "unanswerable" questions of Christianity such as "how did God come to be?" (in the margins Freud writes "*Religiöse Zweifel* [religious doubts]"; S2/MH42), doubts the literal sense of certain dogmas like the Sonship of Jesus (which Freud emphasizes; S3/MH42) and the truth of others like eternal damnation and resurrection ("*Kritik festgehalten* [(he) held tight (to his) criticism]; S3/MH42; while next to the discussion of the "fleeting-improvised-men" Freud writes "*Erklärung Aufersteh[un]g* [explanation (of) resurrection]"; S4/MH42–43n1). These and other such passages (cf. S8/MH46) might have sustained Freud's judgment that "in the Redeemer of to-day much remains of the doubter of yesterday" (12:24).

18. S45/MH69.

19. It may quite legitimately be argued that at times Freud contends that woman is nothing other than a castrated man. In Schreber's case, however, since the castration is delusional, sexual difference is both threatening and threatened.

20. Kant, *Critique*, 97 (A58, B83).

21. Another rhetorical effect of this passage is to represent Freud as a risk-taker, thereby preparing the reader to engage the ensuing narrative of Freud's attempts at interpretation as an adventure story with a happy ending.

22. On Flechsig, see the discussion below. Möbius's work presented a problem for Freud, for the widely known Möbius, too, ascribed a primacy to sexuality in the development of neurosis, albeit with the focus on physiological constitution and heredity—whether the natural inferiority of woman (in his notorious 1901 *On the Physiological Feeble-Mindedness of Women*) or the correlation of hereditary health and normative gender identity ("the healthier the individual is, the more definitively he [or she] is male or female," in *Schwachsinn*, 77, cit. Omran, *Frauenbewegung*, 101). More, his reductive biographies of the pathological sources of so-called creative geniuses (for example, Rousseau, Goethe, Schopenhauer, and Nietzsche) cast a pall over Freud's own efforts with Leonardo and Schreber.

23. The desired supersession of the older discipline by psychoanalysis is no less evident in Freud's marginalia to the *Denkwürdigkeiten*. In a number of passages where Schreber critiques psychiatry or psychiatrists Freud notes in the margins "Bravo" (S59/MH77; S79/MH89–90n42; S82/MH91).

24. Jung, *Psychogenesis*, 179–93.

25. By taking on the Schreber case Freud was perhaps undercutting his heir-apparent, Jung. In their correspondence of the time, however, Freud and Jung seem very much to be enjoying themselves in sharing Schreberisms; there does not seem to be any overt hostility; cf. Freud/Jung, *Letters*, 307–80 (##186J–225F; 17 April–18 December 1910). Still, Jung was ever sensitive to Freud's reception of the "Dementia Praecox" essay, and Gay, *Freud*, 199, holds that after the appearance of "Psychological Notes" their breakup was inevitable. Moreover, after the breakup Jung would return to Schreber (in "On Psychological Understanding" [1914]) and endeavor to one-up Freud.

26. And on occasion Freud notes in the margins of his copy of the *Denkwürdigkeiten*, "Protest" (for example, S57/MH76).

27. Unable to squelch publication, members of the Schreber family and the Schreber Associations did ensure that the memoir's third chapter, which dealt with events in the lives of his extended family, never saw the light of day. That chapter was apparently, at least in part, an elaboration of an earlier discussion that also suffered prepublication censorship. When Schreber is about

to enlarge upon his few hints about the essential nature of soul murder, a parenthetical remark appears: "(the passage which follows is unfit for publication)" (S28/MH58). Freud does receive information from Arnold Georg Stegmann, a psychiatrist from Schreber's home town of Dresden, although Freud did not incorporate all of it into his narrative (see 12:6n1 [on omitting knowledge of Schreber's third illness], 46, 51). For this and other reasons, Freud has often been faulted for not trying to contact Schreber—who was still alive when Freud began writing the case study—his family, or his doctors. The correspondence with Jung, however, shows a Freud desirous of making inquiries. On 1 October 1910 Freud writes to Jung: "Since the man [Schreber] is still alive, I was thinking of asking him for certain information (for example, when he got married) and for permission to work on his story. But perhaps that would be risky. What do you think?" (Freud/Jung, *Letters*, 358 [#214F]). Jung does not seem to have responded.

28. The *Denkwürdigkeiten* chronicles this second attack.

29. S44/MH68.

30. Recall the discussion of Freud the patient in chapter 2, above.

31. Freud, too, had an ambivalent relationship with Flechsig and his physicalist theories of psychic life, which might have affected Freud's understanding of the case. That Schreber never explicitly identifies Flechsig with his father and that Schreber's image of Gd bears more similarity to the working conditions of the anatomist Flechsig than to the orthopedist and pedagogue Schreber *père* leads Gerd Busse to assume there might have been transferential as well as theoretical reasons behind Freud's analysis; "Schreber," esp. 264–65 and note, and *Schreber*; Lothane, *Defense*.

32. Freud is citing from S442/MH308; the ellipsis between "brother" and "is" is courtesy of Freud and not of the *Denkwürdigkeiten*.

33. Freud writes: "In this instance symbolism overrides grammatical gender—at least so far as German goes, for in most other languages the sun is masculine" (12:54).

34. For example, S280/MH207. Cf. Baumeyer, "Fall," 518: "Juli 1898. Dasselbe Verhalten. Oft nackt in seinem Zimmer vor einem Spiegel lachend und schreiend mit bunten Bändern geschmückt [July 1898. The same behavior. Often laughing and screaming naked (except for being) adorned with colored ribbons in front of a mirror in his room.]."

35. Over the last forty years, these appliances and their possible use on his son Daniel Paul have been held responsible for some of Schreber's symptomology; see Niederland, *Schreber*; Schatzman, *Soul*; and Israëls, *Father and Son*.

36. In 1864, three years after the death of Daniel Gottlob Moritz Schreber, the school director Dr. Ernst Innocenz Hauschild set up the first playground in Leipzig's Johanna Park based on the educational principles devised by the

late Schreber *père*. The playground was soon surrounded by small allotments—quickly dubbed "Schreber gardens"—where local people grew vegetables. The plan was copied in many towns. See www.ahsetal.de/ Geschichte_der_Kleingarten/body_geschichte_der_klein g arten.html.

37. Freud is himself citing from an early footnote of Schreber's; S4/ MH42–43n1.

38. On 31 October 1910 Freud writes to Jung of "our dear and ingenious friend Schreber"; Freud/Jung, *Letters*, 368 (#218F).

39. S442/MH308; emphasis added.

40. Although Schreber's concern about his wife's honor could easily be invoked in support of Freud's argument about Schreber's anxiety over the *Schmach* and *Schimpf* (disgrace) that homosexuality entails.

41. Santner, *My Own*, brilliantly discusses the role of performatives in precipitating both Schreber's breakdown and Freud's response to the *Denkwürdigkeiten* as well as being constitutive of both Schreber's delusion and Freud's psychoanalysis; however, while Santner suggests a connection for Schreber between the performative *Ernennung* and *Entmannung* (40–42) he does not attend to *Entmannung's* performative role in Freud's reenactment of the Schreber case.

42. Derrida, "Living On," 100ff.

43. S53/MH73.

44. Technically one cannot speak of an ellipsis without the presence of either an antecedent or subsequent—or, frequently, both an antecedent and subsequent—citation. Moreover, the meaning of an ellipsis—of anything— cannot be determined without consideration of its borders, both within the text and between texts.

45. S36/MH63.

46. Freud/Jung, *Letters*, 358 (#214F; 1 October 1910).

47. Yet considering Freud's discussion of jealousy as one of the permutations of the paranoiac's repressed sentence "I (a man) love him" (12:63–64), Schreber's jealousy might well have supported Freud's argument.

48. S36/MH63.

49. Baumeyer, "Fall," 514.

50. Harsin, "Syphilis," 87.

51. Kraepelin, *Psychiatrie*, 2:604.

52. See Busse, *Schreber*. In "Unmanning" I undertake an extensive analysis of how the trope of syphilis infects the *Denkwürdigkeiten*.

53. S98/MH101; cf. 12:48.

54. S74/MH87.

55. Cf. Gilman, *Jew's Body*, 81–87.

56. As the nineteenth century drew to a close, the European bourgeoisie were terror stricken before the "venereal peril"; see Corbin, *Women*, esp. 261–

75, and Geller, "Blood Sin." Fears of syphilitic infection also played a role in Freud's analysis of the Rat Man.

57. Schreber's first psychiatrist, Flechsig, had been a longtime supporter of female castration (ovarectomies) as a cure for hysteria; see Busse, "Schreber," 268 and note 6.

58. Yet besides this appearance and the later invocation of his father's memory there is only one other reference to Schreber's father in the extant text: Schreber mentions reading his father's *Ärztliche Zimmergymnastick/Medical Indoor Gymnastics*, which Freud greets with an "also!" (S166/MH142). As has been pointed out by many, for a figure who plays such a major function in Freud's etiological scenario, Schreber's father appears to play a rather minor role in the *Denkwürdigkeiten*.

59. Top of S9/MH46–47; cf. S139/MH126n65.

60. S12/MH49.

61. S96/MH100. Thus this suggestion occurs well before the passage on S442/MH308 that Freud claims was discovered after a prolonged search.

62. For Freud to have discussed this paper trail would have also undercut the rhetorical function of evoking a "prolonged search": the narrative of a quest engaged the readers vicariously in the scientific adventure of hypothesis and confirmation. That narrative helped quiet those who assumed that Freud already had the answer, but had not followed Freud's advice to read Schreber's *Denkwürdigkeiten*.

63. The eventual splitting off of Gd from Flechsig is, like Schreber's splitting of Gd into higher and lower personae, a function of paranoia's decomposing tendencies and not of intrinsic differences between figures. "They were all duplications of one and the same important relationship" (12:50). Yet, as Gerd Busse reminded me (personal correspondence, 4 October 1991), while Freud notes at the bottom of a discussion of Gd's "irregular policy" toward Schreber, "*Erheb[un]g des Verfolg[un]gswahn zu Gott* [and] *Gott identif[iziert] mit Flechsig* [sublimation of persecution delusion to Gd (and) Gd identified with Flechsig]" (S62/MH79), and annotates "*bravo! Identific[ation]!*" next to a passage (S82/MH91) that demonstrated in "Psychological Notes" that for Schreber, Flechsig and Gd "were ideas belonging to the same class" (12:49), Freud never explicitly states that Flechsig was *identified* with Gd. Indeed, the discussion of paranoia's characteristic decomposition of identifications and condensations implies that Flechsig and Gd were always distinct figures (12:49–50).

64. Macalpine and Hunter describe "soul murder" as "the most obscure issue in the *Memoirs*" ("Notes," 359). It refers to the advantage or influence exercised by one person over another; "illness, particularly nervous illness, is caused when the soul leaves the body temporarily, or is under another's influence" (ibid.).

65. S20/MH53n13.

66. Freud also refers to the presence of *"Schwesterinzest"*—not *Geschwister-inzest*—in *Manfred* in his 31 October 1910 letter to Jung (Freud/Jung, *Letters*, 369 [#218F]).

67. *Entmannung*'s only previous appearances in Freud's collected works also manifested a conflicted Freud and the heart of a different matter. In the original edition of *Interpretation*, Freud asserts that "Zeus emasculated [*entmannt*] his father [Kronos] and made himself ruler in his place" (4:256). In both *Psychopathology* (6:218 and note) and a 1909 note to *Interpretation*, Freud corrects, with qualifications, his original assertion: "Or so [Zeus] is reported to have done according to some myths. According to others, emasculation [*Entmannung*] was only carried out by Kronos on his father Uranus" (4:256n1). Lukacher, "K(Ch)ronosology," has thoroughly elaborated the implications of Freud's parapraxis, albeit without specific reference to *Entmannung*. Freud is concerned here with more than exemplifying the neglect of filial piety. In addition to providing evidence of Freud's resistance to a theory of castration (cf. Laplanche, "La castration," 635), "The omission of reference to Kronos's role as castrator and the repetition of his role as castrated inscribes in Freud's text the concealed fulfillment of his [Freud's] desire to castrate the father and possess the mother" ("K[Ch]ronosology," 67). Freud's self-analysis had yet another side: the incorporation of the fault, here figured by emasculation, of the father; cf. Balmary, *Psychoanalyzing*.

68. S45/MH74.

69. S8/MH46n3, S17/MH52n10, S20/MH53n13; also cf. S91/MH93.

70. S7/MH45n2.

71. S24/MH56.

72. For example, S4/MH42–43n1.

73. S7 (at top of page) /MH45–46.

74. S28/MH58.

75. S36/MH63.

76. S44/MH68. In a 1911 addition to *Interpretation* (5:392–94), Freud cites a long passage from Rank's 1911 "Zum Thema," in which dental dreams accompanied by nocturnal emissions are tied to auto-eroticism or, at most, "a slight tendency toward homosexuality."

77. S45/MH69.

78. S53–54/MH73–74.

79. S52/MH72–73 and note 29.

80. S54/MH74.

81. Ibid.

82. S71/MH85, S73/MH86, and S91/MH97.

83. Professor Valerie Greenberg (personal correspondence) suggests a fourth: "Freud might have been in such complete agreement with parts of a

text that his concentration did not permit interrupting to make marks. [W]e know he was engrossed by many texts that he did not mark at all." It is indeed possible that Freud was so engrossed in this one page (S53/MH73–74) that his pen remained silent; however, the silence belies his marking practices in this text. For example, on this page rife with biblical, classical, and literary references, even "*Quelle,*" the sign of Freud's ongoing concern with possible sources for Schreber's delusions, is missing.

84. Cf. Gilman, "Struggle."

85. Compare with some of Freud's later works, "History" (17:110–11, on Adler); "'Child'" (17:200–201, on Adler and Fliess); and "Analysis: Terminable and Interminable" (23:250–51, on Adler and Fliess). See the discussion of this last passage in the Afterword, below.

86. Fliess, *Beziehungen*, 223.

87. Gay, *Freud*, 86–87, 204, 274–76.

88. Freud/Jung, *Letters*, 121 (#70F; 17 February 1908).

89. Freud/Ferenczi, *Correspondence*, 221 (6 October 1910).

90. Ibid., 243 (16 December 1910).

91. As Freud's fainting scene in November 1912 in Munich would testify; see Gay, *Freud*, 275.

92. Freud/Jung, *Letters*, 379, 380 (#225F; 18 December 1910).

93. The Jewish Wandering Jew either figures the culmination of Christian salvation history or heralds the liberation of humanity. In the former he is the Jew who, for having cursed Jesus on the way to Calvary, is condemned to wander the earth until his death at the Last Judgment. In the latter he is emblematic of a contemporary *Judentum*; for example, according to Schopenhauer "Ahasuerus, the Wandering Jew, is nothing but the personification of the whole Jewish race" (*Parerga*, 2:261). Eternally marked by its contemptible national or racial character, this incarnation of stubbornness and deceit, of egoism and incessant desire, of amorality and destructive negation, would through its own (self-)destruction (either literally or figuratively by becoming non-Jewish) fulfill its emancipatory telos. Thus, Wagner concludes the first version of his *Judentum in der Musik*: "One only thing can redeem you from the burden of your curse: the redemption of Ahasuerus—Going under [*der Untergang*]!" I explore the historical peregrinations of the Wandering Jew in "Unmanning."

94. S14/MH50.

95. Freud might well have been familiar with the alleged problems of Jewish digestion, anchored empirically, perhaps, in the tendency of Ashkenazim to contract ileitis, but more a function of the abject fascination that Jewish dietary law had for non-Jews: compare the appetitive theory of *Judentum* proffered by one of the favorite authors of Freud's youth, Ludwig Feuerbach. See my "It's 'Alimentary.'"

96. S151/MH133. Another neglected aspect of Schreber's illness is his hypochondria. Both Schreber and his doctors give considerable weight to his hypochondriacal symptoms. Freud does cite Dr. Weber's list of these symptoms (esp. 12:13). Freud also mentions that Schreber developed an "enormous number of delusional ideas of a hypochondriacal nature," and then adds in a footnote that he "shall not consider any theory of paranoia trustworthy unless it also covers the hypochondriacal symptoms by which that disorder is almost invariably accompanied" (12:56 and note 3). But Freud fails to follow through. In his copy of the *Denkwürdigkeiten* Freud, too, emphasizes a number of passages. For example, where Schreber notes that the body changes described in chapter 11 are for him the most vivid and certain of all of his experiences, Freud writes "*Beziehung zur Hypochondrie*" (S150/MH132n68). As might be expected Freud is most struck by the "miracles" related to "emasculation": Freud underlines the word *Entmannung* and notes "*Kastr[ation] Komplex*" next to the ensuing description of changes to Schreber's sex organs and of the removal of single hairs from his beard and moustache (S149/MH132). But none of this material makes its way into the case study. Why does Freud not address this material? Surely psychoanalysis would have no difficulty analogizing Schreber's delusional organ losses with castration. Did Freud fear that by focusing on the body, even the delusional one, he would be transgressing the confines of medical psychiatry? Or did he fear that Schreber's body language would transgress the gendered boundaries of nosological classification and be diagnosed as the "female malady" of hysteria? Such a diagnosis would invalidate both his own diagnosis of paranoia and the concomitant theory of its mechanism. Further, although Freud had essayed the existence of male hysteria in the 1880s, the adverse professional response to his proposal dampened his interest in the matter. On this last matter, see Gay, *Freud*, 53–54.

97. As was already noted in his 3 May 1908 letter to Karl Abraham; Freud/Abraham, *Letters*, 34.

98. Questions arise, such as: Why was Schreber silent about his apparent identification with the "Eternal Jew"? Did Schreber, despite his disclaimer that the "Eternal Jew" was not Jewish, find being transformed into a Jew more difficult to accept than being turned into a woman? Although the figure of the Wandering Jew underwent a series of metamorphoses into Gentile as well as Jewish personae during the nineteenth century (cf. Knecht, "Le mythe"), an increasingly prominent leitmotif, as noted above, identified the Wandering Jew with the entire Jewish people. And more pertinent to this chapter, why until recently had the commentators after Freud ignored (with the exception of Lukacher, "Schreber's," and Prado de Oliveira, "Trois") discussion of the "Eternal Jew"? While Lothane, in his massive work, devotes some notes to antisemitism in Germany, it is not until his unpublished 1993 Postscript that

he addresses the figure, cit. Santner, *My Own*, 107–8 and notes, who then goes on to address Gilman's discussion in *Freud*, 153–54, that drew upon my research during the National Endowment for the Humanities Seminar, "Freud and the Culture of His Time," led by Professor Gilman at the Freud Museum, London, England, 24 June–8 August 1991.

99. S71/MH85; cf. S108/MH107n56, S138/MH125.

100. S177/MH148; cf. S289/MH212.

101. S76–77/MH88–89.

102. The citation is from S293/MH214. Prior to signaling the importance of *Entmannung*, Freud places in a footnote, without commentary, an earlier citation (from S4/MH42–43n1), in which Schreber's having female genitals and being impregnated by Gd are conjoined.

103. In a letter written less than a month before he was able to escape Vienna and join his son Ernst in England, Freud tells his son that "I sometimes compare myself with the old Jacob who, when a very old man, was taken by his children to Egypt. . . . Let us hope that it won't also be followed by an exodus from Egypt. It is high time that Ahasuerus came to rest somewhere"; *Letters of Sigmund Freud*, 442–43 (12 May 1938). Freud's identification is somewhat ambiguous, since the Jewish people, rather than he himself, can also be read as the referent.

104. Bernheimer, "'Castration.'"

105. Ibid. Throughout the essay, Bernheimer tropes the Latin *castrare* (to castrate) with its cognate *castrum* (fortified).

CHAPTER 6: FROM *MÄNNERBUND* TO *URHORDE*: FREUD, BLÜHER, AND THE *SECESSIO INVERSA*

This chapter began its existence as "From *Männerbund* to *Urhorde*: The Colonial and Postcolonial Context of Freud's Theory of Cultural Formation," presented at the 1999 German Studies Association annual meeting. Its next avatar was as "Freud, Blüher, and the *Secessio Inversa*: *Männerbünde*, Homosexuality, and Freud's Theory of Cultural Formation," in *Queer Theory and the Jewish Question*, ed. Daniel Boyarin, Daniel Itzkovitz, and Anne Pelligrini (New York: Columbia University Press, 2003), before passing through this rite of publication.

1. See, inter alia, Wallace, *Anthropology*; Brickman, *Aboriginal*; R. A. Jones, *Secret*.

2. The classic discussion of German male fantasies is Theweleit, *Männerphantasien*. Their colonial reach is explored in Friedrichsmeyer, Lennox, and Zantop, *Imperialist*; their prehistory is examined by Zantop, *Colonial*.

3. Recently there has been a surge of interest in Hans Blüher, especially in relationship to theories of the *Männerbund*; see Brunotte, *Zwischen*; Kurth,

Männer—Bünde; Bruns, "Politik," and "Homosexueller Staatsfreund." They build upon the earlier work of the contributors to Völgler and Welck, *Männerbande*; Sombart, *Deutsche Männer*; Widdig, *Männerbünde*; Geuter, *Homosexualität*; Kreisky, "Stoff"; and Hewitt, *Political*.

4. In *Group Psychology* Freud cites A. L. Kroeber's "Review," 48. On the history of *Totem*'s reception, see Wallace, *Anthropology*. Although, as Wallace recounts, the initial uproar moderated over time, such that even a vociferous early opponent like Kroeber eventually modified his original critique, and indeed found Freud to offer significant insight into human culture, anthropologists are all but unanimous in their denial of what Freud found absolutely necessary—namely, his claims for the historicity of the primal horde.

5. Thus in *Moses* he notes that "more recent ethnologists have unanimously rejected Robertson Smith's hypotheses [on totemism] and have in part brought forward other, totally divergent theories. . . ." Then he defiantly asserts, "But I have not been convinced either of the correctness of these innovations or of Robertson Smith's errors. A denial is not a refutation; an innovation is not necessarily an advance" (23:131; cf. 21:55).

6. The distinction between homosocial and homosexual relationships, between noncarnal and carnal, but in both instances heavily libidinized, male bonds was first brought to critical prominence by the work of Eve Kosofsky Sedgwick, beginning with her *Between Men*.

7. Freud/Abraham, *Letters*, 139 (13 May 1913); *Briefe*, 139.

8. Roustang, *Dire*, and R. Ostow, "Autobiographical." To extend the allegory, the women (*Weibchen*) possessed could be figured by psychoanalysis (*die Psychoanalyse*), theory (*die Theorie*), the psyche (*die Psyche*), or the patients (*die Patientinnen*).

9. Jones, *Life*, 2:354, and Robert, *From Oedipus*, 129.

10. Malinowski, *Sex*, 165: "It is easy to perceive that the primeval horde has been equipped with all the bias, maladjustments and ill-tempers of a middle-class European family, and then let loose in a prehistoric jungle to run riot in a most attractive but fantastic hypothesis"; cf. Brenkman, *Straight*, 112ff., drawing upon the work of Carole Pateman, especially *Sexual Contract*.

11. See Schurtz, *Urgeschichte*, 94–99, and *Altersklassen*, 65–82; Coward, *Patriarchal*; see also Bamberger, "Myth."

12. Freud was not blind to his class position. In a letter (14 June 1907) to Jung, Freud wrote, "if I had based my theories on the statements of servant girls, they would all be negative" (Freud/Jung, *Letters*, 64). Perhaps he forgot about his patient, the innkeeper's daughter Katharina, from *Studies*. See also Stallybrass and White, *Politics*, 152–69, on Freud and the Victorian bourgeois fascination with servant girls, governesses, and nannies—as neurosis-causing seductress, object of desire, and object of identification (citing Freud's 3 October 1897 letter to Fliess), as well as Brenkman, *Straight*.

13. See Carl Schorske's classic, "Politics and Parricide," on psychoanalysis as the retreat of the political into the self and the familial dynamics that determine it.

14. Hocquenghem, *Homosexual*, 60–61: "Freud discovers the libido to be the basis of affective life and immediately enchains it as the Oedipal privatization of the family. . . . At a time when capitalist individualisation is undermining the family by depriving it of its essential functions, the Oedipus complex represents the internalization of the family institution."

15. A typical expression of this sentiment can be discerned in Blüher, "Antifeminismus," 92: "bourgeois society is feminized [*feministisch*]." A less tendentious and more influential depiction of a feminized modernity was proffered by the sociologist Georg Simmel in his 1911 essay "Weibliche Kultur" (excerpted as "Female Culture"). See Bruns and Wolff, *Gegen-Bewegung*, and Kurth, *Männer—Bünde*.

16. As noted by Ellis, *Sex*, 320, 326: "It is, as Krafft-Ebing was accustomed to say, syphilization and civilization working together which produce general paralysis, perhaps in many cases, there is reason for thinking, on a nervous soil that is hereditarily degenerated to some extent. . . . Once undermined by syphilis, the deteriorated brain is unable to resist the jars and strains of civilized life, and the result is general paralysis." Also see Geller, "Blood Sin," and "Le péché."

17. Cf. Blüher, *Wandervogel*, 2:144–45, 3:40. Also see Geuter, *Homosexualität*; Knoll and Schoeps, *Typisch*; Koebner, Janz, and Trommler, "*Mit uns*"; and Lacquer, *Young*.

18. Stauff, *Semi-Kürschner*, 2:98.

19. The classic account of the last days of the Austro-Hungarian Empire and its capital is Robert Musil's encyclopedic novel, *Der Mann ohne Eigenschaften/The Man without Qualities*.

20. See Mogge, "Jugendreich."

21. In late 1906 one of Germany's leading critics and the editor of the independent Berlin weekly *Die Zukunft*, Maximilian Harden, attacked what he called the "Liebenberg Round Table," the group of male friends led by Prince Philipp zu Eulenberg, who formed the closest circle of advisors to Kaiser Wilhelm II. Harden held that the prince's homosexuality inclined him "to advocate weak, pacific policies that undermined the energetic, warlike course more befitting Germany's world power" (Hull, "Kaiser Wilhelm," 193). Harden's public accusations of homosexuality in the highest military and political circles, in particular his "outing" of Eulenberg and Count Kuno von Moltke, led to a rash of tabloid articles and cartoons about the homosexual *camarilla* as well as a series of libel trials against Harden in 1907–9. See Steakley, "Iconography," and Bruns, "Skandale."

22. J. W. Jones, *"We"*; Oosterhuis and Kennedy, *Homosexuality*; Hergemöller, *Mann*, 244–45; and Micheler, *Selbstbilder*, 137–42.

23. Among others, Theweleit, *Männerphantasien*, and Sombart, *Deutsche Männer*.

24. *Heimat und Aufgang/Homeland and Rise* and *Blüte und Niedergang/Blossoming and Decline* were the first two volumes of *Wandervogel*.

25. Cf., inter alia, Widdig, *Männerbünde*, and See, "Politische."

26. Neubauer, "Freud/Blüher."

27. Blüher, *Secessio*, 21ff.

28. Foreword to the second edition of *Wandervogelbewegung*, 14 (dated December 1914).

29. Cf. Blüher, *Traktat*, on psychoanalysis as un-German.

30. Letter to Freud, 2 May 1912; cit. Neubauer, "Freud/Blüher," 133.

31. Freud here suggests a research agenda that, alas, he never takes up: "From the point of view of psycho-analysis the exclusive sexual interest felt by men for women is also a problem that needs elucidating and is not a self-evident fact based upon an attraction that is ultimately of a chemical nature." (Freud, who is known to have possessed a copy of the 1880 edition of Gustav Jaeger's *Die Entdeckung der Seele* [Davies and Fichtner, *Freud's Library*, cd 274] as well as encountering discussions of this work in Blüher's writing [see below], would have been familiar with not only Jaeger's theory of the chemical basis of the antipathy between Jews and Germans, but also his theory of the chemical nature of both hetero- and homosexual attraction; on Jaeger, see Weinreich, *Duftstoff*.) While, according to the note in *Three Essays*, inverted object choice may be universal and while "in general the multiplicity of determining factors [in a person's final sexual attitude] is reflected in the variety of manifest sexual attitudes in which they find their issue in mankind," Freud still here associates those who opt finally for inversion with the archaic, the primitive, and early stages of development.

32. In *Three Essays*, Freud argued that inverts do not manifest the two key characteristics of degeneracy: "(1) *several* serious deviations from the normal are found together, and (2) the capacity for efficient functioning and survival seem to be severely impaired" (7:138; emphasis added).

33. Blüher letter to Freud, 2 May 1912; cit. Neubauer, "Freud/Blüher," 134.

34. Freud letters to Blüher, 10 May 1912, 7 July 1912, 10 July 1912; cit. ibid., 135, 138, and 140.

35. Blüher letter to Freud, 3 July 1912; cit. ibid., 136–37.

36. Freud letter to Blüher 10 July 1912; cit. ibid., 138.

37. Ibid., 139 and note 16. Blüher was not convinced by Freud's gift. That Blüher did not accept the inevitable course of repressed homosexual feelings

that Freud argues in the Schreber case study—"the mechanism of symptom-formation in paranoia *requires* that internal perceptions, or feelings, shall be replaced by external perceptions" such that the proposition "I hate him" becomes, via projection, "He hates (persecutes) me, which will justify me in hating him" (12:63; emphasis added)—is noted below.

38. Neubauer, "Freud/Blüher," 140.

39. See also his 9 April 1935 letter to an American mother concerned about her son's homosexuality, in *Letters of Sigmund Freud*, 423: "Homosexuality is assuredly no advantage, but it is nothing to be ashamed of, no vice, no degradation; it cannot be classified as an illness"—but it still remains arrested development. See also Abelove, "Freud."

40. Cf. Freud/Abraham, *Letters*, 34 (3 May 1908), on Freud's plea for Abraham's tolerance and courtesy in the face of Jung's vacillation on pragmatic grounds ("only by his appearance on the scene that psycho-analysis escaped the danger of becoming a Jewish national affair") as well as the prospect that Jung "should find his way back to the views that he has now abandoned." S. Winter, *Freud*, 235, writes: "Freud also promoted the recognition of psycho-analysis as a discipline by stressing its usefulness to research in other disciplines. In this way Freud solicited academic alliances—'conversions' as well as conquests."

41. The complete passage reads: "Since nothing that men make or do is understandable without the cooperation of psychology, the applications of psycho-analysis to numerous fields of knowledge . . . came about of their own accord, pushed their way to the front and called for ventilation. . . . [Analysts] were no better treated by the experts resident in those fields than are trespassers in general: their methods and their findings, in so far as they attracted attention, were in the first instance rejected. But these conditions are constantly improving, and in every region there is a growing number of people who study psycho-analysis in order to make use of it in their special subject, and in order, as colonists to replace the pioneers" (22:144–45); cit. Winter, *Freud*, 215.

42. Freud letter to Blüher, 10 July 1912; cit. Neubauer, "Freud/Blüher," 139.

43. Blüher, *Werke*, 53: "Moreover one should not forget to which race the overwhelming majority of [Third-Sex sexologists] belong."

44. In the foreword to the 1914 edition of *Wandervogelbewegung*, Blüher ties Hirschfeldian homosexuals to cultural decadence (*Verfall der Kultur*, 10), and describes them as "truly deformed men . . . whose racial degeneracy is marked by an excessive endowment of female substance" (13). Homosexuality runs parallel to the decline and bad race mixing of a people (164 [1918 edition]). By contrast, the physiognomies of the *Wandervogel* exemplify the noblest racial development (*edelste Rassenbildung*; 119 [1918 edition]).

45. On the noncausal relationship between effeminization and homosexualization, see Blüher, *Rolle*, 1:29; cf. Hewitt, *Political*; Keilson-Lauritz, "Tanten"; and Bruns, "Politics."

46. *Wandervogelbewegung*, passim; *Wandervogel*, 2:211, on Jaeger, and 2:326, on "Drei Grundformen."

47. Blüher letter to Freud, 13 July 1912; cit. Neubauer, "Freud/Blüher," 142.

48. Cf. Blüher letter to Freud, 31 July 1913; cit. ibid., 145.

49. I am grateful to Keith Davies of the Sigmund Freud House, Mansfield Gardens, London, who made these two pages from Freud's copy available to me.

50. Blüher, *Studien*, 32.

51. Blüher, "Antifeminismus," 91.

52. See Freud, "Some Neurotic Mechanisms" and "History."

53. Nor are theories that locate the origin in the economy, the spirit [*Geist*], or the herd true either; cf. Blüher, *Rolle*, 3ff.

54. While Blüher acknowledged that female-female attraction does exist, there is no female equivalent of the *Männerheld*.

55. See Blüher, *Wandervogelbewegung*, 70–71.

56. See Hewitt, *Political*, and Widdig, *Männerbünde*.

57. See Freud's (last) letter to Blüher, 8 September 1913; cit. Neubauer, "Freud/Blüher," 146–47.

58. In some accounts of Greek mythology Laius is described as the first pederast. In exile from Thebes Laius fell in love with Chryssipus, King Pelops's youngest son; when his banishment had been rescinded Laius abducted the young boy and brought him to Thebes as his catamite. Chryssipus killed himself out of shame, and Pelops put a curse on Laius: that he would be killed by his firstborn son. See Graves, *Greek Myths*, 2:41–42.

59. A triumphant C. G. Jung. In a letter to Freud on 26 December 1912, Ferenczi comments on Jung's new schism-confirming work, *Symbols of Transformation*, "The *father* plays almost no role in his new work, the *Christian community of brothers* (christlicher Brüdergemeinschaft) takes up all the more room in it" (Freud/Ferenczi, *Correspondence*, 449–50; emphases in original).

60. Freud, "Overview," 18.

61. Ibid., 19–20.

62. Cf. ibid., 20.

63. Blüher continued to draw upon Freud throughout the 1910s. Both the *Internationale Zeitschrift für Psychoanalyse* (Eisler, "Review") and *Imago* (Lorenz, "Review"), in which many of Freud's works—from the four essays of *Totem* to the first two essays of *Moses*—appeared, welcomed publication of Blüher's 1917–18 *Role of the Erotic* by crediting him as the first to found a

theory of society on Freud's views. Still, neither the editors nor Freud could have been happy that his writings came to be representative of psychoanalytic writings; see, for example, Franz Kafka's letter to Max Brod, mid-November 1917, in Kafka, *Letters*, 167. When Erich Leyens, a Jewish member of the youth movement, asked Freud in 1923 how someone like the "now right-wing radical" Blüher could have had been involved with Freud, he responded that Blüher "has nothing to do with analytical science" (Neubauer, "Freud/Blüher," 131).

64. *Wandervogelbewegung*, 102ff.

65. Schmidt, "Nein," and Wilker, "Freieschulgemeinde"; both cited by Geuter, *Homosexualität*, 95.

66. Revised and reissued virtually every year from 1887 until Fritsch's death in 1933, it was later renamed the *Handbook of the Jewish Question*.

67. See Lacquer, *Young*, esp. chap. 9, "The Jewish Question," 74–83, from which these examples derive.

68. "Der Wandervogel ist weder ein Ablagerungsplatz für alte Stieffel die ehemals auf Plattbeinen gesessen haben und nach Knoblauch stinken, noch ist der Wandervogel ein Spekulation für Judenunternehmungen." This passage was cited in the Jüdische Jugendbewegung (Jewish Youth Movement) exhibit at Vienna's Jüdisches Museum held March–April 2001. The mentions of garlic and flat feet are common stereotypical allusions to Jews.

69. *Wandervogel*, 2:241 (on the influence of Langbehn) and 2:98 (on Fischer).

70. Also see Laqueur, *Young*, 21–22.

71. Blüher, *Werke und Tage*, 345.

72. Cf. Blüher, *Wandervogelbewegung*, 70–71.

73. Friedlaender draws upon Karsch-Haack's "Uranismus."

74. Friedlaender, *Renaissance*, 117ff., 214ff. Jaeger (*Entdeckung*) held that there was a chemical basis to the soul—individuals are constantly emitting these molecules of soul-stuff. Human attraction—and repulsion—is a function of the reception or smell of this soul-stuff; see also Weinreich, *Duftstoff*.

75. Cf. Friedlaender, *Renaissance*, 123.

76. Blüher, *Wandervogelbewegung*, 71.

77. See chapter 4, above.

78. Blüher, *Wandervogelbewegung*, 135.

79. Blüher, *Secessio*, 19–20.

80. "Drei Grundformen," 327. In his later memoir, *Werke und Tage*, 346, Blüher writes how the encounter with Schurtz's writing allowed him to articulate what had been implicit to his first consideration of the bases for male groups.

81. Reulecke, "Das Jahre 1902," 1:3–7, and Schweizer, "Männerbünde," 1:23.

82. Schurtz, *Urgeschichte*, esp. 93–99 ("Anfange der Gesellschaft").

83. Schurtz's *Altersklassen* was well received and, for a number of years, frequently cited by Americans like Robert Lowie as well as by German-speaking ethnographers. A few sociologists did not have quite so high an opinion of his text; Marcel Mauss in 1906 wrote that it had been "too soon declared a classic" (*Oeuvres*, 3:59). While the Boas-influenced American anthropologist repudiated its evolutionary and generalizing tendencies, nonetheless Lowie's *Primitive Society*, in its classic supersession of all of his predecessors since Morgan's *Ancient Society*, wrote "to Schurtz above all others belongs the glory of having saved ethnologists from absorption in the sib organization and stirred them to a contemplation of phenomena that threatened to elude their purblind vision. . . . His insistence on the theoretical significance of association must rank as one of the most important points of departure in the study of primitive sociology" (257–58). The almost complete absence of reference to Schurtz after World War II is probably less a function of divergent concerns in anthropology than it is of the appropriation of his term of choice, *Männerbund*, by the Nazi movement and its ideologues, such as Alfred Baeumler.

84. But not only; race, too, constituted a natural difference for Schurtz, albeit as an incidental, unreflected assumption rather than as the lynchpin of social-theory construction. In *Altersklassen* he invokes race-specific odors, including the *foetor Judaicus*, and other ethnic differences as exemplifying the natural formation and exclusivity of homogeneous groups (43); he also expresses his concerns over race mixing. Such "bastardization" (75) leads to the sinking among the descendants of their racial value and culture. See Kurth, *Männer—Bünde*, 142.

85. Blüher letter to Freud, 8 August 1913; cit. Neubauer, "Freud/Blüher," 146: "ich plane für den Winter ein Buch über die Rolle der Erotik in der männlichen Gesellschaft."

86. Blüher, *Rolle*, 2:92ff.

87. Ibid., 2:99.

88. Ibid., 1:7, 6 (emphases in original); cf. Blüher, *Wandervogelbewegung*, 74.

89. Blüher, *Rolle*, 2:170–71; trans. in Hewitt, *Political*, 123, 125.

90. I trace the reception of Spinoza's solution in "Spinoza's Election."

91. This, according to Spinoza, was effected by the principles of Jewish religion, not by circumcision.

92. Blüher, *Secessio*, 49.

93. Blüher, *Rolle*, 2:21; trans. in Hewitt, *Political*, 126.

94. Blüher, *Rolle*, 2:162; on Freud's theory that homosexuality is a form of developmental inhibition, see ibid., 2:166.

95. Ibid., 2:194–98.

96. Zantop, *Colonial.*

97. See, inter alia, Puschner, *Die völkische Bewegung,* and Römer, *Sprachwissenschaft.*

98. *Wandervogelbewegung,* 12.

99. Schnurbein, "Geheime," and Greve, "Die SS," esp. 1:108–9.

100. See Spöttel, *Hamiten,* esp. 113–35.

101. Greve, "Die SS."

102. Since Schur's "Some," and, with increased vehemence following Masson's publication of the complete correspondence between them, Freud's relationship to Fliess has been one of the most discussed aspects of Freud's biography; see chapter 2, above.

103. Friedlaender, "Anhang: Nachfolger Gustav Jägers," in *Renaissance,* 49–50.

104. Fuss, "Identification," 45.

105. The antisemitic turn of Blüher's writing led to increasing consternation among other otherwise sympathetic readers. Not only were his writings among the most provocative contributions to the masculinist political counterculture, but like the work of other antisemitic intellectuals who commanded the respect of a particular generation, such as Weininger (*Sex and Character,* 1903) and Werner Sombart (*The Jews and Modern Capitalism,* 1911) before him, Blüher's work demanded a response. Kafka's letters repeatedly discuss the appeal of his writings as well as confer upon them a certain authoritative status. Thomas Mann records in his diaries (17 November 1919) the profound and positive impact Blüher's lectures and books made upon him; see Widdig, *Männerbünde,* 33–34. When *Secessio* appeared in 1922, Kafka wrote to Robert Klopstock (30 June 1922) of the necessity to respond to its characterizations and proposed solution to the Jewish problem in German cultural life. Kafka considered it a standard against which to read similar studies that differentiate German from Jewish culture/writing, such as Friedrich van der Leyen's *Deutsche Dichtung in neuer Zeit*; Kafka, *Letters,* 330–31. And the psychoanalyst Paul Federn, "Review," felt compelled to dismiss it.

106. Blüher, *Secessio,* 23–24.

107. Freud letter to Leyens, 4 July 19[23]; cit. Neubauer, "Freud-Blüher," 131.

108. Ibid.

109. As noted above, the antisemitic polemicist Stauffer characterized the family very similarly.

110. Cf. Geller, "Mice"; the work of Bhabha, for example, *Location*; and Taussig, for example, *Mimesis.*

111. Blüher, *Rolle,* 2:175.

112. Freud, *Letters of Sigmund Freud,* 375 (30 January 1927).

CHAPTER 7: A PALEONTOLOGICAL VIEW OF FREUD'S STUDY OF *JUDENTUM*:
UNEARTHING THE *LEITFOSSIL* OF AN UNLAID GHOST

This chapter began its existence as a lecture to Professor Mal Diamond's "Religion and Psychology" class at Princeton University during the fall semester, 1987. Its next avatar was "A Paleontological View of Freud's Study of Religion: Unearthing the *Leitfossil* Circumcision," presented to the Person, Culture, and Religion Group at the 1988 American Academy of Religion annual meeting. It then made its way, under the same title, to *Modern Judaism* 13 (1993): 49–70, before running the gauntlet of new readings of *Moses* and finding a resting place here.

1. I prefer the unintentional(?) Shylockian pun of the Katherine Jones translation: "hardly ever been weighed"; Freud, *Moses*, 29.

2. Freud/A. Zweig, *Letters*, 91 (30 September 1934).

3. Ibid.; the translation has been modified.

4. Freud/Andreas-Salomé, *Letters*, 205 (6 January 1935). Cf. 23:105: "problems which have always seemed to deserve attention and which recent events have forced upon our observation anew."

5. Had Freud's readers been privy to the original introduction to his work, uncovered (again—see Grubrich-Simitis, *Early Freud*, 90n1) by Yosef Hayim Yerushalmi, they would have read: "My immediate purpose was to gain knowledge of the person of Moses, my more distant goal to contribute thereby to the solution of a problem, still current today, which can only be specified later on"; cit. Yerushalmi, "Freud," 379.

6. Freud repeats this concern throughout his correspondence with Arnold Zweig about *Moses*: for example, "More important is the fact that this historical novel won't stand up to my own criticism. I need more certainty and I should not like to endanger the final formula of the whole book, which I regard as valuable, by founding it on a base of clay [*auf eine tönerne Basis*]" (Freud/A. Zweig, *Letters*, 97 [6 November 1934]).

7. Actually, as Assman has thoroughly documented in *Moses the Egyptian*, there has been a long tradition of ascribing Egyptian origins to Moses, a tradition not unfamiliar to, if left uncited by, Freud. Freud, too, when discussing water symbolism and the representation of birth in dreams in "Symbolism in Dreams," the tenth of his *Introductory Lectures on Psychoanalysis* (specifically following the invocation of Otto Rank's 1909 *Myth of the Birth of the Hero*— and a text cited by Freud in the first essay of *Moses* [albeit with the proviso: "at that time still under my influence"; 23:10]), had told a joke whose punch line refers to an Egyptian Moses: "an intelligent Jewish boy was asked who the mother of Moses was. He replied without hesitation: 'The Princess.' 'No,' he was told, 'she only took him out of the water.' 'That's what *she* says,' he re-

plied" (15:161). When Freud relates this joke in private, "the intelligent Jewish boy" receives a stock name from the repertoire of Jewish jokes and Gentile stereotypes: Itzig (see Yerushalmi, *Freud's Moses*, 1; also chap. 4 note 75, above).

8. As discussed in the previous chapter, the last had already been floated twenty-five years earlier in *Totem*. It had been assailed to the point of ridicule—as Freud himself mentions in *Moses*. Yet, he adds, "To this day I hold firmly to this construction," and in a defiant act of denial, he asserts: "A contradiction [*Widerspruch*] is not a refutation" (23:131; translation modified).

9. Cf. Freud/Andreas-Salomé, *Letters*, 204 (6 January 1935): "It started out from the question as to what has really created the special character of the Jew."

10. See Freud's letter to Arnold Zweig: "Moses will not let go of my imagination [*Phantasie*]" (Freud/A. Zweig, *Letters*, 106 [2 May 1935]). For additional testimony, see ibid., 91–92 (30 September 1934); 97 (6 November 1934); 104 (14 March 1935); 105 (15 March 1935); and 107 (13 June 1935); as well as Freud/Andreas-Salomé, *Letters*, 204–5 (6 January 1935).

11. In the 30 September 1934 letter that announces the completion of the first *Moses* manuscript, Freud reports to Zweig that the Vatican had closed down Edoardo Weiss's *Rivista Italiana di Psicoanalisis* despite the support of Mussolini; see Freud/A. Zweig, *Letters*, 92. Rather than a historical generality, this very specific instance of suppression is probably alluded to in the first preface when Freud remarks on a prohibition of psychoanalysis: "Such violent methods of suppression are, indeed, by no means alien to the Church" (23:55).

12. Although Freud dismissed his 1927 *Future of an Illusion* as a work of an "old man" in a 1929 letter to French psychoanalyst René Laforgue, adding that "Freud is dead now, and believe me the genuine Freud was really a great man" (cit. Choisy, *Appraisal*, 84), his subsequent works, such as *Civilization*, reveal the resurrection of the "genuine Freud."

13. When Freud begins to construct his analogy between the development of neurosis and the history of the religion(s) of the Jews by describing the forgotten traumatic infantile experiences, he incidentally adds that the infantile amnesia "is usually broken into by a few separate mnemic residues, which are known as 'screen memories'" (23:74). What Freud neglects to add here is that these remarkably clear, yet seemingly innocuous, memories are themselves compromise formations, defensive displacements of forgotten, repressed, experiences. Moreover, as his case studies have shown from the very beginning (cf. the case of Lucy R. in *Studies*, 2:106–24), even the repressed material that analysis dredges up may itself be a screen for more traumatic experiences.

14. "[I]f I am Moses, then you are Joshua and will take possession of the promised land of psychiatry, which I shall only be able to glimpse from afar"

(Freud/Jung, *Letters*, 196–97 [17 January, 1908]). On Freud's identification with Moses, see, inter alia, Goldstein, *Reinscribing*; Grubrich-Simitis, *Early Freud*; and Rice, *Freud and Moses*.

15. Freud's beloved Heine described his last works as written from his "mattress grave." Having contracted spinal tuberculosis (multiple sclerosis, or tertiary syphilis), Heine spent his last eight years of life confined to bed; as the *Jewish Encyclopedia* notes, "it was while on his 'mattress grave' that Heine gave utterance to his most penetrating comments on matters Jewish," as well as writing the *Hebrew Melodies*, *Memoirs*, and *Confessions*.

16. Cuddihy, *Ordeal*, esp. 48–57, appropriates Freud's term to highlight the significance of Freud's being a Jew on the development of psychoanalysis.

17. For example, Van Herik, *Freud*.

18. See Robert, *From Oedipus*.

19. For example, the rather unfunny Oring, *Jokes*.

20. Curiously, while Freud, in large part, draws his conclusion that Moses is an Egyptian by reading the story of Moses' birth to Hebrew slaves and later adoption by the Pharaoh's daughter as an anomalous inversion of the traditional family romance—the child of nobility raised by humble proxies—from a Jewish perspective it is wholly consistent: the child of the chosen people (indeed, of what will become the priestly tribe) is raised by idolatrous gentiles.

21. For example, Krüll, *Father*.

22. For example, Roith, *Riddle*.

23. Zollschan, *Jewish*, 4–5; cit. Efron, *Defenders*, 153.

24. See Santner, "Ethics"; DiCenso, *Other Freud*; P. Schäfer, "Triumph"; Le Rider, *Freud*; and Assman, "Fortschritt," the last of which marks a repudiation of his earlier understanding of Freud's *Moses* in *Moses the Egyptian*. *Geistigkeit* already held center stage in Yerushalmi's characterization of Freud's godless *Judentum*. I address this interpretive trajectory below; my "Not a *Geist*" offers a more extensive discussion of these seers of *Geistigkeit*. The prominence—misplaced, as I argue below—recently ascribed to *Geistigkeit* finally struck me while reading Eliza Slavet's " 'Special Case' " and its offshoot, "Circumcised Supremacy."

25. See Yerushalmi, *Freud's Moses*; Derrida, *Archive*; Bernstein, *Freud*; and Assman, "Sigmund Freud"; see, too, Maciejewski's efforts to meld this thematic to circumcision in *Psychoanalytisches Archiv*. Schäfer, "Triumph," 389, argues that any attempt to nuance Freud's Lamarckism—"there can be no denying of the fact that, in Freud's view, both an individual and a people or an ethnic group shlepp 'fragments of phylogenetic origin' around with them"—or even to focus on the question is besides the point. Santner, in "Ethics," provides a phenomenologically satisfying, but still history-begging, traumatic spin on the issue by understanding the unconscious memory-trace

as structural. Traumatic events, he writes, are "'events' that do not properly take place." Because they are not experienced "within the normative field of object relations" (35–36; or, as I would put it, given meaning and narratively integrated into consciousness or memory or self), they persist as ongoing unsuccessful attempts to describe or make fit what one is not aware are in need of description or fitting. "The 'phylogenetic inheritance,' persists not as this or that set of 'propositional attitudes' or thoughts in deep memory, but rather as the content of the *form*" (40). Such acting out is like the space that is "naturally" perceived as straight but is from another perspective (a perspective not yet attainable by the observer) recognized as continuously distorted by (unseen) forces. Santner seems to be pointing to some mediative performance in the face of ontological difference: acting out the incommensurable desires both to incorporate difference (therefore rendering it no longer different— think parricide) and to have that difference retain its otherness (and yet be knowable—think incest), but that still leaves the question of why—here, now—the content of the form is described in terms of "Oedipal crimes" or the variant under discussion here: Why castration? Here? Now?

26. And sexuality-inflected: the foreclosure of homosexuality from Freud's characterization of the Semitic horde is already discussed in chapter 6, above. For Freud feminization may not be identical to homosexualization, but there is significant overlap as well as significant anxiety on Freud's part about their possible identity; this is evident in a phrase from "Psychological Notes" like "a feminine (that is, a passive homosexual) wish-phantasy" (12:47). As observed in chapter 4, above, Freud worked overtime to represent the "circumcised" Hans as heterosexual. Consequently, the silence with regard to homosexuality in *Moses* is always also connected to his efforts to split off the feminine from *Judentum*.

27. "Defective speech": This phrasing is actually Freud's self-description in a 2 May 1935 letter to Arnold Zweig. As a consequence of the onset of mouth cancer in 1923 Freud had been subjected during the remainder of his life to numerous oral surgeries and fitted with innumerable ill-fitting prostheses. That sharing this plaint with Moses further cemented the identification is doubly indicated by the passage in the letter in which the phrase appears: "I picture myself reading [*Moses*] aloud to you when you come to Vienna, despite my defective speech" (Freud/A. Zweig, *Letters*, 106).

28. See, inter alia, Gilman, "Mental Illness," and Efron, *Medicine*.

29. By others: on the antisemitic representation of the Jew as fossil, see Newman, "Death." Or by Freud, this fossil imagery as well as the depictions of the Hebrews as "the savage Semites" (23:47) and "the primitive masses" (23:63) are held to reflect Freud's feelings toward the Jews, or at least toward *Ostjuden*; see, inter alia, Wistrich, "Last Testament."

30. See Freud, *Outline*, "Splitting," and "Fetishism," and Laplanche and Pontalis, *Language*.

31. Of course, Medusa fell victim herself. Her fate perhaps is a harbinger of that of the Jews: that which allowed them to persist, namely, circumcision, may result in their extinction. See survivor Piotr Rawicz's novel *Blood in the Sky* and Jakov Lind's *Counting My Steps: An Autobiography*, Louis Malle's quasi-autobiographical 1984 film *Au revoir, les enfants* and Agniewska Holland's filming of Solomon Perel's memoir, *Europa, Europa*, among other memoirs, films, and novels where the identities and lives of Jewish boys hiding amid the Gentile population are threatened when Germans pull down their pants to betray their circumcision.

32. Although Freud does not explicitly cite Numbers 12:3 here, his editors make the reference. Freud may well have omitted the explicit reference because of the passage's context. Miriam and Aaron are upset at Moses for having married a Cushite woman. While some contemporary readers may wish to conflate Midian and Cush, the latter is almost always identified with Ethiopia and other regions south of Egypt inhabited by black-skinned peoples. On the other hand, such intermarriage would have correlated with Freud's hypothesis of the merging of two groups at Kadesh.

33. See Carlebach, "Forgotten," 109. Montesquieu appended the label to women in his *Lettres Persanes* (1731).

34. Freud/A. Zweig, *Letters*, 91 (30 September 1934).

35. Zweig, *Bilanz*, 87–96, cit. 89.

36. And, more generally, the relations between divergent groups (Christian-Jew, Aryan-Jew, man-woman, white-black, heterosexual-homosexual, et cetera).

37. As will be discussed below, when Freud returns to how Jews are distinguished from "other peoples" in the second part of the final essay, the singularity of circumcision disappears behind the phrase "by many of their customs" (23:105).

38. Cf. Van Herik, *Freud*, esp. chaps. 11–12.

39. This ideal was also characteristic of the ancient Semites who murdered Moses. On *Judentum*'s alternative model of masculinity, see D. Boyarin, *Unheroic*.

40. Cf. Manuel, *Broken Staff*.

41. Especially the Freud-cited Breasted, *History*, and the curiously uncited Abraham, "Amenhotep." Cf. Shengold, "Parapraxis," and Roith, *Riddle*, 170–74; as well as Abraham's 11 January 1912 letter to Freud and Freud's 14 January 1912 response, in Freud/Abraham, *Letters*, 111–13, in which Abraham's article is discussed.

42. Or to deny credit to Akhenaten's wife? In his copy of Laforgue, *L'influence*, 13, Freud had underlined: "Ikoun Aton n'aurait pu réformer la religion

égyptienne ni proclamer le règne de son dieu unique, sans l'influence de sa femme, qui était d'origine étrangère, aryenne ou babylonienne." Freud's concern is probably less with spousal influence per se than her origin. While he earlier noted that the pharaohs married "Asiatic" princesses or women "from Syria" (23:21–22), Freud may have been uneasy with suggesting either Aryan or Babylonian roots—the latter because it echoed the "Babel and Bible" controversy initiated in 1902 by leading Assyriologist Friedrich Delitsch, who, drawing upon archaeological discoveries and textual decipherings of ancient Mesopotamian material, authoritatively declared Jewish monotheism and ancient Israelite culture to be wholly derivative and later embraced the substitution of the Old Testament with Schwaner's *Germanenbibel* that represented German folk epics and theological writings as holy script; also see Chavalas, "Babel." Hence either origin may have evoked racial antisemitic associations and undermined Freud's claims for *Judentum*'s contribution of *Geistigkeit* to the West.

43. Albright, *Stone Age*, 220, notes that examination of his mummy soon after its discovery in 1907 confirmed the millennia-old depiction of Akhenaten's pathology. Abraham, "Amenhotep," refers to the young king's "soft, delicate body build" (*zartem, schwächlichem Körperbau*; 332) and the "youthful, almost maidenly [*fast Mädchenhafter*] form" (352) of the king on the British Museum relief.

44. See Yerushalmi, "Freud," 378. Freud discussed his reading of the third volume of the eventual tetralogy in a 29 November 1936 letter to Mann and perhaps during a meeting or phone conversation on 15 January 1937; see Molnar, *Diary*, 214, and Freud, *Letters*, 432–34. The admiration was mutual; Herbert Lehnert, "Vorstudien," 479, argues that Freud's work, especially *Totem*, provided primary sources for the tetralogy. Unfortunately, the first volume is missing from Freud's library so it is impossible to investigate whether Freud responded to this passage in its margins.

45. Mann, *Tales*, 48. Mann goes on to tie the sentiments aroused by the mystic significance of circumcision and "a certain degeneracy betrayed in [Joseph's] behavior" (49); Mann thereby connects circumcision with the discourse of Jewish degeneracy. On the Jew as degenerate, see Gilman, "Sexology." We do know that Mann underlined the footnote on circumcision in his copy of *Totem und Tabu*; Lehnert, "Vorstudien," 483n31.

46. Fischer, *Handbuch*, 322.

47. Mereschkovsky, *Geheimnisse*, 105–6.

48. Ibid., 100.

49. Ibid., 99.

50. Ibid. 106. Mereschkovsky's reflection here also makes a gender-coded distinction between the sensual and the *geistig*, albeit the inverse of Freud's

conclusion. Moreover, image-prohibition is not the only practice by which *Judentum* transcends the empirical; the superseded circumcision also achieves this end—again, so long as discretion remains the better part of that virile quality valor.

51. Freud/A. Zweig, *Letters*, 91; cf. 65–66, 86 (letters of 25 February, 15 July 1934). Unfortunately, many liberties have been taken by commentators when confronted by Freud's characterization of his work as "a historical novel." They ignore Freud's own explanation of what he means by the term to that other author of historical novels, Arnold Zweig. For Freud, his historical novel was neither a fictional story of a real person nor a reconstruction of an era through fictional characters; rather, he sees his work as a connecting of the dots, the historical traces strewn about a fragmented, distorted text.

52. In the discussion of the origins of guilt in *Civilization*, "people of Israel," exemplifying for Freud how a group takes upon itself the blame for its misfortune, are contrasted with the fetish that is blamed by "primitive" men for their misfortune (21:26). Did the "people of Israel" assume the position of the fetish with the "German people['s] relapse into almost prehistoric barbarism" (23:54)?

53. In his first letter to Arnold Zweig from his new refuge in London, Freud reports about a letter he had just received from a young American Jew, who had read the first two essays in *Imago*, "imploring [Freud] not to deprive our poor unhappy people of the one consolation remaining to them in their misery" (Freud/A. Zweig, *Letters*, 163 [28 June 1938]). Freud anticipated "an onslaught by the Jews on it" in a postscript to 5 March 1939 letter to his fellow analyst Max Eitingon, cited in Schur, *Freud*, 520. Also like Spinoza, Freud felt that he had been put under the ban (*"Bann"*; 20:9) of the community's powers.

54. Strauss, "Testament."

55. Spinoza, *Tractatus*, 63.

56. In his "too literal" 1841 edition of Spinoza's *Tractatus*, Berthold Auerbach translates *effoeminarent* as *"weibisch machten"* (rendered womanish); later translators, including J. H. von Kirchmann's 1870 *Theologisch-politische Abhandlung*, and Carl Gebhardt's standard edition of the *Traktat*, render *effoeminarent* as *"verweichlichten/verweichlichen"* (made soft or effeminate).

57. "Identification" is to be understood here, above all, in the sense of *Interpretation* (4:319–20): through their relationship of similitude one image is substituted for the threatening other, whereby a partial resemblance becomes a total identity.

58. In the entry for "Women's Movement Jewesses" in his antisemitic biographical encyclopedia of German Jews, *Semi-Kürschner*, 2:98, Phillip Stauff writes that the Jews (*die Juden*) had directed the "originally healthy" women's movement down false paths in order to undermine their hosts (*Wirtsvölker*;

that is, the indigenous population as opposed to the alien guests, the Jews), politically, ethically, and economically.

59. This is not to gainsay the importance of ascribing ethnic or racial difference to the maintenance of the imperialist order that is discussed in the Introduction. Modernity's impossible demand of "clear and distinct" identities is always already subverted by the hybrid of "clear and distinct" race and ethnic, gender and sexual, class and other differences that form those identities; however, this analysis of *Moses* focuses on gender.

60. In his concluding discussion of "blood-bridegroom" and Exodus 4:25–26, Mereschkovsky, *Geheimnis*, 249, describes Israel as a "Man-Woman" (*"Mann-Weib"*).

61. In the first part of the third essay, Freud appears unable to suture his developing theory of splitting with his extant theory of repression, of trauma with drive theory, and as the analogy (subsection C) enters the stage of application (subsection D), repression has returned to dominate Freud's argumentation.

62. "Repetition" is a more accurate translation of *Wiederholung*.

63. Katherine Jones's translation explicitly makes "Summary" the title of the subsection and the *Standard Edition* employs the same font size for "Summary and Recapitulation" and subsection form as the preceding prefatory notes; however, Freud's preliminary table of contents (Grubrich-Simitis, *Early Freud*, 97) ambiguously suggests that it is the title of the entire second part.

64. He even *zweimal* (twice) repeats the word *"zweimal."*

65. Freud, "Fortschritt."

66. See Robertson, "Testament"; Assman, "Fortschritt," 157; and Wistrich, "Last Testament."

67. See note 24, above.

68. Ignaz Zollschan, for example, wrote, "In *Judentum* the consciousness of 'Geist' arose over and against nature. Notions of ethics and law therefore first blossomed in *Judentum. In this fact lies the actual crux of Judentum's significance for world history"* (*Rassenproblem*, 404; emphasis in original). On this general strategy, see Schäfer, "Triumph."

69. As Assman ("Fortschritt,"169) concludes and Schäfer ("Triumph," 399–400n52) seconds: "In returning to the prohibition of images Freud shows that this striving for spiritual liberation is both a profoundly Jewish project and a tradition that he himself with his psychoanalysis claims to be heir to and to surpass."

70. It should be recalled that the "double" is emblematic of the uncanny; see chapter 1, above.

71. The one example that Freud provides of the contempt of the circumcised for the uncircumcised is not the Jew but the "Turk [who] will abuse a Christian as an 'uncircumcised dog' " (23:30).

72. Actually, the super-ego makes a cameo appearance in the first part of the third essay in order to announce its apparent irrelevance: "The fact that later on a special region—the 'super-ego'—is separated off in the ego lies outside our present interest" (23:97).

73. Beyond the theoretical confusion that the dynamic model of sublimation may have presented to Freud's metapsychology, binding sublimation to Jewish *Geistigkeit* may have generated associations to deviant sexuality that Freud would have sought to avoid. When the notion of sublimation first made appearances in his corpus Freud tied it to the transformation of nonnormative sexual aims. In the 1908 essay " 'Civilized' Sexual Morality" Freud comments, "The forces that can be employed for cultural activities are thus to a great extent obtained through the suppression of what are known as the perverse elements of sexual excitation" (9:189), while Freud analyzes Leonardo's "intellectual labor" (*geistigen Arbeit*; 11:74) as an effect of the sublimation of homosexual libido (11:80–81). Perhaps it is no accident that in the midst of that discussion, Freud's only other mention of Spinoza in his corpus appears; he compares Leonardo's "transformation of the instinct" with "Spinoza's mode of thinking" (11:75). See also the discussion of the Freud-Blüher exchange over homosexuality, sublimation, and cultural production in chap. 6, above.

74. As per Assman's original reading in *Moses*.

75. See, for example, Grubrich-Simitis, *Early Freud*, 77–78. Beyond the nexus of race and religion, Freud may have wished to extend the series of displacements that he proffered as the last of the deep motives for antisemitism: If the "misbaptized" have shifted the blame for the renunciations demanded by Christianity onto their purported origin, *Judentum*, and therefore are bearing a grudge against the source, then . . .

76. D. Boyarin, *Unheroic*, 246–48. Or the Egyptians, see Schorske, "Egyptian Dig," esp. 208–9. Van Herik, *Freud*, esp. 183–93, describes how Freud apologetically associates Jewish religion with masculinity, especially in the second part of the third essay.

77. Mann, *Tales*, 1:48.

78. Freud/Andreas-Salomé, *Letters*, 205 (6 January 1935) (translation modified). While Freud claims Sellin's *Moses* as his principal scholarly source for Moses' murder, Robert A. Paul carefully analyzes whether Freud "really 'borrowed' anything from Sellin at all beyond the idea of a murdered Moses" in "Freud," 833.

79. The curiosity is doubled when the original publication site of Rank's monograph is considered: the same volume (3) of *Imago* (1914) as Freud's anonymously published "The Moses of Michelangelo."

80. The young Rank also wrote a Weininger-inspired essay, "The Essence of Judaism," in which he writes that the Jews "are, so to speak, women among

the people and must above all join themselves to the masculine life-source if they are to become 'productive'" (171).

81. In *Jokes* (8:75) and in *Leonardo* (11:77).

82. Freeman, *Insights*, 87. Lydia Marinelli, research director of Vienna's Freud Museum, reports that there is no other evidence or eyewitness account of such a painting ever hanging at Berggasse 19.

83. Hessing, *Spinoza-Festschrift*, 196–97.

84. Klausner, "Jüdischer Charakter," 125.

85. Freud's thank-you letter to Hessing appears in its entirety in Hessing, "Freud's," 229.

86. Andreas-Salomé, *Freud*, 75–76. The references to Spinoza in Andreas-Salomé's diary of a year in Vienna far outweigh those in Freud's entire corpus. The Spinozan critique of Judaism was well-known in the Jewish intellectual circles of Freud's youth, however. Moreover, Hessing, "Freud's," reproduces a letter from Freud to Lothar Bickel, dated 28 June 1931, written in response to an article submitted to him by the latter. Freud writes: "My dependence on the teachings of Spinoza I do admit most willingly. I had no reason to mention his name directly, as I got my presumptions not from studying him, but from the atmosphere he created" (227). Hessing assumes that via his friendship with Andreas-Salomé, Freud may have been "quasi-transformed into a follower of Spinoza . . . establishing a noble link between them" (228). Interestingly, the only reference to either Spinoza or to circumcision that appears in the extant notes to the Vienna Psychoanalytic Society belong to Tausk; see Nunberg and Federn, *Minutes*, 2:328–30 (24 November 1909; on Spinoza) and 4:177 (12 March 1913; on circumcision). Andreas-Salomé was in attendance at the latter session, Tausk's presentation (to Freud's consternation) of subjects much on Freud's mind at the time: patriarchy, the castration of the son by the father (of which circumcision is a residue), and "The Father Problem."

87. On the import and prevalence of male bonds as well as the role of woman as mediating object of male exchange, see the discussion of homosocial desire in Sedgwick, *Between Men*, and Geller, "Contact."

88. Andreas-Salomé, *Freud*, 166–67, 97. The relationship among these three has been the object of controversy with Roazen, *Brother*, on the one hand, suggesting Freud's romantic and intellectual envy of Tausk as well as complicity in Tausk's 1919 suicide, and Eissler, *Talent* and *Suicide*, on the other, defending an idealized Freud and denigrating the hopelessly neurotic Tausk. Roustang, *Dire*, chap. 5, has provided a judicious account of their relationship and calls attention to Tausk's doubling of Freud.

89. She died 5 February 1937. The first essay had just been published, the second would not be completed until August of that year, and the concluding essay would take yet another year before it attained its final form. Cf. editor's note, 23:3–5, and Freud, "Lou Andreas-Salomé," 23:297–98.

90. The 1850 edition of Richard Wagner's *Das Judentum in der Musik* concludes with the contested words "die Erlösung Ahasvers: der Untergang!"

91. Laplanche and Pontalis, *Language*, 59 (s.v. "Castration Complex").

92. Or, even, monotheism. Recall in this context the discussion in chap. 3, above, of Binet's analogy of sexual fetishism with monotheism; Binet, "Le Fétichisme," 143.

AFTERWORD: A FORENSIC ANALYSIS OF SIGMUND'S ROD, OR CRACKING
OPEN THE *GEWACHSENE FELS* OF PSYCHOANALYSIS

1. Homer, *The Iliad*, 8:19, 24–26; Mereschkovsky, *Geheimnisse*, 99. The consort of the lord of Olympus, Juno, would later defiantly lament her stance with the words that became the motto of *Interpretation*: *Flectere si nequeo, Acheronta movebo* (If I cannot bend the Higher Powers, I will move the Infernal Regions; Vergil, *Aeneid*, 7:312).

2. An alternative reading might interpret this section on the interface through Freud's 1913 essay "The Theme of the Three Caskets" and find instead of the interminable analysis effected by biology, the terminable that is death; instead of castration, the mother. As Sprengnether, *Spectral*, 121–23, points out, Freud was working on the earlier essay at the same time as he was attempting to resolve another rivalry—with Jung—and to historically ground his universal algorithm for regulating sexual difference: Oedipus.

3. Cf. Verhaeghe, "Riddle."

4. Cf. Kristeva, *Powers*, 99–100: "By repeating the natural scar of the umbilical cord at the location of sex, by duplicating and thus displacing through ritual the preeminent separation, which is that from the mother, Judaism seems to insist in symbolic fashion . . . that the identity of the speaking being (with his God) is based on the separation of the son from the mother."

5. Had he spoken—called upon Gd's action—instead of using Aaron's rod upon the rock Moses would not have been punished. Curiously, the footnoted unplumbable navel of the Irma Dream is appended to Freud's wish that Irma's friend and not Irma had been the patient in the dream, for "She would then have *opened her mouth properly*, and have told me more than Irma" (4:111; emphasis in original).

6. See the editor's note, 23:32n3.

7. Sachs concludes from his triangulation of Bismarck and Moses that "the prohibited seizing of the rod [*Stockes*] (in the dream an unmistakably phallic one), the production of fluid from its blow, the threat of death—in these we find all the principal factors of infantile masturbation united" (5:380).

8. See D. Boyarin, "Homophobia," 166, and the discussion of his *Unheroic* in the Introduction to the present volume.

9. See M. Freud, *Sigmund*, 70–71, and chapter 4, above. Dr. Stockmann also brandishes an umbrella to drive out the last of the hypocrites in the penultimate scene of *Enemy* (79).

10. Ibsen, *Enemy*, 80.

11. Luther translated Matthew 16:18, "you are Peter . . . and on this rock I will build my church," as "Du bist Petrus, und auf diesen *Felsen* will ich meine Gemeinde bauen" (emphasis added). The leading nineteenth-century German-Jewish theologian-historian, Abraham Geiger, offered his own variant: Christianity "is also completely hewn from the *rock* of the Jewish spirit" (dem *Fels* des jüdischen Geistes; *Judenthum*, 5; emphasis added).

12. Ibid., 82; he also refers to them as "specimens" and "curs."

13. Unlike Stockmann, Freud entrusted his legacy to his daughter Anna, and at least compromised when Anna, unlike Petra, confronted the choice between "masculine" medicine and "feminine" teaching. She became a lay analyst of children.

The Standard Edition of the Complete Psychological Works of Sigmund Freud.
Trans. and ed. J. Strachey. 24 vols. London: Hogarth Press and the
Institute of Psycho-Analysis, 1953–74.
Die Freud-Studienausgabe. Ed. Alexander Mitscherlich, Angela Richards,
and James Strachey, with Ilse Grubrich-Simitis. 11 vols. Frankfurt/M:
S. Fischer Verlag, 1969–75.
Gesammelte Werke. Ed. Alexander Mitscherlich, Angela Richards, and
James Strachey. 4th ed. 19 vols. Frankfurt/M: S. Fischer Verlag, 1993.

I. Writings in the *Standard Edition* [S.E.] (listed in order of appearance
in the *S.E.*, with official original date of publication in parentheses and
date of composition in brackets where different)

Studies on Hysteria (with Josef Breuer) (1895d). [*Studies* or *Studien*]
    On the Psychical Mechanism of Hysterical Phenomena: Preliminary
        Communication (1893; Breuer and Freud). 2:1–17. ["On the Psychi-
        cal Mechanism"]
    Case History of Fräulein Anna O (Breuer). 2:21–47.
    Case History of Frau Emmy von N. (Freud). 2:48–105.
    Case History of Miss Lucy R. (Freud). 2:106–24.
    Case History of Katharina —— (Freud). 2:125–34.
    Case History of Fräulein Elisabeth von R. (Freud). 2:135–81.
    Theoretical (Breuer). 2:183–251.
    The Psychotherapy of Hysteria (Freud). 2:255–305.
Obsessions and Phobias: Their Psychical Mechanism and Their Aetiol-
    ogy." 3:74–139 (1895c [1894]).
"Heredity and the Aetiology of the Neuroses." 3:143–56 (1896a).
"Further Remarks on the Neuro-Psychoses of Defense." 3:162–83
    (1896b).
"The Aetiology of Hysteria." 3:187–229 (1896c).

The Interpretation of Dreams. 4–5:4–627 (1900a). [*Interpretation* or
  Traumdeutung]
The Psychopathology of Everyday Life. 6:1–279 (1901b). [*Psychopathology*]
Fragments of an Analysis of a Case of Hysteria. 7:1–122 (1905e [1901]). [*Frag-
  ments* or *Dora*]
Three Essays on the Theory of Sexuality. 7:123–243 (1905d). [*Three Essays*]
Jokes and Their Relation to the Unconscious. 8:1–236 (1905c). [*Jokes*]
"The Sexual Enlightenment of Children." 9:129–39 (1907c). ["Sexual
  Enlightenment"]
"'Civilized' Sexual Morality and Modern Nervous Illness." 9:177–204
  (1908d). ["'Civilized' Sexual Morality"]
"On the Sexual Theories of Children." 9:205–26 (1908c). ["Sexual
  Theories"]
"Family Romances." 9:235–41 (1909c [1908]). ["Family Romances"]
"Analysis of a Phobia in a Five-Year-Old Boy." 10:1–147 (1909b). ["Anal-
  ysis" or "Little Hans"]
"Notes upon a Case of Obsessional Neurosis." 10: 151–249 (1909d).
  ["Notes" or "Rat Man"]
"Original Record of the Case of Obsessional Neurosis." 10:251–318
  (1955a [1907–8]). ["Original Record"]
Leonardo da Vinci and a Memory of His Childhood. 11:57–137 (1910c).
  [*Leonardo*]
"Psychoanalytic Notes upon an Autobiographical Account of a Case of
  Paranoia (Dementia Præcox)." 12:1–79 (1911c [1910]). ["Psychoana-
  lytic Notes" or "Schreber"]
"An Evidential Dream." 12:269–77. (1913a).
"The Theme of the Three Caskets." 12:291–301 (1913f [1912]).
"'Great Is Diana of the Ephesians.'" 12:342–44 (1911f)
Preface to the Hebrew Translation of *Totem and Taboo.* 13:xv (1934b
  [1930]).
Totem and Taboo. 13:1–161 (1912–13). [*Totem*]
"The Moses of Michelangelo." 13:209–36 (1914b).
"On Narcissism: An Introduction." 14:67–102 (1914c).
"Thoughts for the Times on War and Death." 14:275–301 (1915b).
"Lecture X. Symbolism in Dreams." In *Introductory Lectures on Psychoanal-
  ysis.* 15:149–69 (1916–17 [1915–17]). [*Introductory Lectures*]
"Lecture XII. Some Analyses of Sample Dreams" In *Introductory Lectures
  on Psychoanalysis.* 15:184–98 (1916–17 [1915–17]). [*Introductory Lectures*]
"From the History of an Infantile Neurosis." 17:1–122 (1918b [1914]).
  ["History" or "Wolf-Man"]

"'A Child Is Being Beaten.'" 17:175–204 (1919e). ["'Child'"]

"The Uncanny." 17:217–52 (1919h).

Group Psychology and the Analysis of the Ego. 18:65–143 (1921c). [*Group Psychology*]

"Some Neurotic Mechanisms in Jealousy, Paranoia and Homosexuality." 18:221–32 (1922b [1921]). ["Some Neurotic Mechanisms"]

"Medusa's Head." 18:273–74 (1940c [1922]).

"The Resistances to Psychoanalysis." 19:211–22 (1925e [1924]). ["Resistances"]

"Letter to the Editor of the *Jewish Press Center in Zurich.*" 19:291 (1925b).

An Autobiographical Study. 20:7–70 (1925d). [*Autobiographical*]

Inhibitions, Symptoms, and Anxiety. 20:75–172 (1926d [1925]). [*Inhibitions*]

"Address to the Society of B'nai B'rith, Vienna." 20:273–74 (1941e [1926]).

The Future of an Illusion. 21:1–56 (1927c).

Civilization and Its Discontents. 21:57–145 (1930a [1929]). [*Civilization*]

"Fetishism." 21:147–57 (1927e).

"A Religious Experience." 21:169–71 (1928a).

"Dostoevsky and Parricide." 21:173–94 (1928b [1927]).

New Introductory Lectures on Psycho-Analysis (1933a [1932]).

"Lecture XXXIII: Femininity." 22:112–35. ["Femininity"]

"Lecture XXXIV: Explanations, Applications, and Orientations." 22:136–57.

"Lecture XXXV: The Question of a *Weltanschauung.*" 22:158–82.

"The Acquisition and Control of Fire." 22:187–93 (1932a [1931]).

Moses and Monotheism. 23:1–137 (1939a [1934–38]). [*Moses*]

An Outline of Psychoanalysis. 23:141–207 (1940a [1938]). [*Outline*]

"Analysis: Terminable and Interminable." 23:209–53 (1937c).

"Splitting of the Ego in the Process of Defence." 23:271–78 (1940 [1938]). ["Splitting"]

"Lou Andreas-Salomé." 23:297–98 (1937a).

II. Writings outside of the *Standard Edition* (in presumed order of composition)

"Über Hysterie." *Wiener medizinische Press* 36, 43–44 (27 October, 3 November 1895): 1638–41, 1678–79.

"*Aus älteren Aufzeichnungen* von 1897 an" (1897–98). Container B28 ("Writings, 1877–1985 and n.d."). Sigmund Freud Collection, Library of Congress, Washington, D.C.

L'Homme aux rats. Journal d'une analyse. Ed. and trans. Elza Ribeiro Hawelka, with Pierre Hawelka. Paris: Presses Universitaires de France, 1974. [*L'Homme*]

"Wir und der Tod," *Zweimonats-Bericht für die Mitglieder der österreichischisraelischenHumanitätsvereine B'nai B'rith* 18, 1 (1915): 41–45. "Death and Us." Trans. and intro. Mark Solms. In *Freud and Judaism*, ed. David Meghnagi. London: Karnac, 1993. ["Death"]

"The Overview of the Transference Neuroses." In *A Phylogenetic Fantasy: Overview of the Transference Neuroses*, ed. Ilse Grubrich-Simitis, trans. Axel Hoffer and Peter T. Hoffer. Cambridge, Mass.: Harvard University Press, 1987. ["Overview"]

"Der Fortschritt in der Geistigkeit." *Internationale Zeitschrift für Psychoanalyse und Imago* 24, 1–2 (1939): 6–9. ["Fortschritt"]

Moses and Monotheism. Trans. Katherine Jones. New York: Vintage, 1939.

III. Correspondence

The Letters of Sigmund Freud. Ed. Ernst L. Freud, trans. Tania and James Stern. New York: Basic, 1960. [*Letters of Sigmund Freud*]

A Psycho-Analytic Dialogue: The Letters of Sigmund Freud and Karl Abraham (1907–1926). Ed. Hilda C. Abraham and Ernst L. Freud, trans. Bernard Marsh and Hilda Abraham. London: The Hogarth Press and the Institute of Psycho-Analysis, 1965. [*Letters*]

Sigmund Freud und Karl Abraham. Briefe. Ed. Hilda C. Abraham and Ernst L. Freud. Frankfurt/M: S. Fischer Verlag, 1965. [*Briefe*]

Sigmund Freud and Lou Andreas-Salomé. Letters. Ed. Ernst Pfeiffer, trans. William and Elaine Robson-Scott. New York: Norton, 1985. [*Letters*]

Sigmund Freud and Max Eitingon. Briefwechsel. 1906–1939. Ed. Michael Schröter. 2 vols. Tübingen: edition discord, 2004. [*Briefwechsel*]

The Correspondence of Sigmund Freud and Sándor Ferenczi, 1908–1914. Ed. Eva Brabant, Ernst Falzeder, and Patrizia Giampieri-Deutsch, trans. Peter T. Hoffer. Cambridge, Mass.: Harvard University Press, 1993. [*Correspondence*]

The Origins of Psychoanalysis. Letters to Wilhelm Fliess. Ed. M. Bonaparte, A. Freud, and E. Kris, trans. E. Mosbacher and J. Strachey. New York: Basic, 1954. [*Origins*]

The Complete Letters of Sigmund Freud to Wilhelm Fliess. Ed. and trans. Jeffrey Moussaieff Masson. Cambridge, Mass.: Harvard University Press, 1985. [*Complete*]

Sigmund Freud Briefe an Wilhelm Fließ, 1887–1904. Ed. Jeffrey Moussaieff Masson and Michael Schröter. Frankfurt/M: S. Fischer Verlag, 1986.

The Complete Correspondence of Sigmund Freud and Ernest Jones, 1908–1939, Ed. R. Andrew Paskauskas. Cambridge, Mass.: Belknap/Harvard University Press, 1993. [*Correspondence*]

The Freud/Jung Letters. The Correspondence between Sigmund Freud and C. G. Jung. Ed. W. McGuire, trans. R. Manheim and R. F. C. Hull. Princeton: Princeton University Press, 1974. [*Letters*].

Psychoanalysis and Faith: The Letters of Sigmund Freud and Oskar Pfister. Ed. Heinrich Meng and Ernst L. Freud, trans. Eric Mosbacher. London: The Hogarth Press and the Institute of Psycho-Analysis, 1963. [*Letters*]

The Letters of Sigmund Freud and Arnold Zweig. Ed. Ernst L. Freud, trans. William and Elaine Robson-Scott. New York: Harcourt, Brace and World, 1970. [*Letters*]

Abelove, Henry. "Freud, Male Homosexuality, and the Americans." In *The Lesbian and Gay Studies Reader*, ed. H. Abelove, Michèle Aina Barale, and David M. Halperin, 381–93. New York Routledge, 1993; orig. *Dissent* 33 (Winter 1985–86). ["Freud"]

Abraham, Karl. "Amenhotep IV (Ichnaton): Psychoanalytische Beiträge zum Verständnis seiner Persönlichkeit und des monotheistischen Atonkults." *Imago* 1 (1912): 334–60. ["Amenhotep"]

Abraham, Nicolas, and Maria Torok. *The Wolf Man's Magic Word: A Cryptonomy*. Trans. Nicholas Rand. Minneapolis: University of Minnesota Press, 1986; orig. 1976. [*Wolf*]

Albright, William Foxwell. *From the Stone Age to Christianity. Monotheism and the Historical Process*. Garden City, N.Y.: Doubleday Anchor, 1957; orig. 1940. [*Stone Age*]

Allison, D. B., E. Prado de Oliveira, M. S. Roberts, and A. S. Weiss, eds. *Psychosis and Sexual Identity. Toward a Post-Analytic View of the Schreber Case*. Albany: State University of New York Press, 1988. [*Psychosis*]

Andreas-Salomé, Lou. *The Freud Journal*. Trans. Stanley A. Leavey. New York: Basic, 1964; orig. 1958. [*Freud*]

Andrée, Richard. "Völkergeruch." *Korrespondenzblatt der Anthropologischen Gesellschaft* 5 (1876): 246–47. ["Völkergeruch"]

———. *Zur Volkskunde der Juden*. Bielefeld: Velhagen & Klasing, 1881. [*Volkskunde*]

Anspaugh, Kelly. "Repression or Suppression? Freud's Interpretation of the Dream of Irma's Injection." *Psychoanalytic Review* 82 (1995): 427–42. ["Repression"]

Anzieu, Didier. *Freud's Self-Analysis*. Trans. P. Graham. Madison, Conn.: International Universities Press, 1986; orig. 1975. [*Self-Analysis*]

Appignanesi, Lisa, and John Forrester. *Freud's Women*. New York: Basic, 1992. [*Freud's Women*]

Armstrong, Nancy. "The Occidental Alice." *Differences* 2, 2 (1990): 3–40. ["Occidental"]

Armstrong, Richard H. "Contrapuntal Affiliations: Edward Said and Freud's *Moses.*" *American Imago* 62 (2005): 235–57. ["Contrapuntal"]

Aschheim, Steven E. *Brothers and Strangers: The East European Jew in German and German Jewish Consciousness, 1800–1923.* Madison: University of Wisconsin Press, 1982. [*Brothers and Strangers*]

Assman, Jan. "Der Fortschritt in der Geistigkeit. Sigmund Freuds Konstruktion des Judentums." *Psyche* 56 (2002): 154–71. ["Fortschritt"]

———. "Monotheismus, Gedächtnis und Trauma. Reflexionen zu Freuds Moses-Buch." Chap. 2 of *Religion und kulturelles Gedächtnis.* Munich: C. H. Beck, 2000. ["Monotheismus"]

———. *Moses the Egyptian: The Memory of Egypt in Western Monotheism.* Cambridge, Mass.: Harvard University Press, 1997. [*Moses*]

———. "Sigmund Freud: The Return of the Repressed." Chap. 5 of Assman, *Moses.* ["Return"]

———. "Sigmund Freud und das kulturelle Gedächtnis." *Psyche* 58 (2004): 1–25. ["Sigmund Freud"]

Baeumler, Alfred. *Männerbund und Wissenschaft.* Berlin: Junker & Dünnhaupt, 1934. [*Männerbund*]

Bajohr, Frank. *"Unser Hotel ist judenfrei." Bäder-Antisemitismus im 19. und 20. Jahrhundert.* Frankfurt/M: S. Fischer Verlag, 2003. [*"Unser Hotel"*]

Bakan, David. *Sigmund Freud and the Jewish Mystical Tradition.* Princeton: C. Van Nostrand, 1958. [*Freud*]

Balmary, Marie. *Psychoanalyzing Psychoanalysis: Freud and the Hidden Fault of the Father.* Trans. Ned Lukacher. Baltimore: The Johns Hopkins University Press, 1982; orig. 1979. [*Psychoanalyzing*]

Bamberger, Joan. "The Myth of Matriarchy: Why Men Rule in Primitive Society." In *Women, Culture, and Society,* ed. Michele Zimbalist Rosaldo and Louise Lamphere. Stanford: Stanford University Press, 1974. ["Myth"]

Bar Amitai, *Ueber die Beschneidung in historischer und dogmatischer Hinsicht.* Frankfurt/M: J. S. Hermannische Buchhandlung, 1843. [*Beschneidung*]

Basch, R. von. "Ein Suggestionsexperiment." *Wiener medizinische Presse* 36, 25 (25 June 1893): 1027–29. ["Suggestionsexperiment"]

Baumeyer, Franz. "Der Fall Schreber." *Psyche* 9 (1955): 513–36. ["Fall"]

Benedikt, Moriz. "Ueber Neuralgien und neuralische Affectionen und deren Behandlung." *Klinische Zeit- und Streitfragen* 6, 3 (1892): 67–106. ["Neuralgien"]

Beit-Hallahmi, Benjamin. "Political and Literary Answers to Some 'Jewish Questions': Proust, Joyce, Freud, and Herzl." In *Psychoanalysis, Identity, and Ideology: Critical Essays on the Israel/Palestine Case,* ed. John Bunzl and B. Beit-Hallahmi. Norwell, Mass.: Kluwer Academic Publishers, 2002. ["Political"]

Beller, Steven. *Vienna and the Jews, 1867–1938: A Cultural History.* Cambridge: Cambridge University Press, 1989. [*Vienna*]

Benjamin, Walter. "On Some Motifs in Baudelaire." In *Illuminations*, ed. Hannah Arendt, trans. Harry Zohn. New York: Schocken, 1969. ["Some Motifs"]

Bergman-Carton, Janis. "Negotiating the Categories: Sarah Bernhardt and the Possibilities of Jewishness." *Art Journal* 55, 2 (Summer 1996): 55–64. ["Negotiating"]

Berillon, Edgar. "Psychologie de l'olfaction: La fascination olfactive chez les animaux et chez l'homme." *Revue de l'hypnotisme et de la psychologie physiologique* 23 (1908–9): 98–103, 135–38, 167–69, 196–200, 235–39, 263–67, 303–7. ["Psychologie"]

Berman, Jeffrey. "Review of Gilman, *Freud, Race, and Gender,* and *The Case of Sigmund Freud.*" *Psychoanalytic Review* 82 (1995): 778–83. ["Review"]

Berman, Marshall. *All That Is Solid Melts into Air: The Experience of Modernity.* New York: Simon and Schuster, 1982. [*All*]

Bernheimer, Charles. "'Castration' as Fetish." *Paragraph* 14 (1991): 1–9. ["'Castration'"]

———. "Fetishism and Allegory in *Bouvard et Pécuchet.*" In *Flaubert and Postmodernism*, ed. N. Schor and H. F. Majewski. Lincoln: University of Nebraska Press, 1984. ["Fetishism"]

Bernstein, Richard J. *Freud and the Legacy of Moses.* Cambridge: Cambridge University Press, 1998. [*Freud*]

Beusterien, John L. "Jewish Male Menstruation in Seventeenth-Century Spain." *Bulletin of the History of Medicine* 73 (1999): 447–56. ["Jewish"]

Bhabha, Homi K. *The Location of Culture.* New York: Routledge, 1994. [*Location*]

———. "The Other Question: Difference, Discrimination and the Discourse of Colonialism." In *Literature, Politics, and Theory: Papers from the Essex Conference 1976–84*, ed. F. Barker, P. Hulme, M. Iversen, and D. Loxley, 148–72. London: Methuen, 1986. ["Other Question"]

Bilski, Emily D., and Emily Braun. "The Power of Conversation: Jewish Women and Their Salons." In Bilski, Braun, et al., *Jewish Women and Their Salons: The Power of Conversation*, 1–147. New York: Jewish Museum; and New Haven: Yale University Press, 2005. ["Power"]

Binet, Alfred. "Le Fétichisme dans l'amour." *Revue philosophique de la France et de l'étranger* 24 (1887): 143–67, 252–74. ["Le Fétichisme"]

Birnbaum, Pierre. *Les fous de la République. Histoire politique des juifs d'Etat, de Gambetta à Vichy.* Paris: Fayard, 1992. [*Les fous*]

Bland, Kalman P. *The Artless Jew: Medieval and Modern Affirmations and Denials of the Visual.* Princeton: Princeton University Press, 2000. [*Artless*]

Bloch, Iwan. *Odoratus Sexualis.* New York: Panurge, 1934. [*Odoratus*]

———. *The Sexual Life of Our Time in Its Relations to Modern Civilization.* Trans. M. E. Paul from 6th German ed. London: Rebman, 1909. [*Sexual*]

Blüher, Hans. *Die deutsche Wandervogelbewegung als erotisches Phänomen. Ein Beitrag zur Erkenntnis der sexuellen Inversion.* 3rd ed. Berlin: Verlag Hans Blüher, 1918; orig. 1911–12. [*Wandervogelbewegung* or *Youth Movement*]

———. "Die drei Grundformen der Homosexualität." *Jahrbuch für sexuelle Zwischenstufen* 13 (1913): 139–65, 326–42, 411–44. ["Drei Grundformen" or "Three Basic Forms"]

———. *Die Rolle der Erotik in der männlichen Gesellschaft.* 2 vols. Jena: Eugen Diederichs, 1918. [*Rolle* or *Role of the Erotic*].

———. *Secessio Judaica. Philosophische Grundlegung der historischen Situation des Judentums und der antisemitischen Bewegung.* Berlin: Der weisse Ritter Verlag, 1922. [*Secessio*]

———. *Studien zur Inversion und Perversion.* Schmiden bei Stuttgart: Decker Verlag Nachfolger, 1965. [*Studien*]

———. *Traktat über die Heilkunde, insbesondere die Neurosenlehre.* Jena: Eugen Diederichs, 1926. [*Traktat*]

———. *Wandervogel. Geschichte einer Jugendbewegung.* 3 vols. Prien: Kampmann and Schnabel, 1922; orig. 1912. [*Wandervogel*]

———. "Was ist Antifeminismus." In *Gesammelte Aufsätze.* Jena: Eugen Diederichs, 1919. ["Antifeminismus"]

———. *Werke und Tage.* 1st ed. Jena: Eugen Diederichs, 1920. [*Werke*]

———. *Werke und Tage.* Munich: List, 1953. [*Werke und Tage*]

Blumenberg, Yigal. "'Der Jude ist selbst zur Frage geworden' (E. Jabés) oder: 'die Annahme des Vaters' (S. Freud)." In *Das unmögliche Erbe. Antisemitismus—Judentum—Psychoanalyse,* ed. Wolfgang Hegener, 63–85. Gießen: Psychosozial-Verlag, 2006. ["Jude"]

Boon, James A. "Of Foreskins: (Un)Circumcision, Religious Histories, Difficult Description (Montaigne/Remondino)." Chap. 2 of *Verging on Extra-Vagance: Anthropology, History, Religion, Literature, Arts . . . Showbiz.* Princeton: Princeton University Press, 1999. ["Foreskins"]

Borch-Jacobsen, Mikkel. *Remembering Anna O.: A Century of Mystification.* Trans. Kirby Olson with Xavier Callahan and the author. New York: Routledge, 1996. [*Remembering*]

———, and Sonu Shamdasani. *Le Dossier Freud. Enquête sur l'histoire de la psychanalyse.* Paris: Empêcheurs de Penser en Rond, 2006. [*Dossier*]

Botz, Gerhard. "Die Ausgliederung der Juden aus der Gesellschaft. Das Ende des Wiener Judentums unter der NS-Herrschaft (1938–43)." In Botz, Oxaal, and Pollak, *Zerstörte Kultur*, 285–312. Buchloe: Obermayer, 1990. ["Ausgliederung"]

———, Ivar Oxaal, and Michael Pollak, eds. *Eine zerstörte Kultur. Jüdisches Leben und Antisemitismus seit den 19. Jahrhundert.* Buchloe: Obermayer, 1990. [*Zerstörte Kultur*]

Boyarin, Daniel. "*Épater l'embourgeoisement*: Freud, Gender, and the (De)-Colonized Psyche." *Diacritics* 24, 1 (Spring, 1994): 17–42. [*"Épater"*]

———. "Homophobia and the Postcoloniality of the 'Jewish Science.'" In *Queer Theory and the Jewish Question*, ed. D. Boyarin, Daniel Itzkovitz, and Ann Pellegrini, 166–98. New York: Columbia University Press, 2003. ["Homophobia"]

———. *Unheroic Conduct: The Rise of Heterosexuality and the Invention of the Jewish Man.* Berkeley: University of California Press, 1997. [*Unheroic*]

———. "What Does a Jew Want? or The Political Meaning of the Phallus." In *The Psychoanalysis of Race*, ed. Christopher Lane, 211–40. New York: Columbia University Press, 1998. ["What?"]

Boyarin, Daniel, and Jonathan Boyarin. "Diaspora: Generation and the Ground of Jewish Identity." *Critical Inquiry* 19 (1993): 695–725. ["Diaspora"]

———. *Powers of Diaspora: Two Essays on the Relevance of Jewish Culture.* Minneapolis: University of Minnesota Press, 2002. [*Powers*]

Boyarin, Jonathan. *Thinking in Jewish.* Chicago: University of Chicago Press, 1996. [*Thinking*]

Bradbury, Ray. "The Man in the Rorschach Shirt." In Bradbury, *I Sing the Body Electric*, 181–90. New York: Perennial, 2001; orig. 1969.

Breasted, J. H. *A History of Egypt, from the Earliest Times to the Persian Conquest.* 2nd ed. New York: C. Scribner's Sons, 1912. [*History*]

Brenkman, John. *Straight Male Modern: A Cultural Critique of Psychoanalysis.* New York and London: Routledge, 1993. [*Straight*]

Brickman, Celia. *Aboriginal Populations of the Mind: Race and Primitivity in Psychoanalysis.* New York: Columbia University Press, 2003. [*Aboriginal*]

Brittan, Arthur. *Masculinity and Power.* Oxford: Basil Blackwell, 1989. [*Masculinity*]

Bronner, Stephen Eric. *A Rumor about the Jews: Reflections on Antisemitism and the* Protocols of the Learned Elders of Zion. New York: St. Martin's, 2000. [*Rumor about the Jews*]

Brown, Wendy. *Manhood and Politics: A Feminist Reading in Political Theory.* Totowa, N.J.: Rowman and Littlefield, 1988. [*Manhood*]

Brunotte, Ulrike. *Zwischen Eros und Krieg. Männerbund und Ritual in der Moderne.* Berlin: Verlag Klaus Wagenbach, 2004. [*Zwischen*]

Bruns, Claudia. "Der homosexuelle Staatsfreund. Von der Konstruktion des erotischen Männerbunds bei Hans Blüher." In Nieden, *Homosexualität und Staatsräson.* ["Homosexueller Staatsfreund"]

———. "The Politics of Masculinity in the (Homo-)Sexual Discourse (1880–1920)." *German History* 23 (2005): 306–20. ["Politics"]

———. "Politik des Eros. Der Männerbund als Wissens-, Macht- und Subjektsstrategie vom Kaiserreich zum Nationalsozialismus." Ph.D. diss., Universität-Hamburg, 2004. ["Politik"]

———. "Skandale im Beraterkreis um Kaiser Wilhelm II. Die homoerotische 'Verbündelung' der 'Liebenberger Tafelrunde' als Politkum." In Nieden, *Homosexualität und Staatsräson,* 52–80. ["Skandale"]

Bruns, Claudia, and Kerstin Wolff, eds. *Gegen-Bewegung der Moderne. Verbindungen von Antifeminismus, Antisemitismus und Emanzipation um 1900* (= *Ariadne* 43 [2003]) [*Gegen-Bewegung*]

Brunswick, Ruth Mack. "A Supplement to Freud's 'History of an Infantile Neurosis.'" In *The Wolf-Man by the Wolf-Man*, ed. Muriel Gardiner, 263–307. New York: Basic, 1971; orig. 1928. ["Supplement"]

Bublitz, Hannelore, Andrea Seier, and Christine Henke. *Der Gesellschaftskörper. Zur Neuordnung von Kultur und Geschlecht um 1900.* Frankfurt and New York: Campus Verlag, 2000. [*Gesellschaftskörper*]

Bührmann, Andrea Dorothea. "Die Normalisierung der Geschlechter in Geschlechterdispositiv." In *Das Geschlecht der Moderne. Genealogie und Archäologie der Geschlechterdifferenz*, ed. Hannelore Bublitz. Frankfurt and New York: Campus Verlag, 1998. ["Normalisierung"]

Burckhardt, Jacob. *The Letters of Jacob Burckhardt.* Ed. and trans. A. Dru. New York: Pantheon, 1955. [*Letters*]

Buschan, Georg. "Die beiden Geschlechter innerhalb der einzelnen Rassen." In *Mann und Weib. Ihre Beziehungen zueinander und zum Kulturleben der Gegenwart*, ed. Robby Koßmann and Julius Weiß. 3 vols. Stuttgart, Berlin, and Leipzig: Union Deutsche Verlagsgesellschaft, 1908. ["Die beiden Geschlechter]

Busse, Gerd. *Schreber, Freud, und die Suche nach dem Vater. Über die realitätsschaffende Kraft einer wissenschaftlichen Hypothese.* Frankfurt/M: Peter Lang, 1991. [*Schreber*]

————. "Schreber und Flechsig: der Hirnanatom als Psychiater." *Medizinhistorisches Journal* 24, 3–4 (1989): 260–305. ["Schreber"]

Butler, Judith. *Bodies that Matter: On the Discursive Limits of "Sex."* New York: Routledge, 1993. [*Bodies*]

————. *Gender Trouble: Feminism and the Subversion of Identity.* New York: Routledge, 1990. [*Gender Trouble*]

Caputo, John D. *The Prayers and Tears of Jacques Derrida: Religion without Religion.* Bloomington: Indiana University Press, 1997. [*Prayers*]

Carlebach, Julius. "The Forgotten Connection. Women and Jews in the Conflict between Enlightenment and Romanticism." *Leo Baeck Yearbook* 24 (1979): 107–38. ["Forgotten"]

Carvalho Ribeiro, Paulo de. "Oedipe et castration selon le petit Hans." *Psychanalyse à l'université* 18 (1993): 47–69. ["Oedipe"]

Certeau, Michel de. *L'écriture de l'histoire.* Paris: Éditions Gallimard, 1975. [*L'écriture*]

Chamberlain, Houston Stewart . *Foundations of the Nineteenth Century.* Trans. J. Lees. New York: Howard Fertig, 1968; orig. English. ed., 1910; orig. German ed., 1899. [*Foundations*]

Chavalas, Mark. "Babel and Bible. A Century of Tension." Lecture at Dickinson College, 17 November 2005. Available at www.johnnewtoncenter.org/babel-lecture.doc. ["Babel"]

Cheyette, Bryan. "The Jew Inside." *Times Literary Supplement* 4726 (29 October 1993): 8–9. ["Jew"]

————, and Laura Marcus. "Introduction: Some Methodological Anxieties." In *Modernity, Culture and 'the Jew,'* ed. Cheyette and Marcus. Stanford: Stanford University Press, 1998. ["Introduction"]

Choisy, Maryse. *Sigmund Freud: A New Appraisal.* New York: Philosophical Library, 1963. [*Appraisal*]

Cixous, Hélène. *Portrait of Jacques Derrida as a Young Jewish Saint.* Trans. Beverley Bie Brahic. New York: Columbia University Press, 2004. [*Portrait*]

Classen, Constance, David Howes, and Anthony Synott. *Aroma: The Cultural History of Smell.* New York: Routledge, 1994. [*Aroma*]

Cohen, Shaye. *Why Aren't Jewish Women Circumcised? Gender and Covenant in Judaism.* Berkeley: University of California Press, 2005. [*Why?*]

Connell, R. W. *Gender and Power: Society, the Person, and Sexual Politics.* Stanford: Stanford University Press, 1987. [*Gender and Power*]

————. *Masculinities.* Berkeley: University of California Press, 1995.

Corbin, Alain. *The Foul and the Fragrant: Odor and the French Social Imagination.* Cambridge, Mass.: Harvard University Press, 1986; orig. 1982. [*Foul*]

————. *Women for Hire: Prostitution and Sexuality in France after 1850.* Trans. Alan Sheridan. Cambridge, Mass.: Harvard University Press, 1990. [*Women*]

Cournut-Janin, Monique, and Jean Cournut, "La castration et le féminin dans les deux sexes." In *La castration et le féminin dans les deux sexes,* ed. Paul Denis and Claude Janin, 1353–1558 (= Special Issue of *Revue française de psychanalyse* 57 [1993]). ["La castration"]

Coward, Rosalind. *Patriarchal Precedents: Sexuality and Social Relations.* London: Routledge and Kegan Paul, 1983. [*Patriarchal*]

Crews, Frederick. *The Memory Wars: Freud's Legacy in Dispute.* New York: New York Review of Books, 1995. [*Memory*]

————, ed. *Unauthorized Freud: Doubters Confront a Legend.* New York: Viking, 1998. [*Unauthorized*]

Cuddihy, John Murray. *The Ordeal of Civility: Freud, Marx, Lévi-Strauss and the Jewish Struggle with Modernity.* New York: Basic, 1974. [*Ordeal*]

Daumer, Georg Friedrich. *Der Feuer- und Molochdienst der alten Hebräer als urväterlicher, legaler, orthodoxer Kultus der Nation, historisch-kritisch nachgewiesen.* Braunschweig: F. Otto, 1842. [*Feuer- und Molochdienst*]

David-Menard, Monique, *Hysteria from Freud to Lacan: Body and Language in Psychoanalysis.* Trans. C. Porter. Ithaca: Cornell University Press, 1989; orig. 1983. [*Hysteria*]

Davis, Whitney. *Drawing the Dream of the Wolves: Homosexuality, Interpretation, and Freud's "Wolf Man."* Bloomington: Indiana University Press, 1995. [*Drawing*]

Deleuze, Gilles. "What Is a Dispositif?" In *Two Regimes of Madness: Texts and Interviews 1975–1995,* ed. David Lapujade, trans. Ames Hodges and Mike Taormina, 338–48. New York: Semiotext[e], 2006; orig. 1988–89. ["Dispositif"]

Derrida, Jacques. *Archive Fever: A Freudian Impression.* Trans. Eric Prenowitz. Chicago: University of Chicago Press, 1996. [*Archive*]

————. "Circonfession." In *Jacques Derrida,* Geoffrey Bennington and Jacques Derrida. Paris: Éditions du Seuil, 1991.

————. *The Ear of the Other: Otobiography, Transference, Translation: Texts and Discussions with Jacques Derrida.* Ed. Christie V. McDonald. Trans. Peggy Kamuf. New York: Schocken, 1985. [*Ear*]

————. "Living On: Border Lines." In Harold Bloom et al., *Deconstruction and Criticism.* New York: Seabury, 1979. ["Living On"]

————. *Mal d'Archive: une impression freudienne.* Paris: Éditions Galilée, 1995. [*Mal*]

DiCenso, James J. *The Other Freud: Religion, Culture, and Psychoanalysis.* New York: Routledge, 1999. [*Other Freud*]

Djikstra, Bram. *Idols of Perversity. Fantasies of Feminine Evil in Fin-de-Siècle Culture.* New York: Oxford University Press, 1986. [*Idols*]

Duden, Barbara. *Geschichte unter der Haut. Ein Eisenacher Arzt und seine Patientinnen um 1733.* Stuttgart: Klett-Cotta, 1987. [*Geschichte*]

Efron, John M. *Defenders of the Race: Jewish Doctors and Race Science in Fin-de-Siècle Europe.* New Haven: Yale University Press, 1994. [*Defenders*]

———. *Medicine and the German Jews: A History.* New Haven: Yale University Press, 2001. [*Medicine*]

Eilberg-Schwartz, Howard. *God's Phallus and Other Problems of Men and Monotheism.* Boston: Beacon, 1994. [*Phallus*]

———. "People of the Body: The Problem of the Body for the People of the Book." *Journal of the History of Sexuality* 2 (1991): 1–24. ["People"]

———, ed. *The People of the Body: Jews and Judaism from an Embodied Perspective.* Albany: State University of New York Press, 1992. [*People*]

Eisler, M. J. "Review of Blüher, *Die Rolle der Erotik in der männlichen Gesellschaft.*" *Internationale Zeitschrift für Psychoanalyse* 6 (1920): 180–82. ["Review"]

Eissler, K. R. "A Farewell to Freud's *Interpretation of Dreams.*" *American Imago* 42 (1985): 111–29. ["Farewell"]

———. *Talent and Genius: The Fictitious Case of Tausk contra Freud.* New York: Quadrangle, 1971. [*Talent*]

———. *Viktor Tausk's Suicide.* Madison, Conn.: International Universities Press, 1982. [*Suicide*]

Eliot, George. *Daniel Deronda.* Baltimore: Penguin, 1967; orig. 1876. [*Deronda*]

Ellenberger, Henri F. *The Discovery of the Unconscious: The History and Evolution of Dynamic Psychiatry.* New York: Basic, 1970. [*Discovery*]

Ellis, Havelock. *Sex in Relation to Society.* Vol. 2, part 3, of *Studies in the Psychology of Sex.* New York: Random House, 1936. [*Sex*]

———. *Sexual Selection in Man.* Vol. 4 of *Studies in the Psychology of Sex.* Revised and enlarged ed., Philadelphia: F. A. Davis., 1928. [*Sexual Selection*]

Elms, Alan C. "Freud, Irma, Martha: Sex and Marriage in the 'Dream of Irma's Injection.'" *Psychoanalytic Review* 67 (1980): 63–109. ["Freud, Irma"]

Erb, Rainer. "Die Wahrnehmung der Physiognomie der Juden: Die Nase." In *Das Bild der Juden in der Volks- und Jugendliteratur vom 18.*

Jahrhundert bis 1945, ed. Heinrich Pleticha, 107–26. Würzburg: Königs-
hause & Neumann, 1985. ["Wahrnehmung"]

Erikson, Erik H. "The Dream Specimen of Psychoanalysis." *Journal of the
American Psychoanalytic Association* 2 (1954): 5–56. ["Dream"]

———. "Pseudospeciation in the Nuclear Age." *Political Psychology* 6
(1985): 213–17. ["Pseudospeciation"]

Fabian, Johannes. *Time and the Other: How Anthropology Makes Its Object.*
New York: Columbia University Press, 1983. [*Time*]

Fanon, Frantz. *Black Skins, White Masks.* Trans. Charles Lamm Mark-
mann. New York: Grove Press, 1967. [*Black Skins*]

Feder, Gottfried. "Die Judenfrage." In *Der Jud ist schuld . . . ? Diskussions-
buch über die Judenfrage.* Basel, Berlin, Leipzig, and Vienna: Zinnenver-
lag 1932. ["Judenfrage"]

Federn, Paul. "Review of Blüher, *Secessio Judaica." Imago* 9 (1923): 138–39.
["Review"]

Ferris, Paul. *Dr. Freud: A Life.* London: Sinclair-Stevenson, 1997. [*Dr.
Freud*]

Fichtner, Gerhard, and J. Keith Davies, comps. and eds. *Freud's Library:
A Comprehensive Catalogue/Freuds Bibliothek. Vollständiger Katalog.* London and Tübingen: The Freud Museum/edition diskord, 2006. [*Katalog*]

Fischer, Bernd-Jürgen. *Handbuch zu Thomas Manns "Josephromanen."*
Tübingen and Basel: A. Francke Verlag 2002. [*Handbuch*]

Fischer, Eugen, and Gerhard Kittel, *Das antike Weltjudentum. Tatsachen,
Texte, Bilder.* Hamburg: Hanseatische Verlagsanstalt, 1943. [*Antikes
Weltjudentum*]

Fishberg, Maurice. *The Jews: A Study of Race and Environment.* New York:
Charles Scribner's Sons, 1911. [*Jews*]

Fleming, Lydia. *Freud et ses patients.* Paris: Hachette, 1986. [*Freud*]

Fliess, Wilhelm. *Die Beziehungen zwischen Nase und weiblichen Geschlechtsorganen. In ihrer biologischen Bedeutung dargestellt.* Leipzig and Vienna:
Franz Deuticke, 1897. [*Beziehungen*]

———. *Les relations entre le nez et les organes génitaux féminins. Présentées
selon leurs significations biologiques.* Trans. P. Ach and J. Guir. Paris: Seuil,
1977; orig. 1897. [*Les relations*]

Forrester, John. "A Triumph of Identity Politics." *Medical History* 39, 1
(1995): 97–100. ["Triumph"]

Foucault, Michel. *History of Sexuality. Vol. 1: An Introduction.* Trans. R.
Hurley. New York: Random House, 1978; orig. 1975. [*History*]

———. "Introduction." *Hercules Barbin,* ed. Foucault, trans. R. McDou-
gall. New York: Pantheon, 1980. ["Introduction"]

————. "Le Jeu de Michel Foucault (entretien sur *l'Histoire de la Sexualité*)." In *Dit et écrits 1954–1988. III 1976–1979*, ed. Daniel Defort and François Ewald, 298–329. Paris: Éditions Gallimard, 1994; orig. 1977. ["Le Jeu"]

————. *The Order of Things*. Trans. A. M. S. Smith. New York: Random House, 1973; orig. 1970. [*Order*]

Fraenkel, Josef. "Professor Freud and the Student Society 'Kadimah.'" *The Gates of Zion* 19 (April 1964): 15–17. ["Professor"]

Frankiel, Rita V. "Analysed and Unanalysed Themes in the Treatment of Little Hans." *International Review of Psycho-Analysis* 19 (1992): 323–33. ["Analysed"]

————. "A Note on Freud's Inattention to the Negative Oedipal in Little Hans." *International Review of Psycho-Analysis* 18 (1991): 181–84. ["Note"]

Freeman, Erika. *Insights: Conversations with Theodor Reik*. Englewood Cliffs, N.J.: Prentice-Hall, 1971. [*Insights*]

Freud, Anna. "Beating Fantasies and Daydreams." In *Introduction to Psychoanalysis: Lectures for Child Analysts and Teachers, 1922–1935*, 137–57. Vol. 1 of *The Writings of Anna Freud*. New York: International Universities Press, 1974; orig. 1922.

Freud, Martin. *Sigmund Freud: Man and Father*. New York: Vanguard, 1958. [*Sigmund*]

————. "Who Was Freud?" In *The Jews of Austria: Essays on Their Life, History and Destruction*, ed. Josef Fraenkel. London: Valentine Mitchell, 1967. ["Who?"]

Frevert, Ute. "Bürgerliche Meisterdenker und das Geschlechterverhältnis. Konzepte, Erfahrungen, Visionen an der Wende vom 18. zum 19. Jahrhundert." In Frevert, *Bürgerinnen und Bürger*, 17–48. ["Bürgerliche Meisterdenker"]

————. *Ehrenmänner. Das Duell in der bürgerlichen Gesellschaft*. Munich: C. H. Beck, 1991. [*Ehrenmänner*]

————. "Einleitung." In Frevert, *Bürgerinnen und Bürger*.

————. *Mann und Weib, und Weib und Mann. Geschlechter-Differenzen in der Moderne*. Munich: C. H. Beck, 1995. [*Mann und Weib*]

————, ed. *Bürgerinnen und Bürger. Geschlechterverhältnisse im 19. Jahrhundert*. Göttingen: Vandenhoeck and Ruprecht, 1988. [*Bürgerinnen und Bürger*]

Freytag, Gustav. *Debit and Credit*. New York: Harper and Brothers, 1855. [*Debit*]

————. *Soll und Haben*. Munich: Hauser, 1977; orig. 1855. [*Soll*]

Friedlaender, Benedict. *Die Renaissance des Eros Uranios*. Berlin: Renaissance, 1904. [*Renaissance*]

Friedrichsmeyer, Sara, Sara Lennox, and Susanne Zantop, eds. *The Imperialist Imagination: German Colonialism and Its Legacy*. Ann Arbor: University of Michigan Press, 1998. [*Imperialist*]

Fritsch, Theodor. *Antisemiten-Katechismus. Eine Zusammenstellung des wichtigsten Materiels zum Verständnis der Judenfrage*. Leipzig: Hermann Beyer, 1887. [*Catechism for Antisemites*]

Frosh, Stephen. *Hate and the "Jewish Science": Anti-Semitism, Nazism and Psychoanalysis*. Basingstoke: Palgrave Macmillan, 2005. [*Hate*]

Fuchs, Eduard. *Die Juden in der Karikatur. Ein Beitrag zur Kulturgeschichte*. Munich: Albert Langen, 1921. [*Juden*]

Fuss, Diana. *Identification Papers*. New York: Routledge, 1995. [*Identification*]

Gallagher, Catherine, and Thomas Laqueur, eds. *The Making of the Modern Body*. Berkeley: University of California Press, 1987 (= *Representations* 14 [1986]). [*Making*]

Garrison, Marsha. "A New Look at Little Hans." *Psychoanalytic Review* 65 (1978): 523–32. ["New Look"]

Gates, Henry Louis. "Writing, 'Race' and the Difference It Makes." In *"Race," Writing and Difference*, ed. Gates. Chicago: University of Chicago Press, 1986. ["Writing"]

Gay, Peter. *Freud. A Life for Our Time*. New York: Norton, 1988. [*Freud*]

———. "Freud verstehen: Zu einem Essay von Ilse Grubrich-Simitis." *Psyche* 47 (1993): 973–83. ["Freud verstehen"]

———. *A Godless Jew: Freud, Atheism, and the Making of Psychoanalysis*. New Haven: Yale University Press, 1987. [*Godless*]

Geiger, Abraham. *Das Judenthum und seine Geschichte von dem Anfange des dreizehnten bis zum Ende des sechszehnten Jahrhunderts. In zehn Vorlesungen*. Breslau: Schletter'schen Buchhandlung, 1871. [*Judenthum*]

Geller, Jay. "Blood Sin: Syphilis and the Construction of Jewish Identity." *Fault Line* 1 (1992): 21–48. ["Blood Sin"]

———. "Contact with Persistent Others: The Representation of Woman in Friedrich Schlegel, G. W. F. Hegel, and Karl Gutzkow." Ph.D. diss. Duke University, 1985. ["Contact"]

———. "Fetishism." In *Encyclopedia of Religion*, 2d ed. New York: Macmillan, 2005.

———. "Hegel's Self-Conscious Woman." *Modern Language Quarterly* 53, 2 (1992): 173–99. ["Hegel's"]

————. "It's 'Alimentary': Feuerbach and the Dietetics of Antisemitism." In *Cultures of the Abdomen: Diet, Digestion and Fat in the Modern World*, ed. Christopher E. Forth and Ana Carden-Coyne. London: Palgrave, 2005. ["'Alimentary'"]

————. "*Judenzopf/Chinesenzopf*: Of Jews and Queues." *positions* 2, 3 (1995): 500–37. ["*Judenzopf*"]

————. "Not a *Geist* of a Chance: Laying to Rest an 'unlaid Ghost'?" *Germanic Review* (forthcoming). ["Not a *Geist*"]

————. "Of Mice and Mensa: Antisemitism and the Jewish Genius." *Centennial Review* 38 (1994): 361–85. ["Mice"]

————. "Le péché contre le sang: la syphilis et la construction de l'identité juive." *Revue germanique internationale* 5 (1996): 141–64. ["Le péché"]

————. "Review of Gresser, *Dual Allegiance*." *Journal of Religion* 38 (1996): 510–12. ["Review"]

————. "Some More Additional 'Day Residues': The First Review of *Studien über Hysterie*, Ilona Weiss, and the Dream of Irma's Injection." *Psychoanalysis and History* 2, 1 (2000): 61–75. ["Some More"]

————. "Spinoza's Election of the Jews: The Problem of Jewish Persistence." *Jewish Social Studies* 12 (2005): 39–63. ["Spinoza's Election of the Jews"]

————. "The Unmanning of the Wandering Jew," *American Imago* 49 (1992): 227–62. ["Unmanning"]

Gerhard, Ute. "Andere Ergebnisse." In Frevert, *Bürgerinnen und Bürger*, 211–15. ["Andere"]

Geuter, Ulfried. *Homosexualität in der deutschen Jugendbewegung*. Frankfurt/M: Suhrkamp, 1994. [*Homosexualität*]

Ghillaney, Friedrich Wilhelm. *Der Menschenopfer der alten Hebräer*. Nuremberg: Johann Leonhard Schrag, 1842. [*Menschenopfer*]

Gilman, Sander L. *The Case of Sigmund Freud: Medicine and Identity at the Fin de Siècle*. Baltimore: The Johns Hopkins University Press, 1993. [*Case*]

————. *Difference and Pathology: Stereotypes of Sexuality, Race, and Madness*. Ithaca: Cornell University Press, 1985. [*Difference*]

————. *Freud, Race and Gender*. Princeton: Princeton University Press, 1993. [Freud]

————. *Jewish Self-Hatred: Anti-Semitism and the Hidden Language of the Jews*. Baltimore: The Johns Hopkins University Press, 1986. [*Self-Hatred*]

————. "Jews and Mental Illness: Medical Metaphors, Anti-Semitism, and the Jewish Response." *Journal of the History of the Behavioral Sciences* 20 (1984): 150–59. ["Mental Illness"]

——. *The Jew's Body*. New York: Routledge, 1991. [*Jew's Body*]

——. *Making the Body Beautiful: A Cultural History of Aesthetic Surgery*. Princeton: Princeton University Press, 1999. [*Making*]

——. "Max Nordau, Sigmund Freud, and the Question of Conversion." In *Love + Marriage = Death, and Other Essays on Representing Difference*, 40–64. Stanford: Stanford University Press, 1998. ["Max"]

——. "Salome, Syphilis, Sarah Bernhardt and the 'Modern Jewess'." *German Quarterly* 66 (1993): 195–211. ["Salome"]

——. "Sexology, Psychoanalysis, and Degeneration: From a Theory of Race to a Race to Theory." In *Degeneration: The Dark Side of Progress*, ed. J. E. Chamberlin and Gilman. New York: Columbia University Press, 1985. ["Sexology"]

——. "The Struggle of Psychiatry with Psychoanalysis: Who Won?" *Critical Inquiry* 13 (1987): 293–313. ["Struggle"]

——. "What Looks Crazy. Towards an Iconography of Insanity in Art and Medicine in the Nineteenth Century." In *The Turn of the Century: German Literature and Art 1890–1915*, ed. G. Chapple and H. H. Schulte. Bonn: Bouvier Verlag, 1981. ["What"]

Glenn, Jules. "Circumcision and Anti-Semitism." *Psychoanalytic Quarterly* 29 (1960): 395–99. ["Circumcision"]

——. "Freud's Advice to Hans's Father: The First Supervisory Sessions." In *Freud and His Patients*, ed. Mark Kanzer and Glenn, 121–27. New York: Jason Aronson, 1980. ["Freud's Advice"]

——. "Integrative Summary." In Kanzer and Glenn, *Freud and His Patients*, 128–34. ["Integrative"]

Glick, Leonard B. *Marked in Your Flesh: Circumcision from Ancient Judea to Modern America*. New York: Oxford University Press, 2005. [*Marked*]

Goethe, Johann Wolfgang von. *Goethe's Faust*. Trans. Walter Kaufmann. New York: Anchor, 1961. [*Faust*]

Goldstein, Bluma. *Reinscribing Moses: Heine, Kafka, Freud, and Schoenberg in a European Wilderness*. Cambridge, Mass.: Harvard University Press, 1992. [*Reinscribing*]

Graf, Max. "Reminiscences of Professor Sigmund Freud." *Psychoanalytic Quarterly* 11 (1942): 465–76. ["Reminiscences"]

Grau, Rudolf Friedrich. *Semiten und Indogermanen in ihrer Beziehung zu Religion und Wissenschaft. Eine Apologie des Christentums vom Standpunkte der Völkerpsychologie*. Stuttgart: Liesching, 1867. [*Semiten*]

Graves, Robert. *The Greek Myths*. 2 vols. Harmondsworth: Penguin, 1957. [*Greek Myths*]

Green, André. *Le complexe de castration.* Que sais–je? Paris: Presses Universitaires de France, 1990. [*Le complexe*]

Greenberg, R., and C. Pearlman. "If Freud Only Knew: A Reconsideration of Psychoanalytic Dream Theory." *International Review of Psycho-Analysis* 5 (1978): 71–75. ["If"]

Gresser, Moshe. *Dual Allegiance. Freud as a Modern Jew.* Albany: State University of New York Press, 1994. [*Dual*]

Greve, Reinhard. "Die SS als Männerbund." In Völgler and Welck, *Männerbande,* 1:107–12. ["Die SS"]

Groddeck, Georg. "Le double sexe de l'être humain." *Nouvelle Revue de Psychanalyse* 7 (1973): 195–98; orig. 1931. ["Le double"]

Grosser, Paul E., and Edwin Halperin. *Anti-Semitism: The Causes and Effects of a Prejudice.* Secaucus, N.J.: Citadel Press, 1979. [*Anti-Semitism*]

Grossman, William I. "Some Sources for a Slip in a Translation by Freud." *Journal of the American Psychoanalytic Association* 36 (1988): 729–39. ["Some Sources"]

Grubrich-Simitis, Ilse. *Back to Freud's Texts: Making Silent Documents Speak.* Trans. Philip Slotkin. New Haven: Yale University Press, 1996. [*Back*]

——. *Early Freud and Late Freud: Reading Anew* Studies on Hysteria *and* Moses and Monotheism. Trans. Philip Slotkin. London and New York: Routledge, 1997. [*Early Freud*]

——. *Freuds Moses-Studie als Tagtraum. Ein biographischer Essay.* Frankfurt/M: S. Fischer Verlag, 1994. [*Freuds Moses-Studie*]

Gruman, Harris L. "Freud's 'Forgetting of Foreign Words': The History of the Jews between Parody and Paranoia." *History and Memory* 6 (1994): 125–51. ["Freud's 'Forgetting'"]

Grunwald, Max. *Vienna.* Trans. Solomon Grayzel. Philadelphia: Jewish Publication Society, 1936.

Gubar, Susan. "Eating the Bread of Affliction." In *People of the Book: Thirty Scholars Reflect on Their Jewish Identity,* ed. Jeffrey Rubin-Dworsky and Shelley Fisher Fishkin. Madison: University of Wisconsin Press, 1996. ["Eating"]

Günther, Hans. *Rassenkunde des jüdischen Volkes.* Munich: J. F. Lehmann, 1930. [*Rassenkunde*]

Habermas, Jürgen. *Strukturwandel der Öffentlichkeit. Untersuchungen zu einer Kategorie der bürgerlichen Gesellschaft.* Neuwied: Luchterhand, 1962. [*Strukturwandel*]

Haeckel, Ernst. *Anthropogenie oder Entwickelungsgeschichte des Menschen: Keimes- und Stammes-Geschichte.* Leipzig: Wilhelm Engelmann, 1874. [*Anthropogenie*]

316 Bibliography: Works by Other Authors

Haller, John S., Jr. *Outcasts from Evolution: Scientific Attitudes of Racial Inferiority, 1859–1900.* New York: McGraw-Hill, 1975. [*Outcasts*]

Harrison, Simon. "Cultural Difference as Denied Resemblance: Reconsidering Nationalism and Ethnicity." *Comparative Studies in Society and History* 45 (2003): 343–61. ["Cultural"]

Harrowtiz, Nancy A., and Barbara Hyams, eds. *Jews and Gender: Responses to Otto Weininger.* Philadelphia: Temple University Press, 1995. [*Jews*]

Harsin, Jill. "Syphilis, Wives, and Physicians: Medical Ethics and the Family in Late Nineteenth-Century France." *French Historical Studies* 16, 1 (Spring 1989): 72–95. ["Syphilis"]

Hartman, Frank. "A Reappraisal of the Emma Episode and the Specimen Dream." *Journal of the American Psychoanalytic Association* 31 (1983): 555–86. ["Reappraisal"]

Hartmann, Eduard von. *Das Judentum in Gegenwart und Zukunft.* Leipzig and Berlin: Wilhelm Friedrich, 1885. [*Judentum*]

Hartsock, Nancy. *Money, Sex, and Power: Toward a Feminist Historical Materialism.* New York: Longman, 1983. [*Money*]

Hausen, Karin. "Family and Role-Division: The Polarization of Sexual Stereotypes in the Nineteenth Century—An Aspect of the Dissociation of Work and Life." In *The German Family: Essays on the Social History of the Family in Nineteenth- and Twentieth-Century Germany,* ed. R. J. Evans and W. R. Lee. Totowa, N.J.: Barnes and Noble, 1981. ["Family and Role-Division"]

———. "Die Polarisierung der 'Geschlechtscharaktere.' Eine Spiegelung der Dissoziation von Erwerbs- und Familienleben." In *Sozialgeschichte der Familie in der Neuzeit Europas,* ed. Werner Conze, 363–93. Stuttgart: Klett, 1976. ["Polarisierung"]

Hauser, Otto. *Geschichte des Judentums.* Weimar: Alexander Duncker Verlag, 1921. [*Geschichte*]

———. "Jüdische Rassedivergenzen." In *Juden und Deutsche.* Danzig: "Der Mensch," 1929. ["Jüdische Rassedivergenzen"]

Hechter, Michael. *Internal Colonialism: The Celtic Fringe in British National Development, 1536–1966.* Berkeley: University of California Press, 1975. [*Internal Colonialism*]

Heer, Friederich. *Der Glaube des Adolf Hitlers. Anatomie einer politischen Religiosität.* Munich: Bechtle Verlag, 1968. [*Glaube*]

Hegener, Wolfgang. *Wege aus der vaterlosen Psychoanalyse. Vier Abhandlungen über Freuds Mann Moses.* Tübingen: edition diskord, 2001. [*Wege*]

Heiden, Anne von der. *Der Jude als Medium. 'Jud Süß.'* Zürich and Berlin: diaphanes, 2005. [*Der Jude*]

Heine, Heinrich. *Ludwig Börne. Ein Denkschrift.* In *Beiträge zur deutschen Ideologie.* Frankfurt/M: Ullstein, 1971. [*Börne*]

————. *The Rabbi of Bacharach.* In *Jewish Stories and Hebrew Melodies*, trans. Charles Godfrey Leland with Elizabeth Petuchowski. New York: Markus Wiener, 1987. [*Rabbi*]

Heller, Peter. "A Quarrel over Bisexuality." In *The Turn of the Century: German Literature and Art*, ed. G. Chapple and H. H. Schulte. Bonn: Bouvier, 1981. ["Quarrel"]

Henseler, Heinz. "Einige Gedanken zur Psychodynamik des Antisemitismus." *Sigmund Freud House Bulletin* 10 (1986): 281–87. ["Einige Gedanken"]

Hergemöller, Bernd-Ulrich. *Mann für Mann. Biographisches Lexikon zur Geschichte von Freundesliebe und mannmännlicher Sexualität im deutschen Sprachraum.* Hamburg: MännerschwarmSkript Verlag 1998. [*Mann*]

Herzl, Theodor. "Mauschel." In *Zionist Writings, Vol. 1: January 1896–June 1898*, trans. H. Zohn. New York: Herzl, 1973; orig. *Die Welt*, 15 October 1897.

Herzog, Dagmar. *Intimacy and Exclusion: Religious Politics in Pre-Revolutionary Baden.* Princeton: Princeton University Press, 1996. [*Intimacy*]

Hess, Jonathan. *Germans, Jews and the Claims of Modernity.* New Haven: Yale University Press, 2002. [*Germans, Jews*]

Hess, Moses. *The Revival of Israel: Rome and Jerusalem, the Last Nationalist Question.* Trans. Meyer Waxman. Lincoln: University of Nebraska Press, 1995; orig. 1862. [*Revival*]

Hessing, Siegfried. "Freud's Relation with Spinoza." In *Spinoza Spinozanum, 1677–1977*, ed. Hessing. Boston: Routledge and Kegan Paul, 1977. ["Freud's"]

————, ed. *Spinoza. Dreihundert Jahre Ewigkeit. Spinoza-Festschrift 1632–1932*, 2nd ed. The Hague: Marcellus Nijhoff, 1962; orig. 1933. [*Spinoza-Festschrift*]

Hewitt, Andrew. *Political Inversions: Homosexuality, Fascism, and the Modernist Imaginary.* Stanford: Stanford University Press, 1996. [*Political*]

Hirschfeld, Magnus. *Sexual Pathology: A Study of the Derangements of the Sexual Instinct.* Trans. J. Gibbs. Rev. ed. New York: Emerson Books, 1940. [*Sexual*]

Hirschmüller, Albrecht. *The Life and Work of Josef Breuer: Physiology and Psychoanalysis.* New York: New York University Press, 1989. [*Life*]

————. "Psychoanalyse und Antisemitismus." *Luzifer-Amor* 2 (1988): 41–
54. ["Psychoanalyse"]

Hitler, Adolph. *Mein Kampf.* Trans. R. Manheim. Boston: Houghton
Mifflin, 1943. [*Mein Kampf*]

Hocquenghem, Guy. *Homosexual Desire.* Trans. Daniella Dangoor. London: Allison and Busby, 1978. [*Homosexual*]

Hödl, Klaus. *Die Pathologisierung des jüdischen Körpers. Antisemitismus,
Geschlecht und Medizin im Fin de Siècle.* Vienna: Picus Verlag, 1997.
[*Pathologisierung*]

Hoffman-Krayer, E., and H. Bächtold-Stäubli, eds. *Handwörterbuch des
deutschen Aberglaubens.* 10 vols. Berlin and Leipzig: Walter de Gruyter,
1934–35. [*Handwörterbuch*]

Homer, *The Iliad.* Trans. Michael Reck. New York: HarperCollins, 1994.

Honegger, Claudia. *Die Ordnung der Geschlechter. Die Wissenschaften vom
Menschen und das Weib 1750–1850.* Frankfurt and New York: Campus
Verlag, 1991. [*Ordnung*]

Horkheimer, Max, and Theodor W. Adorno. *Dialectic of Enlightenment.*
Trans. J. Cumming. New York: Seabury, 1972. [*Dialectic*]

Howes, David. "Olfaction and Transition: An Essay on Ritual Uses of
Smell." *Canadian Review of Sociology and Anthropology* 24 (1987): 390–
416. ["Olfaction"]

Hsia, R. Po-chia. *The Myth of Ritual Murder: Jews and Magic in Reformation
Germany.* New Haven: Yale University Press, 1988. [*Myth*]

Hubrich, Peter Heinz. *Gustav Freytags "Deutsche Ideologie" in "Soll und
Haben."* Kronberg, Czech Republic: Scriptor, 1974. [*Gustav*]

Hull, Isabel V. "The Bourgeoisie and Its Discontents: Reflections on
[Mosse's] 'Nationalism and Respectability.'" *Journal of Contemporary
History* 17 (1982): 247–68. ["Bourgeoisie"]

————. "Kaiser Wilhelm and the 'Liebenberg Circle.'" In *Kaiser Wilhelm
II: New Interpretations,* ed. John C. G. Röhl and Nicolaus Sombart.
Cambridge: Cambridge University Press, 1982. ["Kaiser Wilhelm"]

————. *Sexuality, State, and Civil Society in Germany, 1700–1815.* Ithaca:
Cornell University Press, 1996. [*Sexuality*]

Ibsen, Henrik. *An Enemy of the People.* Mineola, N.Y.: Dover, 1999; orig.
1883. [*Enemy*]

Ireland, William W. *Herrschermacht und Geisteskrankheit. Psycho-pathologi-
sche Studien aus der Geschichte alter und neuer Dynastien.* Stuttgart: Lutz,
1887. [*Herrschermacht und Geisteskrankheit*]

Iribarne, J. "Névropathies réflexes d'origine nasale." *Revue de psychothéra-
pie et de psychologie appliqué* 26 (1912): 236–42. ["Névropathies"]

Israëls, Han. *Schreber: Father and Son*. Eng. ed. by the Author. Madison, Conn.: International Universities Press, 1989. [*Father and Son*]

Jacobs, Joseph. "On the Racial Characteristics of Modern Jews." *Journal of the Anthropological Institute* 15 (1886): 23–62. ["Racial"]

Jaeger, Gustav. *Entdeckung der Seele*. Vol. 1. 3rd ed. Leipzig: W. Kohlhammer, 1884. [*Entdeckung, 1*]

———. *Entdeckung der Seele*. Vol. 2. 4th ed. Leipzig: W. Kohlhammer, 1912. [*Entdeckung, 2*]

Jay, Nancy. "Sacrifice as Remedy for Having Been Born of Woman." In *Immaculate and Powerful: The Female in Sacred Image and Social Reality*, ed. C. W. Atkinson, C. H. Buchanan, and M. R. Miles. Boston: Beacon, 1985. ["Sacrifice"]

Jellinek, Adolf. *Studien und Skizzen. Erster Theil. Der jüdische Stamm. Ethnographische Studien*. Vienna: Herzfeld and Bauer, 1869. [*Studien*]

Jewish Encyclopedia. New York: Funk and Wagnalls, 1901–6.

Jones, Ernest. *The Life and Work of Sigmund Freud*. 3 Vols. New York: Basic, 1953–57. [*Life*]

———. "The Psychology of the Jewish Question." In *Essays in Applied Psycho-Analysis*. London: The Hogarth Press, 1951. ["Psychology"]

Jones, James W. *"We of the Third Sex": Literary Representations of Homosexuality in Wilhelmine Germany*. New York: Peter Lang, 1990. [*"We"*]

Jones, Robert Alun. *The Secret of the Totem: Religion and Society from McLennan to Freud*. New York: Columbia University Press, 2005. [*Secret*]

Jonte-Pace, Diane. *Speaking the Unspeakable: Religion, Misogyny, and the Uncanny Mother in Freud's Cultural Texts*. Berkeley: University of California Press, 2001. [*Speaking*]

Judd, Robin. "German Jewish Rituals, Bodies and Citizenship." Ph.D. diss., University of Michigan, 2000. ["German"]

Jüdisches Lexikon. Berlin: Jüdisches Verlag, 1927–30.

Jung, C. G. *The Psychogenesis of Mental Disease*. Vol. 3 of *The Collected Works of C. G. Jung*, ed. H. Read et al., trans. R. F. C. Hull. Princeton: Princeton University Press, 1982; orig. 1960. [*Psychogenesis*]

Kafka, Franz. *Letters to Friends, Family, and Editors*. Ed. Max Brod. Trans. Richard and Clara Winston. New York: Schocken, 1977. [*Letters*]

Kant, Immanuel. *Critique of Pure Reason*. Trans. Norman Kemp Smith. New York: St. Martin's, 1965; orig. 1929.

———. *Religion within the Limits of Reason Alone*. Trans. Theodore M. Greene and Hoyt H. Hudson. New York: Harper, 1960. [*Religion*]

Karsch-Haack, Ferdinand. *Das gleichgeschlechtliche Liebesleben der Naturvölker*. Munich: Verlag E. Reinhardt, 1906. [*Gleichgeschlechtliches Liebesleben*]

———. "Uranismus oder Päderastie und Tribadie bei den Naturvölkern."
  Jahrbuch für sexuelle Zwischenstufen 3 (1901): 72–201. ["Uranismus"]
Katz, D. S. "Shylock's Gender: Jewish Male Menstruation in Early Mod-
  ern England." *Review of English Studies* 50 (1999): 440–62.
  ["Shylock's"]
Katz, Jacob. *From Prejudice to Destruction. Anti-Semitism, 1700–1933.*
  Cambridge, Mass.: Harvard University Press, 1980. [*Prejudice*]
Keilson-Lauritz, Marita. "Tanten, Kerle und Skandale. Die Geburt des
  'modernen Homosexuellen' aus den Flügelkämpfen der Emanzipa-
  tion." In Nieden, *Homosexualität und Staatsräson*, 81–99. ["Tanten"]
Kendrick, Walter. "God Must Be Crazy." *Village Voice Literary Supplement*
  (May 1990). ["God"]
Kirschenblatt-Gimblett, Barbara. "The Corporeal Turn." *Jewish Quarterly
  Review* 95 (2005): 447–61. ["Corporeal"]
Kittel, Gerhard. *Die Judenfrage.* 2nd rev. ed. Stuttgart: W. Kohlhammer,
  1933. [*Judenfrage*]
Klausner, Joseph. "Der jüdische Charakter der Lehre Spinozas." In Hess-
  ing, *Spinoza-Festschrift*. ["Jüdischer Charakter"]
Klein, Dennis B. *The Jewish Origins of the Psychoanalytic Movement.* New
  York: Praeger, 1981. [*Jewish Origins*]
Kleinpaul, Rudolf. *Menschenopfer und Ritualmorde.* Leipzig: Schmidt and
  Günther, 1892. [*Menschenopfer*]
Knecht, Edgar. "Le mythe du Juif errant." *Romantisme* 8, 9, 12, 16 (1974–
  77): 103–16, 84–96, 95–112, 101–15. ["Le mythe"]
Knoll, Joachim, and Julius H. Schoeps, eds. *Typisch deutsch: Die Jugend-
  Bewegung. Beiträge zu einer Phänomenologie.* Opladen: Leske und Bud-
  rich, 1988. [*Typisch*]
Koebner, Thomas, Rolf-Peter Janz, and Frank Trommler, eds. *"Mit uns
  zieht die neue Zeit." Der Mythos Jugend.* Frankfurt/M: Suhrkamp, 1985.
  [*"Mit uns"*]
Koestenbaum, Wayne. "Privileging the Anus: Anna O. and the Collabora-
  tive Origin of Psychoanalysis." *Genders* 3 (1988): 57–81. ["Privileging"]
Kofman, Sarah. *The Enigma of Woman: Woman in Freud's Writings.* Trans.
  Catherine Porter. Ithaca: Cornell University Press, 1985; orig. 1980.
  [*Enigma*]
Kohlbauer-Fritz, Gabriele. "'La belle juive' und die 'schöne Schickse.'"
  In *"Der schejne Jid." Das Bild des "jüdischen Körpers" in Mythos und Ritual,*
  ed. Sander L. Gilman, Robert Jütte, and Kohlbauer-Fritz on behalf of
  the Jüdischen Museums Wien, 109–22. Vienna: Picus Verlag, 1998.
  ["'La belle juive'"]

Kozloff, Max, et al. *New York: Capital of Photography*. New York: Jewish Museum, 2002. [*New York*]

Kraepelin, Emil. *Psychiatrie. Ein Lehrbuch für Studirende und Aertze*. 6th ed. 2 vols. Leipzig: Johann Ambrosius Barth, 1899. [*Psychiatrie*]

Krafft-Ebing, Richard von. *Psychopathia Sexualis. A Medico-Forensic Study*. Trans. H. E. Wedeck. New York: Putnam, 1965. Orig. 1887–. [*Psychopathia*]

Kraus, Karl. "Weib und Kultur." *Die Fackel* 213 (11 December 1906). ["Weib"]

Kreisky, Eva. "Der Stoff aus dem Staaten sind. Zur männerbündischen Fundierung politischer Ordnung." In *Das Geschlechterverhältnis als Gegenstand der Sozialwissenschaften*, ed. Regina Becker-Schmidt and Gudrun-Axeli Knapp. Frankfurt and New York: Campus Verlag, 1995. ["Stoff"]

Kris, Ernst. "Introduction." In *The Origins of Psychoanalysis: Letters to Wilhelm Fliess*, ed. M. Bonaparte, A. Freud, and E. Kris; trans. E. Mosbacher and J. Strachey. New York: Basic, 1954. ["Introduction"]

Kristeva, Julia. *Powers of Horror: An Essay on Abjection*. Trans. L. S. Roudiez. New York: Columbia University Press, 1982. [*Powers*]

Krobb, Florian. *Die schöne Judin. Jüdische Frauengestalten in der deutschsprachigen Erzählliteratur vom 17. Jahrhundert bis zum Ersten Weltkrieg*. Tübingen: Niemeyer, 1993. [*Schöne Judin*]

Kroeber, A. L. "Review of *Totem and Taboo*." *American Anthropology*, n.s., 22 (1920): 48–55. ["Review"]

Krüll, Marianne. *Freud and His Father*. Trans. Arnold J. Pomerans. New York: W. W. Norton, 1986. [*Father*]

———. *Freud und sein Vater: Die Entstehung der Psychoanalyse und Freuds ungelöste Vaterbindung*. Munich: C. H. Beck, 1979. [*Vater*]

Küpper, Heinz. *Illustriertes Lexikon der Deutschen Umgangssprache*. Vol. 6. Stuttgart: Klett, 1984. [*Illustriertes*]

Kuper, Adam, and Alan A. Stone. "The Dream of Irma's Injection: A Structural Analysis." *American Journal of Psychiatry* 139 (1982): 1225–34. ["Dream"]

Kurth, Alexandra. *Männer-Bünde-Rituale. Studentenverbindungen seit 1800*. Frankfurt and New York: Campus Verlag, 2004. [*Männer-Bünde*]

Lacan, Jacques. *The Ego in Freud's Theory and in the Technique of Psychoanalysis, 1954–1955: The Seminar of Jacques Lacan—Book II*. Ed. Jacques-Alain Miller. Trans. Sylvana Tomaselli. Cambridge: Cambridge University Press, 1988. [*Ego*]

Lacquer, Walter. *Young Germany: A History of the German Youth Movement.*
New Brunswick, N.J.: Transaction Books, 1984. [*Young*]

Laforgue, René. *L'influence d'Israël sur la pensée moderne.* Paris: Édition de
la ligue internationale contre l'antisémitisme, 1935. [*L'influence*]

Landes, Joan B. *Women and the Public Sphere in the Age of the French Revolution.* Ithaca: Cornell University Press, 1988. [*Women*]

Lane, Christopher, ed. *The Psychoanalysis of Race.* New York: Columbia
University Press, 1998. [*Psychoanalysis*]

Langbehn, Julius. *Rembrandt als Erzieher.* Leipzig: C. L. Hirschfeld, 1890.
[*Rembrandt*]

Laplanche, Jean. "La castration, ses précurseurs et son destin." *Bulletin de
Psychologie* 27–28, 311, 312, 314 (1973–74): 632–46, 685–709, 145–66.
["La castration"]

———. *Problématiques. 2: Castration, symbolizations.* Paris: Presses Universitaires de France, 1980. [*Problématiques*]

———, and J. B. Pontalis. *The Language of Psycho-Analysis.* Trans. D. Nich-
olson-Smith. New York: W. W. Norton, 1973. [*Language*]

Laqueur, Thomas. *Making Sex: Body and Gender from the Greeks to Freud.*
Cambridge, Mass.: Harvard University Press, 1990. [*Making Sex*]

———. "Orgasm, Generation, and the Politics of Reproductive Biology."
In Gallagher and Laqueuer, *Making.* ["Orgasm"]

Lavater, Johann Caspar. *Essays on Physiognomy: Designed to Promote the
Knowledge and the Love of Mankind.* Trans. H. Hunter. 4 vols. London:
for J. Murray, H. Hunter, and T. Holloway, 1792; orig. 1776. [*Essays*]

Lehman, Alan. "The Impact of Trauma on Freud's Discovery of Psychoanalysis." Ph.D. diss., Union Institute and University, 2002. ["Impact"]

Lehnert, Herbert. "Thomas Manns Vorstudien zur Josephtetralogie."
Jahrbuch der deutschen Schillergesellschaft 7 (1963): 458–520.
["Vorstudien"]

Le Rider, Jacques. *Le Cas Otto Weininger: Racines de l'antiféminisme et l'antisémitisme.* Paris: Presses Universitaires de France,1982. [*Le Cas*]

———. *Freud, de l'Acropole au Sinaï. Le retour à l'antique des modernes vien-
nois,* Paris: Presses Universitaires de France, 2002. [*Freud*]

———. *Modernité viennoise et crises de l'identité.* Paris: Presses Universitaires de France, 1990. [*Modernité*]

Levitt, Laura. "Correcting Men." *Lilith* 31, 1 (Spring 2006): 43–45.
["Correcting"]

Lewinter, Roger. "Groddeck: (Anti)judaîsme et bisexualité." *Nouvelle
Revue de Psychanalyse* 7 (1973): 199–203. ["Groddeck"]

Lichtblau, Albert. "Die Chiffre Sommerfrische als Erinnerungstopos." In *Erinnerung als Gegenwart. Jüdische Gedenkkulturen*, ed. Sabine Hödl and Eleonore Lappin. Berlin: Philo Verlag, 2000. ["Chiffre"]

Lincoln, Bruce. *Theorizing Myth: Narrative, Ideology, and Scholarship*. Chicago: University of Chicago Press, 1999. [*Theorizing*]

Lipowitz, Thanos. *Der "Fortschritt in der Geistigkeit" und der "Tod Gottes."* Würzburg: Königshausen and Neumann, 2005. [*"Fortschritt"*]

Lorenz, E. "Review of Blüher, *Die Rolle der Erotik in der männlichen Gesellschaft*." *Imago* 6 (1920): 92–94. ["Review"]

Lothane, Zvi. *In Defense of Schreber: Soul Murder and Psychiatry*. Hillsdale, N.J.: Analytic Press, 1992. [*Defense*]

Lowe, Donald M. *The History of Bourgeois Perception*. Chicago: University of Chicago Press, 1982. [*History*]

Lowie, Robert. *Primitive Society*. New York: Boni and Liveright, 1920. [*Primitive*]

Lukacher, Ned. "K(Ch)ronosology." *Sub-Stance* 25 (1980): 55–73.

———. "Schreber's Juridical Opera: A Reading of the *Denkwürdigkeiten eines Nervenkranken*." *Structuralist Review* 2, 2 (1981): 3–25. ["Schreber's"]

Lupton, Julia Reinhard. "*Ethnos* and Circumcision in the Pauline Tradition: A Psychoanalytic Exegesis." In Lane, *Psychoanalysis*, 193–210. [*"Ethnos"*]

Macalpine, Ida, and Richard A. Hunter. "Notes." In Schreber, *Memoirs*, 359–67. ["Notes"]

McClintock, Anne. *Imperial Leather*. New York: Routledge, 1995. [*Imperial*]

McGrath, William J. *Freud's Discovery of Psychoanalysis: The Politics of Hysteria*. Ithaca: Cornell University Press, 1986. [*Discovery*]

Maciejewski, Franz. *Psychoanalytisches Archiv und jüdisches Gedächtnis. Freud, Beschneidung und Monotheismus*. Vienna: Passagen, 2002. [*Psychoanalytisches Archiv*]

———. "Zu einer 'dichten Beschreibung' des kleinen Hans. Über das vergessene Trauma der Beschneidung," *Psyche* 57 (2003): 523–50. ["'dichten Beschreibung'"]

Mackenzie, John Noland. "The Pathological Nasal Reflex. An Historical Study." *New York Medical Journal* (20 August 1887): 199–205. ["Pathological"]

———. "Physiological and Pathological Relations between the Nose and the Sexual Apparatus in Man." *Journal of Laryngology, Rhinology, and*

Otology 13 (1898): 109–23. Also appeared in *Johns Hopkins Hospital Bulletin* 82 (January 1898): 10–17. ["Physiological"]

Mahony, Patrick J. *Freud and the Rat Man*. New Haven: Yale University Press, 1986. [*Freud*]

——. "Friendship and Its Discontents." *Contemporary Psychoanalysis* 15 (1979): 55–109. ["Friendship"]

——. "Towards a Formalist Approach to Dreams." *International Review of Psycho-Analysis* 4 (1977): 83–98. ["Towards"]

——. "Le jeu, le travail, et le au-delà." In *L'oreille de l'autre: otobiographies, transferts, traductions, Textes et débats avec Jacques Derrida*, ed. Claude Lévesque and Christie V. McDonald, 83–92. Montreal: VLB éditeur, 1982. ["Le jeu"]

Malchow, H. L. "Review of Gilman, *Freud, Race, and Gender.*" *Journal of Modern History* 67 (December 1994): 898–99. ["Review"]

Malinowski, Bronislaw. *Sex and Repression in Savage Society*. London: Routledge and Kegan Paul, 1927. [*Sex*]

Mann, Thomas. *The Tales of Jacob*. Part 1 of *Joseph and His Brothers*. Trans. H. T. Lowe-Porter. New York: Alfred A. Knopf, 1948; orig. 1933. [*Tales*]

Mannoni, Octave. "Je sais bien, mais quand-même." In *Clefs pour l'imaginaire de l'autre scène*, 9–33. Paris: Éditions du Seuil, 1969. ["Je sais"]

Manuel, Frank E. *The Broken Staff: Judaism through Christian Eyes*. Cambridge, Mass.: Harvard University Press, 1992. [*Broken Staff*]

Marcus, Steven. "Human Nature, Social Orders, and 19th-Century Systems of Explanation: Starting in with George Eliot." *Salmagundi* 28 (1975): 20–42. ["Human Nature"]

Mark, Elizabeth Wyner, ed. *The Covenant of Circumcision: New Perspectives on an Ancient Jewish Rite*. Hanover, N.H.: Brandeis University Press, 2003. [*Covenant*]

Marks, Elaine. "Juifemme." In Rubin-Dworsky and Fisher Fishkind, *People of the Book: Thirty Scholars Reflect on Their Jewish Identity*, 343–53.

Marr, Wilhelm. *Goldene Ratten und rothe Mäuse*. Antisemitische Hefte 2. Chelmnitz: Schmeitzner, 1881. [*Goldene Ratten*]

Marx, Karl. *Capital: Vol. 1*. Introduction by Ernest Mandel. Trans. Ben Fowkes. New York: Vintage, 1977. [*Capital*]

——. "On the Jewish Question." In *Early Writings*. Introduction by Lucio Colletti. Trans. Rodney Livingstone and Gregor Benton. New York: Vintage, 1975. ["Jewish Question"]

Masson, Jeffrey M. *The Assault on Truth: Freud's Suppression of the Seduction Theory*. New York: Penguin, 1985. [*Assault*]

Maugue, Annalise. *L'Identité masculine en crise au tournant du siècle 1871–1914.* Marseilles: Rivages, 1987. [*L'Identité*]

Mauss, Marcel. *Oeuvres. Vol. 3: Cohésion sociale et division de la sociologie.* Paris: Éditions du Minuit, 1969. [*Oeuvres*]

Mautner, Barbara. "Freud's 'Lost' Dream and the Schism with Wilhelm Fliess." *International Journal of Psycho-Analysis* 75 (1994): 321–33. ["Freud's"]

Mayer, Hans. *Outsiders: A Study in Life and Letters.* Trans. Denis. M. Sweet. Cambridge, Mass.: MIT Press, 1982. [*Outsiders*]

Maylan, Charles E. *Freuds tragischer Komplex: Eine Analyse der Psychoanalyse.* Munich: Ernst Reinhardt, 1929. [*Freuds*]

Mehlman, Jeffrey. "The Suture of an Allusion: Lacan with Léon Bloy." *Sub-Stance* 33–34 (1982): 99–110. ["Suture"]

Mendes-Flohr, Paul. *Divided Passions: Jewish Intellectuals and the Experience of Modernity.* Detroit: Wayne State University Press, 1991. [*Divided Passions*]

Mereschkovsky, Dmitri. *Die Geheimnisse des Ostens.* Trans. Alexander Eliasberg. Berlin: Welt-Verlag, 1924. [*Geheimnisse*]

Meyer, Catherine, ed. *Le Livre noir de la psychanalyse: Vivre, penser et aller mieux sans Freud.* Paris: Les Arènes, 2005. [*Livre noir*]

Meyers Konversations-Lexikon. S.v. "Zweikindersystem." 5th ed. Leipzig and Vienna: Bibliographisches Institut, 1893.

Micheler, Stefan. *Selbstbilder und Fremdbilder der "Anderen." Eine Geschichte Männer begehrender Männer in der Weimarer Republik und der NS-Zeit.* Konstanz: UVK Verlagsgesellschaft, 2005. [*Selbstbilder*]

Möbius, Paul Julius. *Über den physiologischen Schwachsinn des Weibes.* Halle: C. Marhold, 1905. [*Schwachsinn*]

Mogge, Winfried. "Von Jugendreich zum Jungenstaat–Männerbündische Vorstellungen und Organisationen in der bürgerlichen Jugendbewegung." In Völgler and Welck, *Männerbande,* 2:103–10. ["Jugendreich"]

Moll, Albert. *Die conträre Sexualempfindung.* Forward by Richard von Krafft-Ebing. 1st ed. Berlin: Fischer's Medicinische Buchhandlung, 1891. [*Die conträre Sexualempfindung*]

———. *Untersuchungen über die Libido sexualis.* Berlin: Fischer's Medicinische Buchhandlung and H. Kornfeld, 1897. [*Untersuchungen*]

Molnar, Michael, ed. and trans. *The Diary of Sigmund Freud 1929–1939: A Record of the Final Decade.* New York: Charles Scribner's Sons, 1992. [*Diary*]

Mosse, George. "Friendship and Nationalism: About the Promise and Failure of German Nationalism." *Journal of Contemporary History* 17 (1982): 351–67. ["Friendship"]

————. *Germans and Jews: The Right, the Left, and the Search for a "Third Force" in Pre-Nazi Germany.* New York: Grosset and Dunlap, 1970. [*Germans*]

————. *The Image of Man: The Creation of Modern Masculinity.* Oxford: Oxford University Press, 1996. [*Image*]

————. "Nationalism and Respectability: Normal and Abnormal Sexuality in the 19th Century." *Journal of Contemporary History* 17 (1982): 221–46. ["Nationalism"]

————. *Nationalism and Sexuality: Respectability and Abnormal Sexuality in Modern Europe.* New York: Fertig, 1985. [*Nationalism*]

Mufti, Aamir R. *Enlightenment in the Colony. The Jewish Question and the Crisis of Postcolonial Culture.* Princeton: Princeton University Press, 2007. [*Enlightenment*]

Nandy, Ashis. *The Intimate Enemy: Loss and Recovery of Self under Colonialism.* Delhi: Oxford University Press, 1983. [*Intimate*]

Neubauer, John. "Sigmund Freud und Hans Blüher in bisher unveröffentlichten Briefen." *Psyche* 50, 2 (1996): 123–48. ["Freud/Blüher"]

Neugebauer, Franz von. "17 Fälle von Koincidenz von Geistesanomalien mit Pseudohermaphroditismus." *Jahrbuch für sexuelle Zwischenstufen* 2 (1900): 224–53. ["17 Fälle"]

Neusner, Jack. *Stranger at Home:"The Holocaust," Zionism, and American Judaism.* Chicago: University of Chicago Press, 1981. [*Stranger*]

Newman, Amy. "The Death of Judaism in German Protestant Thought from Luther to Hegel." *Journal of the American Academy of Religion* 61 (1993): 455–84. ["Death"]

Nicholson, Linda J. *Gender and History: The Limits of Social Theory in the Age of the Family.* New York: Columbia University Press, 1986. [*Gender and History*]

Nieden, Susanne zur, ed. *Homosexualität und Staatsräson. Männlichkeit, Homophobie und Politik in Deutschland.* Frankfurt and New York: Campus Verlag, 2005. [*Homosexualität*]

Niederland, William G. *The Schreber Case.* New York: Quadrangle, 1974. [*Schreber*]

Nietzsche, Friedrich. *The Anti-Christ.* In *Twilight of the Idols/The Anti-Christ,* trans. R. J. Hollingdale. Harmondsworth: Penguin, 1968. [*Anti-Christ*]

————. *Ecce Homo.* In *On the Genealogy of Morals/Ecce Homo,* trans. W. Kaufmann. New York: Random House, 1969. [*Ecce Homo*]

Nordau, Anna, and Maxa Nordau. *Max Nordau: A Biography.* New York: Nordau Committee, 1943. [*Max Nordau*]

Nordau, Max. *Degeneration*. Trans. of 2nd German ed. New York: D. Appleton and Co, 1895. [*Degeneration*]

———. "Muskeljudentum." In *Zionistische Schriften*, 379–81. Cologne and Leipzig: Jüdischer Verlag, 1909; orig. *Jüdische Turnzeitung*, June 1902. ["Muskeljudentum"]

———. "II Kongressrede" (1898). In *Zionistische Schriften*, Cologne and Leipzig: Jüdischer Verlag, 1909. ["II Kongressrede"]

Nordmann, Johannes (pseudonym: H. Naudh). *Die Juden und der deutsche Staat*. Leipzig: H. Beyer, 1883. [*Juden*]

Novick, Peter. *The Holocaust in American Life*. New York: Houghton Mifflin, 1999. [*Holocaust*]

Nunberg, Herman, and Ernst Federn, eds. *Minutes of the Vienna Psychoanalytic Society*. Trans. M. Nunberg with H. Collins. 4 vols. New York: International Universities Press, 1962–75. [*Minutes*]

O'Brien, Mary. *The Politics of Reproduction*. Boston: Routledge and Kegan Paul, 1981. [*Politics*]

Ofrat, Gideon. *The Jewish Derrida*. Trans. Peretz Kidron. Syracuse, N.Y.: Syracuse University Press, 2001. [*Jewish*]

Omran, Susanne. *Frauenbewegung und "Judenfrage." Diskurse um Rasse und Geschlecht nach 1900*. Frankfurt and New York: Campus Verlag, 2000. [*Frauenbewegung*]

Oosterhuis, Harry, and Hubert Kennedy, eds. *Homosexuality and Male Bonding in Pre-Nazi Germany*. Binghamton, N.Y.: Harrington Park Press, 1991. [*Homosexuality*]

Oring, Elliott. *The Jokes of Sigmund Freud: A Study in Humor and Jewish Identity*. Philadelphia: University of Pennsylvania Press, 1984. [*Jokes*]

Ostow, Mortimer. "Sigmund and Jakob Freud and the Philippson Bible (With an Analysis of the Birthday Inscription)." *International Review of Psycho-Analysis* 16 (1989): 483–92. ["Sigmund"]

Ostow, Robin. "Autobiographical Sources of Freud's Social Thought." *Psychiatric Journal of the University of Ottawa* 2 (1978): 169–80. ["Autobiographical"]

Patai, Raphael. *The Messiah Texts*. Detroit: Wayne State University Press, 1979. [*Messiah*]

Pateman, Carole. *The Sexual Contract*. Stanford: Stanford University Press, 1988. [*Sexual Contract*]

Paul, Robert A. "Freud, Sellin and the Death of Moses." *International Journal of Psycho-Analysis* 75 (1994): 825–37. ["Freud"]

———. *Moses and Civilization: The Meaning Behind Freud's Myth*. New Haven: Yale University Press, 1996. [*Moses*]

Pellegrini, Ann. *Performance Anxieties. Staging Psychoanalysis, Staging Race.* New York: Routledge, 1997. [*Performance*]

Philipson, David. *The Reform Movement in Judaism.* New and rev. ed. New York: Macmillan, 1931. [*Reform*]

Pietz, William. "Fetishism and Materialism: The Limits of Theory in Marx." In *Fetishism as Cultural Discourse*, ed. Emily Apter and Pietz. Ithaca: Cornell University Press, 1993. ["Fetishism"]

———. "The Problem of the Fetish I." *RES* 9 (Spring 1985): 5–17. ["Problem I"]

———. "The Problem of the Fetish II." *RES* 13 (Spring 1987): 23–45. ["Problem II"]

———. "The Problem of the Fetish IIIA." *RES* 16 (Autumn 1988): 105–23. ["Problem IIIA"]

Pinsker, Leo. "Auto-Emancipation: An Appeal to His People by a Russian Jew." In Pinsker, *Road to Freedom: Writings and Addresses*, ed. B. Netanyahu, trans. D. S. Blondheim. New York: Scopus, 1944. ["Auto-Emancipation"]

———. *Autoemanzipation. Mahnruf an seine Stammesgenossen von einem russichen Juden.* 2nd ed. Brünn: Verlag der "Kadimah" Wien, 1903. [*Autoemanzipation*]

Planert, Ute. "Der dreifacher Körper des Volkes: Sexualität, Biopolitik und die Wissenschaft vom Leben." *Geschichte und Gesellschaft* 26 (2000): 539–76. ["Dreifache Körper"]

Plaskow, Judith. "Blaming the Jews for the Birth of Patriarchy." *Lilith* 7 (1980): 11–13. ["Blaming"]

Poliakov, Leon. *From the Time of Christ to the Court Jews.* Vol. 1 of *The History of Anti-Semitism.* Trans. R. Howard. New York: Vanguard, 1965. [*From the Time*]

Poovey, Mary. *Uneven Developments. The Ideological Work of Gender in Mid-Victorian England.* Chicago: University of Chicago Press, 1988. [*Uneven Developments*]

Porter, Roy. "Fear and Loathing in Vienna." *New Republic* 210, 8 (21 February 1994): 36–39. ["Fear"]

Postone, Moise. "Anti-Semitism and National Socialism." In *Germans and Jews since the Holocaust*, ed. A. Rabinbach and J. Zipes, 302–14. New York: Holmes and Meier, 1986. ["Anti-Semitism"]

Prado de Oliveira, Eduardo. "Trois études sur Schreber et la citation." *Psychanalyse à l'université* 4 (1979): 245–82. ["Trois"]

Pulzer, Peter. *The Rise of Political Antisemitism in Germany and Austria.* Rev. ed. London: Halban, 1988. [*Rise*]

Puschner, Uwe. *Die völkische Bewegung im wilhelminischen Kaiserreich. Sprache—Rasse—Religion*. Darmstadt: Wissenschaftliche Buchgesellschaft, 2001. [*Die völkische Bewegung*]

Rainey, Reuben M. *Freud as Student of Religion*. Missoula, Mont.: American Academy of Religion, 1975. [*Freud*]

Rank, Otto. "The Essence of Judaism." In Klein, *Jewish Origins*, 170–72; orig. 1905. ["Essence"]

———. "Zum Thema der Zahnreizträume." *Zentralblatt der Psychoanalyse* 1 (1911). ["Zum Thema"]

Rassial, Jean-Jacques, and Adélie Rassial, eds. *La psychanalyse est-elle une histoire juive?* Paris: Éditions du Seuil, 1981. [*La psychanalyse*]

Rathenau, Walter. "Höre Israel." *Die Zukunft* 18 (16 March 1897): 454–62. ["Höre Israel"]

Reik, Theodor. *Der eigene und der fremde Gott. Zur Psychanalyse der religiösen Entwicklung*. Leipzig: Internationaler Psychoanalytischer Verlag, 1923. [*Der eigene*]

———. "Freud and Jewish Wit." *Psychoanalysis* 2 (1954): 12–20. ["Freud"]

Reinach, Solomon. *Cultes, mythes et religions*. 4 vols. Paris: E. Leroux, 1905–13. [*Cultes*]

———. "The Morality of Mithraism." In *Cults, Myths and Religions*, trans. Elizabeth Post. London: David Nutt, 1912. ["Morality"]

———. *Orpheus: A History of Religions*. Trans. Florence Simmonds. Rev. ed. New York: Livewright, 1935. [*Orpheus*]

Reulecke, Jürgen. "Das Jahre 1902 und die Ursprünge der Männerbund-Ideologie in Deutschland." In Völgler and Welck, *Männerbande*, 1:3–7. ["Das Jahre 1902"]

Revue de l'hypnotisme. "Étude médico-sociale sur le nez." *Revue de l'hypnotisme* 4 (1890): 122–24. ["Étude"]

Rice, Emanuel. *Freud and Moses: The Long Journey Home*. Albany: State University of New York Press, 1990. [*Freud and Moses*]

———. "The Jewish Heritage of Sigmund Freud." *Psychoanalytic Review* 81 (1994): 237–58. ["Jewish"]

Rieff, Philip. *Freud: the Mind of a Moralist*. Garden City, N.Y.: Doubleday, 1961. [*Freud*]

———, ed. *The Sexual Enlightenment of Children: The Collected Papers of Sigmund Freud*. New York: Collier, 1963. [*Sexual Enlightenment*]

Riehl, Friedrich Wilhelm. *Die Naturgeschichte des Volkes als Grundlage einer deutschen Socialpolitik*. Vol. 3: *Die Familie*. 5th ed. Stuttgart and Augsburg: Gottischer Verlag, 1858. [*Naturgeschichte*]

Roazen, Paul. *Brother Animal: The Story of Freud and Tausk.* New York: Alfred A. Knopf, 1969. [*Brother*]

———. *Meeting Freud's Family.* Amherst: University of Massachusetts Press, 1993. [*Meeting*]

Robert, Marthe. *D'Oedipe à Moïse. Freud et la conscience juive.* Paris: Calman-Levy, 1974. [*D'Oedipe*]

———. *From Oedipus to Moses. Freud's Jewish Identity.* Trans. Ralph Manheim. Garden City, N.Y.: Anchor, 1976. [*From Oedipus*]

Robertson, Ritchie. "Freud's Testament: *Moses and Monotheism.*" In *Freud in Exile: Psychoanalysis and Its Vicissitudes*, ed. Edward Timms and Naomi Segal, 80–89. New Haven: Yale University Press, 1988. ["Testament"]

Römer, Ruth. *Sprachwissenschaft und Rassenideologie in Deutschland.* Munich: Fink, 1985. [*Sprachwissenschaft*]

Roith, Estelle. *The Riddle of Freud: Jewish Influences on His Theory of Female Sexuality.* London: Tavistock, 1987. [*Riddle*]

Rosenberg, Alfred. *Der Mythus des 20. Jahrhunderts.* Munich: Hoheneichen-Verlag, 1930. [*Mythus*]

Rosolato, Guy. "Le Fétichisme dont se dérobe l'objet." *Nouvelle Revue de Psychanalyse* 2 (Fall 1970): 31–39. ["Le Fétichisme"]

Roustang, François. *Dire Mastery: Discipleship from Freud to Lacan.* Trans. Ned Lukacher. Baltimore: The Johns Hopkins University Press, 1982; orig. 1976. [*Dire*]

Rozenblit, Marsha L. "Jewish Assimilation in Habsburg Vienna." In *Assimilation and Community: The Jews in Nineteenth-Century Europe*, ed. Jonathan Frankel and Steven J. Zipperstein. Cambridge: Cambridge University Press, 1992. ["Jewish"]

———. *The Jews of Vienna, 1867–1914: Assimilation and Identity.* Albany: State University of New York Press, 1983. [*Jews*]

Rubenstein, Richard. "Religion and the Origins of the Death Camps: A Psychoanalytic Interpretation." In *After Auschwitz: Radical Theology and Contemporary Judaism.* Indianapolis: Bobbs-Merrill, 1966. ["Religion"]

Rubin, Gayle. "The Traffic in Women: Notes on the 'Political Economy' of Sex." In *Toward an Anthropology of Women*, ed. Rayna R. Reiter, 157–210. New York: Monthly Review Press, 1975. ["Traffic"]

Rudnytsky, Peter L. "'Does the Professor Talk to God?' Countertransference and Jewish Identity in the Case of Little Hans." *Psychoanalysis and History* 1, 2 (1999): 175–94. ["'Does'"]

———. "'Mother, have you got a wiwimaker, too?' Freud's Representation of Female Sexuality in the Case of Little Hans." In *One Hundred Years of Psychoanalysis: Contributions to the History of Psychoanalysis*, ed.

André Haynal and Ernest Falzeder, 121–33. London: Karnac, 1994 (a special issue of *Cahiers Psychiatriques Genevois*). [" 'Mother' "]

Sadger, Isidore. *Sigmund Freud, Persönliche Erinnerungen.* Vienna: Ernst Wengraf, 1930. [*Freud*]

Said, Edward W. *Freud and the Non-European.* London: Verso, 2003. [*Freud*]

Santner, Eric L. "Freud's *Moses* and the Ethics of Nomotropic Desire." *October* 88 (Spring, 1999): 3–41. ["Ethics"]

————. *My Own Private Germany: Daniel Paul Schreber's Secret History of Modernity.* Princeton: Princeton University Press, 1996. [*My Own*]

————. *Stranded Objects: Mourning, Memory, and Film in Postwar Germany.* Ithaca: Cornell University Press, 1990. [*Stranded*]

Schäfer, Julia. *Vermessen-gezeichnet-verlacht. Judenbilder in populären Zeitschriften 1918–1933.* Frankfurt and New York: Campus Verlag, 2005. [*Vermessen*]

Schäfer, Peter. "The Triumph of Pure Spirituality: Sigmund Freud's *Moses and Monotheism.*" *Jewish Studies Quarterly* 9 (2003): 381–406. ["Triumph"]

Schatzman, Morton. *Soul Murder: Persecution in the Family.* New York: Random House, 1973. [*Soul*]

Schiebinger, Londa. *Nature's Body: Gender in the Making of Modern Science.* Boston: Beacon, 1993. [*Nature's Body*]

Schmidt, Georg. "Nein, nein! Das ist nicht unser Wandervogel." *Wandervogelführerzeitung* 1 (1913): 47–48. ["Nein"]

Schmiersahl, Katrin. *Medizin und Geschlecht. Zur Konstruktion der Kategorie Geschlecht im medizinischen Diskurs des 19. Jahrhunderts.* Opladen: Leske and Budrich, 1998. [*Medizin*]

Schnitzler, Arthur. *My Youth in Vienna.* Trans. Catherine Hunter. New York: Holt, Rinehart, and Winston, 1970. [*My Youth*]

————. *The Road into the Open.* Trans. Roger Byers. Berkeley: University of California Press, 1992; orig. 1908. [*Road*]

Schnitzler, Heinrich. "Briefe Sigmund Freud an Arthur Schnitzler." *Neue Rundschau* 66 (1955): 95–106. ["Briefe"]

Schnurbein, Stephanie v. "Geheime kultische Männerbünde bei den Germanen—Eine Theorie im Spannungsfeld zwischen Wissenschaft und Ideologie." In Völgler and Welck, *Männerbande*, 2:97–102. ["Geheime"]

Schopenhauer, Artur. *Die beiden Grundprobleme der Ethik. Über das Fündament der Moral.* Vol. 4 of *Sämtliche Werke.* Ed. Arthur Hübscher. Wiesbaden: Brockhaus, 1972. [*Grundprobleme*]

————. *Parerga and Paralipomena.* Trans. E. F. J. Payne. 2 vols. Oxford: Clarendon, 1974. [*Parerga*]

————. *World as Will and Representation.* Trans. E. F. J. Payne. 2 vols. Clinton, Mass.: Falcon's Wing, 1958. [*World*]

Schorske, Carl. "Politics and Patricide in Freud's *Interpretation of Dreams.*" *American Historical Review* 78 (1973): 328–47. ["Politics"]

————. "To the Egyptian Dig: Freud's Psycho-Archaeology of Cultures." In *Thinking with History. Explorations in the Passage to Modernism.* Princeton: Princeton University Press, 1998. ["Egyptian Dig"]

Schreber, Daniel Paul. *Denkwürdigkeiten eines Nervenkranken.* Leipzig: Oswald Mutze, 1903. [*Denkwürdigkeiten*—S]

————. *Denkwürdigkeiten eines Nervenkranken.* Ed. Samuel M. Weber. Frankfurt/M: Ullstein, 1973. [*Denkwürdigkeiten*—W]

————. *Memoirs of My Mental Illness.* Trans. and ed. Ida Macalpine and Richard A. Hunter. Cambridge, Mass.: Harvard University Press, 1988; orig. Eng. ed., 1955. [*Memoirs*—MH]

Schur, Max. *Freud: Living and Dying.* New York: International Universities Press, 1972. [*Freud*]

————. "Some Additional 'Day Residues' of 'The Specimen Dream of Psychoanalysis.'" In *Psychoanalysis: A General Psychology—Essays in Honor of Heinz Hartmann,* ed. R. M. Loewenstein, L. M. Newman, Schur, and A. J. Solnit, 45–85. New York: International Universities Press, 1966. ["Some"]

Schurtz, Heinrich. *Urgeschichte der Kultur.* Leipzig and Wien: Bibliographisches Institut, 1900. [*Urgeschichte*]

————. *Altersklassen und Männerbünde. Eine Darstellung der Grundformen der Gesellschaft.* Berlin: Verlag Georg Reimer, 1902. [*Altersklassen*]

Schwaner, Wilhelm, ed. *Germanenbibel. Aus heiligen Schriften germanischer Völker.* 5th ed. Schlachtensee: Volkserzieher Verlag, 1920. [*Germanenbibel*]

Schweizer, Thomas. "Männerbünde und ihr kultureller Kontext im weltweiten interkulturellen Vergleich." In Völger and Welck, *Männerbande,* 2:23–30. ["Männerbünde"]

Sedgwick, Eve Kosofsky. *Between Men: English Literature and Male Homosocial Desire.* New York: Columbia University Press, 1985. [*Between Men*]

See, Klaus von. "Politische Männerbund-Ideologie von der wilhelminischen Zeit bis zum Nationalsozialismus." In Völger and Welck, *Männerbande,* 1:93–102. ["Politische"]

Seidman, Naomi. "Carnal Knowledge: Sex and the Body in Jewish Studies." *Jewish Social Studies* 1 (1994): 115–46. ["Carnal"]

Sellin, Ernst. *Mose und seine Bedeutung für die israelitisch-jüdische Religionsgeschichte*. Leipzig: A. Deichertsche Verlagsbuchhandlung, 1922. [*Mose*]

Sengoopta, Chandak. *Otto Weininger: Sex, Science, and Self in Imperial Vienna*. Chicago: University of Chicago Press, 2000. [*Otto*]

Shapiro, Susan. "*Écriture judaïque*: Where Are the Jews in Western Discourse." In *Displacements: Cultural Identities in Question*, ed. Angelika Bammer. Bloomington: Indiana University Press, 1994. [*"Ecriture"*]

Shell, Marc. "The Holy Foreskin; or, Money, Relics, and Judeo-Christianity." In *Jews and Other Differences: The New Jewish Cultural Studies*, ed. Jonathan Boyarin and Daniel Boyarin, 345–59. Minneapolis: University of Minnesota Press, 1997. ["Holy"]

Shengold, Leonard. "A Parapraxis of Freud's in Relation to Karl Abraham." *American Imago* 29, 2 (1972): 123–59. ["Parapraxis"]

Showalter, Dennis E. *Little Man, What Now?* Der Stürmer *in the Weimar Republic*. Hamden, Conn.: Archon, 1983. [*Little Man*]

Silverman, Eric Kline. *From Abraham to America: A History of Circumcision*. Lanham, MD: Rowman and Littlefield, 2006. [*Abraham*]

Silverman, Kaja. *Male Subjectivity at the Margins*. New York: Routledge, 1992. [*Male*]

Silverman, Martin. "A Fresh Look at the Case of Little Hans." In *Freud and His Patients*, ed. Mark Kanzer and Jules Glenn, 95–120. New York: Jason Aronson, 1980. ["Fresh"]

Simmel Georg. "Female Culture." In *Simmel on Culture: Selected Writings*, ed. David Frisby and Mike Featherstone, 46–54. London: Sage, 1997; orig. 1911. ["Female Culture."]

Simon, Ernst. "Sigmund Freud, the Jew." *Leo Baeck Institute Yearbook* 2 (1957): 270–305. ["Freud"]

Sinha, Mrinalini. *Colonial Masculinity: The "Manly Englishman" and the "Effeminate Bengali" in the Late Nineteenth Century*. Manchester: Manchester University Press, 1995. [*Colonial*]

Slavet, Eliza. "Circumcised Supremacy: Freud's Final Cut." Presented as part of the Joy Ungerleider Lecture: "Freud's Foreskin, A Sesquicentennial Celebration of the Most Suggestive Circumcision in History." Dorot Jewish Division, New York Public Library, 10 May 2006. ["Circumcised Supremacy"]

———. "The 'Special Case' of Jewish Tradition: Immaterial Materiality." Chap. 5 (draft) of "Freud's *Moses*: Memory Material and Immaterial."

Ph.D. diss., University of California, San Diego, 2006. ["'Special Case'"]

Slezkine, Yuri. *The Jewish Century.* Princeton: Princeton University Press, 2004. [*Jewish*]

Smith, Helmut. *The Butcher's Tale: Murder and Anti-Semitism in a German Town.* New York: W. W. Norton, 2002. [*Butcher's*]

Sombart, Nicolaus. *Die deutschen Männer und ihre Feinde. Carl Schmitt, ein deutsches Schicksal zwischen Männerbund und Matriarchatsmythos.* Munich: Carl Hanser Verlag, 1991. [*Deutsche Männer*]

Soussloff, Catherine M. *Jewish Identity in Modern Art History.* Berkeley: University of California Press, 1999. [*Jewish*]

Spinoza, Baruch. *Theologisch-politischer Traktat.* Ed. and trans. Carl Gebhardt. 4th ed. Leipzig: F. Meiner. 1922. [*Traktat*]

———. *Traité des autorités théologiques et politiques.* In *Oeuvres completes,* ed. and trans. Roland Caillois, Madeleine Francès, and Robert Misrahi. Paris: Gallimard, 1967. [*Traité*]

———. *Tractatus Theologico-Politicus.* In *The Political Works,* trans. A. G. Wernham. Oxford: Oxford University Press, 1958. [*Tractatus*]

Spörk, Ingrid. "L'image du juif dans les écrits de Max Nordau." In *Max Nordau (1849–1923). Critique de la dégénérescence, médiateur franco-allemand, père fondateur du sionisme,* ed. Delphine Bechtel, Dominique Bourel, and Jacques Le Rider, 259–69. Paris: Les Éditions du Cerf, 1996. ["L'image"]

Spöttel, Michael. *Hamiten. Völkerkunde und Antisemitismus.* Frankfurt/M: Peter Lang, 1996. [*Hamiten*]

Sprengnether, Madelon. "Mouth to Mouth: Freud, Irma, and the Dream of Psychoanalysis." *American Imago* 60, 3 (2003): 259–84. ["Mouth"]

———. *The Spectral Mother: Freud, Feminism, and Psychoanalysis.* Ithaca: Cornell University Press, 1990. [*Spectral*]

Stallybrass, Peter, and Allon White. *The Politics and Poetics of Transgression.* Ithaca: Cornell University Press, 1986. [*Politics*]

Stauff, Philipp, ed. *Semi-Kürschner oder Literarisches Lexicon der Schrift steller, Dichter, Bankiers, . . . usw., jüdischer Rasse und Versippung, die von 1813–1913 in Deutschland tätig oder bekannt war. . . .* 2 vols. Berlin: Stauff, 1913. [*Semi-Kürschner*]

Steakley, James D. "Iconography of a Scandal: Political Cartoons and the Eulenburg Affair." *Studies in Visual Communication* 9, 2 (1983): 20–51. ["Iconography"]

Steinberg, Leo. *The Sexuality of Christ in Renaissance Art and in Modern Oblivion.* 2nd ed., revised and expanded. Chicago: University of Chicago Press, 1996. [*Sexuality of Christ*]

Stekel, Wilhelm. *Sexual Aberrations. The Phenomenon of Fetishism in Relation to Sex.* Trans. S. Parker. London: John Lane, the Bodley Head, 1930; orig. 1923. [*Sexual Aberrations*]

Stern, David. "The Ego and the Yid." *New Republic* (21 September 1992): 43–49. ["Ego"]

Stern, Menahem, ed. *Greek and Latin Authors on Jews and Judaism.* 3 vols. Jerusalem: Israel Academy of Sciences and Humanities, 1980. [*Greek*]

Steuer, Daniel. "A Book That Won't Go Away: Otto Weininger's *Sex and Character.*" In Weininger, *Sex*, xi–xlvi. ["Book"]

Stoddart, D. Michael. *The Scented Ape: The Biology and Culture of Human Odour.* Cambridge: Cambridge University Press, 1990. [*Scented*]

Stoecker, Adolf. "Unsre Forderungen an das moderne Judentum." In *Christlich-Sozial. Reden und Aufsätze*, 143–54. Bielefeld and Leipzig: Velhagen & Klasing, 1885. ["Unsre Forderungen"]

Stoler, Ann Laura. *Race and the Education of Desire: Foucault's History of Sexuality and the Colonial Order of Things.* Durham, N.C.: Duke University Press, 1995. [*Race*]

Stourzh, Gerald. "The Age of Emancipation and Assimilation—Liberalism and Its Heritage." In *Österreich-Konzeptionen und jüdisches Selbstverständnis. Identitäts-Transfigurationen im 19. und 20. Jahrhundert*, ed. Hanni Mittelmann and Armin A. Wallas. Tübingen: Niemeyer, 2001. ["Age"]

Stratton, Jon. *Coming Out Jewish: Constructing Ambivalent Identities.* London and New York: Routledge, 2000. [*Coming Out*]

———. *The Virgin Text: Fiction, Sexuality, and Ideology.* Norman: University of Oklahoma Press, 1987. [*Virgin*]

Strauss, Herbert A., and Werner Röder, eds. *International Biographical Dictionary of Central European Emigrés 1933–1945.* Volume II/Part 1: *A–K: The Arts, Sciences, and Literature.* Munich, New York, London, and Paris: K. G. Saur, 1983. [*International*]

Strauss, Leo. "Das Testament Spinozas." *Bayerische Israelitische Gemeindezeitung* 8, 21 (1 November 1932): 322–26. ["Testament"]

Sulloway, Frank. *Freud, Biologist of the Mind: Beyond the Psychoanalytic Legend.* New York: Basic, 1979. [*Freud*]

Swales, Peter. "Freud, His Teacher and the Birth of Psychoanalysis." In *Freud: Appraisals and Reappraisals*, ed. P. E. Stepansky. Hillsdale, N.J.: Analytic Press, 1986. ["Freud"]

Swan, Jim. "Mater and Nannie: Freud's Two Mothers and the Discovery of the Oedipus Complex." *American Imago* 31 (1974): 1–64. ["Mater"]

Taussig, Michael T. *Mimesis and Alterity: A Particular History of the Senses.* New York: Routledge, 1993. [*Mimesis*]

Taylor, Gary. *Castration. An Abbreviated History of Western Manhood.* New York: Routledge, 2000. [*Castration*]

Thalmann, Rita. *Être femme sous le IIIe Reich.* Paris: Éditions Robert Laffont, 1982. [*Être femme*]

Theilhaber, Felix A. *Der Untergang der deutschen Juden. Eine volkswirtschaftliche Studie.* Munich: Ernst Reinhardt, 1911. [*Untergang*]

Theweleit, Klaus. *Männerphantasien.* 2 vols. Frankfurt/M: Verlag Roter Stern, 1977–78. [*Männerphantasien*]

Toews, John E. "Fashioning the Self in the Story of the 'Other.' The Transformation of Freud's Masculine Identity between 'Elisabeth von R.' and 'Dora.'" In *Proof and Persuasion: Essays on Authority, Objectivity, and Evidence,* ed. Suzanne L. Marchand, Elizabeth Lunbeck, and Josine Blok, 196–218. Amsterdam: Brepols, 1996. ["Fashioning"]

———. "Refashioning the Masculine Subject in Early Modernism: Narratives of Self-Dissolution and Self-Construction in Psychoanalysis and Literature, 1900–1914." *Modernism/Modernity* 4 (1997): 31–67. ["Refashioning"]

Trachtenberg, Joshua. *The Devil and the Jews: The Medieval Conception of the Jew and Its Relation to Modern Antisemitism.* New Haven: Yale University Press, 1943. [*Devil*]

Tridon, Gustav. *Du molochisme juif. Études critiques et philosophiques.* Brussels: Edouard Maheu, 1884. [*Molochisme*]

Turner, Bryan S. *The Body and Society. Explorations in Social Theory.* Oxford: Basil Blackwell, 1984. [*Body*]

Van Herik, Judith. *Freud on Femininity and Faith.* Berkeley: University of California Press, 1982. [*Freud*]

Van Velzen, H. U. E. T. "Irma at the Window: The Fourth Script of Freud's Specimen Dream." *American Imago* 41 (1984): 245–93. ["Irma"]

Verdery, Katherine. "Internal Colonialism in Austria-Hungary." *Ethnic and Racial Studies* 2, 3 (1979): 378–99. ["Internal Colonialism]

Verhaeghe, Paul. "The Riddle of Castration Anxiety: Lacan beyond Freud." *The Letter: Lacanian Perspectives on Psychoanalysis* 6 (Spring 1996): 44–54. ["Riddle"]

Verein zur Abwehr des Antisemitismus. *Antisemiten-Spiegel. Die Antisemiten im Lichte des Christentums, des Rechtes und der Wissenschaft.* 2nd ed. Danzig: A. W. Kafemann, 1900. [*Antisemiten-Spiegel*]

Völgler, Gisela, and Karin v. Welck, eds. *Männerbande, Männerbünde. Zur Rolle des Mannes im Kulturvergleich.* 2 vols. Köln: Rautenstrauch-Joest-Museum, 1990. [*Männerbande*]

Vogt, Carl. *Lectures on Man: His Place in Creation and in the History of the Earth.* London: Longman, Green, 1864. [*Lectures*]

Volkan, Vamik D. "The Need to Have Enemies and Allies: A Developmental Approach." *Political Psychology* 6 (1985): 219–47. ["Need"]

Volkov, Shulamit. "Antisemitism as a Cultural Code: Reflections on the History and Historiography of Antisemitism in Imperial Germany." *Leo Baeck Yearbook* 23 (1978): 25–46. ["Antisemitism"]

W. "Studien über Hysterie." *Wiener medizinische Presse* 36, 28 (14 July 1895): 1093–96. ["Studien"]

Wallace, Edwin R., IV. *Freud and Anthropology: A History and a Reappraisal.* Psychological Issues no. 55. New York: International Universities Press, 1983. [*Anthropology*]

Walter, Jacques. *La Shoah à l'epreuve de l'image.* Paris: Presses Universitaires de France, 2005. [*La Shoah*]

Wasserman, Jacob. *My Life as a German and a Jew.* Trans. S. N. Brainin. New York: Coward-McCann, 1933. [*Life*]

Weber, Samuel. "Doing Away with Freud's *Man Moses*." In *Targets of Opportunity. On the Militarization of Thinking.* New York: Fordham University Press, 2005. ["Doing Away"]

Weeks, Jeffrey. *Sex, Politics, and Society: The Regulation of Sexuality since 1800.* White Plains, N.Y.: Longman, 1981. [*Sex*]

Wege zum Menschen. "Der Mann Moses." *Zur Religionskritik von Sigmund Freud.* Special issue of *Wege zum Menschen* 51, 4 (1999). [*Wege zum Menschen*]

Weiner, Marc A. "Wagner's Nose and the Ideology of Perception." *Monatshefte* 81 (1989): 62–78. ["Wagner's Nose"]

Weininger, Otto. *Sex and Character: An Investigation of Fundamental Principles.* Ed. Daniel Steuer with Laura Marcus. Trans. Ladislaus Löb. Bloomington: Indiana University Press, 2005. [*Sex*]

Weinreich, Heinrich. *Duftstoff-Theorie. Gustav Jaeger (1832–1917): Vom Biologen zum "Seelenriecher."* Stuttgart: Wissenschaftliche Verlagsgesellschaft, 1993. [*Duftstoff*]

Weiss, Heinrich. "Discussion über den Vortrag S. Freud's: Ueber Hysterie." *Wiener medizinische Presse* 38, 46 (17 November 1895): 1757–58. ["Discussion"]

Widdig, Bernd. *Männerbünde und Massen. Zur Krise männlicher Identität in der Literatur der Moderne.* Opladen: Westdeutscher Verlag, 1992. [*Männerbünde*]

Wilcocks, Robert. *Maelzel's Chess Player: Sigmund Freud and the Rhetoric of Deceit*. Lanham, Md.: Rowman and Littlefield, 1994. [*Maelzel's*]

Wilker, Karl. "Freieschulgemeinde und Wandervogel." *Wandervogelführerzeitung* 1 (1913): 48–50. ["Freieschulgemeinde"]

Williams, Patrick, and Laura Chrisman, eds. *Colonial Discourse and Post-Colonial Theory: A Reader*. New York: Columbia University Press, 1994. [*Colonial Discourse*]

Williams, Raymond. *Marxism and Literature*. Oxford: Oxford University Press, 1977. [*Marxism*]

Windscheid, Dr. "Review of *Handbuch der Neurasthenie*." *Wiener medizinische Presse* 36, 38 (17 September 1893): 1495–96. ["Review of *Handbuch*"]

———. "Review of *Die Hysterie nach der Lehre der Salpêtrière*." *Wiener medizinische Presse* 36, 50 (10 December 1893): 1974. ["Review of *Die Hysterie*"]

Winter, Pierre. "Sur 'Moïse et le Monothéisme.' Psychanalyse de l'antisémitisme." In Rassial and Rassial, *La psychanalyse*. ["Sur 'Moïse'"]

Winter, Sarah. *Freud and the Institution of Psychoanalytic Knowledge*. Stanford: Stanford University Press, 1999. [*Freud*]

Wistrich, Robert S. *The Jews of Vienna in the Age of Franz Joseph*. The Littman Library of Jewish Civilization. Oxford: Oxford University Press, 1990. [*Jews*]

———. "The Last Testament of Sigmund Freud." In *Laboratory for World Destruction. Germans and Jews in Central Europe*, 258–81. Lincoln and London: University of Nebraska Press for the Vidal Sassoon International Center for the Study of Antisemitism, 2007. ["Last Testament"]

Wittels, Fritz. *Sigmund Freud: Der Mann, die Lehre, die Schule*. Leipzig: Tal, 1924. [*Freud*]

Wortis, Joseph. *Fragments of an Analysis with Freud*. New York: Simon and Schuster, 1954. [*Fragments*]

Yerushalmi, Yosef Hayim. "Freud on the 'Historical Novel': From the Manuscript Draft (1934) of *Moses and Monotheism*." *International Journal of Psycho-Analysis* 70 (1989): 374–95. ["Freud"]

———. *Freud's Moses: Judaism Terminable and Interminable*. New Haven: Yale University Press, 1991. [*Freud's Moses*]

———. *Zakhor: Jewish History and Jewish Memory*. Seattle: University of Washington Press, 1982. [*Zakhor*]

Young-Bruehl, Elizabeth. *Anna Freud*. New York: Summit, 1988. [*Anna*]

Zantop, Susanne. *Colonial Fantasies: Conquest, Family, and Nation in Precolonial Germany, 1770–1870*. Durham, N.C.: Duke University Press, 1997. [*Colonial*]

Zollschan, Ignaz. *Jewish Questions: Three Lectures*. New York: Bloch, 1914. [*Jewish*]

——. *Das Rassenproblem*. 2nd ed. Vienna and Leipzig: Wilhelm Braumüller, 1910. [*Rassenproblem*]

Zweig, Arnold. *Bilanz der deutschen Judentum. Ein Versuch*. Amsterdam: Querido, 1931. [*Bilanz*]

'Little Hans,' 2, 4, 26–27, 31, 37–38, 105,
110–31, 134–38, 141, 179, 195, 203,
227n120, 253n2, 255nn23–24, 256–
57n35, 258nn40, 50, 52, 259nn53–55,
57–58, 261nn75–76, 261–62n77,
264n92, 286n26. *See also* "Analysis of a
Phobia . . ."; Graf, Herbert; Graf, Max
Lothane, Zvi, 273–74n98
'Lucy R.,' 78, 85, 284n13
Lueger, Karl, 113
Lukacher, Ned, 252n46, 271n67
Lupton, Julia Reinhard, 222n55, 229n139
Luther, Martin, 212, 238n41, 294n11
Lyotard, Jean-François, 19

Macalpine, Ida, and Richard A. Hunter
140, 270n64; translation of: 265nn3, 8
Maciejewski, Franz, 31, 256–57n35,
285n25
MacKenzie, John Noland, 75
Mahoney, Patrick J., 68, 236n12, 262n88,
264n92
male associations (*Männerbund, Brüderband*), 6–7, 39, 69, 93–94, 162–63,
165, 168–69, 174–79, 181–83, 199–
200, 245–46n145, 274nn2–3, 281n83,
292n87; in ethnography, 162, 164,
178–79, 281n83; in Germanophone
areas, 164–65, 263n89; jealousy, 163,
182; and the political, 7, 162, 174–79;
rivalry, 11, 67, 144, 170, 181–82, 207,
218n18. *See also* Blüher, Hans; *B'nai
B'rith*; family; homosexuality; homosociality and homoeroticism; primal
horde; Schürtz, Hans;
Wandervogelbewegung
Mann, Thomas, 197–98, 204, 282n105,
288nn44, 45
Mannheimer, Isaac Noah, 22
Marcus Aurelius, 72, 237n36
Marcus, Laura, 6
Maria-Theresa (empress of Austria), 48
Marks, Elaine, 20
Marx, Karl, 20, 102, 219n27, 251n34
masculinization of the Jews. *See* gender:
masculinization of the Jews
Mayer, Hans, 33
Maylan, Charles E., 17
medicine, Jewish practice of, 9, 13, 78, 86,
91; doctor-patient relationship, 79, 87,
91, 147, 244n130; Jewish specialties,
71, 78, 89, 91, 221n45, 245n146

Medusa, 193, 247n165, 287n31. *See also*
fetish and fetishism
melitzah. See Freud, Jacob: Hebrew
inscription
memory: as forgetting, 53–57, 263n89;
memory-trace, 14, 25, 30, 41–42, 185,
201, 208, 226n111, 256n27, 285–
86n25; screen memory, 30, 284n13
Mendelssohn, Moses, 49, 251n33
Mendelssohn-Bartholdy, Felix, 222n54,
230n158
Mereschkovsky, Dmitri, 130, 197–98,
211, 288n50, 290n60
Meyer, Conrad Ferdinand, 256n32, 257–
58n40, 262n80
Meyer, Eduard, 189, 257n40
Michelangelo, 23, 233n26
Micheler, Stefan, 220n28
modernity: crises of, 6, 11, 19, 28, 40, 78,
110, 112–13, 176, 188, 207, 220n27,
276n15, 290n59; modernization, 6,
175; postmodern, 19–20, 26, 28, 41.
See also Jews: double bind of Jewish
modernity
Möbius, Paul Julius, 145, 267n22
Moll, Albert, 220n35, 263n89
Moltke, Kuno von, 167, 172, 276n21
Moses, 21–23, 27, 29, 32, 41–42, 184–87,
189–94, 196–98, 200–202, 204–5,
211–14, 224n82, 226n111, 233n26,
246n149, 254n12, 257n40, 261n76,
283nn5, 7, 284n10, 284–85n14,
285n20, 286n27, 287nn32, 39, 291n78,
293nn5, 7
Moses and Monotheism, 5, 12, 15, 17–18,
22–25, 29–30, 33–35, 39, 41–42,
47,110, 112, 115, 182–83, 184–208
passim, 212–13, 221n50, 226n109,
246n149, 257n40, 275n5, 283nn6–7,
284n11, 286n26, 290n59
"Moses of Michelangelo, The," 15, 114,
207, 213, 254n12, 291n79
Mosse, George, 33, 227n113
Much, Rudolf, 178
Mühlmann, Wilhelm E., 178
multiculturalism, 18–21
Musil, Robert, 249n11, 276n19

Nancy, Jean-Luc, 19
narcissism, 46–47, 61, 98, 136, 150, 198,
203, 206, 249n10, 264n92; narcissistic
crisis, 47, 61, 98, 138